TERRORISM AND COUNTERINTELLIGENCE

Columbia Studies in Terrorism and Irregular Warfare

Columbia Studies in Terrorism and Irregular Warfare

Bruce Hoffman, Series Editor

This series seeks to fill a conspicuous gap in the burgeoning literature on terrorism, guerrilla warfare, and insurgency. The series adheres to the highest standards of scholarship and discourse and publishes books that elucidate the strategy, operations, means, motivations, and effects posed by terrorist, guerrilla, and insurgent organizations and movements. It thereby provides a solid and increasingly expanding foundation of knowledge on these subjects for students, established scholars, and informed reading audiences alike.

Ami Pedahzur, *The Israeli Secret Services and the Struggle Against Terrorism*

Ami Pedahzur and Arie Perliger, *Jewish Terrorism in Israel*

Lorenzo Vidino, *The New Muslim Brotherhood in the West*

Erica Chenoweth and Maria J. Stephan, *Why Civil Resistance Works: The Strategic Logic of Nonviolent Resistance*

William C. Banks, *New Battlefields/Old Laws: Critical Debates on Asymmetric Warfare*

TERRORISM AND COUNTER-INTELLIGENCE

HOW TERRORIST GROUPS ELUDE DETECTION

BLAKE W. MOBLEY

To Ed,
Hope your enjoy the book!

Columbia University Press   *New York*

Columbia University Press
Publishers Since 1893

New York   Chichester, West Sussex
cup.columbia.edu

Library of Congress Cataloging-in-Publication Data
Mobley, Blake W.
Terrorism and counterintelligence : how terrorist groups
elude detection / Blake W. Mobley.
p. cm. — (Columbia studies in terrorism and irregular warfare)
Includes bibliographical references and index.
ISBN 978-0-231-15876-3 (cloth : alk. paper) —
ISBN 978-0-231-52809-2 (e-book)
1.   Terrorists.   2.   Intelligence service.   3.   Criminal
methods.   4.   Terrorism—Prevention.   I.   Title.

HV6431.M625 2012
363.325'163—dc23
2011046373

c 10 9 8 7 6 5 4 3

Cover Designer: Thomas Stvan

CONTENTS

ACKNOWLEDGMENTS

I could not have written this book without the support and guidance of many friends, colleagues, and mentors. First and foremost, I owe an extraordinary debt of gratitude to Dan Byman, professor in the Security Studies Program at Georgetown University and chair of my dissertation committee. Dan has been a wonderful mentor and friend, and his ideas and suggestions helped to shape this book. Dan's boundless energy, patience, and kindness have also provided intellectual and personal inspiration.

David Edelstein, associate professor in the School of Foreign Service at Georgetown University, and Andrew Bennett, professor of government at Georgetown University, provided invaluable substantive and methodological support. I am indebted to my good friend Larry Grossback—renowned as one who can turn pulp into poetry—for his substantive comments and editing. I also thank the numerous fellow scholars who helped me to refine my questions and my analysis in seminars and workshops at Georgetown, where I presented my initial research. I am also grateful to a host of analysts and case officers I worked with at the Central Intelligence Agency—unnamed for obvious reasons—who contributed to my understanding of terrorism and counterintelligence over the years. To everyone mentioned here, I offer absolution for any errors and omissions in the text, which are my own.

I thank the two anonymous reviewers and the editorial board at Columbia University Press for their very helpful comments. I also thank Bruce Hoffman, editor of the Terrorism and Irregular Warfare series at Columbia University Press, for his guidance and assistance. Bruce is a luminary figure in this field, and it was a great honor to have his input and support.

My family and friends deserve a special thanks for suffering through my endless preoccupation with non-state-actor counterintelligence. My wife, Sarah, has been my greatest supporter and my best friend. I thank her for her patience and understanding while I spoiled countless nights and weekends in Cairo and Washington while completing this project. Finally, I dedicate this book to my son, Finn—I hope that when he grows up and reads this one day, the threat of catastrophic terrorism will be a thing of the past.

The views expressed here are solely my own and do not reflect the views or opinions of RAND or its sponsors.

TERRORISM AND COUNTERINTELLIGENCE

Jamal Ahmed al-Fadl joined al Qa'ida in 1989. As a founding member, he was a close confidant of Osama Bin Laden and helped the notorious leader to manage al Qa'ida's properties and front companies in Sudan. By the mid-1990s, al-Fadl was entrenched in the upper echelons of al Qa'ida's bureaucracy and by all appearances was ready to lay down his life for the organization. On September 7, 1996, al-Fadl approached the US embassy in Eritrea on foot, undoubtedly rehearsing in his mind a dark plot that had been planned for many months. The ensuing events caught everyone off guard. Al-Fadl's secret plot did not involve attacking the embassy—his plan was to sell al Qa'ida's most treasured secrets to the US government. Above all, al-Fadl's decision to betray al Qa'ida made it clear to all observers that the shadowy terrorist organization was not immune to spies.

Al Qa'ida's problems are not unique. In fact, most terrorist groups face even greater challenges, and many do not survive past their first few years of existence.[1] Some groups lose key leaders, transition to non-violent political entities, or fail to pass on their cause to the next generation of terrorists.[2] All terrorist groups—even those that survive for decades—face an even more basic threat to their existence: the discovery of their activities, members, and plans by government law enforcement and intelligence agencies.

Groups that fail to hide their communications, movements, and plots from a determined adversary will be eliminated quickly. Terrorist groups that survive for years do so because they have developed sophisticated methods for staying hidden. These strategies are often referred to a "counterintelligence." Current studies on terrorism have not systematically addressed this critical issue, and, more important, most terrorist groups that experience crippling counterintelligence problems do not survive long enough to be studied at all. What factors shape a terrorist group's counterintelligence capabilities? The answer to this question has profound implications for homeland security and international counterterrorism efforts.

This book is fundamentally about disrupting terrorist groups. It examines terrorist groups through the lens of counterintelligence and offers lessons for uncovering terrorist plots and manipulating terrorist-group decision making. The book makes a case for elevating the role of counterintelligence analysis in counterterrorism operations. The book specifically explores how we can better monitor, impede, and eliminate terrorist groups by exploiting the weaknesses of their counterintelligence and security practices. Part of the approach involves knowing where to look for their weaknesses. Some counterintelligence pathologies are more likely to accrue to certain types of terrorist groups, whereas some destructive bureaucratic tendencies, such as mistrust and paranoia, pervade all terrorist groups. Being smarter about where to look for weaknesses and how to capitalize on them will allow intelligence and law enforcement agencies to improve how they recruit and manage human penetrations (spies) into terrorist groups, locate and monitor the groups' communications, and analyze and manipulate their decision making.

Scholarship on intelligence and terrorism offers limited insights into terrorist-group counterintelligence. A large portion of terrorism literature focuses on terrorist-group motivations and decision-making as well as on government policy responses. The intelligence literature consists mainly of firsthand accounts of intelligence practitioners and large-scale assessments of the intelligence community. Very few studies attempt to examine carefully and theorize about operational intelligence, and almost none has dealt with terrorist-group intelligence operations. I seek to answer two basic questions: How do a terrorist group's organizational structure, level of popular support, and access to territory it controls affect its counterintelligence strengths and vulnerabilities? How can governments exploit terrorist groups' counterintelligence vulnerabilities to collect more accurate information about them and disrupt their activities?

To investigate either of these questions, we must address an even more basic question: What is terrorist-group counterintelligence? The answer to this question is not as simple as it may initially appear because terrorist-group counterintelligence strategies vary widely among groups. Some strategies can be as simple as avoiding the use of communication technologies that can be intercepted by state adversaries. In planning the attacks of September 11, 2001 (9/11), al Qa'ida operatives occasionally used trusted couriers to transmit sensitive messages rather than risk using telephones or email. A terrorist group may also develop sophisticated counterintelligence procedures if such innovations can provide an important intelligence advantage over the group's adversaries. When British intelligence began paying members of the Provisional Irish Republican Army (PIRA) to spy for the British government, the PIRA responded by recruiting government tax and social security bureaucrats to identify PIRA spies who were earning and spending beyond their "means"—an indication that they were receiving payment as British informants.

I explore how three primary factors shape a terrorist group's counterintelligence capabilities: the terrorist group's organizational structure, its popular support, and its access to territory it controls. The book also shows, to a lesser extent, how the counterterrorism capabilities of the group's adversary and the terrorist group's resources shape its counterintelligence strengths and vulnerabilities. Even a small change in one of these factors can have a dramatic effect on a terrorist group's counterintelligence fitness.

Understanding terrorist-group counterintelligence will lead to a better understanding of terrorist groups and the design of more effective counterterrorism efforts. Anticipating terrorist counterintelligence vulnerabilities will enable governments to monitor and diagnose more effectively a terrorist group's capabilities and weaknesses. Improved monitoring will allow governments to adapt to a terrorist group's counterintelligence strengths and to disrupt more effectively the group's activities. Understanding why and predicting when the key counterintelligence trade-offs arise will allow government law enforcement and intelligence agencies to better detect and exploit them.

KEY FINDINGS

All terrorist groups face counterintelligence dilemmas, or trade-offs, that challenge their ability to function securely. No terrorist group can maintain perfect secrecy and function effectively—every counterintelligence adaptation or new advantage produces new vulnerabilities. The three factors named earlier in particular—organizational structure, popular support, and controlled territory—shape terrorist organizations' counterintelligence practices and are at the heart of the trade-offs their leaders face.

Terrorist groups with a centralized and tight command-and-control structure rather than a loose and decentralized command structure tend to have superior counterintelligence training and compartmentation. Centralization of command gives group leaders greater control over group members, allowing leaders to mandate specific training for the entire organization and to punish those who do not comply. Almost all terrorist groups attempt to train their members in basic counterintelligence skills, which can significantly impact how members and new recruits are monitored and captured by the adversary. The Palestinian terrorist groups Fatah and Black September Organization (BSO) had tight command structures and successfully trained their members in counterintelligence methods. Al Qa'ida had a relatively tight command structure from 1989 to 2001 and was able to train its members in counterintelligence.

Terrorist groups with a tight and centralized command structure are more vulnerable, however, to their adversaries' efforts to develop high-level spies, or "penetrations," and to exploit the groups' standardized counterintelligence procedures. The PIRA improved its counterintelligence training when its organizational structure tightened in the 1970s, but the tightening also allowed British to place a long-term spy in the PIRA's "internal security" department, giving British forces access to a volume of PIRA secrets that they could not have acquired with even their best spies of the early 1970s. Groups with a loose and decentralized command structure are more difficult to train systematically but also are less predictable to the state adversary because they develop fewer standardized organizational procedures. Fatah's use of standard codes for communicating with its operatives allowed the Jordanian government to manipulate the organization by mimicking its communications; had each Fatah unit developed its own codes, the Jordanian government would have had to study and break all of the subgroups' codes instead of just one code.

Terrorist groups with popular support tend to receive more counterintelligence support from the local population. Militant groups that have won their local population's affection are more likely to win their support in intelligence tasks, such as identifying government spies and notifying the group of government raids and investigations. The PIRA received crucial counterintelligence support from its Hen Patrols, made up of members of the community who alerted the Republicans to incoming British patrols and searches.

At the same time, however, terrorist groups that invest in developing popular support are more likely to expose sensitive details about their plans and members in their efforts to generate and maintain their popularity. The growth of video-sharing and user-generated media outlets on the Internet has heightened this publicity dilemma. Outreach to the population, in particular outreach through the media, can reveal details about the group that a clever adversary can piece together to learn about the group's personnel and activities. Al Qa'ida leaders, for example, were in frequent contact with journalists and media organizations, and group members in the West had regular liaison contact with the media. Bin Laden routinely leaked valuable information about his health, locations, and operational intentions in video interviews and tapes released to media organizations. Importantly, for clandestine organizations there is a natural tension between secrecy and popularity. One PIRA member noted that increased secrecy drew PIRA volunteers away from daily interaction with the average citizen of Northern Ireland and that less contact with the population eventually resulted in less familiarity and trust between the PIRA and its base of popular support.[3]

Terrorist groups that control territory rather than living in uncontrolled territory or areas the adversary controls tend to have superior communications security, physical security, and counterintelligence vetting. Operating freely in territory that the adversary has trouble entering and observing allows the group to dominate the local intelligence environment, to move freely between safe houses, and to interrogate locals and outsiders. For the Egyptian terrorist group known as the "Islamic Group" (IG), controlled territory provided a shelter from the Egyptian security forces. Egyptian forces could not adequately police the group's territories and had to rely on mass sweeps and raids when venturing into those areas. Police raids on this scale may have been easy to predict and may have given key leaders and operatives a chance to hide or escape police roundups.

Terrorist groups that control territory are, however, more vulnerable to their adversaries' efforts to concentrate their intelligence and military forces on a discrete and often well-known location. In the case of the Egyptian IG, controlled territories gave Egyptian security forces an area to target, and mass arrests almost certainly netted some operatives and IG sympathizers. Israel found it difficult to track and assassinate Fatah leaders in their controlled territory in Lebanon, but at least Israel knew where to direct their human, signal, and imagery-collection assets to begin looking for targets. In contrast, the rank-and-file members of BSO spread out across Europe and Asia were more anonymous and hidden among tens of thousands of noncombatants with similar biographical profiles. In many cases, BSO operatives were legitimate students and workers in Europe, and BSO operatives who participated in only one mission would leave very few operational footprints.

Among the three key factors, controlled territory stands out as the factor offering the most important counterintelligence advantages. Groups that do not control territory suffer tremendously if they are constantly targeted by hostile intelligence and law enforcement entities or if they live at the mercy of state sponsors that can and often do turn on them at any time. Organizational structure is the second most influential factor. Tightly commanded groups tend to have a counterintelligence advantage over loosely connected groups because they can more efficiently train and discipline their members while centrally coordinating and professionalizing the group's security, investigation, and counterespionage functions. However, groups that do not control territory *and* face an overwhelmingly powerful adversary may prefer the advantages of a loose command structure, which allows for some level of adversary penetration without a catastrophic collapse. In this situation, the tight command structure would promote counterintelligence behavior—centralized counterespionage and record keeping, standardized counterintelligence tradecraft, and the maintenance of secure facilities or safe houses—that would allow a penetration that may fatally wound the group.

DEFINITIONS

The definitions of the two main concepts of the book—"terrorism" and "counterintelligence"—have been vigorously debated. This research does not seek to resolve these controversies. Rather, the definitions selected allow for a broad application of the book's insights into both theory and practice.

Terrorist Group. I use a modified version of terrorism expert Bruce Hoffman's definition of a terrorist group. Hoffman identifies five key elements of terrorism: "ineluctably political in aims and motives," "violent—or equally important, threatening violence," "designed to have far-reaching psychological repercussions beyond the immediate victim or target," "conducted by an organization," and "perpetuated by a subnational group or non-state entity."[4] Terrorism scholar Daniel Byman adds a sixth element in his study of state sponsors of terrorism: "The attack deliberately targets non-combatants."[5] Terrorist groups are those that use terrorism as a core tactic to achieve their objectives.

An insurgent group—defined as a nonstate actor engaged in a political-military campaign seeking to overthrow a government or to secede from it through use of conventional and unconventional military strategies and tactics—may use terrorist tactics to achieve its objectives.[6] In many cases, insurgent groups are not easily distinguished from terrorist groups. In principle, an insurgent group's intention to overthrown a government or to secede from it can distinguish it from a classic terrorist group. In reality, many insurgent groups target civilian populations with terrorist tactics to achieve objectives short of "overthrowing a government." This may be especially true in the cases where an insurgent group conducts its operations in densely populated urban settings or where the line between combatant and noncombatant is blurred or creatively defined by either side.[7] In addition, many terrorist groups participate in internal conflicts designed to overthrow or undermine the stability of a government, often to gain controlled territory. Even an archetypal terrorist group such as al Qa'ida supported the Afghan Taliban in its efforts to undermine Afghanistan's central government after 2001.

Defining a terrorist group as an entity that uses terrorism as a core tactic to achieve its objectives intentionally casts a wide net into murky waters teeming with clandestine, armed groups. This approach reduces the need for highly subjective distinctions among terrorist, insurgent, guerrilla, and revolutionary groups and broadens the applicability of the analysis and conclusions.

In some respects, this broad definition applies—albeit unevenly—to many types of groups that are not typically considered terrorist organizations, including some organized criminal groups, drug-trafficking organizations, and large, transnational street gangs.[8] This book does not address the counterintelligence practices of this broader set of armed, clandestine groups, but a rigorous investigation of these organizations would likely show many similarities.

Counterintelligence. Counterintelligence is the process—or constellation of activities, analysis, and decision-making—that a group engages in to prevent adversaries from acquiring accurate information about its actions, personnel, and plans. Counterintelligence has three subprocesses—basic denial, adaptive denial, and covert manipulation—each building on the previous in sophistication.

Basic denial, the foundational counterintelligence practice, consists of activities that prevent the passage of information, intentionally or unintentionally, from the group to the adversary. Activities in this category are sometimes referred to as "defensive counterintelligence" and often focus on prohibited behaviors. For example, group members may be required to refrain from discussing the group's information with nongroup members, from talking about group activities in electronic or telephonic media, from talking with group members or about group activities in "nonsecure" fora, and from associating with the adversary and its allies. Some basic-denial activities focus on preventing the adversary from seeding spies, or penetrations, into the group's supply of recruits and on thwarting the adversary's efforts to recruit longtime group members to spy.

Counterintelligence vetting of new recruits might include a basic background check to ensure that recruits are associated with the appropriate tribe, family, or neighborhood and do not have current or past affiliations with the adversary's security apparatus or vulnerabilities that an adversary's intelligence service can exploit in a recruitment operation. Counterintelligence checks to ensure that current members are not spying might include an informal system for group members to report any abnormal or alerting behavior of another group member to a higher-ranking member. The subsequent investigation might include questioning of other members in contact with the suspected individual and possibly direct questioning of the member about his alerting behavior. Educating group members about the risks and penalties of spying for the adversary and compartmentalizing the group into cells that do not share information about their operations are typically effective basic-denial techniques as well.

Adaptive denial consists of activities that identify the adversary's unique intelligence-collection methods as well as the terrorist group's own unique counterintelligence vulnerabilities and that promote adjustments to the group's behavior based on this information. Adaptive denial builds on the group's basic-denial techniques, which are not tailored to a specific adversary and its capabilities. Activities in this category include investigation and interrogation of suspected spies, cataloging detailed biographical and lifestyle information about each group member to assist in investigations, keeping track of group members' access to sensitive information to assist in investigations, and conducting damage assessments following a spy case or a leak of sensitive group information in order to learn from past mistakes. More sophisticated adaptive measures include using a double agent to learn about the adversary's intelligence-collection priorities, penetrating the adversary's communications system to learn about its operations, identifying risk factors for traitors in order to proactively investigate or expel members who fit a "traitor" profile, and identifying the adversary's strategies for seeding spies into the group's supply of recruits in order to weed out possible informants before they gain access to sensitive information.

Activities in the adaptive-denial category may also include recruiting human penetrations of the adversary's security apparatus to gain insight into the adversary's activities, personnel, and plans. A group may occasionally recruit a penetration of the adversary who can identify the spies within the group's own ranks—this type of penetration is very rare, but very rewarding. This information would allow the group to cut off the traitor's access to sensitive information or to expel him from the group. The group can also investigate how, why, and when spies were recruited in order to adapt to the adversary's methods and to recover from any damage caused by the information the spies provided to the adversary.

Covert manipulation, the most sophisticated subprocess, consists of activities that provide an adversary with false information about the group's behaviors, personnel, and plans. Manipulation builds on the group's basic- and adaptive-denial efforts. False information about the group may be designed to fool the adversary into wasting resources on false leads, confusing or interrupting operations directed against the group, or steering investigations away from the group's penetrations of its adversary. Covert manipulation is sometimes referred to as "offensive counterintelligence" and usually requires a deep understanding of the adversary's intelligence-collection methods.[9]

A capable adversary will have many pathways for collecting information about the group, including open sources, human penetrations, and interception and monitoring of the group's communications. To manipulate a smart adversary, the group will have to feed information into multiple pathways to corroborate the false information being fed into the main disinformation channel. The group may also have to divulge some true secrets to lure the adversary into believing manipulative information to come. A long-term campaign of effective manipulation probably requires that the group recruit a penetration of the adversary to provide feedback on whether and under what conditions the adversary believes the false information. When a "feedback penetration" is achieved, the group may begin to alter or control some of the adversary's behavior. Figure 1.1 provides a schematic of the three counterintelligence subprocesses.

Activities in the manipulation category include sending false defectors to the adversary with misinformation, allowing false defectors (called "dangles") to be "discovered, developed, and recruited" by the adversary, turning the adversary's spies back against the adversary (double agents), feeding false information through the group's conversations in communications channels or venues that the adversary is known to have compromised, and providing false information to the media in order to manipulate the adversary's open-source collection.

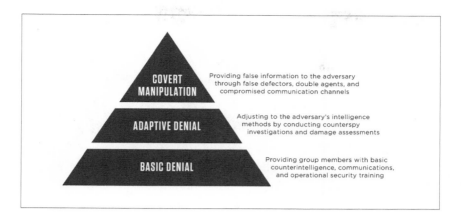

Figure 1.1 Counterintelligence Subprocesses

TERRORIST-GROUP COUNTERINTELLIGENCE

Most terrorist groups practice basic-denial techniques, and some of the more sophisticated groups engage in adaptive denial. An overwhelming majority of terrorist groups do not engage in covert manipulation because of the high level of coordination and successful denial and adaptation required to execute such tasks. In many cases, uniformly implemented basic- and adaptive-denial procedures will be sufficient for survival.

Basic denial, adaptive denial, and covert manipulation are typically designed to deal with five intelligence threats: (1) penetration by the adversary's human spies; (2) the adversary's technical collection of electronic, telephonic, or face-to-face communications; (3) direct observation of group activities by outsiders or locals who have incidental contact with the group in its area of operations or controlled territory; (4) passive observation of group's personnel and activities when they move through hostile territory controlled by either the adversary or an adversary's ally; and (5) exposure of the group's activities and personnel in the media.

The three key factors on which this book focuses—a terrorist group's organizational structure, popular support, and access to controlled territory—significantly shape how and how well a group identifies and mitigates these counterintelligence threats.

Organizational Structure

A terrorist group's organizational structure—specifically, whether the group has a tight and centralized command-and-control structure or a loose and decentralized command structure—determines the extent to which leaders can exercise strategic and tactical control over their personnel. In loosely commanded organizations, leaders exercise mainly strategic control over group personnel, affording lower-ranking members a greater degree of decision-making autonomy.[10]

A tight command structure allows group leaders to coordinate group activities, such as training new recruits in basic-denial techniques, sharing counterintelligence "lessons learned" across geographical and organizational units, and coordinating complex counterespionage investigations. Scholarly research on social movements has frequently highlighted the importance of coordination for group security in revolutions, rebellions, and coup plotting.[11] Mark Irving Lichbach notes that autocratic rebel groups are better able than democratic and decentralized ones to maintain collective dissent.[12] A tight command structure also allows group leaders to implement a strategy known as "compartmentation"— the process restricting the flow of information within an organization to prevent the disclosure of sensitive intelligence to individuals who are not authorized to receive it. For an organization to achieve compartmentation without fragmenting itself into many autonomous groups, a higher degree of coordination at upper levels of the organization is required to compensate for reduced communication and information flow at lower levels.[13] When Italian police began to rout the Italian Red Brigades in the mid-1970s, the Brigades established a rigid territorial hierarchy to facilitate the creation of a highly compartmented structure among its operational cells.[14]

Tight command structures and high levels of strategic coordination have a downside, however, and can create counterintelligence vulnerabilities for a terrorist group. Strategic coordination discourages innovation and potentially useful variation within the organization. The Basque terrorist group Euskadi Ta Askatasuna (ETA, Basque Homeland and Freedom) trained all its recruits to evade government surveillance by communicating with couriers and anonymous exchange points, known as "dead drops," rather than with landline telephones and the postal service.

As a result, however, Spanish police could more easily identify ETA couriers—and perhaps ETA personnel and facilities—by studying the standardized methods of a subset of the group's couriers.

Popular Support

For almost every terrorist group, there is a natural tension between gaining popularity and maintaining secrecy. The Greek terrorist group November 17, for example, once released a detailed account of how it assassinated a US official in Greece by taking advantage of the Greek police's counterintelligence vulnerabilities. November 17 released the account in order to take credit for the operation and to enhance its popularity, but because of that account Greek security forces were provided an opportunity to learn about the terrorist group's operational procedures and improve police communications security. Both Fatah and the PIRA struggled to balance the benefits of gaining the population's trust with the risks of exposing its personnel and operational goals.

Terrorist-group leaders often devote considerable time to improving their public image to increase popular support, improve group morale, and attract financial support and recruits. The leader of the Filipino Abu Sayyaf Group spent substantial time with local media organizations bragging about his battles with Filipino security forces.[15] A group's popularity may increase through media outreach, but group leaders occasionally bask in the media spotlight to develop a personal popularity, which does not directly serve the group. Palestinian leader Yasser Arafat had a huge appetite for publicity and gave many interviews to Western reporters. Although these interviews most likely resulted in some increase in popular support for Arafat's terrorist group, they also provided his adversaries with valuable assessment data on his location and health in addition to valuable information about his group.

Gaining popular support, however, can be very beneficial to a group's counterintelligence fitness. Passive popular support—for example, a population's refusal to provide information to the adversary about a terrorist group—can facilitate the group's basic-denial activities.[16] The absence of passive popular support can compel a terrorist group to engage in overzealous "spy hunting" among the local population, which can further erode the group's popularity. Active forms of support include the provision of safe houses and storage facilities and the identification of outsiders and counterintelligence threats in the terrorist group's territory. It can also include information provided by sympathetic government informants, as in the PIRA case.

Access to Controlled Territory

Controlled territory is a geographical space with defined boundaries that a terrorist group polices and within which the group regularly imposes its will, much like a traditional law enforcement entity.[17] The term *controlled territory* is not synonymous with *safe haven*. The latter is typically used to describe a geographic space where a terrorist group finds refuge from its adversaries. It connotes a semipassive occupation of territory by the terrorist group—perhaps as a result of a state sponsor's patronage or the utter remoteness of the territory—but nonetheless does not indicate how the territory is acquired or managed.

The term *controlled territory*, in contrast, describes a space that a terrorist group actively patrols and manages. The territory is managed occasionally, but not always, with the support of a state sponsor or additional nonstate actors, such as local militias, insurgents, or criminal groups. When a terrorist group does not have the state's consent to control territory within that state's borders, the group may nonetheless control space if the state is too weak to challenge the group. Operating outside of or without controlled territory occurs when the terrorist group's operatives live, plan operations, or carry out a significant portion of operational acts in a geographical space that they do not police or in which they do not regularly impose their will.

Territory allows the group to train, communicate, meet face to face, and make connections with supporters and journalists with a degree of freedom not available in hostile, uncontrolled territory. These capabilities allow the group to better manage its counterintelligence environment. For example, in the 1970s the Palestinian terrorist group Fatah protected the secrecy of its communications and operational plans far more effectively in its controlled territory in Beirut than in the uncontrolled territory of the West Bank, which was deluged with Israeli security agents and collaborators. Controlling territory also allows a group to monitor who is traveling in and out of the region, which can help the group to identify interlopers or group members who are traveling outside of the territory to meet with hostile intelligence services.

Controlled territory, however, can confine a group and give the adversary a fixed target to monitor and against which it can array its military and intelligence forces. Al Qa'ida used its controlled territory in Afghanistan in the 1990s to conduct secure training and enhanced vetting of its recruits, but this same controlled territory gave the United States a well-defined and high-impact target to strike following the 9/11 attacks. A state adversary with territory adjacent to that of a terrorist group can set up checkpoints on their common border to monitor with technical and human assets any movement in and out of the area. Individuals of interest can then be followed into the state adversary's territory to identify contacts and activities. Furthermore, if the adversary can recruit a group member or a local with access to the terrorist group's controlled territory, the adversary can use that individual to collect targeting information about the group more easily than it would if it recruited an asset in uncontrolled territory. An asset within the group's controlled area will have better access to information about the group's activities and about other individuals within the territory who are worth recruiting.

A terrorist group that controls territory is also likely to come under greater pressure to maintain popular support in part to retain its control—particularly if it wishes to deter collaborators who are assisting its adversaries from developing and thriving within its territory. Controlling territory is intimately linked to popular support. Some terrorist and insurgent groups control territory by coercing and intimidating the local population, but many groups are forced to win direct or indirect support from key segments of the population to control territory for an extended period.

Other Factors Shaping Counterintelligence Practices

In addition to the influence of organizational structure, popular support, and controlled territory, the adversary's counterterrorism capabilities and the terrorist group's resources shape the group's counterintelligence strengths and vulnerabilities.

Terrorist groups face a wide variety of adversaries, which differ significantly in their counterterrorism capabilities. A state adversary with strong counterterrorism capabilities will employ a strategy that involves diligent police work (rather than heavy-handed sweeps and mass arrests), good coordination between police and intelligence agencies, and the prudence to avoid costly overreactions to terrorist activities. A state adversary that does not perform diligent police work, foster coordination between police and intelligence agencies, or avoid costly overreactions may permit the terrorist group to evade capture and capitalize on a windfall of popular support.

The terrorist group and its state adversary are often engaged in a competitive and dynamic relationship, often matching innovations. A move or innovation by a terrorist group will frequently result in a countermove or counterinnovation by the state adversary. Because the state typically outmatches its terrorist adversary in military or paramilitary strength, the terrorist group will work to stay hidden and operate clandestinely by constantly improving its counterintelligence practices. For example, when Indonesian law enforcement started efforts to intercept the communications of the Indonesian terrorist group Jemaah Islamiyya in the 1990s, the group responded by adopting sophisticated communications encryption standards.[18] A terrorist group that does not adapt to its adversary's intelligence-gathering innovations can be defeated more quickly, whereas one that does adapt can benefit from the lessons it learns. Hoffman describes this process as one of "natural selection . . . whereby every new terrorist generation learns from its predecessors, becoming smarter, tougher, and more difficult to capture or eliminate."[19]

A terrorist group's resources also shape its counterintelligence fitness. A group with more financial and human capital can dedicate more resources to counterintelligence and security practices. A well-funded terrorist group can purchase better technologies, recruit more spies, bribe more officials, and better secure its communications and facilities. Additional personnel can be assigned to focus solely on counterintelligence tasks when recruitment increases. State sponsorship is a unique and important component of terrorist-group resources. State sponsors can provide a terrorist group with money, intelligence, and logistical support to aid the group in its intelligence and counterintelligence efforts.[20] State sponsorship can, however, be a double-edged sword. A strong state supporter can enhance a group's capabilities directly by training the terrorist group in counterintelligence methods and sharing state-collected intelligence, or it can help indirectly by providing the group with safe-haven and logistical counterintelligence assistance. But if a state supporter has mixed motives and seeks to control the group or, worse yet, turns antagonistic, it can heighten a terrorist group's exposure by compromising information about the group in order to manipulate and ultimately control it.

BOOK STRUCTURE AND CASE SELECTION

The book is composed of in-depth case studies of four major terrorist groups as well as a few minor ones. Chapters 2 through 6 focus on individual terrorist groups and describes how all three of the key factors shaped each group's counterintelligence fitness. Each case study documents a change over time in one or two key factors—such as a group shift from a decentralized to centralized command structure—and how the group responded. Each of these shifts is examined closely to demonstrate how it directly affected the group's counterintelligence capabilities.

Chapter 2 examines the PIRA from 1969 to 1994 and focuses on how organizational structure impacts counterintelligence practices. Chapter 3 chronicles Fatah and the BSO from 1964 to 1984, highlighting the effects of controlled territory on terrorist counterintelligence fitness. Chapter 4 focuses on al Qa'ida from 1988 to 2003 and the counterintelligence ramifications of popular support and media outreach. Chapter 5 details the activities of the Egyptian IG from 1989 to 1998 and explores how popular support impacted the group's counterintelligence capabilities. Chapter 6 examines four terrorist groups whose counterintelligence tactics failed so catastrophically that they did not survive past their first few years of existence. Finally, chapter 7 summarizes the main findings and identifies avenues for exploiting terrorist counterintelligence vulnerabilities.

The cases selected for the book fall short of capturing all of the complexities of terrorist groups but feature a variety of geographic regions, ideologies, historical time periods, and sophistication of counterintelligence capabilities. Some of the terrorist groups examined, such as the PIRA and Fatah, at times exhibit many characteristics of a classical insurgent group. Other groups, such as al Qa'ida and the BSO, have characteristics considered to be representative of leaner, transnational terrorist organizations.

A broad definition of "terrorist group" allows for an investigation of the counterintelligence practices of many types of terrorist groups, such as those that behave like insurgencies and those that behave like lean, transnational organizations. It is important to note that terrorist-group types *vary systematically* along the key factors—organizational structure, popular support, and controlled territory. This systematic variation does not negate or alter the impact of the key factors but suggests there may be a tendency for certain terrorist-group types to fit a particular counterintelligence profile. For example, an insurgent-type group's decision to "overthrow a government or secede from it" rather than to pursue some other political agenda may indicate that the group is more likely to seek to control territory.[21]

The spectrum of terrorist-group behavior, motivation, and strategy is vast, which poses a challenge to the generalizability of any study of terrorism. This study's findings on terrorist-group counterintelligence, however, are uniquely generalizable because terrorist groups are sufficiently similar in ways that affect counterintelligence trade-offs, including that they all are violent nonstate organizations that need to recruit and train members, conduct operations, live in a controlled or uncontrolled territory, manage publicity, and avoid being spied on or disrupted by adversaries.

As a result, the findings are very likely applicable both to terrorist groups that are highly centralized, such as the South Asian group Lashkar-e-Tayyiba, and to those that operate with a more decentralized "franchise" model, such as al Qa'ida and its affiliates. The findings also apply to organizations that are part terrorist and part insurgent, such as the Taliban in Afghanistan and Hamas on the Gaza Strip. Although Lashkar-e-Tayyiba and Hamas are different in many respects, the fact that both have tight command-and-control structures should facilitate their efforts to create uniform counterintelligence training for their members but at the same time make each more vulnerable to long-term, high-level penetrations.

In the early 1970s, British security forces were steadily dismantling the Provisional Irish Republican Army (PIRA). British interrogators were collecting confessions and details of terrorist plots from PIRA detainees and using the information to locate and capture senior PIRA leaders. By 1978, however, arrests and detentions of PIRA personnel had dropped dramatically, and those who were captured gave less information to their British interrogators. How was the PIRA able to improve its counterintelligence capabilities so dramatically and rapidly? The answer is that it chose to tighten its organizational structure in response to the British government's increasingly effective counterterrorism tactics, significantly improving its counterintelligence training and compartmentation. However, in doing so, it also exposed itself to a typical counterintelligence trade-off by increasing its vulnerability to high-level penetrations by the British government.

This chapter breaks the PIRA's counterintelligence history into three parts, as shown in table 2.1. The first part depicts the PIRA in its earliest stages, from 1969 to 1972, when its organizational structure was relatively loose and the British government's counterterrorism capabilities were relatively weak. The second part describes the PIRA from 1972 to 1976, when its organizational structure remained relatively loose, but British counterterrorism capabilities improved significantly. The third part describes the PIRA from 1976 to 1994, when its organizational structure became tight and compartmented, and British counterterrorism capabilities remained strong. Figure 2.1 shows Northern Ireland and highlights the PIRA-controlled territory from 1969 to 1994. The three parts illustrate the impact of Britain's improved counterterrorism capabilities

Table 2.1 Provisional Irish Republican Army (PIRA)
Case Study: Key Factors

PIRA	Organizational Structure	Popular Support	Controlled Territory	Resources	Adversary Counterterrorism Capability
1969–1972	Loose	High	Yes	High	Low
1972–1976	Loose	High	Yes	High	High
1976–1994	Tight	High	Yes	High	High

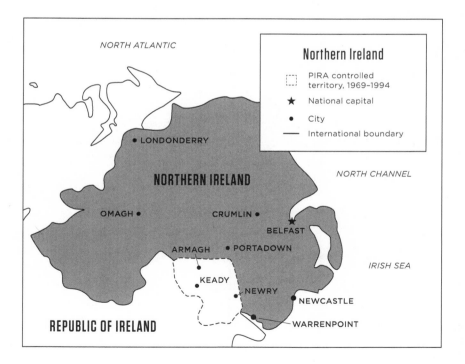

Figure 2.1 Northern Ireland

and how the PIRA's intelligence and counterintelligence capabilities changed in relation to its organizational structure. The three sub-cases allow for the isolation of two of the three factors driving counterintelligence capabilities.

OVERVIEW OF THE PROVISIONAL IRISH REPUBLICAN ARMY

The PIRA was established in Northern Ireland in 1969 as a splinter faction of the Irish Republican Army (IRA). PIRA members, also known as the "Provisionals" or "Provos," sought to defend the mostly Catholic, Irish "Nationalist" communities of Northern Ireland from what they viewed as British imperialism and belligerent pro-British "Unionist" activism.[1]

The PIRA's split from the IRA occurred against the backdrop of the civil rights movement in Northern Ireland, which began in the mid-1960s. The civil rights movement, which aspired to secure greater voting and employment rights for Catholics, turned violent in 1968 and 1969 when pro-British Unionist communities and law enforcement authorities in Northern Ireland increasingly clashed with Nationalist protestors. The Unionist communities, in response to the growing unrest, established Loyalist militia groups, such as the Ulster Volunteer Force, to deter and fend off attacks from Nationalist, Republican activists. The IRA, which had traditionally defended the Nationalist communities, offered a tepid political response to the Republican calls for self-defense.[2]

In August 1969, the police force in Northern Ireland, known as the Royal Ulster Constabulary (RUC), violently engaged Republican protestors marching in the city of Derry, setting off riots across Northern Ireland. The IRA was caught flat-footed, without the weapons, personnel, or strategy to respond to the law enforcement attacks. Later that month several members of the IRA's Belfast branch assembled and created the PIRA. These first members—Gerry Adams, Sean MacStiofain, Billy McKee, Joe Cahill, Leo Martin, and Seamus Twomey—decided that the PIRA would more forcefully defend the Nationalists and Republicans of Northern Ireland.

The PIRA slowly gathered recruits and weapons and by 1972 had established a collection of urban and rural strongholds from which it

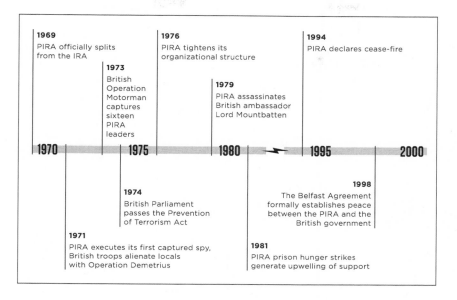

Figure 2.2 Abbreviated Timeline of Key Provisional Irish Republican Army (PIRA) Activities and Events

launched militant operations against British and Northern Ireland's security forces.[3] The British responded by increasing their military, policing, and intelligence operations against the PIRA. In July 1973, the British conducted an urban counterterrorism campaign called "Operation Motorman," which rounded up sixteen of the PIRA's senior leaders and dramatically reduced the group's urban strongholds. In response, the PIRA restructured itself in the mid-1970s and increased its security and lethality. Over the following decade, the PIRA and the British fought to a stalemate by adapting to each other's tactics and leaving only brief periods where one side had a significant strategic advantage. Figure 2.2 offers a summary of key events for the PIRA.

The PIRA and the British shifted their focus to the peace process in the early 1990s. The PIRA declared a cease-fire in August 1994 and gave its political wing, Sinn Fein, greater latitude to seek a political solution with the British and the pro-British authorities in Northern Ireland. Republican frustration with the pace of negotiations grew steadily until in 1996 the PIRA detonated a large bomb in London to show the British that it was capable of renewing its terrorist campaign if the political process did not yield results. The bombing backfired and lost PIRA key supporters, including some among the Nationalist community. From then on, Sinn Fein's political negotiations with the British and Irish governments would determine the future of Northern Ireland and the PIRA.[4] A peace agreement, known as the Belfast Agreement, was reached in 1998, and the PIRA publicly announced several years later that it was abandoning its armed struggle and would commit to surrendering its weapons.

THE PIRA'S BEGINNINGS: 1969–1972

Key Factors

Organizational Structure. The PIRA's leadership consisted of an elected twelve-member Executive, which then elected a seven-member Army Council. The Army Council, which included the General Headquarters Staff, elected Sean MacStiofain the provisional chief of staff—the primary position of authority within the PIRA.[5]

Borrowing from the IRA's structure, the PIRA was modeled after the British army, with brigades, battalions, and companies.[6] In Belfast, the PIRA had three battalions under its influential Belfast Brigade: the First Battalion covering Upper Falls and Ballymurphy; the Second Battalion covering the Lower Falls and Clonard; and the Third Battalion covering Crumlin Road and the Short Strand.[7] Every company was designated to have a commanding officer, a training officer, a quartermaster, and an intelligence officer, in addition to the rank-and-file PIRA members, known as "volunteers."[8]

Despite the paramilitary structure, PIRA leaders exercised loose command and control over the organization and had relatively little tactical or operational control over the activities of PIRA companies. J. Bowyer Bell, a scholar of the Republican movement, describes the PIRA leadership style as "control by consensus": units worked within a rough framework, and decisions were made by those "close to the pointed end of the stick, often at the last possible moment."[9] PIRA scholar Ed Moloney supports Bell's characterization, noting that there was virtually no central control of the PIRA from Dublin or even from the Belfast Brigade: "Companies were encouraged to go their own way. . . . [T]his led to a large amount of operations. . . . [A] bank would be robbed, a bomb downtown, a booby trap for the Brits, snipes, a float—where three or four heavily armed IRA members would drive randomly around their streets in the hope of encountering a British army patrol to fire upon."[10]

During this early period, the General Headquarters Staff suffered from a lack of control over PIRA volunteers and the inability to co-ordinate operations among battalion commanders. In one incident, Gerry Adams, then commander of the Ballymurphy units, had to detain a Belfast unit at gunpoint to keep it from meddling with military affairs in his area of operations.[11] In another incident, undercover PIRA volunteers assassinated three young off-duty British soldiers in March 1971 despite PIRA guidelines not to target off-duty soldiers. The killing was so heinous that the PIRA immediately issued a denial of responsibility.[12]

Throughout 1971, PIRA attacks against police officers and soldiers became increasingly careless, endangering civilians and bystanders.[13] It became clear to lower units that guidelines issued by Dublin were mal-leable and that transgressing them would not result in disciplinary ac-tion.[14] This interpretation became painfully clear to PIRA leaders when they offered a truce to the British in the summer of 1972 but subsequently could not prevent their members from conducting terrorist operations. During the fourteen days of the so-called truce, PIRA volunteers were suspected of killing at least six Protestants, so, not surprisingly, the PIRA leadership denied responsibility and even alleged that some of the kill-ings might have been done by freelancing elements.[15]

One advantage the PIRA gained from this lack of control, Bell ar-gues, is that PIRA units could keep a very high operational attack tempo because of considerable operational freedom at low levels. This higher tempo worked in favor of PIRA interests when PIRA leaders needed to sustain or escalate its efforts.[16]

Popular Support. The PIRA's level of popular support from 1969 to 1972 was intimately related to the British government's failed counter-terrorism policy in Northern Ireland. The British army's policy of ag-gressive house-to-house searches was one of the greatest sources of anger in Catholic communities.[17] The PIRA's ability to play a law enforcement role in its controlled territories, punishing criminals and deterring crime in areas where traditional law enforcement forces had pulled back, gave it additional local support.[18] The British government's blunders in

Northern Ireland—the large-scale raids, the bombing of roads at the Irish border, and Bloody Sunday in January 1972—ultimately led to a surge of support for the PIRA. Gerry Adams described the outcome: "Thousands of people who had never been republicans now gave their active support to the IRA; others, who had never had any time for physical force now accepted it as a practical necessity."[19]

The PIRA knew that British military's tendency to overreact aided the Republican cause, and so it often sought to induce security crackdowns. It successfully compelled British forces to increase security operations outside of the Catholic ghettoes and in the Loyalist and economic centers of Northern Ireland; PIRA bombings in Belfast forced the British to set up a series of checkpoints that included body searches and vehicle searches in the heart of the city's economic center that many civilians found offensive and tedious.[20] PIRA volunteers are alleged to have made anonymous telephone calls to the security forces and misidentified people in Catholic areas as PIRA members, causing a surge of arrests of innocent Catholics, for which the British would be blamed.[21] The PIRA also suffered from its own missteps, however. Bloody Friday, a PIRA bombing incident that accidentally killed seven civilians and two soldiers in Belfast, allowed the British to initiate a series of ambitious raids against the PIRA with relatively little public backlash in Northern Ireland.[22]

The PIRA also used policing and intimidation to garner population support or to enforce compliance with its views in this early period. Most intimidation and "kneecapping" was directed at criminal elements in the population and both solidified the PIRA's control and generated support by keeping local communities safe. The PIRA also forced others to adhere to their views. For example, it targeted Catholic women that fraternized with British soldiers on the streets or in army discos.[23] If Catholic women were caught fraternizing with British soldiers in the street or in the British army's discotheques, they were sometimes tied to a lamp post, and hot tar was poured over their head and upper body—a technique known as "tarring and feathering."[24]

Controlled Territory. One of the PIRA's most important resources was its access to controlled territory. Following the unpopular internment debacle in 1971, where the British army and the RUC arrested and detained suspected PIRA members en masse, the PIRA was able to develop a number of "no go" areas for the British where PIRA could "operate openly," its units "patrolling the streets with weapons on display" and controlling the entire area with barricades and checkpoints.[25] One of the benefits of operating openly was that PIRA volunteers could engage in a wider range of training and testing activities. The volunteers often used their controlled territory in South Armagh to test new weapons and prototype bombs.[26]

The PIRA's ability to establish and control territory varied by region. County Derry, for example, became home to PIRA-controlled "no go" areas because the county shared a border with the Republic of Ireland, whose population was 75 percent Catholic.[27] Belfast's Catholic population, in contrast, was far smaller and less suitable for PIRA control. Even so, the heavily Catholic ghettos of Belfast became effective "no go" areas for British forces.[28]

Other Important Factors

Resources. When the PIRA split from the IRA in 1969, its resources, in terms of recruits and finances, were relatively meager. There were an estimated 50 to 60 members in Belfast, and few weapons were available to them.[29] At the time of the August 1970 riots, when the popular sympathy for Republicans reached new heights, there were an estimated 100 to 120 volunteers in Belfast and between 300 and 500 Republican supporters in the population, known as "auxiliaries," who could be relied upon to relay a message or to hide weapons.[30] The PIRA quickly amassed a deep reservoir of recruits, weapons, and financial supporters, however, due to the British government's inept and heavy-handed response to PIRA activity in Northern Ireland.

Revelations of detainee abuse following the British army counter-terrorism raid Operation Demetrius resulted in the coming forward of many new recruits in Belfast and in areas where the PIRA previously had little support.[31] The PIRA enjoyed a web of safe houses, supportive medical personnel, and around 1,000 "auxiliary" volunteers.[32] By 1972, the organization was inundated with weapons, collected from sympathetic Irish American communities, partners in the Middle East, and international arms markets.[33] PIRA companies were growing so large that they were forced to split, and new members came to outnumber the veteran volunteers needed to train and test them.[34] With its ranks swollen, the PIRA's terrorist activity reached a high point in May 1972 with twelve hundred military operations.[35]

Adversary Counterterrorism Capabilities. Prior to 1969, the British had amassed considerable counterinsurgency experience in Malaya, Kenya, and Cyprus, and they had created the English Intelligence Center in Sussex to serve as the historical storehouse of British counterinsurgency experience.[36] They had difficulty translating these lessons to the Northern Ireland battlefield, however. The British army, the RUC's Special Branch, the British Internal Security Service (MI5), and the British Special Intelligence Service (MI6) were the British government's main counterterrorism forces in Northern Ireland, and each faced challenges in gathering intelligence, coordinating policing and intelligence activities, and resisting military overreaction to the PIRA's terrorist operations.

Between 1969 and 1972, the British government's intelligence on the PIRA was severely lacking. When the conflict began, the RUC's Special Branch, a police intelligence unit, had only twenty officers.[37] The Special Branch's intelligence gathering had historically been focused on the IRA and produced very little intelligence on the new young PIRA hardliners.[38] Special Branch files were based on the IRA's previous military campaign in the late 1950s and contained information that "largely concerned families that had IRA connections in the country districts" in the 1950s.[39] An MI5 team sent to Northern Ireland in the early 1970s to supplement Special Branch activities found that Special Branch did not have a single current address for any high-ranking PIRA personnel.[40]

The British army's intelligence gathering was also unsophisticated. The army relied on a policy of "tea and sympathy." Army officers on patrol would stop and chat with locals in an effort to gain their confidence, which would be followed up with a visit from an intelligence officer if the locals seemed willing to provide information on the PIRA. The British developed their initial picture of Republican activity through unsystematic, casual contact with locals and the occasional detainment of Republican suspects.[41]

British security forces also suffered from inept policing and counterterrorism techniques. British counterterrorism activities were initially relatively passive, relying heavily on fostering good community relations. The British strategy until late 1970 was to avoid confrontation with the broader Catholic community in Northern Ireland by keeping a low-profile in Catholic areas and opening lines of communication to representatives of the Catholic minority.[42] The policy inadvertently created "no go" areas for British forces, which the PIRA exploited to extend its influence in the Catholic communities. The British strategy also meant fewer arrests, patrols, and house searches, which allowed the PIRA to operate openly in these critical "no go" areas.[43]

When the PIRA-led rioting began in the summer of 1970, the British army overcorrected its permissive counterterrorism policy. In July 1970, it imposed a curfew on a prominent Catholic thoroughfare, the Falls Road—an incident that later became known in Republican circles as the "Rape of the Lower Falls."[44] Standoffs and gun battles between PIRA and British soldiers led to an even more severe British reaction, including widespread arrest and internment operations. In August 1971, the British initiated Operation Demetrius, in which British forces were permitted to arrest any individual "under suspicion of acting, having acted, or about to act in a manner that disturbed the peace in Northern Ireland."[45] Operation Demetrius was a disaster largely because of the British government's poor intelligence on the PIRA. The British army rounded up hundreds of innocent people but only a few key PIRA members, thus further alienating the Catholic population.[46]

Operation Demetrius also failed because of poor British counterintelligence. The British failed to apprehend many PIRA volunteers because the PIRA knew the operation was coming. The British army had "telegraphed" the operation by conducting a series of dry runs and "tryout" swoops in late July—an obvious sign to the Republican community that a big operation was imminent.[47] The overt preparations and a possible tip-off from unspecified clandestine sources gave the PIRA advance warning of the British plans.

A second mistake the British made was to increase heavy-handed interrogations of PIRA suspects. As the conflict with the PIRA heated up, the British began more aggressive use of the "five techniques" of interrogation, which included subjecting the suspect to hooding, sleep deprivation, white noise, and a starvation diet, as well as making the suspect stand spread eagle against the wall for hours and assaulting him with verbal harassment and occasional blows. A public inquiry exposed the interrogation abuses and left the Catholic community feeling increasingly alienated from the British government and sympathetic toward the PIRA.[48]

The PIRA's car-bomb innovation further complicated the British government's policing efforts. In order to stop the flow of car bombings in Northern Ireland, the British sealed off traffic from city centers and established numerous checkpoints. This effort placed a large burden on the security force's resources yet failed to prevent many car bombings.[49]

Intelligence and Counterintelligence Outcomes

Intelligence. In the 1969–1972 period, PIRA intelligence gathering was ad hoc and haphazard but was often good enough to serve the PIRA's immediate goals of terrorizing the British and Protestant communities of Northern Ireland. Importantly, PIRA intelligence was focused on simple military operations rather than on assessing the political climate in Britain or Northern Ireland.[50] In 1970, the core of the PIRA campaign involved a series of bombs aimed at economic targets, which would have required only basic surveillance.[51] The strategy worked well because the PIRA had access to plenty of explosives, and the British could not defend every building.[52]

For many targets, extensive preoperational "intelligence" was unnecessary for PIRA units. PIRA volunteer Martin Meehan describes the daily routine for PIRA units in the Ardoyne in this early period: "Members [would] set off in pairs, usually by car, to cruise the narrow streets in search of a target. . . . [I]nstructions were vague. . . . They [the members] were simply under orders to engage any troops who entered the district."[53] PIRA volunteer Brenden Hughes describes this technique as a "float": "That's a two-man car with one man driving and one man in the back with a particular weapon. . . . They'd be floating around waiting until a target came along. . . . [S]ome [operations] would have been opportunistic."[54] The PIRA's targets were sometimes carefully chosen, though—army foot patrols and vehicle convoys would be monitored to find patterns, and hoax warnings were used on occasion to lure soldiers into an ambush.[55]

In this early period, the PIRA received a great deal of intelligence support from sympathetic local populations. In areas where population support was very strong, such as South Armagh, PIRA units relied on locals to gather details of troop activities.[56] In the "no go" areas, where the population was staunchly Republican, PIRA units could openly patrol the streets and check the identities of everyone coming in or out of the area.[57] In some areas, British soldiers would be greeted by Hen Patrols— local women and children rattling garbage can lids, blowing whistles, and following the patrols alley to alley—in order to alert PIRA units to impending raids.[58]

Additional popular support for PIRA intelligence came from the young men who lived in the areas of operation. Men who were too young to serve as PIRA volunteers were used as couriers or lookouts for snipers.[59] Former British army colonel Michael Dewar recalls that in one operation boys signaled to "hidden PIRA members when a British patrol had entered a kill zone, allowing the PIRA members to keep a safe distance for concealment and quick escape."[60]

There is little evidence to support the claim that the PIRA penetrated the security services or the British government during the 1969–1972 period, despite PIRA member Joe Cahill's allegations that the PIRA was tipped off to Operation Demetrius by a PIRA mole working in the office of the minister of home affairs. Cahill and PIRA volunteer Sean Mac-Stiofain allegedly traveled to different company areas forty-eight hours before the operation, telling volunteers not to sleep in their own houses.[61] Though the claim seems sensational, it is corroborated by the fact that the vast majority of key PIRA volunteers eluded British capture by going on the run well before the operation began.[62]

Counterintelligence: Basic Denial. Prior to 1972, PIRA counterintelligence was ad hoc and disorganized, but it was also relatively effective when pitted against British capabilities. The PIRA did not have a counterintelligence staff or unit in this period, so every PIRA unit and volunteer was informally responsible for detecting informers.[63] This counterintelligence posture was likely sufficient for the period given the PIRA's reliance on small, local units that maintained a high operational tempo. Former PIRA official Brenden Hughes argued that because a unit would undertake a series of operations every day, any unexplained absence by an individual member would have raised suspicion among other members of the unit.[64]

The British did not seem to have any significant penetrations of the PIRA in this early period, so the PIRA could survive with haphazard counterintelligence tradecraft. Potential PIRA volunteers would directly contact a local recruiter and would then attend an overt Sinn Fein political meeting, where they could volunteer to join the violent side of the movement.[65] The advantage of recruiting locally was that most volunteers would be known in their community and vetted by their neighbors.[66]

Despite the PIRA's haphazard counterintelligence practices, it was able to stay a step ahead of the British in many cases. Tipped off to Operation Demetrius in August 1971, PIRA volunteers escaped to safe houses. The PIRA also exploited local support to maintain personal security. PIRA scholar Tony Geraghty recalls asking PIRA leader Leo Martin where he slept at night, to which Martin held up a key ring with thirty different door keys.[67] The PIRA also benefited from recruiting volunteers who had no Republican background, called "unknowns" or "sixty-niners," to assure that some portion of the organization would be unknown to the Special Branch.[68] The natural counterintelligence advantage fell to the PIRA in this case because many of the most recruitable volunteers, the young and unemployed, were also those about whom the Special Branch had little intelligence.[69]

Population support also provided the PIRA with a counterintelligence advantage in a number of cases. The medical assistance provided by sympathetic populations within the Republic of Ireland proved invaluable because medical personnel in Northern Ireland would sometimes report suspicious injuries to the police.[70] Controlling territory in the countryside, such as South Armagh, allowed the PIRA to relax its counterintelligence profile and to operate more openly.[71] Staying "hidden" in urban areas was more challenging. Some PIRA leaders realized early on that South Belfast, a religiously mixed area with a large transient student population, was an ideal hiding ground and so decided to use the area as a base.[72]

Some of the PIRA's counterintelligence advantages were based on more coercive practices. Starting in the autumn of 1970, the PIRA took measures against members of the community who socialized with British soldiers. As described earlier, young girls caught socializing with soldiers would sometimes be tied to a lamp post with a placard hung around their neck announcing their offense.[73] The organization dealt even harsher penalties to "touts," volunteers suspected of passing information to the British. The PIRA carried out its first execution in January 1971. John Kavanagh had ignored warnings to avoid contact with the police and so was apprehended, tried in a PIRA "court," and then shot in the back of the head.[74]

During the 1969–1972 period, the PIRA also suffered from counter-intelligence sloppiness. Following a PIRA gun battle with British soldiers in South Armagh, two volunteers proceeded to brag about the operation while drinking in a bar and were subsequently arrested.[75] Many PIRA members made no attempt to conceal their PIRA affiliation, in some cases walking in public wearing balaclavas and stopping cars at check-points with weapons drawn.[76] During the halt in hostilities in 1972, many of the PIRA volunteers who had previously guarded their affiliation openly mixed in public with known PIRA men, all of which British intelligence observed and later exploited.[77]

The PIRA's disciplining and public condemnation of group members who made unsanctioned contact with the adversary was a basic-denial tactic. It would have been adaptive denial had the PIRA investigated the contacts of volunteers such as John Kavanagh to learn what made him vulnerable to British recruitment. The PIRA's windfall of recruits from populations that did not have Republican backgrounds can also be characterized as a basic-denial technique to the extent that it was an intentional recruiting strategy.

Summary. In the 1969–1972 period, the PIRA maintained a loose or-ganizational structure built on a wealth of financial and human re-sources and expanded the territory it controlled. The PIRA also benefited from a relatively weak adversary that was prone to military overreaction and unpopular mass arrests. The PIRA's operational and counterintelli-gence postures were ad hoc rather than standardized, but they were often sufficient given the weakness of British counterterrorism efforts. The PIRA occasionally exposed its personnel and political agenda in its efforts to generate popular support through open Sinn Fein meetings in the local communities, but overall it built organizational and opera-tional momentum during this time.

THE DECENTRALIZED PIRA SUFFERS HEAVY LOSS: 1972-1976

Key Factors

Organizational Structure. The PIRA's command-and-control structure in the mid-1970s remained loose and nominally organized in brigades, battalions, and companies. By 1973, British forces began to capture many PIRA leaders, but the PIRA's loose command structure allowed it to recover quickly from these losses in some cases. Bell notes that when the British captured Gerry Adams, commanding officer of the Belfast Brigade, the brigade took "only a week or so to recover." The Belfast unit's ability to recover quickly was severely tested in this period—following Adams's arrest in July 1973, its next five commanders were arrested in succession within a year.[78]

The PIRA's resilience was due in part to its units' operational independence. Units in the countryside in particular had little or no operational connection to any other PIRA units and sometimes no contact with the Army Council or a representative from the General Headquarters Staff for six months at a time.[79] Units in East Tyrone and South Armagh were effectively under the control of their respective clan chieftains, Kevin Mellon and Tom Murphy.[80] Scholar Ed Moloney quotes a rural PIRA volunteer's description of the relationship between these units and central leadership: "The leadership would never try to give them orders. . . . There was virtually no control from the center. They mounted operations against the British, and the job of the leadership was to provide resources, training, guns, explosives."[81] PIRA units deployed in London also exercised considerable autonomy. In 1974, the London unit was averaging about one attack a week in spite of limited communication with the PIRA's "overseas operations" headquarters in Dublin.[82]

The relative autonomy of PIRA units also made them difficult to control. Units throughout Northern Ireland would often act without clearance from the General Headquarters Staff, seeking revenge for sectarian killings or conducting special operations. In one case, the PIRA unit in Andersonstown kidnapped a German businessman without official authorization, and when the German died of a heart attack, the PIRA disowned the attack out of embarrassment.[83] Lack of control also imperiled some of the PIRA's political strategies. On February 9, 1975, its Army Council announced a cease-fire after discussions with British officials, but only a month later a PIRA unit in Derry killed an RUC constable.[84]

The loose command-and-control structure also affected personnel management. The flood of PIRA recruits was incorporated, sometimes haphazardly, into this structure.[85] Talented individuals were not easily shared or transferred to where they might be needed most.[86] In addition, there was no formal plan for "retiring" PIRA members who had served a full career with the PIRA and were looking to return to the nonmilitant lifestyle. Former PIRA member Sean O'Callaghan recalls that volunteers came and went all the time, and their absence was sometimes not even noticed.[87] The PIRA continued to lack a formal training plan for its recruits between 1972 and 1976.[88] O'Callaghan notes that when he was a young volunteer in the mid-1970s, training was informally conducted by a member of his unit and focused mostly on weapons skills.[89]

Popular Support. Popular support for the PIRA also did not shift significantly from the early to the mid-1970s. Local support continued to be an important asset in PIRA intelligence and counterintelligence operations. One of the most important forms of support from the population was "nondenunciation," or denial of any knowledge of PIRA personnel or activities, which stymied British investigations and intelligence collection.[90]

Popular support also aided intelligence collection. PIRA spies in Northern Ireland's tax and social security offices passed useful information to the group, such as the home addresses of police officers and personal information about members of the Loyalist paramilitaries.[91] In 1973, a telephone engineer with PIRA sympathies offered to tap British army communications when his company assigned him to install a new back-up telephone exchange at the army's Lisburn headquarters.[92] The engineer was not a member of the PIRA but had developed strong sympathies for the PIRA after he saw the British army kill a protestor in Andersonstown.[93]

The PIRA also continued to use intimidation and other "heavy-handed" techniques to force the population's acquiescence. Police informers were dealt with harshly, and knowledge of the PIRA informant policy was enough to compel many citizens to lend their cars and houses for PIRA operations without question.[94] The majority of residents did not approve of the organization's intimidation methods but preferred to tolerate them rather than resist the PIRA.[95] Former PIRA member Raymond Gilmour recalls that people who knew each other fairly well might talk about PIRA policies freely in the confines of their own homes, but talking about the PIRA in public was considered dangerous.[96] There was no appreciable decline in the PIRA's overall popular support in this period, but sympathy for the PIRA was probably beginning to thin as the shock of internment wore off, and reckless PIRA thuggery in the ghettoes continued.[97]

Controlled Territory. One big change for the PIRA in the early to mid-1970s was its loss of urban "no go" areas.[98] As the British improved their counterterrorism capabilities, they began to challenge the PIRA's controlled territory more effectively. Operation Motorman, one of the British government's most important urban counterterrorism operations, worked well because it was politically sensitive and reduced PIRA "no go" areas in the city centers of Belfast and Derry.[99] The operation took place on July 31, 1973, and was largely successful because it followed a particularly violent PIRA attack known as "Bloody Friday"—an operation that killed six civilians, including two Catholics and two children. The attack gave the British license to reclaim some of the PIRA's urban controlled territory and to construct military forts in some of these areas, both of which restricted the PIRA's freedom of movement and allowed the British to surveil thousands of civilians with Republican sympathies. The British grip on the PIRA strongholds in West Belfast grew so tight that the PIRA was forced to move its operational headquarters to the southern fringes of the city. Areas bordering the Republic of Ireland, however, continued to offer safe haven to PIRA units.[100]

Other Important Factors

Resources. PIRA resources did not shift significantly from the early 1970s to the mid-1970s; the PIRA still had a flood of recruits, often too many to deploy. British counterterrorism operations did put some strain on the group. The number of PIRA suspects arrested, interned, or charged with criminal offenses increased from one hundred to one thousand from 1972 to 1973. On a single day in July 1973, the PIRA saw at least sixteen of its most experienced leaders arrested by the British, including the entire staff of the Third Brigade.[101] Following Operation Motorman, the British set up security checkpoints in urban centers and security towers in the countryside. Urban units continued their bombing campaigns at a reduced level, and although the countryside was still considered "bandit country," PIRA volunteers had to move about more cautiously or operate only at night.[102]

Adversary Counterterrorism Capabilities. As the increase in arrests shows, by 1973 the British government's counterterrorism capabilities had dramatically improved and continued to improve through 1976.[103] Specific counterterrorism improvements included intelligence collection through house raids, interrogations, and penetrations of the PIRA as well as better coordination between routine policing and more politically sensitive military interventions.

House raids conducted by British forces reached a peak in 1973, when security forces searched one-fifth of all houses in Northern Ireland.[104] Raids and interrogations were reoriented toward gathering information about future PIRA operations rather than gathering evidence to facilitate criminal prosecution of past operations.[105] The British Parliament passed the Prevention of Terrorism Act in 1974, which aided British counterterrorism efforts by allowing terrorist suspects to be detained for up to seven days.[106] The week-long interrogations allowed under the Prevention of Terrorism Act proved an intelligence windfall for the British. A secret PIRA document confiscated in 1977 from a high-ranking PIRA leader revealed that British detentions were taking a severe toll on the organization: "The three-day and seven-day detention orders are breaking volunteers and it is the Republican Army's fault for not indoctrinating volunteers with a psychological strength to resist interrogation."[107] The PIRA's assessment highlights the advantage of having a tighter organizational structure that permits the standard indoctrination of lower-level members. The PIRA's loose structure made this sort of routine counterintelligence training difficult.

British penetrations of the PIRA also improved.[108] British forces recruited many cash-deprived young Catholics during their interrogation by offering them a financial reward for spying on the PIRA.[109] British authorities also stepped up their effort to penetrate the Irish community in Great Britain, hoping to forestall support to PIRA units.[110] British forces skillfully used their interrogation centers to meet with PIRA informants. Uniformed British battalions sometimes staged mass arrests to identify new informers and to provide cover for meetings with ongoing informants.[111]

In one case, the British recruited the Belfast Brigade quartermaster, Eamon Malloy, during an interrogation but knew that releasing him back to the street quickly without a criminal trial would raise suspicion in the PIRA ranks. The British invented a cover story for Malloy, which was that he had escaped through a door that was carelessly left unlocked at the interrogation facility. The story was good enough to get Malloy back into the PIRA ranks, from which he was able to provide British forces with details about arms dumps and the location of hard-to-smuggle weaponry—intelligence that decimated the PIRA arsenal.[112] The British worked hard to recruit quartermasters during this time because they would "know where weapons were" and, up until the PIRA's reorganization, "who was using them."[113]

MI5 hired many new officers and employed new techniques in order to improve surveillance operations against the PIRA. It also began to plant listening devices in suspects' cars and homes; in one scenario, it would covertly "award" a suspect with a weekend holiday trip through a staged radio contest and then wire the house with microphones once the individual left for the weekend.[114] British forces used creative intelligence analysis to improve operations against the PIRA. Special Branch and other intelligence offices worked out which units were responsible for which operations based on the PIRA's well-defined geographical distribution. They used this analysis to aid interrogations and achieve more precise targeting.[115]

British intelligence agencies also employed more sophisticated offensive intelligence operations, which targeted internal PIRA morale. The British frequently announced that informant information had led to an arrest even when it had not or exaggerated the figure of the spoils of a PIRA bank robbery, a ploy designed to raise suspicions of betrayal, which sometimes resulted in a spate of internal PIRA punishment shootings.[116] A PIRA spokesperson aptly summed up the British counterterrorism capabilities in this period, referring to a specific British operation: "We were had. We knew we had fallen for it. It was very much in the mould of the [British army intelligence] operations, clever, well-planned and brilliantly executed. . . . They almost destroyed us. They created paranoia in the ranks and left us severely damaged."[117]

Intelligence and Counterintelligence Outcomes

Intelligence. The PIRA's intelligence-collection capability in this period was at times quite sophisticated, such as when for several months the PIRA tapped key British army intelligence unit phones at the army's Lisburn headquarters.[118] The PIRA's intelligence collection mostly supported basic operations against static or soft targets. Successful operations included locating the London home of the British army's adjunct general, the bus ferrying British soldiers between Manchester and Catterick Camp, British army headquarters at the Grand Central Hotel, the Special Branch chief in Omagh, Judge Rory Conaghan, and Magistrate Martin McBirney.[119] In some cases, soft civilian targets required even less operational intelligence—pubs frequented by off-duty soldiers were easy surveillance targets.[120]

Even the PIRA's more sophisticated intelligence operations were performed in a relatively ad hoc and haphazard manner. The successful bugging of the army's Lisburn headquarters depended on the fortuitous access gained by a Republican sympathizer who through trial and error eventually tapped the line that led to the army's intelligence unit "G2 Int." The tap itself was "not sophisticated," consisting of a "voice-activated tape recorder" and a descrambling device stolen from army headquarters.[121]

Even the relatively successful London operations in the mid-1970s were based on ad hoc intelligence collection. Units would get intelligence, orders, and suggestions from headquarters through couriers but would usually choose their own targets and gather the critical operational intelligence only weeks before the operation.[122]

Although PIRA intelligence collection was basic and often disorganized, the PIRA used some of its incarcerated members to perform intelligence analysis. Long Kesh prison, home to many arrested PIRA volunteers, developed its own command and leadership structures and became a de facto think tank for the organization.[123] Some of the PIRA's most innovative analysis, including that which inspired the PIRA's reorganization, was prepared by prisoners at Long Kesh.[124]

Counterintelligence: Basic Denial, Some Adaptive Denial. PIRA counter-intelligence in this period was also relatively ad hoc and disorganized and was made increasingly haggard by improvements in British counter-terrorism efforts. In spite of being unstructured, though, it was sound, and so PIRA enjoyed several counterintelligence successes. Some PIRA units continued to recruit volunteers with no criminal records who were unlikely to be known to British forces.[125] The PIRA also occasionally forced nonvolunteers to drive truck bombs to their targets in order to keep PIRA volunteers out of the reach of security forces.[126] For some operations, PIRA units would change the license plates and paint jobs of cars to be used in operations to keep from drawing the suspicion of security forces.[127]

The PIRA continued to enjoy counterintelligence support from the Catholic and Republican community. The community's knowledge of what the PIRA did to police informants was often enough to keep them from offering information to security forces.[128] The British government's "confidential phone" operation, in which any citizen could leave an anonymous message about PIRA activities, was a failure for the British.[129] Gerry Adams argued that it was impossible for the majority of Catholics to see the PIRA from the same perspective as British forces did: "It's not staff officer Paddy Maguire," Adams explained, "it's Mrs. Maguire's boy."[130] The PIRA also recognized the counterintelligence threat that came from operating in areas where it lacked popular support, such as in England. By the early 1970s, the British had infiltrated many pro-Republican organizations in England, and as a result Sinn Fein did not allow its British supporters to open overseas branches.[131]

The PIRA would occasionally offer amnesty to informants if they told the PIRA everything about their activities and other British informants.[132] This strategy was particularly clever, in theory, because it potentially al-lowed the PIRA to reduce the number of informants in their ranks, assess damage done by British informants, and adjust PIRA operations to reduce damage from current and future British intelligence operations. The trade-off for the PIRA was that by offering amnesty, it might be reducing a volunteer's perceived risk of becoming British informant.

The PIRA further bolstered its counterintelligence posture by exploiting the talents of volunteers in prison. PIRA inmates at Long Kesh analyzed a string of British counterterrorism successes and discovered that PIRA volunteer Kevin Malloy was most likely an informer. Inmates passed this message to the leadership outside, and Malloy was eventually tricked into admitting his role as an informer.[133] PIRA inmates would debrief and interrogate newly arrived inmates and in one case prompted two "fake" inmates in the Crumlin Road jail to confess to working as informants for the RUC's Special Branch. Interrogations were sometimes brutal—a warden at Long Kesh prison discovered that PIRA interrogation devices included piano wire and electric current.[134]

The PIRA used interrogations to enhance its counterintelligence practices outside of the prisons as well. It learned from informant Kevin Malloy that the British had PIRA leader Brenden Hughes and an important PIRA safe house under constant surveillance.[135] Hughes claims to have used information gleaned from the PIRA's phone tap at Lisburn to inform at least one counterespionage investigation.[136] The PIRA also learned of several major British covert-action programs by interrogating suspected informants Kevin McKee and Seamus Wright.[137] In addition to revealing the presence of more British informants among the PIRA, McKee and Wright alerted the PIRA to a laundry service run by British spies to test the clothing of Republicans for explosives residue.[138] These counterintelligence victories demonstrate the PIRA's effective interrogation practices but also reveal that it had limited systematic counterintelligence capabilities because the penetrations were detected as a result of nonroutine counterespionage interrogations.[139]

The PIRA's disorganized and ad hoc counterintelligence practices cost the organization dearly. Part of the problem stemmed from the PIRA's growing membership—as the organization grew, security tended to slacken.[140] In some areas, such as the Divis Flats, security problems arose because PIRA volunteers were easy to target as they patrolled streets openly with weapons displayed.[141] Lack of training and sloppiness also contributed to counterintelligence problems. British police named this sloppiness the "Paddy factor."[142] PIRA scholar Tim Pat Coogan argues that in the mid-1970s anyone could stroll into a PIRA establishment, such as a bar in Andersonstown, and observe PIRA volunteers and supporters mixing together and singing about the battalion to which they belonged—a potential intelligence windfall for any police agent present.[143]

The British government's most lethal counterterrorism platforms during this period were its interrogation "holding centers" at Castlereagh, Gough Barracks, and Strand Road. One PIRA volunteer recalled: "Men were breaking in the police stations. We'd hear of people handing over 25 or 30 names at a time."[144] The British used this intelligence to arrest top PIRA leadership, including Sean MacStiofain (November 1972), Sean Keenan (November 1972), Martin Meehan (November 1972), Ruairi O'Bradaigh (December 1972), Martin McGuinness (December 1972), Joe McCallion (December 1972), Anthony Doherty (January 1973), Leo Martin (January 1973), John Martin (February 1973), Seamus Twomey (September 1973), Kevin Mallon (September 1973), and Ivor Bell (April 1974), to name only a few.[145] In June 1973, British forces arrested twenty-three known PIRA volunteers and thirteen known officers in a period of five days. In July, security forces arrested seventeen members of the Belfast Brigade, including the three most wanted men in Belfast—senior PIRA leaders Gerry Adams, Tom Cahill, and Brenden Hughes. The PIRA was so weakened by the string of arrests that PIRA leaders Gerry Adams and Martin McGuinness regarded this time in PIRA history as the closest the organization came to defeat.[146]

The PIRA's decision to refrain from opening political branches in England to avoid being infiltrated by British spies could be characterized as adaptive denial. It is unclear, however, that the PIRA made this decision specifically as a result of a confirmed case of British intelligence infiltrating an overseas cell. The group's use of interrogations, the Lisburn phone tap, and analysis conducted in prisons to make operational adjustments is clearly an example of adaptive denial. Most of the PIRA's counterintelligence practices in this period, however, can be categorized as basic denial.

Summary. From 1972 to 1976, the PIRA maintained a loose organizational structure, a high level of resources, and access to shrinking controlled territory. The major change in this period was that British counterterrorism capabilities dramatically improved, presenting the PIRA with a significant, existential challenge. The PIRA's operational and counterintelligence training and practices remained ad hoc, and PIRA leaders were systematically captured as a result. The British government's ability to take advantage of the PIRA's lack of training, also known as the "Paddy factor," is a clear example of the critical importance of standardized counterintelligence training for terrorist groups.

THE PIRA CENTRALIZES ITS COMMAND: 1976–1994

Key Factors

Organizational Structure. The PIRA's command-and-control structure changed dramatically from the second to the third period. The structural change began in the fall of 1976 and involved a tightening of command and control over the organization, which increased the top PIRA leaders' control of PIRA volunteers and included the compartmentation of PIRA Active Service Units (ASUs) into cells.[147] The PIRA made these structural changes as a direct response to improvements in British counterterrorism practices. Its restructuring strategy memo, known as the Staff Report, was found on arrested PIRA member Seamus Twomey in December 1977.[148] The document spelled out the motivation for and the ramifications of PIRA restructuring: "This old system with which the Brits and the [Special] Branch are familiar has to be changed. We recommend reorganization and remotivation. . . . We emphasize a return to secrecy and strict discipline. Army men must be in total command of all sections of the movement. . . . Anti-interrogation lectures must be given in conjunction with indoctrination lectures. . . . Cells of four volunteers will be controlled militarily by the Brigade's/Command Operations Officer. . . . Cells should operate as often as possible outside of their own areas: both to confuse Brit intelligence (which would increase our security) and to expand out operational areas."[149]

The PIRA was able to tighten its command-and-control structure by compartmenting PIRA units.[150] Compartmentation was designed to keep most of the members of one cell from knowing the members of another cell and to keep the individual cells dependent on top leadership for resources and direction. Cells would have one leader who reported to the brigade operations officer so only the leader of the cell

would be in contact with members of the brigade staff.[151] Compartmentation, it was hoped, would make it difficult for a British interrogator to extract much information from a captured volunteer.[152]

The PIRA's second organizational shift involved dividing the PIRA
into two commanding units, the Northern Command and the Southern Command, and subordinating the previously influential Southern
Command to the northern leadership. The Northern Command, created in 1976, gave leaders from the North much greater control over
daily operations in the six counties of Northern Ireland and the four
border counties of the Republic of Ireland, where the majority of fighting occurred.[153] The Southern Command retained control over military
action abroad and was responsible for facilitating weapons procure-
ment for the northern fighters.[154] The position of northern commander
became the most important position in the PIRA, and the individual
occupying that post had the final say in strategic and operational matters.[155] Over time, the Northern Command's control over the PIRA grew;
by 1986, the Northern Command was vetting most operations, and area
commanders were expected to describe prospective operations to the
chief of staff in detail.[156]

The PIRA also restructured its prison command-and-control structures. Inmates could no longer select a commanding officer by vote
but instead would submit a list of candidates to the Army Council,
which would then select one of the nominees to assume the role of
commander—a move that significantly increased the influence of the
Army Council in the prisons.[157]

The effort to tighten and compartmentalize the PIRA was largely successful, but it was neither complete nor problem free. Because the PIRA
remained relatively dependent on public support for its operations, volunteers were in some cases known to the local population and to each
other.[158] Volunteers also broke with secrecy practices during the hunger-
strike protests, for which they had to go public, and the marches, when
they could be seen talking and marching together in the open.[159]

The restructuring increased PIRA leaders' knowledge of and power
over the organization, which made them more enticing targets for
British forces. Because the PIRA depended more heavily on this cadre
of leaders, every leadership loss would affect the PIRA more deeply.[160]
Compartmentation reduced contact between PIRA leaders and low-level

volunteers, but it increased contact between PIRA leaders and midlevel volunteers, making those volunteers a more valuable target for the British. PIRA volunteer Raymond Gilmour, a midlevel driver and intermediary for his cell, became an ideal British informant because he was in regular contact with a wide range of PIRA members throughout Derry.[161] Midlevel PIRA counterespionage officer Freddie Scappaticci became another key British informant because he had access to the PIRA's innermost secrets—upcoming missions, arms cache locations, travel and security details, bombing and assassination targets, and which PIRA volunteers were suspected of being informants. Scappaticci was able to protect himself from suspicion by rigging counterespionage investigations and framing "innocent" PIRA members.[162]

Compartmentation occasionally generated operational coordination problems. In theory, cell leaders would deconflict their operations by coordinating their activities via the brigade commander. At times, however, one cell's operations could compromise another clandestine cell's logistical base or safety.[163]

Increased top-down command and coordination also blunted the PIRA's spontaneous edge.[164] Unpredictability had made the PIRA a hard target in the 1970s, and some of that unpredictability was lost when PIRA leaders standardized the organization's operations and tradecraft.[165] The PIRA in South Armagh had resisted sharing its radio-controlled bomb technology with the rest of the PIRA for fear of having it captured and studied by the British—which is exactly what happened when Northern Command forced South Armagh to share the bomb technology with other PIRA units.[166]

In spite of these challenges, the restructuring was on balance a success for the PIRA. The compartmented structure provided a host of counterintelligence advantages, and the PIRA was able to exert greater control over its personnel. A higher degree of control allowed the Northern Command to coordinate attacks throughout Northern Ireland and to make "rapid alterations in military tactics more feasible."[167] Improved control also equipped the organization to support advanced training and increased specialization in PIRA units.[168] Finally, the PIRA was better prepared to increase or scale back operations to maximize public support for its campaign.[169] Perhaps the most convincing evidence on this ledger was the British government's admission that the PIRA had become significantly more sophisticated. Humphrey Atkins, secretary of state for Northern Ireland, spoke about the PIRA in July 1979: "The first six months of this year have shown a marked rise in the level of terrorism and have demonstrated that we are up against a more professional enemy, organized on a system of self-contained, close-knit cells which make it difficult to gather information."[170]

Popular Support. The PIRA popular support remained high from 1976 through 1994. The countryside, including border areas and South Armagh, continued to offer the greatest source of popular support. Many of these areas initially wished to remain neutral in the conflict in order not to attract police attention, but rough searches, planting of weapons, and abrasive checkpoints turned the population against the police.[171] In the Republic of Ireland, the PIRA had an estimated fifty thousand to one hundred thousand sympathizers, which included individuals who attended funerals and memorials, signed petitions, or were simply outspoken.[172]

The PIRA had by the late 1970s grown even savvier about cultivating public support. The top leadership required that any potentially contentious operation, such as an assassination or operation that endangered civilians, receive top-level clearance.[173] This care was reflected in the dramatic decline in civilian deaths caused by the PIRA in this period; whereas security-force deaths remained approximately the same between 1976 and 1977, civilian deaths dropped from 243 to 67.[174] The PIRA's "Green Book"—a manual on the organization's mission and intelligence and counterintelligence procedures—stated: "Resistance must be channeled into active and passive support with an on-going process through our actions, our education programmes, our policies of attempting to turn the passive supporter into a dump holder, a member of the movement."[175] The PIRA also sought to undermine its adversaries' popular base. PIRA analysis in 1977 estimated that a terrorist campaign in Northern Ireland might evoke a Loyalist overreaction and thereby reduce popular support for Protestants.[176]

The PIRA's reorganization both helped and hindered its quest to win popular support. The reorganization allowed the PIRA to plan and coordinate operations that did not alienate the public, but the stricter compartmentation and the increased secrecy drew PIRA volunteers away from daily interaction with the average citizen of Northern Ireland.[177] One PIRA volunteer argued that less contact with the population eventually led to less familiarity and trust between the PIRA and the public.[178]

Controlled Territory. Border and countryside areas, such as South Armagh, remained the main territories controlled by the PIRA. RUC sources claimed that there was an almost total lack of informants in South Armagh.[179] A British military assessment from the time remarked that there were areas in Northern Ireland and the Republic of Ireland where the PIRA could act with relatively impunity: "The Republic [of Ireland] provides many of the facilities of a classic safe haven so essential to any terrorist movement."[180]

In contrast, noncontrolled territories were far more vulnerable to British surveillance. J. Bowyer Bell argues that Nationalist areas of the city began to resemble low-security prisons: "There were cameras and night sights, hidden spotters, bought informants, erratic patrols and undercover police, computer banks and those who kept track of milk delivered and clothes taken to the cleaners."[181] Belfast traffic was forced through choke points and roadblocks and constantly monitored from hidden observation posts.[182]

Other Important Factors

Resources. The PIRA retained access to sufficient resources between 1976 and 1994. The PIRA's rosters were purposely slimmed down following reorganization, commanding between three hundred and four hundred active-duty volunteers in Northern Ireland by the early 1980s.[183] The PIRA continued to draw on one thousand "auxiliary" supporters who provided safe houses and transportation assistance.[184] Full-time active-service members were expected to be ready to participate in an operation at all times and were even paid by the PIRA—though only about twenty pounds per week. The PIRA assured itself of a steady supply of recruits through its PIRA "boy scouts" movement.[185]

The PIRA also did not lack for weapons in this period. By October 1986, it had smuggled approximately three hundred tons of Libyan weapons into Northern Ireland and had hidden the weapons in secret dumps.[186] This cache was supplemented with a steady stream of weapons smuggled from the United States in small shipments that were hard for law enforcement to detect.[187] The PIRA always wanted more weapons, but it always seemed to have plenty to continue its campaign.[188]

The quality of PIRA personnel and their expertise increased from 1976 to 1994. By the 1990s, the average PIRA volunteer was in his midtwenties to late thirties, in contrast to the earlier periods when the average volunteer was in his late teens.[189] Volunteers improved their technological sophistication, deploying more deadly bombs and preventing more volunteer deaths due to premature detonations.[190] In 1993, police discovered a PIRA electronics engineering lab in the Republic of Ireland, where the PIRA had put young electronics graduates to work on making and testing homemade electronic detonators.[191]

Adversary Counterterrorism Capabilities. British counterterrorism capabilities remained high and even steadily improved from 1976 through 1994. British security forces continued to coordinate operations successfully, extract information through interrogation centers, recruit informants, and moderate military activity to garner public sympathies.

The RUC took the lead in the war against the PIRA in 1976—the job that had previously fallen to the British army—which led to increased cooperation between the RUC and other military and intelligence agencies.[192] The RUC's Special Branch and military intelligence were sharing information with other intelligence units and running some agents together by the mid-1980s.[193] The RUC turned itself into a top-notch policing and intelligence organization, having developed the most comprehensive network of informants in Northern Ireland, a world-renown forensic science department, and its own equivalent of the British Special Air Service (a surveillance unit known as Echo 4 Alpha), which increased collaboration between the police, the RUC, and MI5.[194] Supplementing the RUC's work was the Force Research Unit, a British military intelligence squad, which managed its own spies and informants.[195] The British army also fielded the Military Reconnaissance Force, which conducted surveillance and intelligence operations against the PIRA.[196] Beginning in the mid-1980s, the Special Air Service increased its operations in Northern Ireland and used sophisticated electronic surveillance and informants to plan and conduct ambushes and captures.[197]

British interrogation centers continued to produce information on the PIRA, but they also became increasingly fertile ground for recruiting informants. The British focused on recruiting vulnerable PIRA volunteers—captured volunteers would be given the choice of a long jail sentence or money and protection if they agreed to spy on the PIRA; not surprisingly, some chose to spy.[198] Interrogation centers such as Castlereagh also benefited from a brutal reputation, and some captured volunteers would quickly give up information to avoid the RUC's infamous "torture" practices.[199]

Through the 1990s, the RUC was getting a large portion of its daily intelligence on the PIRA from informants run by Special Branch, estimated to have been in the hundreds.[200] The British government also began to use "supergrasses"—informants who were offered amnesty, a new life, and a pension—to provide evidence in court against PIRA volunteers.[201] British forces cleverly targeted senior PIRA officers who had left the organization under a cloud of disagreement because these individuals were more vulnerable to a recruitment pitch.[202] The British also started rumors of informants in the PIRA—the British knew that PIRA cells would tend to lie low for up to several months after such an incident for fear of being betrayed by the phantom informant.[203]

The British infused their counterterrorism strategy with an increasing technological sophistication. When the RUC took the counterterrorism helm in 1976, it centralized collected intelligence in massive databases; the personal information about every suspect brought into the police station—including aliases, nicknames, neighborhood, accent, scars, and tattoos—would be loaded into a database.[204] By the late 1980s, intelligence agents would plant listening devices in suspects' houses that could transmit for months and upload recorded material to a helicopter flying overhead.[205] The Royal Air Force provided aerial photography to British forces and used infrared and thermal imaging to search for subterranean arms caches.[206] The British also used sophisticated computer software to monitor large numbers of telephone calls, including all cross-border calls and all calls to known Republicans.[207] The increased surveillance capability made it difficult for the PIRA to operate in the open, even in its countryside strongholds.[208]

Intelligence and Counterintelligence Outcomes

Intelligence. The PIRA increased the sophistication of its tactical intelligence-collection operations from 1976 to 1994. It probably never acquired a capacity to gather strategic or political intelligence systematically because the organization's survival rarely depended on this type of intelligence collection even after political negotiations with the British government began in 1994.[209] The PIRA's military operations usually followed the same basic procedure: scouting teams would case an area, safe houses would be rented, explosives would be moved in, cars used for the operation would be acquired, intelligence would be gathered by volunteers conducting basic foot surveillance, and then the bomb would be delivered to its target.[210] Intelligence collection did not need to be highly sophisticated to be effective.

The PIRA eased the tactical intelligence burden by selecting targets that were generally vulnerable to observation. PIRA soft targets included civil servants, government contractors, telecommunications companies, shipping and bus companies that transported soldiers, and retired members of the various British security forces.[211] Harder targets included British soldiers, members of the RUC and Ulster Defense Regiment, and members of Loyalists paramilitaries.[212] Even an RUC officer, however, had considerable vulnerabilities—he was easy to spot and follow because he walked around in an official uniform and was stationed in an immobile base.[213] The PIRA also grew more proficient at tracking troop patrol and police movements. Its operations would often follow the path of least resistance, seeking vulnerable targets close to home—targets that required relatively less sophisticated intelligence collection. Bell puts this strategy succinctly: "If the lights in London were to be turned off, the IRA bombed the power stations rather than tinkered with the computers."[214]

Static targets were preferred because they were more easily observed and, by definition, could not be hidden or moved. The PIRA mounted attacks on Downing Street, the Grand Hotel in London, a Royal Air Force officer's club in Germany, and RUC stations across Northern Ireland.[215] The PIRA also successfully targeted VIPs. Among their favorite targets were British judges involved in prosecuting PIRA volunteers. The organization assassinated Judge William Doyle, Magistrate William

Staunton, Magistrate Martin McBirney, Judge Rory Conahan, and Lord Chief Justice Sir Maurice Gibson, Northern Ireland's second most senior judge.[216] Other victims of PIRA assassinations included several Ulster politicians, the assistant governor of Long Kesh prison, the director of an American-owned Dupont factory in Derry, the British ambassador to the Netherlands, a prominent retired British ambassador, and the prominent author of *The Guinness Book of World Records* after he had offered a one-hundred-thousand-pound reward for information leading to the arrest of PIRA volunteers.[217]

PIRA surveillance continued to be strong in this period. RUC stations and bases were regularly watched, and the model and license plates of RUC vehicles were recorded.[218] Detectives working against the PIRA could be observed as they gave evidence against the organization in court.[219] Patient PIRA surveillance occasionally produced dramatic operational successes. In 1979, surveillance of British convoy activity in County Down allowed the PIRA to ambush a British truck convoy, killing eighteen soldiers.[220] Also in 1979, patient observation of former British ambassador Lord Mountbatten and the Gardai forces protecting him allowed the PIRA to assassinate him on his private boat while he vacationed in Ireland.[221]

The PIRA also benefited from improvements in technical surveillance collection. In June 1979, the RUC raided three houses in Andersonstown and stumbled upon a command post filled with radios, unscrambling equipment, sophisticated monitors, military-grade transmitters, position-fixing devices, and telephone taps routed through the British Telecom network.[222] Most surprisingly, the RUC discovered detailed transcripts of the RUC's Operation Hawk—a major surveillance operation against the PIRA initiated in early 1979.[223] Operation Hawk had been tracking PIRA leadership, and the PIRA had been listening in and adjusting its operations. PIRA leadership had even deliberately moved their people around to discover what code names the RUC was using for them.[224] It seems likely that the PIRA leadership used this technique to discover which volunteers were unknown to the RUC and therefore more useful for particularly sensitive activities or operations. By listening to RUC postoperation assessments, the PIRA also used this technical collection capability to call off compromised operations, to move out of unsafe locations, and to refine its bombing tactics.[225]

The PIRA had actually begun to acquire radio equipment capable of breaking into police and army communications networks in the early 1970s, but it was not until the late 1970s that it acquired the number of radios and the technical expertise to sift quickly through security-force frequencies and lock in on a particular target. This technical surveillance capability also allowed the PIRA to cut back on the number of volunteers conducting labor-intensive foot surveillance.[226]

There is some evidence that the PIRA used open sources to supplement secret collection activities. Bell argues that a close reading of open sources helped the PIRA to conduct several operations, including the attempted assassination of Margaret Thatcher at the Grand Hotel.[227] Former PIRA volunteer Raymond Gilmour indicates that checking the local news was a trusted source of intelligence: "Every IRA man tuned in to the BBC's early morning Northern Ireland bulletin . . . [which] always gave a catalogue of all the previous night's bombings, shootings, hijackings, knee-cappings, riots, arrests, and arms finds."[228] It is alleged that PIRA volunteers sometimes used public sources, such as the *Who's Who* book, to gather biographical information for assassination operations.[229]

There is also evidence that the PIRA occasionally collected human intelligence through interrogations and penetrations of British security elements, including the RUC.[230] The PIRA used a seductress, also known as a "honey trap," to control a vulnerable Maze prison guard, John Christopher Hanna, who was subsequently given a life sentence for helping the PIRA.[231] Prisons, the organization's "think tanks," turned out to be a good source of intelligence analysis and collection for the PIRA. The PIRA's Green Book was written by PIRA prisoners in the mid-1970s and later smuggled out.[232] The PIRA regularly used false priests in order to lure new prisoners into confessing to acting as informants for the British.[233] Prisoners frequently used visits from friends and family to pass intelligence to the organization in the field.[234] PIRA prisoners reported gathering valuable intelligence from Loyalist prisoners—one PIRA prisoner commented: "The Loyalists generally talk in jail. . . . Half of them haven't even got a clue that they are giving away information."[235]

Interrogations proved to be a fruitful source of intelligence. By interrogating confirmed RUC informant Peter Valente in 1981, the PIRA was able to get the names of six more British informants.[236] Interrogations were also used to control damage caused by British capture and interrogation of PIRA volunteers. It was standard practice to subject volunteers to an extensive debriefing after they were released from a British interrogation center.[237] Debriefers could evaluate the state of RUC intelligence by learning what questions the RUC was asking PIRA captives and what captives told it.[238]

In its later years, the PIRA collected more intelligence in support of reducing unintended civilian casualties. In 1992, the PIRA bombed the Baltic Exchange, causing eight hundred million pounds in damage. However, because the bomb was timed to harm no one, it killed only three people.[239]

The PIRA reorganization had a noticeable effect on the PIRA's intelligence operations. PIRA operations were far less hectic than in the early 1970s, with more planning and operational dry runs.[240] Compartmentalization protected senior PIRA leaders from the routine arrests and detentions they were subject to in the early 1970s, which helped them keep valuable experience and knowledge in the field and out of British prisons.[241] The reorganization also allowed the PIRA to train its volunteers more thoroughly in intelligence techniques and to impress upon them the valuable role they played as the organization's "eyes and ears."[242]

Counterintelligence: Basic and Adaptive Denial, Limited Manipulation. The PIRA counterintelligence capabilities increased dramatically from the second period to the third period. After its reorganization was initiated in 1976, the hemorrhage of volunteer arrests slowly subsided. By 1978, there were 465 fewer charges for paramilitary offenses than in the previous year.[243]

The PIRA leadership's increased control of the organization played a key role in counterintelligence improvements. For the first time, volunteers from across the organization were given strict orders to "keep a low profile," not to be seen in "each other's company or in the company of known Republicans," and to refrain from activities that "would draw attention to themselves."[244] All recruits were required to go through a series of background checks and to read the PIRA's counterintelligence-heavy Green Book before they could be officially admitted into the organization.[245]

By the 1980s, all PIRA units in Northern Ireland had a "security" officer who enforced secrecy standards, and the PIRA established a security department to vet recruits and conduct counterespionage investigations and interrogations. One of the security department's first investigations exposed volunteer Peter Valente as an RUC informant in 1980. Within the PIRA, security department volunteers became as unpopular as policemen, lurking around bars in Belfast to develop hunches and pick up investigative leads. The security department executed "confirmed" informants and deliberately left these executed individuals in public places as a warning to others.[246] Former PIRA volunteer Raymond Gilmour recalls that when he was suspected of being an informer, security department officers parked outside his house and "were hovering about, watching for any sign of tension or break in routine. . . . They made no attempt at concealment since visibility was part of their game: crank up the pressure, see if he panics."[247]

Increased control over the rank-and-file PIRA volunteers permitted the organization to reach a level of compartmentation that produced numerous counterintelligence benefits. After compartmentation, the average member's knowledge of the organization's plans and personnel became severely limited.[248] Raymond Gilmour recalls that his ASU leader did the mission planning, and ASU volunteers would typically learn about the operation only a short time before it was to take place.[249] Another benefit of compartmentation was that information about PIRA arms caches was more limited. Even if the British could find an informant who knew where an arms cache was, that informant would not know how or by whom the arms were delivered.[250] Compartmentation also allowed the PIRA leaders to investigate leaks and informant activity more easily—the list of suspects with access to particular compartments was small, so spies had less room to maneuver.[251]

With increased control, the PIRA leadership was able to standardize and oversee counterintelligence training for its recruits. Counterinterrogation training was a primary focus. The Green Book informed recruits about many British interrogation tactics, including the use of verbal and physical abuse to "soften up" captors and the "top-secret file" technique wherein interrogators tried to convince their detainee that they already had a complete file of all his or her crimes and activities.[252] Gilmour was trained to dump his weapon, dump his getaway car, change his clothes, and give his clothes a good wash to "get rid of forensics" following every operation. He was also taught to say nothing during interrogation and to remember the interrogators' questions for his PIRA counterintelligence debriefing following his release.[253] By 1977, the RUC became aware that the PIRA was training its members in counter-interrogation techniques, and detectives at Castlereagh alleged that they had recovered documents and tapes to prove it, including notes of debriefings by PIRA intelligence officers.[254] One of the techniques the PIRA volunteer would employ was naming the interrogation tactic being used by his British questioner—a technique that psychologically empowered the PIRA volunteer and frustrated British interrogators because many interrogators themselves did not know the names of the techniques they were using.[255]

The PIRA's operational procedures in this period better reflected counterintelligence training and awareness. ASUs would pick up weapons, disguises, and vehicles at safe houses prior to an operation and then drop them at "wash houses" following the operation, where volunteers would also get debriefed and then burn or wash their clothes to remove forensic evidence.[256] During operations, ASUs would work in code, using the jargon of taxi drivers to avoid getting ensnared in the RUC's electronic surveillance nets.[257] ASUs would mask the identity of their vehicles by changing license plates to match those of vehicles registered in another county or region.[258] Following operations, volunteers were taught to act discretely, not to brag about operations, and to avoid getting drunk.[259]

The PIRA also began to develop an impressive counterforensics capability. Collecting information from volunteers who were captured and put on trial, PIRA forensic experts were allegedly able to put together a nine-thousand-page document on avoiding detection. The document details the RUC's formidable forensic capabilities, describes how the RUC would commonly take fibers from washing machines and waste from water pipes in suspected wash houses, and notes that volunteers should wear nylon or denim rather than wool clothing because wool sheds fibers easily and readily retains fibers from other materials. Perhaps the PIRA's most sophisticated counterforensic operation involved concealing a bomb in a car taken into the Northern Ireland forensics laboratory—the "Trojan horse" car was then remotely detonated, destroying much of the forensic evidence held in the RUC laboratory.[260] PIRA ASUs began using "drogue" bombs in the late 1980s, which would first punch a hole through an armored vehicle and then detonate a second explosive to destroy any forensic evidence left on the bomb.[261] In instances where forensic evidence was believed to be successfully destroyed, the PIRA would sometimes falsely announce the death of a high-value member, which would allow the organization the opportunity to "resurrect" that member for special operations.[262]

The PIRA continued to use population support in this period as a counterintelligence advantage. The British Special Air Service found it extremely difficult to operate clandestinely against the PIRA in areas such as South Armagh because locals paid close attention to outsiders and suspicious behavior.[263] Gilmour, a member of a Derry-based PIRA unit, reports that any strange individual hanging out in a local pub would be watched closely, chased out, or possibly detained and interrogated.[264] Anti-British sentiments in PIRA strongholds were so strong that British soldiers would not risk directly challenging an attack on an RUC or army base in these areas, which in turn allowed ASUs to escape undetected after an operation.[265] Keeping the army and the RUC on constant alert and under heavy fortification limited their intelligence-collection and offensive operations against the PIRA in these strongholds.[266] Population support also facilitated PIRA investigations of informants. The PIRA used "snitches" to keep tabs on how much money locals had in their shops, who was relocating to certain areas, and which women were spending time with British soldiers.[267] In the early 1980s, locals would provide support for high-level meetings by scanning police frequencies to alert leaders to threatening police activities.[268]

Aggressive interrogations and investigations of informants also increased. Following a failed mission or operational surprise, the PIRA assumed that someone had betrayed the organization.[269] By one estimate, 70 percent of all informants caught by the PIRA during the entire troubles were executed after 1977.[270] Analysis of recovered informant bodies, such as that of British agent Robert Nairac, suggests that in some cases informants were tortured before being executed.[271] Former PIRA volunteer Sean O'Callaghan reported that investigations of informants sometimes entailed passing them false information and then monitoring the police reaction.[272] Compartmentation made investigations of "leaked" operations even easier because the list of volunteers with access to preoperational information about a subsequently compromised mission was usually very small.[273]

When the PIRA discovered that an informant had penetrated the organization, it acted to limit the damage the informant could cause. When the British supergrass informants threatened to cause serious damage in the early 1980s, the PIRA communicated to the supergrasses through their families that if they retracted their testimony, they would be granted amnesty.[274] The PIRA also sent "solicitors" to meet with arrested PIRA volunteers under the ruse of providing legal advice in order to assess how much the prisoner had told interrogators and how likely it was that he would break under additional interrogation; because the "defending lawyer" was entitled to see everything the prisoner had told interrogators, he could ascertain whether the volunteer had been compromised.[275]

The PIRA also demonstrated some capability to manipulate British intelligence operations. Using its technical surveillance equipment, the PIRA discovered key RUC strengths and weaknesses by running operations and watching the RUC's operational responses.[276] Former PIRA volunteer Stephen Lambert recalled that a member of the security forces offered him remuneration to spy against the group and that he himself then subsequently worked with PIRA leadership to clandestinely tape future meetings with the British agent to get information about British informant-recruitment procedures.[277]

During the 1976–1994 period, the PIRA improved its prison counterintelligence practices. PIRA prisoners were strictly prohibited from speaking to non-PIRA prisoners, and each floor would designate one member to speak with prison officials.[278] New prisoners would be debriefed or interrogated to prevent the British from "planting" informants in the PIRA prison community.[279] Some PIRA prisoners taught each other a variation on Irish Gaelic, known as "Jailic," so that they could converse openly without being understood.[280] PIRA prison leadership in some instances controlled the information available to the rank-and-file prisoners. One PIRA prisoner recalled that they would get a censored Sunday paper, with complete pages taken out by their own PIRA leaders.[281]

In spite of its counterintelligence advances, the PIRA continued to face several challenges and experienced several setbacks. Compartmentation was not adopted comprehensively throughout the organization, which the British supergrass informants made painfully obvious when they gave evidence against former colleagues in court.[282] During the hunger strike in the early 1980s, volunteers who had once strictly observed nonfraternization rules now openly attended marches and conversed with other volunteers in public, overcome by the emotion of the day.[283]

Centralization generally made the PIRA less vulnerable to informants among the rank and file but increased its vulnerability to informants in high-level or sensitive positions. The RUC's Special Branch and British army intelligence had long identified the PIRA's security department as a leading target for infiltration. Because the security department was privy to many compartmented programs, an informant in the department would be able to pass valuable information about PIRA personnel and plans.[284] Moreover, the security department was the vetting and counterespionage shop for the PIRA, so a well-positioned informant could more easily redirect, terminate, or otherwise manipulate an investigation to exonerate himself. Centralization also allowed the British to concentrate their resources against key high-value operatives and leaders instead of dispersing resources against hundreds of lower-value targets.[285]

Standardization of intelligence and counterintelligence procedures made the PIRA more predictable to British security forces. Prior to reorganization, each area of Northern Ireland had its own training camps and procedures. After PIRA's reorganization, British forces could better assess PIRA's standard operating procedures by surveilling a single camp.[286] This ability ultimately revealed the key counterintelligence trade-off that came with centralization: centralization allows a group to establish uniform, high-quality tradecraft that, once cracked by the adversary, is significantly more transparent and predictable.

Finally, the PIRA's culture of counterintelligence at times stifled the organization. Following high-profile British counterterrorism operations, the PIRA would stall operations in order to conduct investigations to discover informants.[287] Counterintelligence proved to be a good strategy for preserving leaders and talent but militated against a quicker operational tempo.

Many of the PIRA's notable counterintelligence successes in this period did not result from sophisticated adaptive-denial techniques, but rather from the uniform and disciplined application of basic-denial practices, such as compartmentation and security training. The group gained an additional counterintelligence edge, however, by actively investigating its members and their contacts, anticipating and defeating the British forensic investigations, and using the British legal system to get transcripts of interrogations of PIRA's detainees. The PIRA's use of known informants to pass the British false information in order to monitor their reactions can be categorized as covert manipulation. The group's technical infiltration of RUC's Operation Hawk—which the group used to identify which group members and safe houses were known to the RUC—is a clear example of covert manipulation of the adversary's intelligence-collection system.

Summary. The PIRA's resources and controlled territory as well as its adversary's capabilities stayed constant from 1976 to the 1990s, but the PIRA's organizational structure tightened significantly in direct response to the British government's counterterrorism improvements. Although the PIRA was able to reduce the steady flow of information to British security forces through superior training and compartmentation, the group also suffered from several devastating high-level penetrations. The PIRA's popular-support campaigns also routinely exposed critical information about the group's personnel and plans.

KEY FACTORS REVISITED

Organizational Structure. By adopting a tight command-and-control structure, the PIRA was able to develop superior counterintelligence and counterinterrogation training and compartmentation. There is some evidence that PIRA volunteers were better prepared to resist interrogation as a result of this training. The PIRA volunteers' increased attention to counterforensic techniques also reflects the benefits of improved training. In addition, as a direct result of compartmentation, British infiltrations of PIRA ASUs by the late 1970s provided the British with a more limited picture of PIRA activities as a direct result of compartmentation.

However, the PIRA's tight command-and-control structure also made the group more vulnerable to its adversary's efforts to develop high-level penetrations and to exploit the group's standardized counter-intelligence procedures. British infiltration of sensitive cells in the late 1970s, such as the security department, provided British forces with a volume of information on the PIRA that they could not have acquired with their best penetrations of the early 1970s. The PIRA's standardization of training, for example, allowed the British to glean more about the PIRA through infiltrating a single camp than it could in the early 1970s.

Popular Support. The PIRA leveraged its popular support to gain counter-intelligence assistance from the local population. It received crucial counterintelligence support from its Hen Patrols, made up of members of the community who alerted Republicans to incoming British patrols and raids. It also capitalized on its popular support as members of the community volunteered vital human and technical intelligence to the group. Its campaign to win and maintain popular support occasionally resulted in the exposure of the group's personnel and plans, though. The PIRA routinely exposed its personnel and plans at its marches, rallies, and pubs despite nonfraternization rules banning the mingling of known and unknown PIRA members.

Controlled Territory. The PIRA had superior communications security, physical security, and counterintelligence vetting in its controlled territories. Its controlled territories allowed the group to train its members more effectively and to coordinate its operations while analyzing its counterintelligence strengths and weaknesses.

The PIRA's controlled territory also gave its adversary a discrete territory to monitor and against which it could array its military and intelligence forces. British security forces were consistently able to produce intelligence from close observation of areas of high PIRA member concentration. Checkpoints and surveillance cameras near urban controlled territories allowed known PIRA members to be tracked and suspected PIRA members to be monitored for connections to confirmed PIRA entities. Security towers in the PIRA's rural controlled territories offered the British a similar surveillance advantage.

ADDITIONAL LESSONS FROM THE PIRA CASE

The PIRA's experiences over the full time frame from 1969 to 1994 offers some additional insights into terrorist counterintelligence. First, tightening a terrorist group's structure can affect its popular support. For example, tightening and centralizing command of the group may allow the group to better vet and control operations that influence popular opinions of the group—for instance, by mandating that civilians not be targeted in group operations. Conversely, tightening and compartmentation can reduce popular support by giving the terrorist organization's community leaders and civic activities a lower public profile and limited contact with the wider population.

Second, the case suggests that the quality of a terrorist group's intelligence apparatus can directly affect the quality of its counterintelligence capabilities. If a terrorist group has intelligence on what its population desires and on its adversaries vulnerabilities, then it can select targets and conduct operations that achieve its population's objectives. With better operations, the terrorist group will increase its popular support, which will reduce the adversary's ability to stage aggressive military, policing, and intelligence operations against the terrorist group. In addition, a terrorist group that performs better operations and garners high popular support will produce fewer disaffected and disillusioned members who are vulnerable to the adversary's recruitment pitches.

Third, prisons can play an important role in the quality of a terrorist group's intelligence capabilities. For the PIRA, prison sentences were sometimes a great benefit for the organization because the time in jail allowed some volunteers to ponder PIRA strategy and tactics—in particular counterintelligence issues that may have lead to their arrest—in a face-to-face venue with other volunteers.

Fourth, centralization may affect how quickly a terrorist group's capabilities can evolve as its adversary's counterterrorism capabilities evolve. The terrorist group and its state adversary are engaged in a competitive and dynamic relationship—a move or innovation by one side frequently results in a countermove or counterinnovation by the other. Terrorist groups that can initiate intelligence and counterintelligence innovations, as opposed to simply reacting and adapting to the adversary's innovations, will be better positioned to take advantage of its adversary's vulnerabilities. Centralized organizations appear more capable of transmitting lessons learned to the whole organization and thereby of increasing the organization's overall capacity for innovation.

The Palestinian terrorist group Fatah successfully used territory it controlled in the 1960s to recruit and train its personnel and to launch attacks against Israel. In the early 1970s, Fatah became more aggressive and sent terrorist operatives into "uncontrolled territory" across Europe, Asia, and the Middle East to attack Israeli interests abroad. Israel answered by dispatching assassination squads to hunt down Fatah's international leaders, many of whom were successfully tracked and killed. Although Fatah had adapted to the challenges and advantages of its controlled territory, the uncontrolled territory of Europe and the Middle East offered an entirely new set of benefits and drawbacks. Fatah leveraged critical counterintelligence advantages when operating outside of its controlled territory to remain effective, but despite the advantages of working across the globe, Fatah leaders were often more secure within Fatah's controlled territory (shown in figure 3.1) because they could insulate themselves with multiple layers of personal security among tightly knit communities.

Fatah's counterintelligence story can be told in three parts, as summarized in table 3.1. The first part depicts Fatah when it operated without controlled territory and minimal popular support in the West Bank and Gaza Strip between 1964 and 1967. The second part describes Fatah when it operated within its controlled territory with high popular support in Jordan and Lebanon between 1967 and 1982. The third part depicts a smaller core of Fatah members, known as the Black September Organization (BSO), operating outside of Fatah's controlled territory in Lebanon and dispersed among the Palestinian diaspora communities of Europe from 1971 to 1978. The shift from the first era to the second

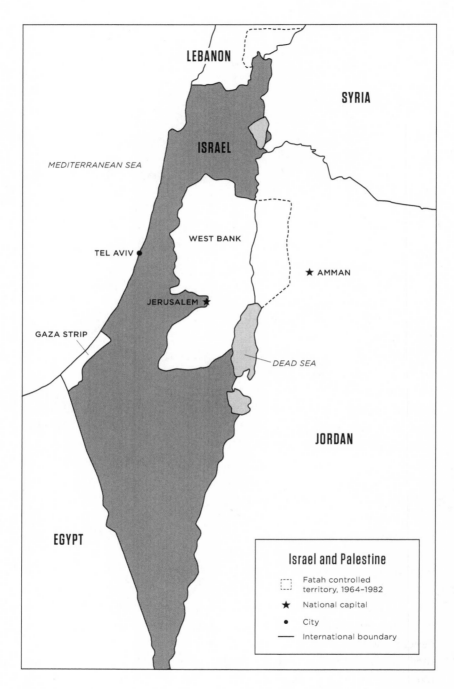

Figure 3.1 Lebanon, Syria, Israel, Gaza Strip, West Bank, and Jordan

Table 3.1 Fatah and Black September Organization (BSO)
Case Study: Key Factors

Fatah/ BSO	Organizational Structure	Popular Support	Controlled Territory	Resources	Adversary Counterterrorism Capability
Fatah 1964–1967	Tight	Low	No	High	High
Fatah 1967–1982	Tight	High	Yes	High	High
BSO 1971–1978	Tight	High	No	High	High

era demonstrates the counterintelligence gains accrued as Fatah increased both its controlled territory and its popular support. The history of BSO shows the counterintelligence implications of expanding operations beyond a group's home base.

OVERVIEW OF FATAH AND THE BLACK SEPTEMBER ORGANIZATION

Fatah, which was also known as the Palestinian National Liberation Movement, formed in the late 1950s among Palestinian students at universities in the Middle East and Europe.[1] Its founders, which included Yasser Arafat, aspired to liberate Palestine from Israel's military occupation through armed struggle carried out by Palestinians.[2]

In the early 1960s, Fatah concentrated on increasing its membership, developing secret cells, raising funds, and distributing revolutionary literature, but it did not engage in guerrilla attacks. It was not until January 1965 that Fatah conducted its first terrorist attack—an attempted sabotage of an Israeli national water carrier near the village of Eilabun—and so began its long, violent struggle against the State of Israel.[3]

By 1965, Fatah had established itself in the Gaza Strip and the West Bank and used this territory to recruit fighters and launch a more active and violent campaign of terrorist warfare against Israel. Israel responded with superior firepower and local intelligence, and by 1967 the majority of Fatah's ranks had been arrested, killed, or driven into Jordan.[4] Fatah was also eventually driven from Jordan by the Jordanian military and intelligence services, but not before winning public-relations victories and an upwelling of sympathy. Fatah fighters and refugees then turned to Lebanon, which turned out to be a more durable safe haven for Fatah—by the 1970s, Fatah controlled significant portions of southern Beirut, strips of southern Lebanon, and the Palestinian refugee camps in these areas.

The Israeli and Jordanian militaries continued to assault Fatah, even in the depths of its most secure, controlled territories. In May 1970, Israeli military forces attacked Fatah's strongholds in Lebanon. The Jordanian military also stepped up its efforts to eliminate the Fatah fighters remaining in Jordan by shelling terrorist facilities throughout the country. Jordan's military campaign against Fatah, which culminated in September 1971, was so brutal that the Fatah Central Committee was inspired to establish a new covert arm, the Black September Organization (BSO), to commemorate and avenge Fatah losses that month.[5]

BSO was established to strike back at Israel and its allies in unexpected venues outside of Fatah's traditional theater of operations. It was designed to be disconnected from Fatah's traditional hierarchy, but it probably consulted regularly with Fatah leaders, received funding regularly from it, and relied heavily on Fatah connections to build its networks. BSO remained operationally distinct, however, insofar as its operations and training camps were geographically dispersed and not directly launched from Fatah's controlled territory in Lebanon.

BSO first gained global attention when it kidnapped and killed several Israeli athletes at the Munich Olympics in 1972. Israel responded aggressively with military and intelligence operations across Europe and the Middle East. In April 1973, Israeli commandos launched Operation Spring of Youth, in which they clandestinely penetrated Fatah's stronghold in Beirut and assassinated numerous Fatah and BSO terrorist operatives.[6] Israeli agents also systematically tracked down and killed BSO operatives in Europe over the following several years. BSO's leaders

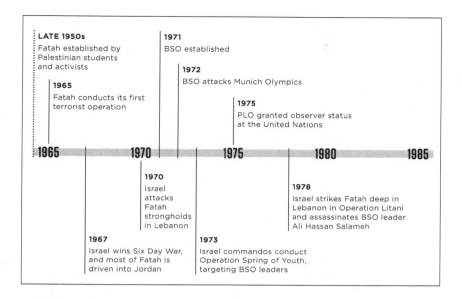

Figure 3.2 Abbreviated Timeline of Key Fatah Activities and Events

and rank-and-file members were decimated and out of commission by the mid-1970s, and Fatah became increasingly less violent until it was recognized internationally as a nonterrorist entity in the late 1980s.[7] Figure 3.2 offers a summary of key events for Fatah and BSO.

FATAH ESTABLISHED, STRUGGLES FOR SUPPORT AND TERRITORY: 1964–1967

Key Factors

Organizational Structure. From 1964 to 1967, Fatah's organizational structure was mostly tight, with leaders exercising a relatively high degree of command and control over the organization. When Fatah operated predominantly out of the West Bank in the mid-1960s, terrorist cells were often cut off from Fatah's top leaders, who were based in Syria. Fatah leaders, as a result, imposed strict regulations on their cells when it came to choosing targets and methods of attack. Fatah's leadership in Syria and its cells in the West Bank would communicate through couriers and liaisons when they had the opportunity.[8]

Fatah's control over its cells was largely due to the force of Yasser Arafat's charismatic leadership. Arafat was personally organizing underground networks, coordinating and mediating between various units, and determining their objectives by intermittently shuttling between the West Bank and Damascus.[9] He maintained some contact with almost all units, according to the many terrorists captured by the Israelis.[10] Despite Fatah's mostly tight structure, the group faced some organizational discipline challenges during its time in the West Bank. Some terrorists, for example, joined Fatah without being sufficiently coordinated or supervised by senior members.[11]

Popular Support. Fatah was relatively unpopular among West Bank inhabitants between 1964 and 1967. In 1964, Fatah created a political base from the Palestinian intelligentsia and enjoyed some support in the refugee camps of the West Bank and Gaza—though not as much as it would gain after 1967.[12] Fatah's West Bank command established its headquarters in Nablus.[13] Unrest in Palestinian refugee camps, where an estimated 200,000 of the 400,000 refugees lived under United Nations sponsorship, provided a large recruiting pool for Fatah.[14] Fatah also tried tapping into a network of Arab Fatah sympathizers within Israel, who helped carry out acts of sabotage.[15] In this period, there were approximately 440,000 Arabs living in Israel, but only a small fraction would end up in Israeli prisons or detention camps for real or alleged cooperation with Palestinian guerrillas.[16] Many Israeli Arabs did not support Fatah and instead aligned themselves with the Israeli government or with popular Egyptian leader Gamal Nassar, who openly opposed sabotage activities.[17]

Several factors impaired Fatah's ability to gain popular support in the West Bank in the mid-1960s. Fatah's code of secrecy interfered with the group's effort to gather a following among the population.[18] Israeli counterinsurgency efforts also capped the amount of support Fatah could attain because villages were often reluctant to pass information or provide shelter to Fatah terrorists.[19] Fear of being caught and punished by Israel compelled many Palestinian residents to limit their assistance to Fatah to providing food and advice on local conditions.[20] Arafat would spend a great deal of time escaping Israeli forces, which were being aided by Palestinian informants.[21] By the late 1960s, it was clear to Fatah that the local population was not receptive to a popular uprising against Israel.[22]

Controlled Territory. Fatah did not have controlled territory in the 1964–1967 period. It used a small number of refugee camps for training and recruiting and took advantage of Lebanon's weak central government to establish a few training sites near Palestinian refugee camps in Lebanon.[23] The overcrowded camps of the Gaza Strip provided Fatah terrorists with some limited cover and sanctuary while they launched attacks against Israel, but Fatah did not police the camps, nor did it control movement in and out of the camps.[24] Israel policed the West Bank and Gaza Strip aggressively and moved quickly to challenge Fatah guerrillas, which eventually forced Fatah to relocate to Jordan.

Other Important Factors

Resources. During Fatah's initial campaign in the West Bank, it drew upon potential recruits gathered in the refugee camps of Lebanon and among men who regularly sold information to Arab intelligence services.[25] Recruits were trained in terrorist techniques based on Algerian and Vietnamese programs of unconventional warfare. Recruits were trained on Kalashnikov rifles and indoctrinated in Palestinian and Arab history and Fatah's philosophy.[26] This concentrated pool of recruits allowed Fatah to initiate a moderate operational tempo. In late 1967, Fatah organized sixty military operations in the West Bank, mostly against civilian targets such as farms, apartment buildings, and factories.[27]

Throughout its existence, Fatah was well financed. In its early days, members of the Qatari ruling family and wealthy and influential Saudis provided funds to Fatah.[28] As Fatah grew, it began to receive donations from other Arab governments and remittances from Palestinians working throughout the world. In Lebanon, Fatah forced some Lebanese businesses to pay protection fees, and some Fatah members ran illicit arms and drugs networks.[29]

Adversary Counterterrorism Capability. Powerful state adversaries hounded Fatah from its inception in the late 1950s. When Fatah emerged as a political movement run by Egyptian university students in the late

1950s, the Egyptian government moved quickly to deport its leaders.[30] In 1965, Israel's aggressive policing of the West Bank and Gaza prevented Fatah from controlling the territory. Israel was able to arrest and imprison many of Fatah's recruits in the West Bank and Gaza Strip.[31] Using informers in the West Bank and Jordan, Israel infiltrated Fatah and disrupted its operations as they were being planned.[32]

In addition to collecting information from informants, Israel broke up newly formed Fatah cells and kept abreast of the population's political mood.[33] Israel's swift retaliation made many would-be Fatah recruits reluctant to join the terrorist organization.[34] It involved demolitions of Palestinian houses, curfews, and restrictions on movements, so that Palestinians became reluctant to pass on information or to provide food or shelter to Fatah fighters and in general inclined to distance themselves from Fatah.[35] Israel bolstered its intelligence collection on Fatah during the Six Day War in June 1967 when it captured the Jordanian army intelligence branch's files on all the fedayeen (commandos) and sympathizers in the West Bank, along with their detailed histories and photographs.[36]

Despite Israel's control over the Gaza and West Bank territories, Fatah continued its terrorist operations mostly against civilian targets. By November 1967, however, "the majority of Fatah personnel in the West Bank" had been "killed, captured, or driven" into Jordan.[37] By 1968, Israeli security patrols kept the border between Jordan and the West Bank virtually sealed off and carefully scrutinized all militants organizing in the West Bank and the Gaza Strip.[38] As a result, Fatah had limited manpower—by one estimate, Fatah had no more than one hundred fighters.[39]

Intelligence and Counterintelligence Outcomes

Intelligence. Fatah's intelligence capabilities were fairly basic during the 1964–1967 period. Target surveillance was a staple of the Fatah's intelligence operations. As early as 1964, Fatah was running reconnaissance missions into Israel to gather intelligence for sabotage operations. Before Arafat relocated to the West Bank, couriers shuttled intelligence to him in Damascus from Fatah cells in Beirut and the refugee camps. By 1965, Syrian government intelligence training for Fatah militants was beginning to have an impact on Fatah's intelligence capabilities—intelligence units became more efficient and better able to provide information on targets and perform preoperational surveillance.[40]

Fatah's early intelligence operations were partially shaped by the *Minimanual of the Urban Terrorist*. Israeli Arab expert Steve Posner claims the manual was required reading for Fatah and Palestine Liberation Organization (PLO) recruits. The manual counseled terrorists to take personal responsibility for gathering intelligence against the adversary: "The urban terrorist must have a great ability for observation. . . . [H]e must be well-informed about . . . the area in which he lives, operates, or travels through." The manual also noted that local populations that oppose the government and its security forces were an excellent source of information.[41] In the mid-1960s, Fatah tried to establish "village cells," modeled after the Viet Cong intelligence system, to provide such information on Israeli security forces.[42] Fatah recruited some of the Arabs living inside of Israel, but the Israeli internal security services were effective at monitoring these populations and at limiting the support that Fatah gained from them. A small network of Fatah informants allegedly operated in Israel in 1967 and passed intelligence on potential targets to Fatah liaison men waiting in Jordan.[43]

Counterintelligence: Basic Denial. Fatah's counterintelligence capabilities varied between 1964 and 1967, though counterintelligence and security probably were always a central focus for the group. Even before Fatah was formed, Arafat was learning how to evade Arab intelligence services by compartmenting his small, radical student organization in Kuwait.[44]

When Fatah formed in the early 1960s, the group concentrated on developing secret, compartmented cells that would distribute pro-Palestinian literature.[45] From the beginning, Fatah leaders also adopted aliases.[46] Arafat's alias was "Abu Amar," and Fatah initially adopted a group alias, "al Assifa" (the Storm).[47] Fatah's leaders reasoned that the group alias would allow Fatah to avoid embarrassment and continue with secret military and propaganda operations if its initial attacks failed.[48] At this early stage, Arafat chose not to reveal his identity in order to maintain his safety.[49] Fatah's security consciousness was reinvigorated in the first few months of 1965 in the wake of several counterintelligence lapses and betrayals.[50]

Fatah leaders took numerous precautions in vetting new members. Potential recruits had to be recommended by two or three active members. Recruits also had to demonstrate that they had severed ties with Arab political parties, probably to prevent infiltrations by Arab intelligence services. They were interviewed at length and then had to take an oath of allegiance, wherein they promised not to give away Fatah's secrets. One Fatah member recalled: "We kept our secrets so close that the word Fatah would not be mentioned except to a member. Only Fatah members could see our two basic documents, the organizational structure and the political program."[51]

Fatah was occasionally burned by bad counterintelligence practices in this early period. One of these setbacks involved Fatah's habit of cataloging lists of members and operational details. In May 1966, a Jordanian informant in Fatah's ranks fled to Jordan with a list of Fatah's members, "details of the organization, their leaders, and operational plans." Many of Fatah's cells in the West Bank were rolled up soon thereafter. The Jordanians also used the compromised information to broadcast "fake code signals calling terrorists" in Syria to Jordan, where the Jordanian security forces subsequently captured the terrorists and their weapons at the border.[52]

Fatah implemented several counterintelligence innovations in this period, such as its use of throw-away aliases. Fatah coordinators assembled cell members for operations in an ad hoc manner and issued members one-time aliases for the operation, which would change for their next mission.[53] This system impaired a spy's ability to report key details about his fellow members and challenged Israeli analysts who were probably listening to intercepted Fatah radio communications. Fatah also established a formal counterespionage capability. Counterespionage personnel focused on capturing Arabs in the refugee camps suspected of cooperating with Israeli security forces.[54] Arafat also developed personal-security procedures, using several go-between security officers to vet any group member who requested an audience with him.[55] He relied on messengers and couriers and allegedly never used the telephone or telegraph.[56] Fatah in some cases communicated with its rank and file by sending coded signals via its Cairo Radio station, which broadcast to Egypt, Jordan, and Syria.[57]

Fatah faced a serious counterintelligence setback in August 1967 when Israeli forces advancing into the Jordanian-controlled West Bank seized Jordanian intelligence and police files on Fatah.[58] The intelligence files included detailed histories and mug shots of many Fatah terrorists.[59] Israeli security forces used the information to capture Fatah operatives as they tried to reenter the West Bank.[60] Israel also conducted a "cave" survey in the West Bank, capturing and interrogating many terrorists. Security forces encircled villages where suspected terrorists were hiding and by January 1968 had almost completely shut down sabotage operations launched from the Palestinian territories.[61]

Fatah responded to Israel's increased intelligence by ferociously hunting down informants—Israeli figures indicate that terrorists were targeting suspected collaborators as often as they were targeting Israelis in the late 1960s.[62] Fatah set up a special counterespionage unit, called the "Jihaz al Razd," which was run by Arafat's confidant Saleh Khalef, also known as "Abu Iyad."

When the infamous BSO terrorist Ali Hassan Salameh joined Fatah as a young man in 1967, one of his first assignments was to track down Fatah members who were working for the Israeli security forces. Salameh, working for the Jihaz al Razd, would review the file of each new recruit and conduct a background check. Abu Iyad and Salameh would sometimes test suspected informants' loyalty by making them "undertake particularly dangerous missions behind Israeli lines." Salameh would threaten to broadcast a tape of the terrorist confessing to being an informant if the terrorist did not return from the mission.[63]

Only a few terrorists confessed to collaborating with Israel, and many suspected informants were brutally killed—twenty in Salameh's first year in the Jihaz.[64] Arafat dealt with informants in a heavy-handed fashion, but he refrained from punishing local community leaders in the West Bank to avoid a backlash among the prominent tribes and families in the area.[65] Israel had the critical advantage of believing it could treat anyone in these territories in a heavy-handed fashion, so it was able to wipe out Fatah's networks in the West Bank. It was able to do so more easily because the comfortable, middle-class Palestinians of Nablus, Ramallah, and Jerusalem, with some important exceptions among young people, did not desire to live the life of clandestine guerrillas.[66]

Fatah engaged in basic denial by compartmenting its operations, using aliases, forcing members to take an oath of secrecy, using coded signals for communications, vetting recruits for connections to security services, and terrifying recruits with the shadowy counterespionage unit Jihaz al Razd. Fatah was not learning enough about Israel's intelligence-collection methods to engage in adaptive-denial techniques, however.

Summary. Until 1968, Fatah maintained a tight organizational structure and enjoyed high resources, but it had low popular support and no controlled territory, and it contended with a very capable adversary. Operating without controlled territory offered at least the one counterintelligence advantage of forcing Israel to locate and monitor Fatah operatives across large swaths of neutral territory. However, Fatah's lack of controlled territory did not make it easy for the group to hide its personnel and logistics because it operated in territory that Israel effectively policed. Fatah's lack of direct popular support contributed to its counterintelligence failures in that residents of the West Bank and Gaza Strip feared Israel's wrath more than they supported Fatah's activities.

FATAH GAINS TERRITORY: 1967–1982

Key Factors

Organizational Structure. From 1967 to 1982, Fatah maintained a tight organizational structure, with leaders exercising a relatively high degree of command and control over the organization. Arafat maintained control over the Fatah movement even as it shifted its bases from the West Bank to Jordan and Lebanon. Couriers kept some Damascus-based Fatah leaders in touch with the organization's cells throughout Lebanon, allowing Fatah leaders to direct recruitment campaigns and operation activities "carried out from Lebanese territory."[67]

Popular Support. Israel's counterterrorism efforts forced Fatah to move its bases from Gaza to Jordan, where the group began building refugee centers, training camps, schools, clinics, and orphanages.[68] King Hussein of Jordan eventually recognized that Fatah was building its own state within his kingdom. He could not take military action against the group, however, because the Jordanian public was largely sympathetic to Fatah's cause.[69] Fatah ruled the Palestinian refugee camps, where Jordanian officials and soldiers were not allowed to enter. Fatah's popularity among indigenous Jordanians, however, was limited because many resented the Palestinian refugees.[70]

Fatah's popularity increased following the Battle of Karameh, in which Israel carried out one of its largest attacks against the Fatah stronghold in Karameh on March 21, 1968.[71] Karameh was a clear tactical victory for Israel, but Fatah postbattle propaganda made the event a huge strategic victory for the terrorist group. In Jordan, "pro-Fatah posters showing Palestinian guerrillas defeating the Israeli army" filled many shop windows.[72] Fatah's perceived victory drew five thousand recruits within forty-eight hours of the battle. Up to this point, Fatah had maintained secrecy about its organization, origins, and membership. After Karameh, it became clear to Fatah's leaders that good publicity could yield huge dividends. Quickly thereafter, Arafat's appetite for publicity seemed unbounded. Arafat gave interviews to Western reporters, released mythologized versions of his life to the media, and allowed himself to be filmed living in caves with his fighters.[73]

Fatah began to invest more in its public image, using a radio station in Cairo for a short period every day to broadcast threats and communiqués designed to inspire Arabs.[74] Arafat attempted to generate widespread public support in Jordan's East Bank, hoping to achieve what he had failed to do in the West Bank. However, when Fatah incursions from Jordan drew Israeli troops into the East Bank, many residents of the Jordanian Valley were forced to flee their homes and move away from the border.[75] Fatah's publicity push faced additional obstacles when the group began to fear that Israeli assassination squads were exploiting Fatah's openness in order to track down its leaders.[76]

Fatah found fertile ground for its activities in Lebanon because the Lebanese population initially lent support to it.[77] It used many tactics to gain popular support. For example, in Sidon, a town south of Beirut, students would receive education credits only if they were members of Fatah.[78] Fatah and the PLO also co-located their headquarters and training facilities with large refugee populations.[79] Refugee camp co-location made Israeli air strikes more difficult because any strike against Fatah facilities and personnel could also result in the deaths of innocent refugees.

Indeed, when Israel bombed refugee camp military bases in Lebanon in 1980, thousands of innocent refugees were killed and injured, generating an upwelling of anger toward Israel.[80]

Controlled Territory. Fatah controlled territory in Jordan from 1967 to 1971 and in Lebanon from 1972 to 1984. It regulated physical access to and security within large segments of that territory. When it was forced to relocate to Jordan in 1967, Arafat moved his headquarters to Karameh. Many of the commanders and networks of the West Bank were moved to Jordan's East Bank.[81] Fatah found fertile recruiting ground among the 450,000 Palestinians living in Jordan.[82] By 1968, its membership probably reached into the thousands.[83] At first, the group controlled only the refugee camps in Jordan, but it gradually began to take over towns and villages close to the border with Israel.[84]

When Israel launched its offensive on Karameh, most terrorists retreated across the River Jordan from the East Bank.[85] The Israeli military withdrew from Jordan after violent confrontations with Fatah terrorists ended, and Fatah was subsequently flooded with money and recruits.[86] Overwhelmed by the hundreds of recruits joining the group, it experienced a shortage of militant trainers, which probably degraded the quality of its training for at least a year.[87] It also moved its headquarters and some training camps to Es Salt, outside the range of Israeli commando raids. The Jordanian government had limited control over the camps, and Israel launched air strikes against Es Salt in August 1968.[88] Israeli air strikes were designed to prevent Israeli military losses, boost domestic morale in Israel, and compel the Jordanian regime to restrict the terrorists' movements—the policy's intended effect on Jordan, however, was not immediate.[89]

King Hussein of Jordan offered a truce to Fatah in November 1968 that allowed Fatah to expand its area of control. Fatah agreed not to create trouble for Hussein's regime, and Hussein in turn agreed not to restrict the terrorists' movements within Jordan. He also permitted Fatah members to "retain their own travel documents," which were "honored by the Jordanian authorities." By 1970, Fatah had achieved a high level of organization in Jordan, administering its own hospitals and advertising its care of widows, orphans, and the disabled. Jordanian authorities estimated that Fatah commanded approximately five thousand members in 1971.[90]

However, King Hussein soon became wary of Fatah's growing influence in Jordan and its unchallenged control over swaths of Jordanian territory, including the northern areas of Jerash and Ajloun. As a result, he ordered Jordanian security forces to attack Fatah elements, and many terrorists chose to flee to Syria and southern Lebanon rather than directly confront Jordanian troops.[91] By the end of 1971, the Jordanian army had killed or driven most Fatah members from the country.[92]

Fatah's relationship with the Lebanese government became equally complex. Fatah established a foothold in the small Arkoub region of Lebanon, which became known as "Fatahland."[93] Fatahland was an area of approximately thirty square miles in the foothills of Mount Hermon near the borders of Israel and Syria.[94] The Lebanese had fought terrorist elements to a stalemate in southern Lebanon in November 1968, which led to the Cairo Agreement in November 1969.[95] The agreement allowed the PLO and by extension Fatah to establish a military presence in the refugee camps in southern Lebanon and to provide refugees with security.[96] By 1972, more than three thousand Fatah members had settled in Palestinian refugee camps in southern Lebanon.[97]

Arafat continued to embrace the Cairo Agreement in 1972, realizing that a clash with the Lebanese forces would inflict significant damage on the PLO and Fatah. The Lebanese government tolerated the terrorist presence in Fatahland mostly because the Lebanese army was unable to decisively challenge the PLO's military power.[98] The PLO and Fatah gradually assumed administrative control over the Palestinian camps in Lebanon, running schools and hospitals.[99] By 1975, they controlled southern Beirut, southern strips of Lebanon, and Palestinian refugee camps.

Fatah continued to receive support from Syria, though the relationship remained rocky. Israeli air raids on Syria in 1972 and 1973 convinced Syria to restrict Fatah's freedom of movement in Syria and Lebanon in order to avoid future Israeli strikes.[100] On June 6, 1982, the Israeli military launched a major ground offensive against the PLO and Fatah infrastructure in southern Lebanon, and the outgunned terrorists abandoned their safe haven.[101] With the loss of its controlled territory, Fatah lost its ability to train members and prepare for battle, to educate its youth and recruit them to the PLO ranks, and to protect arms caches.[102]

Other Important Factors

Resources. From 1967 to 1982, Fatah had access to ample funding, outside training, and a large pool of recruits. In 1968, it sent five hundred volunteers from the West Bank to be trained in Syria, Iraq, and Algeria.[103] In some instances, Fatah camps in Syria were even staffed with Syrian military personnel and stocked with Syrian arms and ammunition.[104] Arafat dispatched a select group of terrorists to train in Egyptian military and intelligence schools.[105] Fatah also made a push to recruit Palestinian students in Europe for operations in the Middle East.[106]

Fatah's fund-raising efforts during this period increased as the group focused on establishing links to Palestinian worker, student, and professional organizations throughout the Middle East.[107] It also received some financial assistance from the Chinese and Soviet governments.[108] In the mid-1970s, it had enough money to pay every adult male member of the organization a monthly stipend of between seven hundred and one thousand Lebanese pounds—approximately what an average Lebanese farmworker would earn.[109] Fatah was also aggressively training the next generation of terrorists. Its youth movement, the Lion Cubs, would train twelve-year-olds in basic military skills, including hand-to-hand combat, explosives, and shooting.[110]

Fatah continued to rely on Syrian support once it had established itself in Lebanon, though its relationship with Syria remained unstable because Damascus would occasionally alter its support in order to advance its own objectives. Around three thousand fedayeen fled Jordan to seek refuge in Syria, but the Syrian government imposed onerous restrictions on them.[111] A road leading from Fatahland to Damascus, known as the "Yasser Arafat Trail," became Fatah's main supply route in the late 1960s.[112] As Fatah's strength in Lebanon grew, Syrian president Hafaz al-Asad struggled to keep Fatah in check, viewing Lebanon as Syria's prize. Finally, in June 1976 the Syrian army invaded Lebanon and conquered almost all the areas previously held by Fatah. Despite the setbacks experienced, the PLO's umbrella groups committed more than 8,000 terrorist acts between 1969 and 1985—435 of them abroad—killing more than 650 Israelis and 28 Americans.[113]

Adversary Counterterrorism Capability. Challenged by Israel's dominance of the West Bank and Gaza Strip, Fatah relocated to Jordan and

Lebanon by 1968 and returned to launching operations against Israel.[114] It found refuge in Jordan in part because the Jordanian army was still recovering from the Six Day War, and Jordan's leaders did not want a confrontation with the country's large pro-Palestinian population. Fatah seized control of territory in Jordan, and, as noted, the city of Karameh became the centerpiece of its strongholds. Israel could not infiltrate and police Karameh and other Fatah strongholds in Jordan, so it mounted large military attacks against these territories. Israeli security forces also set up ambushes on frontier paths to catch Fatah militants traveling to and from the Jordan.[115]

Fatah terrorists also began to battle with Jordanian security services. Jordan's King Hussein became increasingly angered as Fatah sought to control large swaths of Jordanian territory. Despite King Hussein's proposed truce in 1968, Fatah's conflict with Jordan "steadily escalated throughout 1969 and 1970."[116] Guerrilla groups proliferated in Jordan during this time, making negotiation between Jordan and the Palestinian factions very difficult. George Habash's Marxist Popular Front for the Liberation of Palestine further complicated the picture, calling for revolution against Jordan and its ruling family.[117]

Jordan finally took decisive action when the Popular Front hijacked three planes in 1970. It "declared martial law and demanded the guerrillas leave Jordan's cities." Arafat responded by commanding his troops to "topple" King Hussein. Jordan's army attacked Palestinian refugee and guerrilla camps, forcing Fatah's fighters into the streets, where they were easily gunned down. Jordan battled the guerrillas so ruthlessly that some Fatah fighters were authorized by their commanding officer to seek refuge in Israel rather than allow themselves to fall into the hands of the Jordanian army. Many of Fatah's guerrillas retreated to Syria, southern Lebanon, the West Bank, and the hills of northwest Jordan.[118] The Jordanian army continued to methodically destroy Fatah and other fedayeen elements in Jordan. Jordan's brutal tactics, including executing terrorists without trial and mutilating their bodies, began to take a toll on Fatah.[119] The Jordanian army had killed, captured, or driven Fatah rebels out of the country largely by the end of 1971.[120]

In the early 1970s, southern Lebanon became the critical front in the war between Fatah and Israel. Following a fedayeen attack on an Israeli school bus in May 1970, Israel invaded Fatahland with two thousand troops and two hundred tanks. They paved roads into the area so they could set up fortified positions and elevated observation posts.[121] This action did not dissuade the Fatah migration to Lebanon. By 1972, more than three thousand Fatah members had settled in Palestinian refugee camps in southern Lebanon, joining the more than two hundred thousand Palestinians who had been in southern Lebanon since 1948.[122] Israel again briefly occupied southern Lebanon in 1972 following the Fatah-led Munich Olympics massacre.[123]

Israel used undercover intelligence collectors in Lebanon throughout the 1970s and 1980s to gather information on Fatah and PLO leadership and facilities. One well-placed spy provided the Israeli army with the positions of terrorist targets and photographs of harbors in the Lebanese cities of Tyre, Sidon, and Ras-a-Shak that were subsequently used in Israeli naval raids.[124] Israeli security services working in Lebanon tracked terrorists and assisted in special-forces raids. Knowing well the modus operandi of the Lebanese services, they kept the Lebanese authorities from meddling in some Israeli raids. To keep the Lebanese out of one Israeli raid in 1973, Israeli commandos called the Lebanese police from various public phones in Beirut, falsely claiming that Palestinian factions were engaged in gun battles—from which Lebanese police kept their distance, as the Israelis had predicted.[125]

By 1975, Fatah and the PLO controlled significant portions of Beirut and key portions of Lebanon. Guerrillas set up roadblocks, took over buildings, protected fugitives, commandeered vehicles, opened shops and nightclubs, and issued Fatah passes and permits.[126] Despite the Lebanese government's numerous victories against Fatah, the group retained control of large areas in Lebanon with relatively little challenge.

Israel, meanwhile, continued its military incursions into southern Lebanon throughout the late 1970s and early 1980s, culminating in the massive invasion in 1982 that led to Fatah's effective expulsion from Lebanon.[127]

Intelligence and Counterintelligence Outcomes

Intelligence. Fatah's intelligence capabilities continued to be fairly basic in the 1967 to 1982 period. Fatah collected intelligence for sabotage operations directed mainly against civilian targets, such as factories, private homes, cinemas, buses, restaurants, and open markets. Given its tactics, the most valuable intelligence for it was information on how best to approach and attack these soft targets. In addition to basic surveillance, Fatah continued to use Israeli Arabs as guides and to get access to storage areas and accommodations inside Israel.[128]

The *Minimanual of the Urban Terrorist* emphasized two types of espionage: information gathered from recruited informants within the adversary's ranks and information gathered from unwitting members of the local population. The manual noted: "The urban terrorist, living in the midst of the population and moving about among them, must be attentive to all types of conversations and human relations, learning how to disguise his interest with great skill and judgment. In places where people work, study, and live, it is easy to collect all kinds of information on payments, business, plans of all kinds, points of view, opinions, people's state of mind, trips, interior layout of buildings, offices and rooms, operations centers, etc."[129] Although there is no evidence that Fatah penetrated the Israeli security forces, Israeli Arabs working with Fatah most likely gathered intelligence through the methods described in the manual. Fatah did manage to penetrate the Jordanian army in 1968, successfully recruiting a number of middle-ranking officers.[130] With these penetrations, it is possible that Fatah indirectly gained some access to Israeli military information that had been shared with the Jordanian armed forces.

When Fatah and the PLO controlled territory in Lebanon in the 1970s, their intelligence capabilities improved. They moved from almost exclusively targeting civilian infrastructure to targeting more commercial and military infrastructure, including oil installations, embassies, and airports.[131] They used their private prisons, including their largest in Sidon, to gather intelligence through the interrogation of detainees.[132] Fatah also developed the ability to communicate intelligence rapidly to vital parts of its organization. Soon after the Israeli raid of Beirut in April 1973, Fatah broadcast urgent messages to its followers to scatter and seek shelter because Israeli agents were assumed to be looking for key Fatah members in Beirut.[133]

The counterintelligence assessment of Fatah is broken here into three sections: (1) 1967–1972, (2) 1972–1982, and (3) a comprehensive look from 1967 to 1982 to better highlight the key counterintelligence events and key factors.

Counterintelligence: Basic Denial, 1967–1972. After Fatah's propaganda victory following the Battle of Karameh in March 1968, the group relaxed its counterintelligence posture in order to capitalize on its increased popular support. Senior Fatah leaders gave interviews to the press, appeared on television, and appeared in public with their bodyguard entourage. The locations of leaders and units were still kept secret, and junior leaders and rank-and-file terrorists were not allowed to seek individual publicity.[134] Arafat was almost captured by Israeli security forces in West Bank in the late 1960s, but he escaped his Ramallah compound as it was being stormed and managed to hide in a Volkswagen parked nearby.[135]

Arafat's affiliation with Fatah was first announced in April 1968, when he was appointed the organization's official spokesperson, though his birthplace and family and political background were kept secret. Fatah's Damascus headquarters were also kept secret, in addition to the group's structure and size. All Fatah leaders had aliases and contacted members in the Persian Gulf, Europe, and Lebanon through couriers and liaison men using crudely coded letters.[136]

Over the next several years, Fatah would gain a renewed appreciation for maintaining strong counterintelligence awareness. One of Fatah's most vexing security problems was the exposure of its bases to its Arab and Israeli adversaries. In 1969, Israeli air strikes inflicted a significant portion of Fatah's loses—nearly 10 percent—causing the terrorists to have to search frequently for new hiding places.[137] Following a demonstration in Tripoli, Lebanon, in 1969, the Israeli air force conducted air strikes against PLO bases in the region. In May 1970, Israeli forces attacked Fatahland, destroying nineteen terrorist bases and killing about one hundred terrorists.[138] Also in 1970, the Jordanian army began its campaign against Fatah, shelling terrorist bases in Amman and other Jordanian cities.[139] Terrorists were instructed, as a result, to keep on the move from cave to cave. Fatah also obtained antiaircraft weapons, dug underground trenches, and strictly enforced the use of camouflage.[140]

By interrogating captured Fatah terrorists, Israel sometimes gained a huge advantage; one Fatah member exposed an entire network in the early 1970s, turning over the names of seventy Fatah members.[141]

In some cases, Fatah cells infiltrated into the West Bank were instructed not to form relationships with the local population because it was feared that informants were lurking among the locals. Some Fatah elements were instructed not to conduct recruitment campaigns because leaders worried that rapid expansion would lead to a lapse in security.[142]

When the Jordanian army began to rout Fatah in 1971, Fatah leaders advocated a return to greater secrecy, shunning the publicity of the late 1960s.[143] The problem facing Fatah, however, was that its leaders were already known to the Arab and Israeli security forces, so going back "underground" would be nearly impossible for these individuals.[144]

Counterintelligence: Basic and Adaptive Denial, 1972–1982. Fatah moved to the controlled territory in Fatahland after being driven from Jordan. The large controlled territory offered numerous benefits. By 1975, Arafat reigned supreme over this territory in southern Lebanon and the southern districts of Beirut. Free of Lebanese government interference, Fatah could provide its leaders with unfettered security as well as intelligence on activities in its territory.[145] For example, when BSO leader Salameh stayed in Beirut in the early 1970s, he would always travel with a large bodyguard entourage, which made it difficult for the Israelis to assassinate because he rarely was left unprotected or defenseless.[146]

A second benefit of the controlled territory was that it allowed Fatah a brief respite from control by its state sponsors. As Fatah launched terrorist operations from Lebanon's southern border, Israel warned the Lebanese government that Israel would continue to occupy and carry out attacks in southern Lebanon as long as Fatah remained.[147] The Lebanese government, however, could do little to impede Fatah and PLO terrorist activities, in contrast to the governments of Jordan and Syria, which could more easily control the terrorists in their territories.[148]

The controlled territory also presented a number of counterintelligence drawbacks, however, which the Israelis were quick to exploit. The chief drawback was that Fatah and PLO bases and supply routes were plainly observable to the adversary and thus vulnerable to air strikes and shelling. In 1969, the Israeli air force was easily able to bomb Fatah bases deep inside Jordan.[149] Following the BSO attack at the Olympic Games in Munich in 1972, Israel attacked numerous Fatah and PLO positions and refugee camps, including the supply routes emanating from Fatahland.[150] During Operation Litani in March 1978, Israel struck

Fatah and PLO targets deep inside Lebanon, including bases, refugee camps, ammunition dumps, and training facilities in a sports stadium in southern Beirut.[151] When the Israeli military moved into southern Lebanon, it was able to locate arms caches and target refugee camps for mass arrests.[152]

The Israelis likely were able to learn about Fatah's capabilities from overhead and ground imagery intelligence. Fatah's attempts to disguise military vessels, equipped with cranes for lowering rubber dinghies, as ordinary fishing vessels docked in Lebanese harbors was probably an attempt to deceive such intelligence collection.[153] Fatah's concentration of personnel—as well as training and administrative facilities—in this controlled territory probably permitted Israel to array its most productive intelligence-collection platforms against this discrete geographical space.

A second drawback was that controlled territory drew Fatah into complacency and occasional counterintelligence sloppiness. In spite of the *Minimanual*'s admonition that the urban terrorist "must not write or hold any documents," Fatah kept many files and occasionally failed to destroy them during Israeli raids. When Israeli security services captured Fatah files of terrorists, supporters, and sleepers during a Beirut raid in 1973, the capture resulted in a massive roundup of terrorists within days.[154] During Operation Litani in 1978, Israeli security services were able to capture PLO registration lists, which allowed them to locate key terrorist leaders and support elements in southern Lebanon.[155]

Fatah's controlled territory made the organization a harder target for Israel's security services, but it was still vulnerable to Israel's human intelligence-collection methods. Israel skillfully used human spies to infiltrate Fatah's safe haven in order to pinpoint bombing targets in Beirut and collect intelligence on Fatah leaders.[156] This infiltration allowed Israel to increase the accuracy of its air strikes and increasingly avoid destroying purely civilian installations, within which Fatah and the PLO had traditionally embedded themselves. One Israeli spy was able to get close to the lieutenant of Fatah leader Abu Iyad (Saleh Khalef) in Beirut by serving as his family's baby-sitter. This access allowed her to photograph documents in his house detailing the "names of PLO members, forged ID papers, and the time and location of impending attacks."[157] Israel probably knew that its priority Fatah leadership targets were all within a few neighborhoods of one another in Beirut. Therefore, when developing a plan to find spies close to these targets, the Israelis probably focused on gathering basic data about these neighborhoods and eventually found a few spies with the appropriate access and motivations. Rather than spreading their intelligence operatives across entire countries or continents, the Israelis could thus focus their collection energies on a few—albeit very well-protected—neighborhoods in Beirut.

Much like controlled territory, Fatah's reliance on outside sponsors also led to counterintelligence challenges. Syria was one of Fatah's key sponsors, but Damascus's hold on the group occasionally placed Fatah at a major counterintelligence disadvantage. Syria arrested and jailed Arafat in the mid-1960s when he was perceived to be acting too independently.[158] Syrian intelligence may also have supported Palestinian terrorist Sabi Khalila Bana, also known as "Abu Nidal," in his campaign to intimidate and discredit PLO leaders in the mid-1970s, probably to reign in Arafat further.[159] In 1983, Syria recruited Fatah leader Said al-Muragha, known as "Abu Musa," to rebel against Arafat, although the Syrian-inspired coup ultimately failed.[160] Syria also intervened militarily against the Palestinians in Lebanon in 1976.[161] Damascus almost certainly used its extensive knowledge of Fatah and PLO military and leadership structures to attack the group more effectively. Fatah probably enjoyed a partial respite from Syrian meddling when it occupied Fatahland, although Syria continued to harass and compromise Fatah assets throughout the group's lifetime.

Up to 1982, Fatah appears to have adopted methods detailed in the *Minimanual of the Urban Terrorist*. Counterespionage is a key focus in the *Minimanual*: "[T]he enemy encourages betrayal and infiltrates spies into the terrorist organization. The urban terrorist's technique against this enemy tactic is to denounce publicly the spies, traitors, informers and provocateurs. For his part, the urban terrorist must not evade the duty— once he knows who the spy or informer is—of physically wiping him out."[162] In accordance with this philosophy, Fatah tortured and killed many informants in public.[163] The *Minimanual* also stressed setting up a formal counterintelligence service, which Fatah initiated in the late 1960s: "For complete success in the battle against spies and informers, it is essential to organize a counter-espionage or counter-intelligence service."[164] Before Fatah sent new recruits to training, every new member was interrogated by Fatah's counterespionage service, the Jihaz al Razd.[165]

Fatah and the PLO responded to Israeli counterterrorism efforts by increasing its counterintelligence and security efforts. After Israel raided Beirut in April 1973, terrorist leaders were instructed to change their apartments at least once a month, to keep their new addresses secret, and to discontinue use of official PLO vehicles. Every time Israel pulled off an intelligence success, Fatah and the PLO would initiate a flurry of counterespionage activity to root out potential informants.[166] Fatah used brutal interrogations to get intelligence out of captured informants and spies. It tortured one Israeli spy by burning her skin with cigarette butts and her mouth with a hot electric curling iron. This same spy was also subject to mock executions, where she was forced to write a farewell letter to her family, convinced she would soon be killed.[167]

Arafat continued to develop strategies for keeping himself secure. He would sleep in the back of cars and be on the move constantly, and he frequently abandoned appointments in order to keep an unpredictable schedule.[168] He would periodically try to feed his adversaries misinformation through suspected informants and thus reduce the adversaries' confidence in their human sources. This misinformation can be categorized as covert manipulation, but it was likely sporadic, and it is unknown whether it successfully fooled the Israelis.

Summary. For the most part, Fatah had a tightly organized command structure, significant resources, and strong adversaries in this second period. Fatah's leaders were much better protected inside its controlled territories of Jordan and Lebanon than in the uncontrolled territory of the Gaza Strip and West Bank, due at least in part to the fact that West Bank communities were not as supportive as those in Jordan and Lebanon.

Fatah provided its members with training in intelligence and counterintelligence. Although some of this training took place in Palestinian refugee camps, more advanced training for elite members probably took place outside Fatah's controlled territories in places such as Syria and Egypt. Some of Fatah's counterintelligence advantage came from recruiting guerrillas with experience in hiding from Arab intelligence services. The training Fatah provided its members was almost certainly better when it controlled territory.

THE BLACK SEPTEMBER ORGANIZATION'S EMERGENCE AND DEMISE: 1971-1978

Key Factors

Organizational Structure. The BSO was established in 1971 as a covert arm of Fatah. It was designed to be operationally compartmented from Fatah, but the two entities remained connected ideologically and financially. Fatah's leaders selected ten young men to head the BSO, which was designed to be small, well trained, and able to strike Israeli targets abroad.[169] BSO's creation was a reflection of Fatah's frustration with its secrecy and counterintelligence lapses, and Fatah hoped BSO would better harness the advantages of the secret "underground."[170] A significant factor in their relationship was that BSO leaders nominally existed outside of the Fatah hierarchy but almost certainly adhered to Arafat's overarching strategy and vision. Arafat also hoped that Fatah could plausibly deny culpability for BSO terrorist operations that drew public ridicule or embarrassment.[171]

BSO relied on a small council of leaders rather than a single chief to make its day-to-day decisions.[172] Many of the key leaders, including Salameh and Abu Iyad, had served in Fatah's Jihaz al Razd intelligence service. Abu Iyad was BSO's most senior leader, and Mohammed Abu Najjer, also known as "Abu Yussef," took charge of BSO's overall strategy.[173] Fakhri al-Omri served as Abu Iyad's confidant and right-hand man.[174]

The group had a cell-based infrastructure, and family affiliations were likely important to group cohesion and organization. The group was highly compartmentalized, and operatives selected for a mission knew few operational details until the mission was in progress.[175]

BSO recruited Palestinians and Arabs who had lived in Europe for years as students, teachers, diplomats, and businessmen, often for short-term service only.[176] These individuals knew nothing about BSO operations beyond their personal assignments. BSO "employed" close to one hundred people of this type.[177] Mahmoud Hamshiri, Fatah's chief in Paris, built a French Fatah network that included native Frenchmen and non-Arab anarchists.[178] It is likely that most BSO operatives were brought into the group for special missions, at which point they would go into training and swear allegiance to BSO.[179]

When BSO took hostages at the Saudi Arabian embassy in Khartoum, Sudan, in 1973, the operation was planned and organized by one BSO member, Fawaz Yassin, Fatah's representative in Khartoum. As one of the few obvious culprits of the operation, Yassin flew out of Sudan a few hours before the operation began. A few of the support personnel were Sudanese nationals.[180] One operative was a local Palestinian news reporter who worked on the *Voice of Palestine* program on Sudanese radio.[181] The other six operatives were flown in on Jordanian passports and briefed on the operation only the day before the attack.[182]

Popular Support. Fatah laid the foundation for BSO's European and Middle Eastern support networks years before BSO was created. Throughout the 1960s, Arafat used the Palestinian Students' Federation in Cairo, Baghdad, and West Germany to collect funds and recruits for Fatah.[183] The approximately six thousand Palestinians living in West Germany offered an ample population of sympathizers.[184] Munich was home to many Arab guest workers, including approximately eight hundred Jordanians, and German security services did not monitor this population until after the Olympic Village attack.[185] Although BSO tapped sympathizers to provide safe houses, funding, and intelligence, it recruited only a few of them to undertake terrorist missions.[186]

Two Palestinian brothers, Khalid and Hani al-Hassan, organized thousands of Palestinian students in Stuttgart, a city that became a principal center for Fatah activity in Europe in the 1960s.[187] Khalid and Hani established firm connections with left-wing Palestinian student groups in Germany and other European countries.[188] Students in Germany, Austria, Italy, and Spain were occasionally selected to take short training courses in Algeria in the use of arms and sabotage techniques. Once BSO was created, some of these students were sent to Lebanon, Syria, and Jordan, where they were trained to participate in BSO operations against Israel.[189]

Fatah had also gained sympathy among Palestinian students in Lebanese and Algerian universities. Some of these students spoke European languages after studying in European universities or at the American University in Beirut, and the few who were recruited by BSO almost certainly became valuable assets as a result of their language skills.[190]

By 1972, BSO was tapping into Fatah's vibrant and deep European connections and was able to call on a few select scholars and students of the region for special missions as needed. Rome, which had a population of approximately two thousand Arab university students, became a headquarters for BSO in Europe due to its proximity to the Middle East and the generally relaxed security practices of the local police services.[191] BSO operatives from all over Europe would use Rome for secure meetings, and BSO sympathizers in Rome provided the group with safe houses and funds.[192]

Paris also became an important operational and communications center for BSO operations in Europe.[193] BSO found sympathizers and a few recruits among the thousands of Algerian and Moroccan workers living in Paris, some of whom were part of the left-wing intelligentsia who had supported Algerians in their war against the French occupation in the late 1950s and early 1960s. BSO operative Mohammed Boudia recruited a French woman who did not fit a terrorist profile to carry out one BSO attack.[194] Geneva also became a favored operating environment due to BSO's ability to blend into the large foreign and diplomatic community. It also served as a transit point for BSO operatives moving to and from the Middle East.[195]

BSO never established a presence in Great Britain, most likely for two reasons. First, unlike Germany, Britain did not have a large Arab student population, nor did it have a large Arab worker population like France to provide BSO operatives with camouflage. Second, the British strictly regulated movement and documentation in the United Kingdom, in contrast to continental Europe, where movement and documentation controls were more relaxed.[196]

BSO did not have to mount a massive independent campaign to generate popular support within Europe because it needed only a few dedicated individuals among the Palestinian diaspora.

Controlled Territory. BSO did not reside in or launch operations from Fatah's controlled territory in the 1970s. BSO leaders, however, occasionally returned to the security of the pro-Fatah communities of the Fakhani District of West Beirut and Fatahland to avoid being monitored or tracked down in uncontrolled territory.[197] BSO operatives and supporting units were spread out among the populations of Europe and the Middle East, commanding no specific territory. BSO did not regulate physical access to or security within its operating environments in Europe and in fact was often monitored or harassed by European and Arab law enforcement and intelligence agencies.

Other Important Factors

Resources. BSO was probably well funded and well stocked with recruits throughout its existence. Fatah seconded many high-quality recruits from the Jihaz al Razd to the BSO. The recruits were usually university graduates who could speak foreign languages and operate in foreign capitals without raising suspicion.[198] Abu Iyad recruited Ahmed Afghani, also known as "Abu Motassin," to "look after" BSO's "finances and supplies." Iyad hired Ghazi el Husseini, an engineer, to develop and "obtain sophisticated weaponry and equipment."[199]

State sponsorship played an important role in BSO's training and operations. Ten BSO members, including Salameh and Mohammed Daoud Odeh, also known as "Abu Daoud," were given special intelligence training in Cairo as BSO was being formed.[200] The Egyptian intelligence service taught the multimonth course on unconventional intelligence operations, including modules on intelligence recruiting and sabotage. Libya also provided BSO with support in Europe via various Libyan embassies. In exchange, BSO and Fatah tracked down and assassinated several Libyan exiles in Europe. Algerian and Libyan diplomats carried weapons, explosives, and communications to BSO operatives in Europe, and their embassies issued passports and identity papers to BSO members. Algerian embassies may have supplied BSO with intelligence reports produced by their security services.[201] Libyan embassy employees are alleged to have assisted BSO in some terrorist operations, including an operation in Sudan, after which the Sudanese government arrested and charged two employees of the Libyan embassy in Khartoum.[202]

Some BSO leaders worked closely with the Soviet KGB and the East German Stasi. Abu Iyad, code-named "KOCHUBEY" by the KGB, met with the KGB in Moscow in June 1978.[203] Hussein Abu Khair was working as a liaison to the KGB when he was assassinated by Israeli security elements in Cyprus in 1973.[204] Abu Daoud often stayed in the Palast

Hotel in East Berlin, where the Stasi helped him to hide, providing him with an around-the-clock security detail.[205]

Adversary Counterterrorism Capability. Throughout its lifespan, BSO was hunted by the very capable Israeli intelligence services. Early in 1972, Israel was preoccupied with Fatah terrorists operating in the Middle East and was not yet hunting down BSO operatives in Europe.[206] Fatah's decision to create the BSO to operate outside its controlled territory paid off. One of BSO's first European operations was the kidnapping of several Israeli athletes during the 1972 Munich Olympics, most of whom were later killed during a German rescue attempt. The success of BSO's kidnapping operation was due in part to the lenient security at the Olympic Village, but BSO also benefitted from the lack of Israeli security as well as from strategic surprise.[207]

Following the Munich Olympics, Israel initiated Operation Wrath of God, dispatching a team of Israeli assassins to Europe to hunt down BSO members. Mike Harari, leading the Israelis, conducted the initial reconnaissance in the Middle East and Europe, picked the assassination teams, and then moved the teams to safe houses in Paris. Israel used about fifteen agents divided into five squads: two assassins, two backups, two logistics men for renting safe houses and cars, seven agents conducting surveillance, and two communications specialists.[208]

Israel methodically assassinated key BSO members throughout Europe and the Middle East. The first assassination was Wael Zwaiter, who worked in Rome at the Libyan embassy and organized BSO attacks in Italy. The second to fall was Dr. Mahmoud Hamshiri, head of BSO in France, killed in Paris in 1972. In January 1973 in Cyprus, the Israeli squad killed Hussein Abad al Chir, a senior Fatah official and liaison with the Soviet KGB. In April 1973, the squad returned to Paris and killed Dr. Basil al Kubaissi, BSO's quartermaster in Europe, who arranged for the transfer of weapons and explosives to BSO operatives. In May 1973, Israeli commandos stormed a BSO-hijacked flight after it landed in Israel, killing and capturing several BSO terrorists.[209]

Israel hit more challenging BSO targets as well. In April 1973, Israeli security forces launched Operation Spring of Youth, successfully tracking and assassinating several key BSO leaders in the heart of their Beirut stronghold. Just hours after the Beirut operation, Israeli agents in Athens killed Zaiad Muchasi, head of BSO in Cyprus. Israel then killed two junior BSO members in Rome and Mohammed Boudia, the new head of BSO in France.[210] Yasser Arafat estimated that more than sixty BSO operatives were killed between September 1972 and July 1973.[211]

As Israeli security forces began to overwhelm BSO in Europe, BSO leaders shifted their focus to softer targets in Southeast Asia, Africa, and the Persian Gulf.[212] For years, Israeli squads stalked key BSO leader Ali Hassan Salameh, finally killing him with a roadside car bomb in Beirut in 1978 when he relaxed his security procedures.[213] Eight innocent bystanders were also killed in this operation, highlighting the difficulty of killing targets within their controlled territory, in contrast to Europe, where Israel completed many assassinations with few innocent bystanders killed.

Black September came to an end sometime in the late 1970s from the combination of Israeli counterterrorism efforts and Arafat's desire to shut the group down after the PLO was granted observer status in the United Nations in 1975. Arafat partially accomplished this task by marrying off approximately one hundred BSO operatives to Palestinian women in Lebanon and providing them with an apartment, a salary, and a nonviolent PLO job. As former operatives were married and started families, their desire to continue terrorist operations was curtailed, according to a former deputy to Abu Iyad.[214]

Intelligence and Counterintelligence Outcomes

Intelligence. BSO's intelligence capabilities, though in many instances not directly observable, can be gleaned in part from the quality of its operations. Its assassination of several targets, including an Israeli intelligence officer in January 1973 and an Israeli deputy military attaché in Washington in June 1973, required sophisticated surveillance or insider knowledge. In 1971, BSO killed the Jordanian prime minister Wasfi Tal while he was attending the Arab League summit in Cairo and almost killed the Jordanian ambassador in London. For Prime Minister Tal's assassination, BSO members Essat Rabah and Monzer Khalifa flew in from Beirut before the attack and waited for Tal in the lobby of his hotel. In the early 1970s, BSO also attacked a number of factories in Germany and gas installations in the Netherlands that were allegedly connected to Israeli interests.[215] Attacking these individuals and installations indicates that BSO employed relatively successful methods for surveilling its targets.

BSO used a network of accomplices in Europe to gather intelligence. A BSO operation to blow up the transalpine oil pipeline in Italy in August 1972 involved an Italian and two Frenchmen.[216] The oil pipeline was targeted because it served as a main feeder point for Middle Eastern and North African oil flowing into Europe.[217] Salameh in particular tapped into a network of radical European groups for some of his intelligence.[218] BSO in Germany used its extensive links to Palestinian students and the General Union of Palestinian Workers to improve its intelligence gathering.[219]

BSO's preoperational reconnaissance for the Munich Olympics mission reflected its reliance on both BSO leaders and locals to gather intelligence. One of the architects of the Munich operation, Abu Daoud (Mohammed Daoud Odeh), began reconnaissance for Munich in July 1972. Abu Daoud arrived in Munich, familiarized himself with the city streets, and began collecting "information on hotels and flights into and out of the city." Intelligence gathering for the Munich operation continued with two Palestinian operatives, Luttif Afif and Yusuf Nazal. Afif, also known as "Issa," had lived in Germany for five years, had attended the University of Berlin, and took a job as a civil engineer in the Olympic Village to surveil BSO targets. Nazal had worked for a Munich oil company and took a job in the Olympic Village as a cook to conduct surveillance. These "temporary jobs" allowed the men to "roam freely through the village," case the Israeli athletes' living quarters, and gather information about the athletes themselves.[220]

Finding Israeli agents and collaborators was an intelligence priority for BSO. It tracked down an Italian employee of Israel's El Al Airline, who BSO suspected was an Israeli agent, and assassinated him in April 1973.[221] A few weeks after BSO's Munich operation, BSO operatives tracked down and assassinated a Syrian radio reporter who was working as an informant for Israel.[222] BSO also used its network of European agents to track down and assassinate the Israeli intelligence officer Baruch Cohen in 1979.[223]

Counterintelligence: Basic and Adaptive Denial, Very Limited Covert Manipulation. BSO considered security and counterintelligence a high priority throughout its existence. Arafat's denial that BSO was a Fatah proxy group was itself a counterintelligence tactic designed to distract Israeli security services from drawing connections between Fatah and BSO leaders.[224] Many BSO leaders had experience in counterintelligence because they were seconded from Fatah's counterespionage and intelligence group. Others had been longtime members of the secretive Muslim Brotherhood, including Khalil Ibrahim al-Wazir, known as "Abu Jihad," and Abu Iyad.[225]

BSO maintained strict compartmentation and disseminated information on a "need-to-know" basis. Beyond Abu Iyad, few were allowed to see the complete picture of BSO's operations and strategy.[226] BSO operatives were organized into compartmented cells, and, although acquainted with fellow cell members, they probably never knew BSO leaders or members of other cells.[227] In some cases, Fatah terrorists recruited for BSO missions were not aware they were embarking on a BSO mission until after it was initiated.[228] Some BSO leaders did not know the group's top leadership or where their headquarters were located.[229] BSO probably assigned its operatives aliases for most of its big operations.[230]

BSO operatives involved in the Munich Olympics operation were trained and dispatched to Germany in this manner. The six BSO operatives selected for the operation were told they were to take special training in Libya but were instructed not to tell their families where they were going. They received about a month of advanced military training in Libya, some of which involved jumping over high walls—they probably figured that the training was for scaling Israeli military bases, but in fact it was for jumping over the wall at the Olympic Village. They were then flown to Germany and briefed into the operation only hours before it was to begin. After they were briefed, they had to surrender their money, passports, and everything else that could reveal their identities. As an added counterintelligence benefit, many of the operatives had grown up in the refugee camps together, trained together in Libya, and thus trusted one another.[231] The chance that an informant could slip in among them was slim.

BSO differed dramatically from Fatah in its approach to publicity. When BSO was formed, Abu Iyad argued to the Fatah Central Committee that secret methods and operations would actually increase popular support for and the mystique of the movement. In striking contrast to

Fatah's publicity-hungry leaders, BSO operatives shunned publicity.[232] The group never had an official spokesperson—which is unusual even for a clandestine militant group.[233] BSO would, however, occasionally conduct bogus interviews to plant disinformation.[234]

Israeli security services had great difficulty tracking BSO operatives in the early 1970s because of BSO's tight security. After information began to trickle into the Israeli services, they discovered that BSO leader Salameh was somewhere in Europe, though they did not know exactly where. BSO also ran a double-agent operation against Israeli security services in 1973. Mohammed Rabah, a Moroccan, contacted Israeli services in the early 1970s to help them find Fatah targets in Europe. After Munich, an undercover Israeli agent, Zadik Ophir, agreed to meet Rabah at a café in Brussels, whereupon Rabah shot Ophir at point-blank range.[235]

BSO security and counterintelligence shifted its focus when group members operated within the Fatah-controlled areas of Lebanon. Salameh traveled alone, using forged passports, when he worked abroad but would surround himself with armed bodyguards when he worked in Lebanon. This change in behavior suggests that Salameh felt comfortable enough in Lebanon to increase his operational profile by traveling with an entourage, but not comfortable enough to travel without physical protection. The BSO leader knew not only that he could be tracked to Beirut, but also that he could not easily be attacked once inside the Fatah territory. Salameh also constantly kept on the move in Lebanon and rarely spent more than one night in the same apartment.[236] Abu Iyad changed his apartment constantly when he was in Beirut, sometimes changing hideouts in the middle of the night.[237] As a testament to the advantage of security in controlled territory, Israel spent thousands of man-hours in the hunt for Salameh—Israel's longest and most costly mission.[238] Israeli agents also spent two decades unsuccessfully chasing Abu Iyad, who secured himself in the PLO's Tunis safe haven.[239]

One of BSO's greatest counterintelligence advantages was its ability to blend into the Middle Eastern community in Europe while planning and conducting operations. In Munich, BSO employed the services of Abdullah al Franji, an official at the Arab League's office in Bonn, whom German officials linked to BSO after finding incriminating documents and bomb materials in his apartment.[240] During the Munich Olympics operation, BSO operatives dressed in tracksuits to allow them to blend in with other athletes climbing over the Olympic Village gates after a late night—a disguise that was so effective that they were actually helped over the fence by a group of returning athletes.[241]

BSO operatives often used forged passports and identity papers to move about Europe and the Middle East.[242] Some BSO operatives became adept at disguising themselves. Mohammed Boudia, head of BSO in France, constantly changed his identity and even dressed as a woman to throw off the French security agents assigned to monitor his movements.[243] Salameh took advantage of the natural cover available to BSO operatives in Europe to recruit intellectual elites who could use their unblemished records, connections to the local elites, and sophistication to avoid being suspected or targeted by security services.[244] BSO's European quartermaster, Basil al-Kubaissi, relied heavily on his status as a professor of law at the American University in Beirut to keep himself above suspicion, although he also employed elaborate ways of communicating covertly and avoiding surveillance.[245] When Kubaissi was assassinated in 1973, he had nine forged passports in his possession.[246] BSO also used Libyan and Algerian embassy personnel to take care of logistics and acquire identity documents.[247]

Salameh was not only a master of disguise but probably was also adept at using deception to throw security services off his scent. It is possible that he actively planted rumors among Palestinians in Europe that he had gone to live in Scandinavia. Israeli security services picked up rumors in Geneva, Zurich, and Paris that Salameh had moved to Scandinavia, and the rumors ultimately led to Israeli agents' assassination of an innocent man living in Sweden.[248] BSO likely appreciated the importance of the counterintelligence tactic known as "damage control." When Jordanian authorities caught key BSO member Abu Daoud in 1972, it was a counterintelligence disaster for the group. Abu Daoud revealed details of a projected BSO operation as well as sensitive details about BSO operations in general.[249] BSO leaders were infuriated by Abu Daoud's confessions and went to great lengths to secure his release from Jordanian prison so that they could execute him and prevent him from providing their adversaries with additional sensitive information. The "Punishment Group" took thirteen hostages at the Saudi Arabian embassy in Paris in September 1973 as leverage to demand Abu Daoud's release, though it was not granted.[250]

BSO experienced other counterintelligence setbacks as well. In one operation, compartmentation led to a serious operational backfire. A mixed Japanese–Palestinian BSO group attempted to hijack a Japanese airliner in July 1973, but the mission planner was killed during the initial aircraft takeover. Because no other member of the hijacking team was fully briefed on the mission, the remaining terrorists had to abandon the operation.[251]

Israeli intelligence efforts were sometimes able to defeat BSO's counterintelligence strategies. In January 1973, Salameh was planning to shoot down the Israeli prime minister's plane as it landed in Rome. He used multiple passports to arrange for surface-to-air missiles to be smuggled from Dubrovnik to Rome and then stored at a PLO safe house in Rome. Israeli security services were able to thwart the operation due to three sources of intelligence. First, an Israeli informant working in the PLO gave Israel information that an operation was being planned. Second, telephone intercepts from a PLO safe house in Rome tipped off Israel on the timing of the operation and the use of missiles. Third, an Israeli surveillance patrol in the vicinity of the prime minister's landing plane found the BSO's missiles ready to launch out of two suspicious-looking chimneys on a food cart.[252]

BSO also, however, demonstrated its adaptiveness and counterintelligence resilience in this period. During Operation Spring of Youth in 1973, Israeli commandos captured three filing cabinets in Beirut housing part of Fatah's and BSO's archives and operational files.[253] Although this capture could have been a massive counterintelligence setback for BSO, the group adjusted quickly to limit the damage. Unsure of the extent of the compromised information, BSO replaced agents, changed codes, and abandoned missions "in the planning stages."[254] Following the Israeli operation in Beirut, BSO increased the protective detail for its leaders and instructed them to change their address at least once a week.[255] As BSO leaders were assassinated in Europe, the remaining leaders increased their security precautions. After Wael Zwaiter was killed, Mahmoud Hamshiri increased his countersurveillance procedures and refrained from making precise appointments.[256]

BSO was also able to use some of Israel's human intelligence networks to deceive Israeli security services. In the mid-1970s, BSO discovered a Palestinian student intelligence network that Israel had developed in

Madrid.[257] At first, BSO used the network to feed false information to Israeli security services through Israel's case officer Baruch Cohen. When Cohen began to suspect that several of his contacts were working for BSO, the group decided to assassinate him. On January 23, 1979, Cohen was shot and killed by a twenty-five-year-old Palestinian medical student as the student was being "debriefed."[258] These BSO double-agent operations clearly demonstrated the sophistication of BSO's counterintelligence methods.

Most of BSO's techniques can be characterized as basic denial. The group's strict compartmentation prevented members from learning much about the group's plans. BSO's choice not to establish an official spokesperson was atypical for a terrorist group, but also effective at preventing information loss through the media. The group employed some adaptive-denial techniques, such as changing codes and replanning missions following the compromise of its files and materials during Israel's Operation Spring of Youth. There is some evidence that it engaged in covert manipulation when its operatives assassinated two Israeli security officers in separate incidents by acting as double agents, which would have required an understanding of how and what to feed the Israeli intelligence-collection apparatus in order to lure each officer to a meeting.

Summary. BSO had a tightly organized command structure, a high level of resources, strong adversaries, and popular support, but it had limited access to Fatah's controlled territories for operational purposes. BSO was able to hide its logistical and operational plans from Israel, and its operatives had a relatively easy time blending into their European and Middle Eastern environments. Israeli agents tracked down and killed a number of BSO operatives. However, these individuals were known to the Israeli security service or were prominent members of the Palestinian community, whereas the relatively anonymous rank-and-file BSO members were far more secure.

BSO used locals and their knowledge of local targets to collect intelligence for its operations. Sympathetic diaspora communities provided fertile ground for gathering information about the operational environment. BSO did not conduct campaigns to increase its publicity or popular support, in part due to the fact that the group tapped into Fatah's popular base of support for recruiting, financing, and intelligence-collection purposes.

KEY FACTORS REVISITED

Organizational Structure. Both Fatah and BSO had tight organizational structures, and both groups were thus able to train their members in intelligence and counterintelligence procedures more effectively. Fatah and BSO were also somewhat vulnerable to their adversaries' efforts to develop high-level penetrations and exploit the groups' standardized counterintelligence procedures. Jordan partially exploited Fatah's standardized counterintelligence procedures when it broadcast fake code signals calling guerrillas to Jordan, where they were arrested. BSO almost fell victim to standardization when Israel captured BSO documents during Operation Spring of Youth. However, the BSO's tight structure allowed it to respond quickly to the document leakage by replacing its agents and changing its codes. However, had BSO counterintelligence and operational procedures not been standardized or centrally coordinated, the group would not have had to spend precious resources to adapt after the document leakage.

Popular Support. Fatah enjoyed greater counterintelligence support from the local populations when it had high popular support. Its leaders could easily relocate from apartment to apartment in Beirut in the 1967–1984 period, but the group was regularly exposed in the West Bank and Gaza in the 1964–1967 period. Fatah also was more likely to expose sensitive details to the media in its effort to maintain popular support. Its leaders craved publicity, particularly between 1968 and 1971. They gave interviews to the press, appeared on television, and appeared in public with their bodyguard entourages. They tried to increase the group's secrecy after 1971 but found it difficult to go back "underground" after exposing themselves and the group organizational structure to the public. Fatah also had to appease local tribes and families in order to keep their support, which sometimes meant not reprimanding local tribal leaders who might be collaborating with Israel. BSO, in contrast, assiduously shunned publicity and rarely had to deal with overexposure to the media. However, some BSO leaders in Europe were well known in their respective academic and professional circles and as a result were easier to locate, monitor, and capture.

Controlled Territory. Controlled territory allowed Fatah to develop superior communications security, physical security, and counterintelligence vetting. Israel found it difficult to track and assassinate Fatah leaders in Lebanon because they were surrounded by bodyguards and were able to move between safe houses with ease. Had Israel tried to strike at Fatah leaders in these conditions, they would likely have been caught in a firing match, which would have caused a great deal of very public, collateral damage. The pro-Fatah community in Beirut and Fatahland could have alerted Fatah to Israel's efforts to surveil and track Palestinian targets. To surveil a terrorist for assassination required weeks of careful observation in close proximity to the individual and his entourage of well-armed bodyguards. Thus, Israel would have to divert energy away from tracking its targets to increasing its own counterintelligence posture when it operated in this hostile territory. Israel took such a risk in Operation Spring of Youth, in which Israeli special-forces units raided an apartment in Beirut and killed several high-ranking Fatah members. The half-hour-long operation cost Israel two of its soldiers and required hundreds of hours surveillance of buildings and neighborhoods. The Israeli operation also left in its wake a large amount of collateral damage, which could have been worse had the Israeli commandos been forced to engage the Lebanese security forces or the PLO guards that chased after them as they were exfiltrated from Beirut.[259]

In contrast, BSO leaders in Europe had less personal protection, and once Israel located them, they were tracked and killed with relative ease. BSO leaders in Europe could not change houses every night and travel with an entourage of bodyguards as Fatah leaders could in the group's controlled territory. From 1964 to 1967, Fatah did not control territory, so the group's physical and operational security suffered as a result.

Controlled territory also made Fatah more vulnerable to its adversaries' efforts to concentrate its intelligence-collection and military resources against a fixed, geographical space. Israel could more easily track the movement of persons, weapons, and supplies to and from Fatah safe havens than it could track BSO personnel, weapons, and supplies through and between its operations in Europe and the Middle East. Israel sealed the border between the West Bank and Jordan, ambushed militants on guerrilla passes in Jordan, and set up observation posts in Lebanon to better monitor and apprehend Fatah members. By watching particular territories, it could estimate Fatah's relative manpower, communications, and weapons supplies.

In contrast, the rank-and-file members of BSO were more anonymous and hidden among tens of thousands of noncombatants with similar biographical profiles. In many cases, BSO operatives were legitimate students and workers, and BSO operatives who participated in only one mission would leave very few operational footprints. The difficulty of locating BSO operatives made estimation of BSO's overall manpower, communications, and weapons supplies very difficult. Even BSO members with a large operational footprint were difficult to locate—Israel spent thousands of man-hours in the hunt for Salameh. Once these BSO operatives were located, however, it proved easy for the Israeli services to apprehend them.

In contrast to BSO efforts in Europe, Fatah gained little advantage from operating outside of controlled territory in the mid-1960s. It was centralized within territory that was controlled by Israel, which allowed Israel to locate and monitor the group with relative ease. A terrorist group can capitalize on operating outside of controlled territory only if its adversary does not control the territory of operation.

ADDITIONAL LESSONS FROM THE FATAH/BLACK SEPTEMBER CASE

The Fatah and BSO case offers additional insights into terrorist counter-intelligence. First, having access to controlled territory had both advantages and disadvantages. Controlled territory allowed Fatah to police a geographical area within which it could track and capture informants, conduct background checks on recruits, increase its popular support, insulate its leaders from foreign security services, and develop a media function to inspire and communicate intelligence to its members. Controlled territory also produced some complacency, though, which decreased Fatah's counterintelligence posture. Fatah kept paper records and files on its members and operations without developing a means of destroying them in an emergency, which proved disastrous on a number of occasions when these records were captured by Jordanian and Israel security forces.

Second, state sponsorship similarly had both advantages and disadvantages for counterintelligence practices. On the one hand, state sponsorship provided Fatah and BSO with high-quality training, protection from hostile security services, financial assistance, identity papers and logistical support for operations, and even raw intelligence on targets. On the other hand, key state sponsors such as Syria often tried to control and weaken Fatah when the group acted against the state's interests.

Third, campaigns to increase popular support may be a necessary evil for clandestine terrorist groups, but they come with a counterintelligence cost. They provide valuable targeting data to the adversary and make it very difficult for terrorist leaders to return "underground" once they become popular.

In the early 1990s, al Qaʾida had relatively little international popular support but enjoyed a high level of local security in its controlled territory in Sudan. In the mid-1990s, it dramatically increased its publicity campaigns and attacks against its adversaries and as a result significantly increased its international popular support. This popular support led directly to improvements in its international intelligence and counterintelligence capabilities. At the same time, though, al Qaʾida began to suffer from many new security and counterintelligence problems in its local controlled territory. Why did al Qaʾida's campaign to increase its popular support simultaneously advance its international counterintelligence capabilities and impede its local counterintelligence efforts?

This case study shows that al Qaʾida's campaign to increase its international popular support introduced numerous counterintelligence and security challenges in its local controlled territory. These challenges arose as it raised its operational profile to connect with media organizations and to inspire its international supporters with details about its leaders and terrorist plans. In addition, the case shows that al Qaʾida's efforts to improve its local counterintelligence posture occasionally introduced counterintelligence problems for the group's international operations.

The al Qaʾida case study is broken into three parts, as noted in table 4.1. The first part depicts al Qaʾida from its inception in 1988 until its departure from Sudan in 1996, when the group had relatively little international and local popular support. The second part depicts al Qaʾida from 1996 until the initiation of US military operations in Afghanistan

Table 4.1 Al Qa'ida Case Study: Key Factors

Al Qa'ida	Organizational Structure	Popular Support	Controlled Territory	Resources	Adversary Counterterrorism Capability
1988–1996	Loose	Low	Yes	High	Low
1996–2001	Tight	Low	Yes	High	High
2001–2003	Loose	High	Yes	High	High

in 2001, when it enjoyed relatively high international popular support and some controlled territory (as shown in figure 4.1) but relatively little local popular support. The third case focuses on the group from 2001 until 2003, when it enjoyed high levels of both international and local popular support.

To sharpen the differences between al Qa'ida's local and international conditions, the group's resources, popular support, intelligence, and counterintelligence are addressed separately for each period in local and international subsets.[1]

OVERVIEW OF AL QA'IDA

Al Qa'ida formed in August 1988 under the leadership of Osama Bin Laden, a Saudi veteran of the anti-Soviet insurgency in Afghanistan in the 1980s. Bin Laden and the Palestinian cleric Abdullah Azzam led the precursor to al Qa'ida, the Bureau of Services, which helped to funnel volunteer jihadists into Afghanistan to fight the Soviet armed forces. When the Soviet Union withdrew from Afghanistan, Bin Laden and Azzam believed that the Bureau of Services should continue its mission of supporting jihadists, from which al Qa'ida derived its original inspiration.[2]

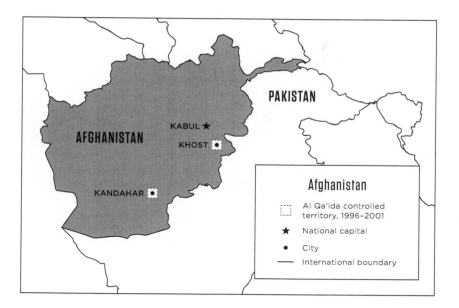

Figure 4.1 Afghanistan

Bin Laden's most trusted advisers came together to form al Qaʾida's "advisory council," which consisted mostly of Egyptians, including a doctor named Ayman al-Zawahiri, who had extensive experience harassing and evading the Egyptian government. These men created the group's by-laws and a mission statement: "To establish truth, get rid of evil, and establish an Islamic nation."[3] A special terrorist-training center near Khost, Afghanistan, known as "al Faruq camp," trained some of al Qaʾida's first recruits after they signed an oath of loyalty to Bin Laden and promised to keep the group's affairs secret.[4]

The government of Sudan invited Bin Laden to establish a base of operations in Sudan in 1990 in return for helping the country wage an internal war in southern Sudan and assist with various infrastructure projects. That year Bin Laden sent representatives to Sudan to purchase property and in the following year moved himself there after fleeing Saudi Arabia when the government seized his passport.[5] He had begun to denounce the Saudi government for allowing US troops to station themselves in the kingdom during and following the Gulf War. The US military presence in Saudi Arabia seemed to galvanize Bin Laden's interest in attacking the West, and in 1992 al Qa'ida issued a fatwa, or religious edict, that called for attacks on US forces.[6]

The international pressure on the government of Sudan to expel Bin Laden grew steadily through the 1990s, until the Sudanese president, Omar al Bashir, believed he could no longer win US favor and investment dollars while Bin Laden was his official guest.[7] Bin Laden and most Sudan-based members of al Qa'ida left the country in May 1996 with the goal of reestablishing themselves in Afghanistan. Bin Laden achieved this goal after the Afghan Taliban captured the Afghan cities of Kabul and Jalalabad in September 1996 and extended an offer of safe haven to al Qa'ida; in return, al Qa'ida gave the Taliban an estimated $10 million to $20 million a year.[8]

In late 1996, al Qa'ida revamped its media strategy and began to reach out to international and English-language media to deliver edicts and warnings. The new zeal of al Qa'ida's media efforts was matched with a string of devastating terrorist attacks, including bombings at the US embassies in Tanzania and Kenya in August 1998 and the bombing of the USS *Cole* in October 2000. Al Qa'ida's media outreach and battlefield success filled its ranks with recruits—probably tens of thousands of individuals visited al Qa'ida training camps in Afghanistan between 1996 and 2001.[9]

It is likely that Bin Laden approved the September 11, 2001, operation sometime in late 1998 or early 1999, although the man responsible for planning and managing the operation, Khaled Sheikh Muhammed (KSM), had proposed the plan to Bin Laden sometime in 1996 or 1997.[10] Al Qa'ida successfully executed its attacks on New York City's World Trade Center and the Pentagon in September 2001, and the United States responded swiftly by putting US and international military and intelligence forces in Afghanistan in October 2001 with Operation Enduring Freedom.

Al Qa'ida suffered many setbacks following the US and international intervention in Afghanistan but also managed to execute additional terrorist operations across the globe—including in Kenya, Morocco, Saudi Arabia, and Turkey—between 2001 and 2003.[11] By the end of 2003, the battle for control of territory, media space, and allies raged on between al Qa'ida and the West. Figure 4.2 offers a summary of key events for al Qa'ida.

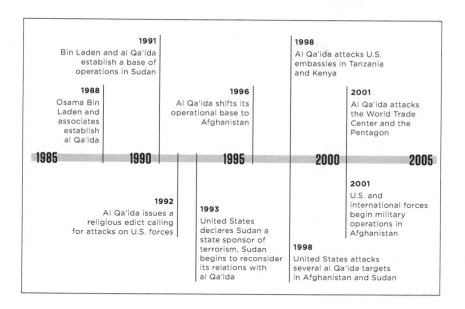

Figure 4.2 Abbreviated Timeline of Key al Qa'ida Activities and Events

AL QA'IDA'S INCEPTION: 1988–1996

Key Factors

Organizational Structure. Al Qa'ida's organizational structure in the 1988–1996 period was relatively hierarchical and tightly commanded and managed. (For the purposes of this chapter, al Qa'ida is defined as Bin Laden, his advisers and deputies, individuals pledging allegiance [*bayat*] to him or to his deputies, and individuals using this core group's funding and training to conduct attacks in the name of al Qa'ida.) Bin Laden was the group's first leader, commanding the group's intelligence branch, a military committee, a financial committee, a political committee, a media committee, and the Advisory Council that comprised Bin Laden's inner circle.[12] The Advisory Council had between seven and ten members who advised Bin Laden on operational goals and political considerations and were considered the highest authority in al Qa'ida next to Bin Laden and his deputy.[13]

Popular Support: Local. Al Qa'ida did not enjoy a significant amount of local popular support in Sudan in the 1988–1996 period. Because the government allowed Bin Laden to set up al Qa'ida's headquarters and camps in Sudan, there was no pressing need to develop local popular support.

Bin Laden cultivated relationships with Sudan's business community, political leaders, and intelligence and military communities. He became close to Hassan 'Abd Allah al-Turabi, leader of the National Islamic Front political party in Sudan; to Sudan's president, Omar al-Bashir; and to some government ministers.[14]

Support for al Qa'ida among the general Sudanese population was limited though not completely absent in this period. Some of this popularity was directed at Bin Laden as an individual. Bin Laden had fought alongside Arabs and Afghans in the trenches of Afghanistan and had become respected and renowned for such bravery.[15] Bin Laden also held regular lectures at his guesthouse and mosques in Khartoum, where group members and recruits could hear him speak about jihad and al Qa'ida.[16]

Al Qa'ida did not embrace the terrorist image during this period and forbade its members from claiming credit for attacks or publicly identifying the organization for fear of drawing attention from its adversaries.[17]

Al Qa'ida's lack of popular support and its dependence on Sudan ultimately backfired on the group. Sudan was under constant pressure from the United States, Egypt, and Saudi Arabia to expel Bin Laden. The government of Sudan likely estimated that the Sudanese public would not react unfavorably to al Qa'ida's expulsion, which gave it leverage over al Qa'ida.[18] The president of Sudan, Omar al-Bashir, came under increased international pressure to expel Bin Laden in 1996 but did not face a countervailing local pressure demanding Bin Laden's protection. The president believed that he would not be able to win US favor or investment dollars as long as Bin Laden was in Khartoum.[19] As a result, Bashir informed Bin Laden that al Qa'ida needed to leave Sudan in 1996.

Popular Support: International. From its inception, al Qa'ida attempted to inspire the "feeling of jihad" on a global scale.[20] The group was partially successful in this endeavor in the 1988–1996 period.

Bin Laden came to al Qa'ida with experience in media and propaganda, having run the Bureau of Services with Abdullah Azzam. Beginning in 1984, the Bureau of Services, published *Jihad* magazine, which provided a monthly assessment of the war in Afghanistan and focused on how Arabs contributed to the struggle against the Soviets. Bin Laden distinguished the group's philosophy from those of its militant cohorts by focusing on overthrowing governments in the Muslim world that were deemed "apostate." In the late 1980s, members of the newly named al Qa'ida began to meet at Bin Laden's residence in Peshawar, Pakistan, and invited journalists and relief agencies to put Bin Laden and al Qa'ida in the media spotlight.[21]

Bin Laden carefully managed his public persona, commissioning documentaries of his life in Afghanistan in 1988, which showed him "eating poor food and living in caves" in the Afghan hills. He funded a newspaper in Pakistan and cultivated "influential" journalists.[22] He became close to Saudi Arabian journalist Jamal Khashoggi, for example, who wrote about Bin Laden's exploits in Afghanistan and took the first published photograph of the al Qa'ida leader.[23] Al Qa'ida's media committee started a weekly newspaper called *Nashrat al Akhbar* and established a media-liaison wing in 1994, known as the Advice and Reformation Committee, based in London.[24]

Bin Laden loyalist Khaled al-Fawwaz moved from Sudan to London in 1994 to establish and manage the Advice and Reformation Committee. Fawwaz began disseminating al Qa'ida condemnations of the Saudi and US governments.[25] Bin Laden's hatred for the Saudi regime and the United States increased dramatically in the early 1990s when the US military based itself in Saudi Arabia to fight the 1991 Gulf War.[26] His vitriolic attacks on the Saudi regime increased his popularity among Muslim youths throughout the Arab world and earned him the moniker "Sheikh Osama."[27]

Bin Laden granted an interview to *Time* magazine correspondent Scott MacLeod in May 1996 in Khartoum, probably to combat his emerging "terrorist" image in the popular media. He argued that he was a simple businessman who was working nonviolently to reform the Saudi regime.[28] At the time, however, US authorities suspected he had played a role in the bombing of a US-run National Guard training center in Riyadh, Saudi Arabia. Bin Laden changed his rhetoric after being expelled from Sudan in 1996, issuing his first declaration of jihad against the United States via the London-based newspaper *al Quds al Arabia*. (It is not exactly clear, though, why Bin Laden was motivated to change al Qa'ida's rhetoric at this point.)

Controlled Territory. Sudan provided al Qa'ida with territory and safe haven for much of this first period. In 1990, National Islamic Front leader Hassan al-Turabi invited Bin Laden to use Sudan as a safe haven after he was expelled from Saudi Arabia in 1991.[29] Turabi then dispatched Sudanese intelligence officers to meet with Bin Laden and facilitate his move to Sudan.[30] Sudan was an ideal terrorist territory. The border with Egypt was largely unguarded, and Islamic militants from all over the Middle East and from Egypt, Pakistan, and Afghanistan in particular had used Sudanese territory for terrorist training since the mid-1980s.[31]

In 1989, Sayf al-Adl, a high-ranking member of al Qa'ida and a former Egyptian army officer, purchased two farms in Sudan for al Qa'ida military training—one in Port Sudan for $250,000 and the other near Khartoum for $180,000.[32] Turabi provided al Qa'ida with two hundred passports and semiofficial status, allowing group members to travel outside of Sudan with relative ease under alias identities.[33] Sudan also allowed foreign militants to enter the country. By 1993, "young men from many countries" were traveling to al Qa'ida's Soba Farm, ten kilometers south of Khartoum, to meet Bin Laden and begin their terrorist training.[34] Bin Laden paid for 480 Islamic fighters to move from Pakistan to Khartoum in the spring of 1993.[35]

An officer in the Sudanese army, Muqadem Abdul Basit Hamza, supplied al Qa'ida with a system of radios for internal communications.[36] During this period, Bin Laden also had access to a satellite phone.[37] Even when Sudan expelled al Qa'ida in 1996, the Sudanese intelligence service tasked its Peshawar station with scouting out a suitable new base for Bin Laden in Afghanistan.[38]

Other Important Factors

Resources: Local. Al Qa'ida had access to money, high-quality personnel, and controlled territory in this early period. Bin Laden's confidant Ayman al-Zawahiri brought with him a cadre of "highly disciplined" Egyptian fighters. His recruits were "doctors, engineers, and soldiers," and many were "used to working in secret." These men joined recruits from the large pool of Arab Afghans left over from the war against the Soviets.[39] Recorded in the minutes of al Qa'ida's first meeting in August 1988 was the group's plan to have 314 militants trained by mid-1989.[40]

In 1988, Zawahiri and Egyptian Islamic Jihad leader Sayyid Imam al Sharif, also known as "Dr. Fadl," established the "al Faruq" camp near Khost, Afghanistan, to recruit and train elite fighters that would become part of al Qa'ida. The group had enough money in this period to pay its married members $1,500 per month and its single members $1,000 per month.[41]

Al Qa'ida received support from other militant groups as well. In 1991, the organization was still relatively small and occasionally relied on the expertise and resources of more established militant groups, such as Egyptian Islamic Jihad.[42] Sometime between 1991 and 1993, veterans of the Afghan war compiled the *Encyclopedia of Jihad*, an eleven-volume collection of terrorist and guerrilla tactics, which al Qa'ida used to improve its operational tradecraft.[43]

Resources: International. Al Qa'ida had access to an international recruiting network in this early phase. Mosques and schools throughout the world that had served as recruiting stations for the Afghan–Soviet War continued to attract radical Islamic militants. Bin Laden was also familiar with global recruitment strategies and logistics because he had helped to set up the Bureau of Services, which had channeled recruits into Afghanistan during the war against the Soviets.[44] However, al Qa'ida had not yet gained international notoriety, nor was it able to use its name recognition to draw recruits to its cause.

Al Qa'ida had access to money in this period, although probably not the $300 million Bin Laden fortune as some analysts have claimed. The Saudi government froze Osama Bin Laden's assets and forced his family to share his portion of the company, so Bin Laden probably had access to only $30 million in Sudan.[45]

Al Qa'ida's international recruits reflected its global ambitions. Many al Qa'ida members settled in Sudan in part because they could not return to their home countries—in particular Egypt, Algeria, Libya, Syria, and Iraq—for fear of government persecution.[46] Al Qa'ida was headquartered in Sudan, but it retained training camps in Afghanistan and had members training in Bosnia, Yemen, and the Philippines.[47]

One of al Qa'ida's most important early resources was a former Egyptian military officer, Ali Adbelseoud Muhammed, also known as "Abu Omar." Abu Omar had served in the Egyptian military from 1971 to 1984, where he had received special-forces and intelligence training. He had also worked for Egyptian Airlines from 1984 to 1986 as a counterterrorism specialist. In 1986, Abu Omar immigrated to the United States, enlisted in the US Army, and was assigned to the John F. Kennedy Special Warfare School at Fort Bragg in North Carolina. At this time, he stole US military training manuals, translated them into Arabic, and used his knowledge of special warfare and intelligence to train al Qa'ida fighters.[48] Al Qa'ida's manuals were probably considered useful and disseminated widely among the group, as indicated by the fact that several operatives were in possession of these materials when they were apprehended. In 1993, an operative involved in the first attack against the World Trade Center was detained at JFK Airport in New York City with a bag full of these terrorist-training manuals.[49]

In this early phase, al Qa'ida was already using its international resources to prepare for the embassy bombings attacks that would occur in 1998. In 1994, its cells were setting up in Nairobi and Mombasa, Kenya, and preparing the initial phases of surveillance for the embassy attacks.[50]

Adversary Counterterrorism Capability. From its beginnings in 1988, al Qa'ida faced capable adversaries. In this first period, however, its adversaries did not always take aggressive military action against the group. The United States, one of al Qa'ida's most powerful adversaries, relied mainly on nonmilitary counterterrorism measures to keep the group in check after it established itself in Sudan in 1991.

First, the United States pressured Sudan to expel several terrorist groups, including al Qa'ida. The governments of Egypt, Syria, Jordan, and Libya also pressured Sudan to cut off its support to al Qa'ida. In 1993, the United States designated Sudan a state sponsor of terrorism and placed Bin Laden on a terrorist watch list, which prevented him from obtaining a visa to enter the United States. US counterterrorism authorities were trying to keep track of Bin Laden's activities, but they ultimately considered him an extremist financier rather than a terrorist.[51] International pressure on Sudan continued to mount until the

Sudanese government forced Bin Laden and al Qa'ida to move its head-quarters out of the country in 1996. Meanwhile, preparations for al Qa'ida's earliest terrorist operations in Saudi Arabia, Kenya, and Tanzania continued undetected because US authorities had limited motivation to gather counterterrorism intelligence in these locations.[52]

Intelligence and Counterintelligence Outcomes

Intelligence: Local and International. Al Qa'ida's intelligence capabilities were modest in this period, primarily because the group was just beginning its intelligence activities to support planned terrorist operations. In Sudan, al Qa'ida was using relatively sophisticated, hand-held radios provided by the Sudanese military to pass information between the group's members.[53] In 1992, Abu Omar was training al Qa'ida members in surveillance and intelligence-gathering techniques.[54] Portuguese al Qa'ida member Paulo Jose de Almeida Santos, "Abdullah Yusuf," asserted in 2002 that he was part of an al Qa'ida open-source intelligence group that provided political analysis to al Qa'ida leaders based on newspaper articles.[55]

Outside of Sudan, al Qa'ida intelligence efforts were gathering steam. Zawahiri had tasked Abu Omar to penetrate US intelligence in the early 1990s. Abu Omar used his access to the Special Warfare School at Fort Bragg to steal training manuals and then copy them at Kinkos.[56] In 1993, Bin Laden sent Muhammed Atef, one of his top military commanders at the time, to Somalia to determine how best to attack US forces based there. Atef reported back to Sudan, and al Qa'ida dispatched a mortar specialist to Somalia. Atef also returned to provide military training and assistance to Somalis fighting against US forces.[57]

In the mid-1990s, Bin Laden dispatched Abu Omar to Nairobi to surveil targets for the upcoming embassy attacks. Abu Omar surveilled the French Cultural Center and the British-owned Norfolk Hotel as well as the Israeli embassy and the Israeli El Al Airline office, but he determined that the Israeli targets were too heavily protected to be attacked. Abu Omar used several cameras as he surveilled the US embassy in Nairobi and noted traffic patterns, the rotation of security guards, and the location of closed-circuit television cameras. He developed the photographs himself, drafted a plan of attack on his personal laptop, and then made his presentation to Bin Laden in Khartoum.[58]

Local Counterintelligence: Basic Denial. Al Qa'ida faced only few major security threats in the 1988–1996 period, but it nevertheless devoted resources to improving its counterintelligence fitness. Some of its counterintelligence awareness was a product of its members' guerrilla fighting and "underground" experience. Zawahiri, for example, had led a clandestine underground organization in Egypt before he was sixteen and had spent years evading Egyptian security services.[59]

Zawahiri's security consciousness was evident when he met Bin Laden in 1988. Bin Laden was giving a lecture on boycotting American goods, and Zawahiri warned Bin Laden that he was provoking a powerful enemy and advised him to increase his security posture. The Egyptian recruits that Zawahiri brought to al Qa'ida were also security conscious, and many were used to working in secret.[60]

Al Qa'ida received direct and indirect counterintelligence support from the Sudanese government. Al Qa'ida trainers showed recruits how to create false passports and alter documents, and Sudan gave the group hundreds of passports.[61] Sudanese intelligence provided perimeter security for Bin Laden, and his personal bodyguards provided close proximity security.[62]

In return for Sudan's support, al Qa'ida offered Sudan counterintelligence. As early as 1992, al Qa'ida members were tasked to the Sudanese intelligence service's "Delegation Office," where people coming into Sudan were interviewed and given a background check to make sure they were not a threat to Sudan.[63] As a by-product, al Qa'ida's service in the Delegation Office provided the group with valuable intelligence on who was coming into Sudan.

Bin Laden and his top officers also carefully considered their personal security. Bin Laden employed guards to watch his house in Khartoum and accompany him when he left the capital. He also required his chief of security to secure the guesthouses and farms where he stayed.[64] He kept a database where he stored information about members' families, their aliases, how much money they made for al Qa'ida, and whether they participated in military operations. He used these files to determine which individuals were best suited for a particular task.[65]

Communications security was also important to the group. Jamal Ahmed al-Fadl, a Sudanese member of al Qa'ida, testified during a trial regarding the US embassy bombings that al Qa'ida relied on radio-based communications because they considered radios to be more secure than telephones.[66]

Al Qa'ida had some counterespionage capabilities in this period, although they were not systematic or sophisticated. Through its work in the Delegation Office in Sudan, it could monitor specific threats to the group and vet recruits who were coming into Sudan to join al Qa'ida. Jamal al-Fadl, as chief of security for Bin Laden, was responsible for checking individuals who were meeting with Bin Laden.[67]

Al Qa'ida relied in part on kinship and trusted referrals to recruit and vet new members.[68] According to the minutes from one of al Qa'ida's first meetings in August 1988, one requirement for entering the group was a referral from a trusted source.[69] Egyptian members of al Qa'ida were tasked with screening new recruits in their first few weeks of training, but this screening was probably designed to assess their skill and intelligence rather than their trustworthiness.[70]

Al Qa'ida experienced several counterintelligence setbacks in this period. First, it suffered two major espionage cases. The most damaging was al-Fadl, one of Bin Laden's most trusted aids, who was caught stealing money from al Qa'ida in 1995. When Bin Laden confronted al-Fadl, al-Fadl decided to leave al Qa'ida rather than return the money and then sold information about al Qa'ida to a variety of intelligence services in the Middle East. US officials first encountered al-Fadl at the American embassy in Eritrea in 1996, where he became a Federal Bureau of Investigation (FBI) informant and eventually a key witness in the 1996 US embassy bombings trial. A second espionage case involved L'Houssaine Kherchtou, one of Bin Laden's personal pilots. Kherchtou turned on al Qa'ida after Bin Laden refused to give him $500 for his wife's Caesarean section.[71] Al Qa'ida caught at least three other informants in this period, sent two of them to prison, and executed the third, according to al-Fadl's testimony at the US embassy bombings trials.[72]

Bin Laden also had at least one serious security breach in which he was nearly assassinated. In 1994, the assassins, led by a Libyan, sped by Bin Laden's Khartoum residence and sprayed the building with machine gun fire.[73] In response, Bin Laden made several renovations to his security protocol. First, he tasked Abu Omar with training an elite force of bodyguards to protect him around the clock. Egyptians made up most of Bin Laden's inner ring of bodyguards, probably to ensure greater loyalty or control.[74] Interestingly, Bin Laden relied on nationality to some extent for vetting. Sudanese intelligence personnel provided perimeter security at his Khartoum home, alongside additional armed guards and roadblocks to prevent traffic from passing too close to the compound.[75]

Another counterintelligence vulnerability for Bin Laden was his large family. When he moved to Sudan in 1992, he brought his four wives and seventeen children with him.[76] This left a large footprint and gave an adversary's intelligence service more individuals to target for surveillance and recruitment.

The final counterintelligence vulnerability was al Qa'ida's closeness to its state sponsor, Sudan. Sudan had the ability to compel al Qa'ida to act in ways that made the group more vulnerable. For example, al Qa'ida was forced to expel its Libyan members when Sudan promised the Libyan government that it would cease providing sanctuary to enemies of Libya—a move that angered the Libyan al Qa'ida members and prompted them to renounce their connections to Bin Laden.[77]

Sudanese officials and the government's intelligence service in particular also knew a great deal about al Qa'ida's modus operandi, personnel, resources, and plans. In 1996, Sudan allegedly offered to give the United States its intelligence files on al Qa'ida, with details of the groups personnel and networks, in exchange for better diplomatic and economic relations.[78] Sudan may or may not have been prepared to give the United States such damaging information. Regardless, an able adversary would only have needed to penetrate the Sudanese intelligence service or perhaps a Sudanese military or law enforcement entity to access sensitive information about al Qa'ida's personnel, plans, and networks.

International Counterintelligence: Basic Denial. The al Qa'ida cell in Nairobi was aware of its counterintelligence vulnerabilities, in some cases to the point of extreme paranoia. Cell manager Harun Fazul faxed a report to American al Qa'ida member Wadi al-Hage warning that the cell members in East Africa were probably under telephonic and physical surveillance by agents of the US, Egyptian, and Kenyan governments.[79]

In addition to being aware of its counterintelligence weaknesses, al Qa'ida also appreciated its adversaries' vulnerabilities. From its inception, it was interested in recruiting individuals who carried US passports because, it was assessed, they would be given less scrutiny and would raise less suspicion in their travels.[80] Al Qa'ida members also used aliases and cover identities.[81] When Zawahiri traveled to the United States in 1993 to raise money for al Qa'ida, he went as a Kuwaiti Red Crescent representative with the alias "Dr. Abdul Mu'iz."[82] Al Qa'ida advised some of its members to carry cigarettes and cologne in their travel bags in order to appear "Western" and nonradicalized in case they were questioned and searched by customs officers.[83] Although this strategy is fairly unsophisticated and easily detected, it was probably sufficient at the time to avoid attracting scrutiny.

Al Qa'ida had additional counterintelligence vulnerabilities in its international operations in this period. First, it did not conduct extensive background checks on its recruits but instead relied in part on kinship and friendship ties to determine if members could be trusted.[84] The system of informal "vouching" would later lead to counterintelligence setbacks for al Qa'ida, including the leakage of information by a husband of one of Bin Laden's nieces. Second, al Qa'ida members did not always practice good computer security in Kenya and the Philippines. Police seized al Qa'ida computers in those countries, and it is plausible that law enforcement exploited sensitive information on those hard drives. Keeping sensitive files on computers is probably unavoidable for a terrorist organization, but the counterintelligence vulnerability comes from not having a method for hiding or destroying computers and computer files before the hard drives are seized.

Al Qa'ida's use of aliases and cover identities is a good example of a basic-denial technique. Members' practice of planting cologne and cigarettes in their luggage to avoid scrutiny at borders and ports is possibly an indication of adaptive denial, although it is not clear that al Qa'ida had concrete evidence that possession of these items would produce less scrutiny.

Summary. From its beginnings in 1988, al Qa'ida faced powerful adversaries, though these adversaries were not always militantly proactive against the group. It had access to a high level of financial resources, high-quality personnel, controlled territory, and an international re-cruiting network. It did not enjoy a significant amount of local popular support in Sudan mostly because Bin Laden was able to purchase the loyalty and protection of the Sudanese government. Al Qa'ida attempted to inspire a global following but was successful to only a limited extent in this endeavor. Its intelligence capabilities were also limited. Although it developed a typically adequate counterintelligence capability in this period, that capability was not systematic or sophisticated. However, its relatively tight organizational structure and access to controlled territory allowed it to train its members and boost its intelligence and counterintelligence capabilities.

Al Qa'ida did not have a high level of popular support and there-fore could not convert such goodwill into intelligence and counter-intelligence from locals. It also did not create an overwhelming counter-intelligence burden from publicity campaigns because it did not focus too heavily on promoting itself in this period.

AL QA'IDA CONDUCTS MAJOR ATTACKS AND GAINS CAPABLE ADVERSARIES: 1996–2001

Key Factors

Organizational Structure. Al Qa'ida's structure in the 1996–2001 period remained relatively hierarchical, though the operatives deployed out-side of Afghanistan retained some operational autonomy. The inner core, which swore loyalty to Bin Laden, had clearly defined positions and salaries.[85] The core in Afghanistan and the al Qa'ida camps was tightly managed. One of its master recruiters, Zayn al Abidin Muhammed Husayn, also known as "Abu Zubaydah," kept files on all the members, made their travel arrangements, assigned them to camps, and assigned them tasks appropriate to their training.[86] By the late 1990s, Muhammed Atef, also known as "Abu Hafs al Masri," was al Qa'ida's senior opera-tional planner and commanded a group of overseas field commanders with help from al Qa'ida member Sayf al-Adl.

Al Qa'ida called this management model the "centralization of deci-sion and decentralization of execution." Its leaders would select the targets and provide funding for the operations in many cases. However, the field commanders would make the day-to-day decisions about logistics and planning.[87] Some have described this system as a "terrorist venture-capital model," where terrorist entrepreneurs would approach al Qa'ida with ideas for operations, and leaders would decide on which "projects" they would fund.[88]

Field commanders adopted al Qa'ida's goals and took assignments from Bin Laden and Atef, but they retained operational autonomy in the field and in some cases did not swear a formal oath of loyalty to Bin Laden. KSM (Khalid Sheikh Muhammed), Riduan Isamuddin ("Hambali"), and Abd al Rahim al Nashiri were three such commanders. KSM proposed the 9/11 operation to Bin Laden sometime in the 1990s, but it was not until late 1998 that Bin Laden gave KSM the green light to plan and manage the operation. KSM, unlike Atef and al-Adl, never formally swore his loyalty to Bin Laden but nonetheless was given the responsibility to manage al Qa'ida's most ambitious and elaborate operation.[89] While KSM planned and executed the operation, Atef and al-Adl continued to manage al Qa'ida's worldwide operations. In this planning period, KSM had relative autonomy from the al Qa'ida leadership and even resisted Bin Laden's requests on three occasions to execute the operation ahead of schedule.[90]

Hambali, considered Bin Laden's lieutenant in Southeast Asia, was affiliated with the Indonesian terrorist group Jemaah Islamiyya and retained a degree of independence from the al Qa'ida leadership in Afghanistan. Hambali objected when al Qa'ida leaders attempted to assign Jemaah Islamiyya fighters to al Qa'ida operations without notifying him.[91]

Nashiri became a key al Qa'ida operations planner in Yemen in 1998 after proposing a plan to strike a US Navy vessel. Bin Laden directed Nashiri to begin planning the operation and provided him with recruits and money. Nashiri consulted with Bin Laden before he planned the attack but selected the recruits and planned the operation specifics on his own.[92]

Al Qa'ida's field commanders did not cut themselves off from al Qa'ida's leaders once operational planning began, however. The cell in Nairobi interacted regularly with the media branch in London, sent security reports to headquarters in Afghanistan, and requested secure communications equipment from the group's leaders.[93] Ziad Jarrah, one of the 9/11 operatives, visited al Qa'ida camps in Afghanistan in 2001 to report to senior leaders and take back new instructions for the cells in the United States.[94]

Al Qa'ida probably adopted the "decentralization of execution" policy as a result of the logistical difficulty of commanding operations from Afghanistan and the security danger of frequent contact between "known" operatives in Afghanistan and "unknown" operatives in cells around the world.[95] The group began to remedy its disconnect with overseas operatives by increasing its communications and training presence on the Internet, though it was not until after 9/11 that this strategy was fully implemented.[96]

Popular Support: Local. In the 1996–2001 period when al Qa'ida was based in Afghanistan, its local popular support remained relatively low. The group relied on the strategy of purchasing the loyalty of local leaders rather than campaigning to win the hearts of the local population. It eventually developed very close ties to the Taliban, but relations between the two were not close initially. When al Qa'ida arrived in Jalalabad in 1996, the area was controlled by a regional council of Pashtun tribal leaders and former guerrillas.[97] Al Qa'ida had not yet developed a relationship with the Taliban, and the two groups were probably not collaborating at this time.[98] In 1997, Taliban chief Mullah Muhammed Omar asked al Qa'ida to move from Jalalabad to Taliban-controlled Kandahar, probably so that the Taliban could keep a closer watch on Bin Laden.[99]

Al Qa'ida's relationship with the Taliban grew increasingly important for both parties—al Qa'ida supplied the Taliban with funds and guerrillas, and the Taliban provided al Qa'ida with a safe haven within which to establish controlled territory. US officials estimate that al Qa'ida was supplying $10 to $20 million per year to the Taliban.[100] The group also provided the Taliban with Arab fighters fresh out of al Qa'ida training camps, which the Taliban used to fight its war against Ahmed Shah Massoud's Northern Alliance.[101] Al Qa'ida developed a special guerrilla unit, Brigade 055, dedicated specifically to helping the Taliban fight the Northern Alliance.[102]

Al Qa'ida reaped some indirect popular support as a result of its association with the Taliban. The Taliban had originated as a small vigilante militia in Kandahar in 1994 and slowly developed the support of powerful Durrani Pashtun traders and cheiftans.[103] As the Taliban consolidated control over and brought order to Afghanistan, it gained legitimacy and popular support.[104] By September 2001, it controlled about 90 percent of Afghanistan.[105]

Al Qa'ida's relations with the Taliban were occasionally rocky. The group frequently angered the Taliban with its publicity campaigns because the campaigns brought negative international attention to the Taliban's role in providing a safe haven to the group. Mullah Omar requested that Bin Laden halt his international media campaign in 1996, and Bin Laden agreed to remain silent. However, in 1998 he reneged on the agreement, issuing a second fatwa and holding numerous press conferences.[106] The Taliban became internally divided about how to deal with al Qa'ida's provocative media strategy. Some Taliban officials, including Foreign Minister Wakil Muttawakil, wanted to expel Bin Laden from Afghanistan, whereas others, such as Mullah Omar, opposed expelling the group.[107]

The US embassy bombings in Tanzania and Kenya led to a US cruise-missile attack on Afghanistan in August 1998 and further taxed the patience of some elements of the Taliban.[108] For other elements of the Taliban, however, the US attacks in 1998 brought them even closer to al Qa'ida and Bin Laden. But then Bin Laden again antagonized some Taliban officials by giving an inflammatory interview to television network al Jazeera's bureau chief in Pakistan in December 1998.[109]

Al Qa'ida also had internal debates about the merits of a media campaign that could potentially get the group expelled from Afghanistan. In an internal al Qa'ida memo from 1999, two Syrian members in Kabul considered the downside of a campaign for popular support: "In short, our brother Abu Abdullah's [Bin Laden] latest troublemaking with the Taliban and the Leader of the Faithful [Mullah Omar] jeopardizes the Arabs, and the Arab presence, today in all of Afghanistan, for no good reason. . . . The strangest thing I have heard so far is Abu Abdullah's saying that he wouldn't listen to the Leader of the Faithful when he asked him to stop giving interviews. . . . I think our brother [Bin Laden] has caught the disease of screens, flashes, fans, and applause."[110]

Bin Laden compensated for this antagonism by developing strong personal ties to Mullah Omar. In the spring of 2001 Bin Laden and

Mullah Omar hosted a gathering of Taliban supporters where Bin Laden announced that he had sworn his loyalty and allegiance to Mullah Omar.[111] The Taliban ultimately continued to protect Bin Laden and al Qa'ida, alleging that it had lost track of the terrorist leader, which was almost certainly untrue.[112]

Despite al Qa'ida's relative inattention to local popular support beyond that offered by the Taliban, the group orchestrated some small-scale public-support campaigns. In 1998, Bin Laden circulated hundreds of 100-rupee notes that featured his face and a caricature of an American request for information about him.[113] Several posters widely available in Pakistan allegedly featured Bin Laden riding on a white horse, thus reminding the viewer of the Prophet Muhammed, who had ridden a white horse into battle.[114] Bin Laden had to limit his "public" exposure in the al Qa'ida camps, however, due to security concerns, and although many aspiring jihadists would come to hear him speak, probably only a few were allowed to see him.[115]

Popular Support: International. Al Qa'ida's international support increased substantially between 1996 and 2001. The increase was the result of a boost in inflammatory public statements and a series of successful al Qa'ida attacks. The group's public communications—including articles, videos, audiotapes, and interviews—increased from an average of 1.3 per year between 1993 and 1995 to 6.5 a year between 1996 and 2001.[116]

Beginning in the winter of 1996, al Qa'ida made big changes to its media strategy. Bin Laden began to reach out to international and English-language media to deliver sermons and warnings.[117] In some cases, he responded to international media organizations asking for interviews. Bin Laden considered the shift in al Qa'ida's media strategy critical to its success as a international terrorist organization. Sometime between 1997 and 1998, he wrote Mullah Omar a letter in which he stated: "Many international media agencies corresponding with us [request] an interview with us [al Qa'ida]. We believe that this is a good opportunity to make Muslims aware of what is taking place [in] the land of the two Holy Mosques [Saudi Arabia] as well as what is happening here in Afghanistan. It is obvious that the media war in this century is one of the strongest methods; in fact, its ratio may reach 90 percent of the total preparation for the battles."[118] Bin Laden thus hypothesized that 90 percent of al Qa'ida's guerrilla campaign was a battle for the hearts of the Muslim world.

Al Qa'ida's message of expelling foreign influence from Muslim lands stayed constant throughout the 1990s, but its focus on expelling Americans in particular increased. Bin Laden believed that terrorist groups focused solely on attacking local rulers and Israel did not go far enough because they missed the opportunity to attack the "head of the snake."[119]

The group's first international declaration of jihad against the United States came in 1996. Bin Laden argued in his 1996 decree that the Muslim world was being overrun by an "alliance of Jews, Christians, and their agents." He issued an escalatory fatwa on May 26, 1998, claiming that the United States had made a "clear declaration of war on God, his messenger, and Muslims." His fatwa announced the formation of the "World Islamic Front for Jihad Against the Jews and Crusaders," which included al Qa'ida, Egyptian Islamic Jihad, and several other regional Islamic militant groups. The goal of World Jihad was to encourage Muslims throughout the world to target American civilians and military personnel.[120]

Al Qa'ida began courting international and English-speaking news organizations in order to get its message to a wider Muslim audience. Bin Laden granted interviews to CNN, ABC, and al Jazeera.[121] He instructed the al Qa'ida media representative in London to invite British journalist Robert Fisk and *al Quds al Arabia* journalist Abdel Bari Atwan to Afghanistan to interview the terrorist leader.[122] To impress foreign journalists, al Qa'ida would sometimes put on a show to herald Bin Laden's arrival for his interviews. In one instance, according to Pakistani journalist Ismial Khan, Bin Laden arrived in a three-car escort, and his bodyguards fired machine guns and rocket-propelled grenades into the surrounding hills the moment he stepped out of the car.[123]

Al Qa'ida's tactical interaction with its international media contacts also became more sophisticated in the 1996–2001 period. Bin Laden's February 1998 fatwa was dictated over a satellite phone to Fawwaz in London, who then delivered it to *al Quds al Arabia*. In May 1998, Atef faxed Fawwaz another fatwa issued by a group of sheikhs in Afghanistan. Fawwaz was instructed to send the fatwa, along with Bin Laden's comments, to *al Quds, al Sharq al Awsat, al-Moharer,* and *al Hayat.* Atef told Fawwaz that it would be best if Bin Laden's comments on the fatwa were published separately, probably to maximize exposure.[124] Both the fatwa and Bin Laden's comments appeared a week later in *al Quds.*[125] Al Qa'ida followed up the fatwa with a press conference in Khost, Afghanistan. Its foot soldiers transported foreign journalists from Pakistan to the press conference, and local guerrillas heralded its presence by firing their machine guns into the air.[126]

Later that month Bin Laden gave a video interview in Afghanistan to *ABC News.* In August 1998, at least a few days before the attacks on US embassies in East Africa, al Qa'ida faxed a claim of responsibility for the attacks to a joint al Qa'ida–Islamic Jihad office in Baku, Azerbaijan, with orders to prepare to transmit the message to *al Quds* when the office got the word from headquarters.[127]

Al Qa'ida leaders also increased their personal contacts with journalists. Zawahiri conversed regularly with Pakistani journalist Rahmullah Yusufzai via a satellite telephone, including immediately before and after the 1998 US cruise-missile strikes on Afghanistan in retaliation for the embassy bombings. Bin Laden called *al Quds* editor Atwan after the missile strikes to assure Atwan that he and his deputies had survived the strikes.[128] All the while, he and his committee crafted his public image with precision. In one *al Quds* interview, Bin Laden did not allow the interviewer to record their conversation so that if he made a mistake, the recording could not be used to tarnish his image.[129]

Al Qa'ida's media committee played an important role in delivering the group's message. It was responsible for issuing statements and reports in support of the group's operations.[130] An internal al Qa'ida document recovered by the US military highlighted the committee's central role in providing information to Muslims about the plans of al Qa'ida's adversaries.[131]

The media committee worked closely with the operational side of al Qa'ida. KSM, the chief operative and manager of the 9/11 attacks, occasionally worked with the media committee during his career and was appointed by Bin Laden in October 2000 to head the committee.[132] Al Qa'ida's media representative in London, Fawwaz, also played an important role in the group's publicity campaign. Fawwaz delivered Bin Laden's 1998 fatwa to media outlets in London, keeping in contact with top al Qa'ida leaders via satellite phone. From 1998 to 2000, members made more than two hundred calls to Fawwaz, probably to discuss and calibrate the media strategy and to arrange for journalists to meet with Bin Laden in Afghanistan.[133]

It appears that al Qa'ida's media strategy paid off in some instances and attracted Muslims as far afield as Europe and the United States. For example, Abdessater Dhamane came to Afghanistan in 2000 to join the group after being inspired by a news program on Bin Laden in Denmark. Dhamane would assassinate Ahmed Shah Massoud, the leader of the Northern Alliance opposition to the Taliban in Afghanistan, on September 9, 2001, for al Qa'ida.[134]

Although al Qa'ida's statements and rhetoric were important for international support, its terrorist attacks also increased its popular appeal. It used the successful attack on the USS *Cole* in 2000 to increase support and improve recruiting. Following the attack, KSM produced a video reenactment of the attack spliced with pictures of al Qa'ida training camps and Muslims suffering in Chechnya and Palestine. The video was widely disseminated and inspired many young men from Saudi Arabia and Yemen to travel to Afghanistan for al Qa'ida training, according to US officials.[135] The US embassy in Nairobi was chosen as a target for the attack in 1998 because the ambassador was a woman, which al Qa'ida reasoned would give the attack more media coverage.[136]

US attacks against al Qa'ida also proved to be a powerful driver of popular support. US cruise-missile attacks in Afghanistan in 1998 generated large demonstrations in Pakistan and Egypt and led to a wave of pro–Bin Laden iconography across the Muslim world.[137] Pakistani journalist Rahmullah Yusufzai argued that the US cruise-missile strikes made Bin Laden a cult hero in Pakistan.[138] Journalist Jason Burke argues that donations to al Qa'ida, which had been lagging, increased markedly after the strikes.[139]

This method of attracting international support would seem to be in conflict with al Qa'ida's desire to maintain local popular support. Although being attacked was good for international support and sympathy, the local people might resent al Qa'ida for attracting such deadly attention to their region. There is a gap in our understanding of how strikes against al Qa'ida influenced the sentiment of the locals who were affected by the strikes. Given that al Qa'ida privileged international popular support over local popular support, due in part to the Taliban's protection, it is not surprising that the group accepted this trade-off.

Al Qa'ida had other means of attracting popular support. The group relied on informal support networks in places such as Saudi Arabia and Yemen to radicalize young men and direct them toward al Qa'ida. Some of the Saudi operatives involved in 9/11 were likely recruited through sympathetic contacts at universities and mosques in Saudi Arabia.[140] In 2000, Bin Laden married his fifth wife, who hailed from the northern tribes of Yemen. Al Qa'ida already had close relations with the Islamic Army of Aden, a group from southern Yemen, and Bin Laden's new marriage solidified his contacts with the northern Yemeni al Islah Party.[141]

Al Qa'ida's media strategy introduced several operational vulnerabilities in the 1996–2001 period. At the strategic level, its inflammatory media statements ultimately had to be backed with action against the group's declared enemies. In an interview with *al Quds* in Tora Bora in Afghanistan in November 1996, Bin Laden defended the fact that al Qa'ida had not yet attacked any targets despite its proclamation to do so in August 1996: "Preparations for major operations take a certain amount of time, unlike minor operations. If we wanted small actions, the matter would have been easily carried out immediately after the [August 1996] statement."[142]

Al Qa'ida also came under pressure from Taliban leader Mullah Omar to discontinue its media campaign. The Taliban were coming under increased scrutiny by the international community, and Mullah Omar relayed this concern to Bin Laden when al Qa'ida launched its media campaign in 1996 but was ultimately unsuccessful in getting Bin Laden to remain quiet.[143]

Controlled Territory. Al Qa'ida's access to controlled territory continued in the 1996–2001 period. When the group initially relocated from Sudan to Jalalabad, Afghanistan, in 1996, Bin Laden had local support from warlords in Jalalabad. He uprooted al Qa'ida once more in 1996 and moved the entire group to Kandahar at the Taliban's behest.[144] The Taliban allowed al Qa'ida to open up terrorist-training camps in Kandahar, Khost, and Kabul, which for al Qa'ida turned out to be one of the most important benefits of controlling territory.

Other Important Factors

Resources: Local. Al Qa'ida's access to financial resources and high-quality personnel continued in the 1996–2001 period. A core of its militants traveled with Bin Laden from Khartoum to Afghanistan in 1996, and although Bin Laden's bank accounts had been drained by then, the group received financial backing from wealthy individuals in the Persian Gulf.[145]

Al Qa'ida's focus on training allowed it to create more technically proficient terrorists. For a brief time in 1999, the Mes Aynak training camp in Kabul was al Qa'ida's only training facility. Trainer Salah al Din complained in this period that the number of recruits in the camp exceeded the training capacity, but Bin Laden insisted that they all be trained.[146] Al Qa'ida opened al Faruq camp near Kandahar with the Taliban's authorization sometime after 1998. Al Faruq offered advanced terrorist training for select members. Training included courses on security, intelligence collection, counterintelligence, and hijacking. An even more select group of members were trained in setting up clandestine cells and planning terrorist and assassination operations.[147] Al Qa'ida member Muhammed Rashed Daoud al-Owhali testified that he received training in several camps in recruitment, surveillance, countersurveillance, site surveys, and intelligence collection with video and still photography.[148]

Before attending these camps, members would have to pass basic training and an additional guerrilla warfare course that lasted forty-five days. As a reference, al Qa'ida trainees could access a 180-page manual on weapons training, security, and espionage titled *Military Studies in the Jihad Against the Tyrants*.[149]

Some recruits could also access videotapes of terrorism and security training given by al Qa'ida member Abu Mousab al Suri. In six videotapes recovered from Afghanistan after 2001, Suri is "viewed in front of a whiteboard addressing a class" on how to set up clandestine cells and create "contingency plans" if their original operation fails.[150] Bin Laden was also able to rely on veterans of the Afghan–Soviet War to serve as trainers and administrators in al Qa'ida camps.[151]

Resources: International. Al Qa'ida's international resources grew steadily in the 1996–2001 period. The sophistication of the group's attacks in this period, both successful and unsuccessful, offer one indicator—albeit imperfect—of its extensive resources. The most prominent attacks were the embassy bombings in 1998; the millennium plots in Amman, Jordan, and the Los Angeles Airport in December 1999; the two attacks against US Navy ships in 1999 and 2000; the Christmas Eve bombings in Manila, Philippines, in December 2000; the Christmas market bombing plot in Germany in December 2000; and the 9/11 attacks.[152] These attacks required well-forged documents, trained and dedicated operatives, well-oiled logistical networks, and relatively large amounts of cash for a small clandestine organization.

Perhaps the group's most impressive resource was the number of individuals it trained between 1996 and 2001. In this period, tens of thousands of individuals are estimated to have visited its training camps in Afghanistan.[153] Bin Laden's reputation was an important factor in drawing militants to Afghanistan. Journalist Peter Bergen argues that "something of a bin Laden cult was taking shape in [this] period" that "helped fuel an unprecedented volume of recruits to al Qa'ida's camps."[154] Al Qa'ida's rhetoric about attacking the United States, coupled with its success in attacking US diplomatic and military assets in the late 1990s, spurred its legendary status in the Islamic world.[155]

Al Qa'ida suffered some financial setbacks following its move to Afghanistan in 1996. Bin Laden lost a number of his businesses after their connection to him was leaked to the Saudi Arabian government.[156] However, al Qa'ida continued to rely on its network of wealthy financiers from Saudi Arabia, the United Arab Emirates, Kuwait, and the Persian Gulf—known as the "Golden Chain"—for donations that were collected via charities, nongovernmental organizations, and front companies.[157]

The US government estimated that it cost al Qa'ida $30 million per year to sustain its activities in this five-year period, almost all of which was raised through donations.[158] Fund-raisers used banks to store and transfer their money, a process that was most likely facilitated by corrupt individuals working at these banks as well as by lax regulation at banks in the United Arab Emirates and Pakistan. Operations were generally cheap—the 1998 embassy bombings cost around $10,000 and the elaborate 9/11 attacks cost around $500,000—but the group also had the overhead costs of maintaining camps as well as recruiting and evaluating members.[159]

After moving to Afghanistan in 1996, al Qa'ida began to rely more heavily on *hawala* networks—informal banking and money-transfer systems prominent in the Middle East, North Africa, and South Asia—in part because Afghanistan's primitive banking sector did not provide the group with many alternatives. *Hawala* banking also allowed al Qa'ida to move its finances without government scrutiny or a paper trail of financial transactions.[160]

Al Qa'ida relied on logistical support networks outside of Afghanistan as well. Support networks in Europe provided assistance in several operations. A Dublin-based charity gave material support to the al Qa'ida operatives involved in the US embassy bombings in East Africa, and operatives who assassinated Ahmed Shah Massoud in Afghanistan received forged document assistance from a European cell.[161] The Hamburg cell of the 9/11 operation relied on logistical and communications resources provided to them, sometimes unwittingly, by local Germans.[162] Al Qa'ida's network in Yemen assisted its operatives with transportation and logistical support.[163]

Operatives overseas were also using training manuals, such as the *Encyclopedia of Jihad*, to aid them in tradecraft and terrorist operations. The seven-thousand-page *Encyclopedia of Jihad* was allegedly transferred to computer disk in the mid-1990s and was "circulating widely in radical Islamic circles" by 1999.[164] The Jordanian al Qa'ida members captured before they could conduct their millennium terrorist attack in December 1999 carried with them an al Qa'ida training manual on CD-ROM.[165]

Adversary Counterterrorism Capability. Al Qa'ida was unique in that it developed powerful adversaries both in the Middle East and in the West. It believed that in order to defeat the "near enemies" such as Saudi Arabia and Egypt, the group had to challenge the "far enemies," such as the United States.[166]

The United States was al Qa'ida's most powerful adversary in the 1996–2001 period. Bin Laden issued a declaration of jihad against the United States in 1996 after moving from Sudan to Afghanistan. The United States sketched out the first of several plans to seize and detain Bin Laden in 1997. It mapped out his Tarnak Farms facility in Kandahar, including the buildings where he was most likely to be sleeping. Working with some local tribal leaders, it rehearsed the seizure operation in the fall of 1997.

It cancelled the operation, however, after assessing that the tribal personnel would be unlikely to complete the mission. It recognized the
dangers of the operation: millions of dollars lost, a bloody shootout
that might be made public, and perhaps a violent backlash among radicals in Pakistan.[167]

After al Qa'ida successfully bombed the US embassies in East Africa
in August 1998, the United States once again made plans to strike at al
Qa'ida's leaders, this time at a terrorist-training camp in Khost, Afghanistan. It initially assessed the strike as worth the risk, given that the
camp was far from civilian population centers and almost certainly
contained Bin Laden and his chief lieutenants. US Navy vessels in the
Arabian Sea launched cruise missiles at the targets in Afghanistan, but
Bin Laden and his lieutenants survived.[168]

The United States received information in December 1998 that Bin
Laden was spending the night at the governor's residence in Kandahar.
Again, plans were drawn up to strike him with cruise missiles. The plan
was shelved, however, after several US officials expressed concern over
the quality of the information and the likelihood of killing or injuring
more than three hundred bystanders.[169]

In the fall of 1999, the United States increased its counterterrorism
efforts against al Qa'ida. It began a program to hire officers with more
counterterrorism skills, recruit more assets, penetrate al Qa'ida's ranks,
and continue disruption and rendition operations worldwide. It also
began to increase its contacts with the Northern Alliance rebels fighting the Taliban in Afghanistan as well as to increase signals and imagery collection against al Qa'ida.[170]

Despite the US assets arrayed against al Qa'ida prior to 9/11, the
United States remained deficient in intelligence on al Qa'ida's top leaders, operational planners and plans, and camps. Feroz Ali Abassi, an
al Qa'ida member captured in Pakistan after the fall of the Taliban in
2001, asserted that it was common knowledge in the camps just prior to
9/11 that there was a large imminent operation against a US target, so
he was surprised that there were no American strikes against al Qa'ida
camps in Afghanistan before 9/11.[171]

Intelligence and Counterintelligence Outcomes

Intelligence: Local and International. Al Qa'ida's intelligence capabilities were more sophisticated in the 1996–2001 period because the group conducted intelligence collection in support of its terrorist operations. Al Qa'ida's local intelligence efforts remained fairly basic and consisted mostly of physical surveillance of its facilities and open-source collection to support intelligence analysis by its leaders. One internal al Qa'ida memo gives Atef's assessment of foreign reconnaissance aircraft activity near an al Qa'ida compound.[172] This memo suggests that al Qa'ida not only provided surveillance support for its facilities but also may have kept formal records of incidents and patterns.

Throughout this period, al Qa'ida kept track of world events and provided leaders with intelligence reports based on open sources. In the late 1990s, KSM was part of the effort to collect news articles for al Qa'ida leaders.[173] Al Qa'ida members sometimes learned of operations after hearing about them from international news agencies, such as al Jazeera.[174] Leaders would sometimes send operatives to Internet cafés to collect open-source information. At an Internet café in Karachi, Pakistan, operative Iyman Faris searched for information on ultralight aircraft at the behest of a top al Qa'ida leader in 2001.[175] Faris then provided a hard copy of the open-source report to this individual. In many cases, top leaders probably received clippings from Arab and foreign newspapers or breaking news from daily wire services. After visiting Bin Laden in Afghanistan, *al Quds* editor Abdel Bari Atwan reported that Bin Laden had a huge archive of data in both hard-copy and soft-copy formats, including press clippings.[176] Al Qa'ida's Nairobi cell also assiduously followed local and international press reporting.[177]

Al Qa'ida's intelligence-collection operations for its international operations increased in sophistication in the 1996–2001 period. It probably developed an intelligence-collection protocol for its terrorist cells during this period. Al Qa'ida operative Muhammed Rashed Daoud al-Owhali testified that the terrorist cell's intelligence chief was the most important member of the cell. The intelligence chief, according to Owhali, assessed the operational environment and then assigned deputies to manage and conduct the tasks needed to complete the mission.[178]

After the cell conducted surveillance of a series of targets, the intelligence was then sent to Afghanistan, where al Qa'ida leaders would study the information and decide whether to move ahead with the operation, according to Bin Laden pilot L'Houssaine Kherchtou. The leaders seemed to have played a role in the analysis of intelligence for several operations, including the US embassy attacks. Cell members in Nairobi would type up security and intelligence updates and then fax the reports to Pakistan. From Pakistan, the reports were delivered to leaders by courier.[179] Al Qa'ida was probably using the Internet by this time to transmit some of its collected intelligence. In an internal memo from an operative known as "Abu Huthayfa" (actual name unknown) to Bin Laden in June 2000, Abu Huthayfa noted that Web sites such as www.driveway.com allowed users to send up to one hundred megabytes of data to one another in a single transmission.[180]

Although cells probably had specific targets in mind when beginning intelligence collection, there is evidence that they also used surveillance to search for targets of opportunity. The cell responsible for the attack on the USS *Cole* set up a surveillance post in the hills overlooking the Aden harbor with the intention of finding a vulnerable US vessel.[181]

Al Qa'ida also collected intelligence by conducting "dry runs" of operations to detect the security reaction to provocative or suspicious behaviors. Operative Khallad bin Attash tested security on an international flight from Malaysia to Hong Kong in 1999 by bringing box cutters in his toiletries kit. During one of his flights, he removed his toiletries kit from his carry-on bags and noted the reaction of passengers and flight stewards.[182] Bin Laden originally asked bin Attash to conduct this intelligence collection, and it is likely that bin Attash reported this information back to him.

Open sources remained a staple of al Qa'ida intelligence collection. The al Qa'ida manual *Military Studies in the Jihad Against the Tyrants* argues that 80 percent of intelligence relevant to the terrorist mission is available in open sources. The manual notes that the percentage varies depending on the openness of the government, but that it is possible to get most information from newspapers, magazines, books, periodicals, and broadcasts.[183] The report produced by the National Commission on Terrorist Attacks Upon the United States (9/11 Commission) in 2004 cites four instances where KSM and his 9/11 operatives used the Internet to gather information or to facilitate communications.[184] In addition, operatives could reference the *Encyclopedia of Jihad*, the fifth chapter of which is dedicated to lessons on spying, military intelligence, sabotage, communication, security within jihad, and secret observation.[185]

Al Qa'ida used local support networks to gather intelligence as well. The cell in Nairobi used a local operative to learn about Nairobi and gather intelligence.[186] The operative named Muhammed Sadiq Odeh testified that locals relied on to gather intelligence did not have to be full-fledged members of al Qa'ida.[187]

There is limited evidence of al Qa'ida espionage operations against key adversaries during this period. In one instance, however, the group recruited a US naval enlistee to collect information on the movement of US battle groups. Operative Babar Ahmed ran a jihadist Web site and received information from the enlistee via that Web site about the US destroyer on which the enlistee was stationed, the USS *Benfold*. The enlistee was sympathetic to al Qa'ida's mission but had no prior connections to the group. He provided Ahmed with information about his ship's movements, its battle-group formation, and details about the best way to attack the ship with a small boat and RPGs.[188]

Local Counterintelligence: Basic Denial and Some Adaptive Denial. Al Qa'ida increased the sophistication of its local counterintelligence procedures in the 1996–2001 period.

Al Qa'ida's controlled territory offered key counterintelligence and security advantages. Although al Qa'ida could move freely in and out of Taliban-controlled areas of Afghanistan, most of its adversaries probably encountered some difficulty recruiting sources and preparing operations in these areas. Journalist Steve Coll reports that the group's adversaries had an easier time recruiting Afghan agents in the Jalalabad region, where the Taliban's control was weak.[189]

The Taliban's agenda occasionally differed from al Qa'ida's, but the Taliban often helped the group improve its security. Following a series of security threats in Jalalabad in 1996, Mullah Omar asked Bin Laden to move his organization to the Taliban-controlled area of Kandahar.[190] Omar almost certainly used this "invitation" to keep a better eye on the publicity-hungry Bin Laden, but al Qa'ida would also benefit from the closer ties to the ruling Taliban.

With the volume of recruits flowing into al Qa'ida camps, the group developed systematic camp security and counterintelligence procedures. Al Qa'ida operative Owhali testified that when he first arrived at the Khaldan training camp in Afghanistan, he immediately began to use an alias and was told by the camp supervisor that camp members would never again use their real names.[191] Shadi Abdalla, who served as Bin Laden's bodyguard in Afghanistan in 2000, reported that member Ramzi Bin al Sheibh wore a veil at training camps because he feared that there could be spies among the recruits.[192] Al Qa'ida operative Iyman Faris told US authorities that some members at the training camps wore black scarves, probably to mask their identity.[193] According to an internal document known as the "New Recruits Form," recruits were required to leave all forbidden items out of the camp, including tape recorders, radios, cameras, and video equipment,[194] indicating that al Qa'ida leaders believed that photographs of its personnel and facilities could pose a threat to camp security.

Al Qa'ida vigorously cultivated its connections to select media organizations and journalists and took great care to manage and monitor these entities when they came into its camps. After *ABC News* reporter John Miller taped an interview with Bin Laden, al Qa'ida's technical experts seized the tape, erased the faces of several group members caught on tape during the interview, and then returned the tape to Miller.[195] CNN journalist Peter Bergen and CNN correspondent Peter Arnett had to pass a number of security checks before interviewing Bin Laden in 1997. They first had to travel to London to be vetted by al Qa'ida representative Fawwaz, who asked them if they worked for the US government. When they were approved to meet with Bin Laden a month later, the two men were greeted in Afghanistan by a coterie of al Qa'ida security guards, who told them they could not bring their own camera for security reasons.[196] To prevent the journalists from retracing their steps to al Qa'ida's facilities, the men were blindfolded and driven to the camp, switching vehicles several times.[197] Just before entering the camp, the journalists were told that if they had tracking devices, they would be killed unless they declared them to al Qa'ida security immediately.[198] Bergen reported that they were also swept for electronic devices.[199]

Other journalists' accounts of meeting with Bin Laden corroborate these data. *Al Quds* editor Abdel Bari Atwan was instructed to fly to Peshawar, Pakistan, where he was contacted secretly by an intermediary before he met with Bin Laden. Atwan was moved from Peshawar to a safe house in Jalalabad and finally taken to an al Qa'ida camp. Atwan recalls that the camp was well protected, with antiaircraft guns, armored vehicles, and a heavily controlled approach road.[200]

The group took extraordinary precautions to protect Bin Laden in particular. He sometimes had fourteen bodyguards at a time, all armed with automatic weapons. When Saudi Arabia sent an assassin to kill Bin Laden in 1998, his armed entourage easily captured the man.[201] Al Qa'ida selected only trusted Arabs to serve as bodyguards for Bin Laden in order to eliminate the chances that a "turned" Afghan or Taliban bodyguard would try to kill or spy on the group's leader.[202] Former Bin Laden bodyguard Shadi Abdalla reported that bodyguards were trusted only after they had served for an extended time in Bin Laden's entourage. Before Abdalla was fully trusted, he was allowed near Bin Laden only when the leader was on the move. Bin Laden also had special protection from new recruits. Any recruit who wanted to meet with Bin Laden had to go through additional vetting.[203]

Bin Laden "rarely spent two nights in the same place" and would move around Afghanistan in a "convoy of up to twenty vehicles" armed with rocket launchers, surface-to-air missiles, and automatic weapons.[204] He would travel very secretly, often showing up by surprise after his security detail cleared and guarded the route he was planning to take. For the most part, his arrival was not heralded by fanfare and rocket fire, unless al Qa'ida was making a propaganda film or trying to impress journalists.[205] However, Steve Coll reports that Bin Laden's journey's within Afghanistan sometimes followed a predictable path: he would move from Kandahar to Ghowr Province, where there was a valley he enjoyed visiting, and then to Jalalabad and back to Kandahar.[206]

Bin Laden's living quarters were relatively easy to secure given the remoteness of the al Qa'ida camps. He lived in a concrete compound surrounded by a ten-foot wall in the middle of an isolated desert on the outskirts of Kandahar.[207] An attempt to breech this fortress would probably have been easy for Bin Laden's security detail to detect.

Al Qa'ida had effective local security procedures for its members as well. Following their terrorist operations, members anticipated US retaliation strikes at the camps and would flee the camps. Leaders fled Kandahar for the countryside after the US embassy bombings in 1998. General camp warnings were issued two weeks before the USS *Cole* attack in 2000 and ten days before the 9/11 attacks. During such an alert, members would leave the camps with their families, and Bin Laden would remain sequestered until the alert was cancelled.[208] For the USS *Cole* attack, Bin Laden split up his top leaders, sending Atef to a location in Kandahar and Zawahiri to Kabul, thereby reducing the odds that the group's top leaders would be killed in a single strike. Before the 9/11 attacks, Bin Laden and Zawahiri fled to the mountains near Khost.[209]

To protect the group against espionage and information leakage, al Qa'ida expected high security awareness among its recruits and mid-level managers. An internal al Qa'ida memo lists the qualities of potential leaders of the group's information committee. Every leader was required to have five years of work experience and be able to keep a secret.[210] Another al Qa'ida memo provides details of a computer system used to track al Qa'ida personnel matters. The memo stated that each recruit had to have "continuous personnel follow-up which accompanies him to any place he is transferred." According to the same memo, recruits were encouraged to take courses in member security, group security, and communications security.[211] Al Qa'ida established special training courses at some of its camps to improve recruits' security practices and their ability to set up and run a clandestine cell.[212] New arrivals in the camps were given extra scrutiny. Before these newcomers were granted access to the camp, they had to surrender their personal belongings. In some cases, camp supervisors would personally assess a newcomer to determine if the recruit was sincere in his commitment to al Qa'ida's goals.[213]

Al Qa'ida practiced good communications security in this period as well. Internal communications recommended that members not use email or the telephone, but faxes and couriers instead.[214] It is unclear why al Qa'ida believed that fax machines were more secure than telephones. Before 9/11, Bin Laden used Inmarsat satellite telephones and possibly two electronic scramblers to encrypt his conversations.[215]

The group also adapted its communication security procedures to changes in its adversaries' methods. When several individuals connected to al Qa'ida abroad were compromised in 1998, al Qa'ida members in Afghanistan began to rely more heavily on a communication coding system called the "one-time pad system"—a simple cryptographic mechanism used by the Allied and Axis powers in World War II that pairs individual letters with randomly selected numbers and letters available only to the sender and the recipient. The group also changed code names for personnel and facilities.[216] The 9/11 Commission determined that al Qa'ida's senior leadership stopped using a particular means of communication almost immediately after a leak to the *Washington Times*, which made it more difficult for US authorities to eavesdrop on their conversations.[217]

Al Qa'ida developed more systematic methods for securing its documents and files. An internal recommended keeping personnel files in a safe place in the main office of headquarters. The same memo was itself classified as "Very Secret," suggesting that the group altered the way it protected a document based on its sensitivity.[218] An al Qa'ida computer recovered after the fall of the Taliban in 2001 provided even more detail of the group's document security practices. The computer, probably belonging to Zawahiri, contained approximately one thousand text documents, encrypted and protected with passwords, written in what one journalist assessed as "an elliptical and evolving system of code words."[219]

Al Qa'ida's most dangerous local counterintelligence threats resulted directly from its campaign to garner international popular support—specifically, its contact with international media and its methods for claiming credit for attacks. Its contact with the media introduced numerous counterintelligence vulnerabilities. First, group members had to interact with the media over the telephone, by Internet, or in person to convey their message or threat. Atef called *al Quds* editor Atwan on August 21, 1998, after US cruise missiles hit Afghanistan, to tell Atwan that Bin Laden and key group leaders were still alive.[220] Al Qa'ida needed to make this call to reassure its base of international supporters that its leaders were still in business, but the phone call itself could have provided valuable targeting information to the group's adversaries.

Bin Laden and Zawahiri also used their phones to contact the media following these 1998 strikes.[221]

Second, al Qa'ida allowed certain interviews to be videotaped, which occasionally offered valuable information about the group's location, faces of unknown al Qa'ida operatives, and the health of key individuals. During the *ABC News* interview in 1998, al Qa'ida technical experts had to black out the faces of two of its operatives who accidentally got in the picture with Bin Laden. The two Saudis were Muhammed Rashed Daoud al-Owhali and Jihad al Azzam, who would fly to Kenya to join the al Qa'ida cell responsible for the US embassy bombing in Nairobi.[222] Had the technical experts not caught the mistake, the identity of these two men could have been used to apprehend them before the attack. Moreover, the fact that al Qa'ida needed to employ technical experts introduces a counterintelligence vulnerability. These individuals could be targeted and recruited by intelligence services at universities before or after they joined al Qa'ida.

Al Qa'ida's need to claim responsibility for its attacks also introduced vulnerabilities. Before the 9/11 attacks, Bin Laden insinuated to some trainees and high-level visitors that al Qa'ida was planning a large attack against the United States. KSM and Atef urged Bin Laden to exercise greater discretion and refrain from bragging about the upcoming mission.[223] In some cases, al Qa'ida transmitted its claim of credit before the attack occurred, possibly to ensure that another group would not make the first claim of credit. Perhaps if law enforcement had closely monitored these transmissions, they would have raised security alert levels at probable targets prior to any attack.

Al Qa'ida's campaign to reach out to the international media imperiled its relationship with the Taliban at times.[224] Elements of the Taliban were set against Bin Laden because his inflammatory statements brought negative international attention to the Taliban regime. Taliban foreign minister Muttawakil ordered that Bin Laden be placed under surveillance and asked Mullah Omar to reign in the terrorist leader. Bin Laden allegedly used to say of Muttawakil: "Two entities are against our jihad . . . one is the US, and the other is the Taliban's own foreign ministry."[225]

The group's record keeping also brought some counterintelligence setbacks. Al Qa'ida recruiter Abu Zubaydah kept files on recruits, which he used to match individuals with required tasks.[226] It is probably necessary for a group to keep records of its personnel, and such records perhaps can even improve the group's counterespionage capabilities by keeping track of security violators. However, improper storage and destruction of such files backfired for al Qa'ida when members evacuated Kabul on November 12, 2001. Journalist Alan Cullison purchased two al Qa'ida computers containing sensitive organizational and operational information that had been looted from al Qa'ida's central office after the evacuation.[227]

Al Qa'ida also suffered from espionage in its camps and adversary recruitment of its lower-level members. Bin Laden's chief bodyguard in 2001, Nasser al-Bahri, also known as "Abu Jandal," told reporters that an Afghan cook working for a foreign intelligence service provided information about Bin Laden's movements in August 1998.[228]

The nature of al Qa'ida's controlled territory in Afghanistan also brought security vulnerabilities. Its members lived and trained in camps far removed from urban centers, and, as a result, it was easier for the United States to justify large-scale strikes against the group.[229] Had al Qa'ida been based in an urban center, the United States may have hesitated to strike the group to avoid generating unacceptable collateral damage.

Most of al Qa'ida's counterintelligence practices consisted of basic denial. Efforts to mask the identities of its operatives at training camps, to carefully screen recruits and journalists trying to meet with Bin Laden, and to code and encrypt communications fall into this category. The group's practice of asking training camp visitors to fill out the New Recruits Form, which aimed to document counterintelligence problems the recruits encountered on their way to the camps, would have facilitated adaptive denial if it had allowed al Qa'ida to learn about its unique vulnerabilities and adjust accordingly.

International Counterintelligence: Basic Denial and Some Adaptive Denial. Al Qa'ida's international counterintelligence capabilities in the 1996– 2001 period were increasingly sophisticated and systematic.

The group established a formal system for evaluating individuals coming to train at the camps in Afghanistan. Before candidates received training, they were screened and vetted at guesthouses and camps.[230] They would transit through Peshawar or Karachi, Pakistan, where they waited for up to two weeks while their papers were verified and their backgrounds scrutinized.[231]

Al Qa'ida had each newcomer fill out a New Recruits Form, where he would indicate his security status in his country of origin, whether he could return to his country, how he arrived in Afghanistan, and the problems he encountered while traveling to Afghanistan.[232] Recruits were asked to write an account of their trip to Afghanistan, presumably to assess other counterintelligence concerns associated with the newcomer and to catalog the counterintelligence vulnerabilities likely to encumber future travelers.

Once at the camps, recruits were kept away from sensitive facilities and individuals. Islamic conferences or summits were held in isolated buildings or tents in the camp so that trainees and other bystanders could not see who was attending.[233] One al Qa'ida training manual reminds recruits that keeping secrets and concealing information from even the closest of friends and relatives are necessary qualifications for membership.[234] Recruits were also given advice on how to blend in and avoid surveillance once they were operating overseas. When US authorities captured al Qa'ida operative Ahmed Omar Abu Ali, they found on him a six-page document on how to avoid various forms of surveillance by government and private entities.[235] Operatives sometimes received further counterintelligence instruction from al Qa'ida members familiar with the country to which they would be deployed. Operatives Ramzi Bin al Sheibh and Muhammed Atta received training in security precautions specific to the United States from KSM in 2000 in Karachi.[236]

The al Qa'ida manual *Military Studies in the Jihad Against the Tyrants* also provides members with counterinterrogation tips. It instructs members to have prepared answers to questions about the purpose and length of their trips when traveling through airports. It tells members about what a common interrogation looks like and what techniques an interrogator will use to elicit information, including blindfolding and torture. Members are told that they should not speak to anyone in their prison cell because some prisoners might be enemy agents. Finally, the manual suggests that members memorize the procedures and content of the interrogation so that other members can learn from the experience.[237]

Al Qa'ida exhibited good operational security in the 1996–2001 period. First, the group compartmented its operational cells. The 9/11 attacks offer an example of the degree to which al Qa'ida restricted information about the operation among its cells. Only Bin Laden, KSM, Atef, and a few senior hijackers knew about the specific timing, targets, operatives, and method of attack. According to KSM, the thirty-four individuals involved in the 9/11 attacks were divided into five groups with varying access to operational details. The first group, the principal decision makers, consisted of Bin Laden, KSM, Atef, Bin al Sheibh (the communications link between KSM and Atta), and Abu Turub al-Urduni (the trainer of the "muscle" hijackers).[238] These individuals would have known almost all the sensitive details of the operation.

The second group, the principal hijackers, consisted of Atta, Marwan al Shehhi, Hani Hanjour, Ziad Jarrah, Nawaf al-Hamzi, and Khalid Mihdhar. These individuals were privy only to operational details that concerned their respective missions. The third group consisted of the other thirteen hijackers, all of whom were "muscle" hijackers. These individuals did not learn much about the operation, including the information that they would be flying hijacked airplanes into buildings, until Atta briefed them on the operation in August 2001.[239]

The fourth group consisted of four individuals who handled logistical, financial, and training aspects of the operation, and these individuals knew only that they were involved in an al Qa'ida operation against the United States. The fifth group consisted of the seven "muscle" hijackers who were unable to get into the United States, and these men knew only that they were to be involved in a suicide operation inside the United States.[240]

The US embassy operation in 1998 followed a similar protocol. Al Qa'ida technical adviser to the Nairobi attack, Muhammed Sadiq Odeh, never met al Qa'ida cell member Owhali, who constructed the bomb and participated in the attack.[241] All the while, the cell would report back to al Qa'ida headquarters with security updates and requests for logistical support. One report back to headquarters, captured off of Fawwaz's computer, provided a security assessment and reported the cell's desire to secure cell communications with a satellite telephone.[242]

It is possible that many other operations were compartmented in this manner. When camp graduates made their requests for operational and logistical support from al Qa'ida, they did so separately and directly to Bin Laden and Atef. Thus, very few individuals were in a position to see al Qa'ida's full operational picture.[243]

Al Qa'ida cells also enhanced operational security by blending into their local environments. Operation planners tried to select environments where blending in would be easy. While casing flights in 1999, al Qa'ida operative Khallad bin Attash traveled to Malaysia because Malaysians did not heavily scrutinize Saudi Arabians or suspected Islamist jihadists.[244] Saudis were also used for the 9/11 attacks because the United States did not scrutinize them as heavily as others coming from the Middle East.[245] The Hamburg cell distanced themselves from Islamist extremists, wore Western clothing, and shaved their beards.[246] Operatives used code names and names starting with "Abu" to further increase security. Operative Owhali could not provide the FBI with the true names of his colleagues when he became a US informant because he knew only their code names.[247]

Al Qa'ida's operational security protocol included moving nonattack personnel out of the area of operations prior to the attack. Before the USS *Cole* operation, the senior commander of the attack left Yemen.[248] Said Bahaji, the logistical support element for the Hamburg cell, fled to Pakistan several days before the 9/11 attacks.[249] Several days before the US embassy bombings, most cell members not involved in the attack had left East Africa.[250]

Elements of al Qa'ida enhanced operational security by securing internal documents that could give away sensitive details about the group. One al Qa'ida cell member reported that he had collected the cell's sensitive files and moved them to a secure location when he thought law enforcement personnel were watching the group.[251]

The group also practiced good communications security. Operational planners consistently demonstrated good communications-security awareness. Fawwaz demanded that Nairobi cell members not call him on his telephone because he was certain that it was "tapped."[252] Only select members of the Nairobi cell were allowed to make international telephone calls, according to al Qa'ida member Odeh.[253] Atta reported to KSM that he had forbidden his 9/11 hijackers from calling their families to say good-bye to them before the attack.[254] Very sensitive communications were conducted via couriers when possible. KSM was informed of the date of the 9/11 attacks by al Qa'ida courier Zakariya Essabar, who had hand carried the letter from Germany to Afghanistan.[255] The 9/11 hijackers used anonymous mail and Internet centers such as Kinkos and Mail Boxes Etc. to send electronic and paper messages.[256]

Al Qa'ida couriers were typically recruited from among al Qa'ida members who could maintain a low profile. Couriers would probably not know the purpose or end user of their "package" and in some cases would hand off the "package" to another courier. Al Qa'ida used couriers to transfer funds as well as messages. It reportedly used a Pakistani-based *hawala* broker, known as a *hawaladar*, to move $1 million from the United Arab Emirates to Pakistan, at which point another *hawaladar* passed the money to a courier who smuggled the funds into Afghanistan.[257]

Al Qa'ida also used encryption and coded messages to enhance communications security. Messages found on an al Qa'ida computer recovered from Afghanistan were encrypted, sometimes with the one-time pad system or coded in the language of multinational firms.[258] Odeh reported to US authorities that members in Kenya referred to jihad as "work," weapons as "tools," hand grenades as "potatoes," and bad documents as "papers."[259] Bin Laden was referred to as the "contractor," and US and UK intelligence services were referred to as "foreign competitors." The al Qa'ida cell leader for the USS *Cole* attack sent a coded pager message to the operative in charge of filming the attack to indicate that the attack was imminent.

Owhali made a telephone call to his logistical contact in Nairobi following the attack and could not use coded language, so he instead spoke cryptically to request a passport and money to get out of Kenya.[260] KSM actually advised his cells to use code words sparingly because he believed overuse would attract the attention of hostile intelligence services. He asked his operatives to keep their messages as normal and as short as possible. He also delegated operational authority to his subordinates in order to keep his communication with his cells to a minimum.[261]

Al Qa'ida helped its operatives stay clandestine by providing them with forged documents. The al Qa'ida manual recommends that every member have forged identity cards and passports.[262] The group tried to forge or steal high-quality papers, particularly from Western countries.[263] Its office of passports and host-country issues, based at the Kandahar airport and managed by Atef, altered passports, visas, and identification cards.[264] Operatives probably received some training to alter documents on their own. Al Qa'ida operative Ahmed Omar Abu Ali received training in document forgery in Saudi Arabia.[265] As a testament to their training and preparation, al Qa'ida operatives involved in the 9/11 operations carried a cache of alias documentation and "pocket litter" that supported their false identity, including ID cards and medical, banking, and educational records.[266]

Al Qa'ida probably enjoyed enhanced operational security as a result of the close ties between individuals in its cells. Nairobi cell member Kherchtou testified that he joined al Qa'ida with four of his friends. Training camps in Afghanistan also helped to bring members together with a shared experience, building confidence and creating esprit de corps. Although there is no direct evidence that this closeness resulted in counterintelligence benefits, it is probable that members were less likely to betray their cell and their friends once these relationships were formed. However, it is possible that closeness would lead to informality and more nonessential communication, which could produce counterintelligence vulnerabilities. Hamburg cell members, for example, frequently emailed one another to share experiences and jokes, which helped them foster and maintain an "emotional closeness."[267] Thus, the closeness of individuals may have made them less susceptible to espionage but more susceptible to eavesdropping.

Al Qa'ida may have engaged in more sophisticated counterintelligence practices, such as deception and rapid adaptation to security procedures. The al Qa'ida manual counsels its members to mislead the adversary with fake telephone conversations if the adversary is monitoring calls.[268] However, though the Nairobi cell believed its phones were tapped, there was no evidence its members engaged in deceptive communications. The manual also recommends that operatives agree on a purposefully misleading cover story in the event they are captured and interrogated.[269] Deception operations require lots of coordination and preplanning and therefore are less likely to have been used by al Qa'ida, particularly in any systematic manner.

On occasion, al Qa'ida rapidly adapted its security procedures to prevent the leakage of sensitive information or to stay one step ahead of its adversaries' counterterrorism efforts. When al Qa'ida member Khallad bin Attash was captured in Yemen before the USS *Cole* operation, Bin Laden contacted Yemeni officials and successfully negotiated bin Attash's release. Bin Laden was worried that bin Attash would break under interrogation and reveal Nashiri's plans to hit a US naval vessel in Yemen.[270] KSM anticipated the US security response to the 9/11 attacks and planned a second wave of attacks that relied on non-Arab-country passport holders to conduct the mission.[271]

Al Qa'ida also faced its share of counterintelligence setbacks in the 1996–2001 period. First, as al Qa'ida spread itself out across the world and remained centrally controlled, the need for its leaders to keep in touch with operatives via telephone and the Internet increased.[272] Connections between the individuals made them vulnerable to monitoring and targeting by savvy intelligence services. For the US embassy bombing operations, al Qa'ida operative Ahmed Abdallah in Tanzania used a cell phone to keep in touch with overall operational commander Mahmoud Abdelkader Es Sayed, also known as "Abu Saleh," in Nairobi.[273] Al Qa'ida member Fawwaz called the London-based media outlet *al Quds al Arabia* and spoke to its representative for more than thirty minutes in February 1998 to dictate Bin Laden's fatwa to the newspaper.[274] Yemeni telephone records from 1998 to 2000 show that the operatives involved in the USS *Cole* attack were talking to operatives involved in the US embassy bombings.[275]

Al Qa'ida experienced a similar vulnerability as a result of its need to claim credit for its attacks. In many cases, al Qa'ida relayed its claim of credit for an attack before the operation took place. For the US embassy bombings, al Qa'ida videotaped one of its would-be suicide bombers, Owhali, in Pakistan before he made the final trip to Kenya to prepare for the operation.[276] Al Qa'ida headquarters then sent its media contact in London a letter claiming responsibility for the upcoming attack. They assumed Owhali would complete his suicide mission and so claimed in the letter that two Saudis in Nairobi and one Egyptian in Dar Es Salam, Tanzania, had perished in the attacks; the Nairobi bomb was detonated, but not until after Owhali jumped out of the truck and run off.[277] Before the operation, the Nairobi cell also sent a fax to the Cairo office of *al-Hayat* newspaper from Egyptian Islamic Jihad threatening an imminent attack against US interests.[278]

For this operation in particular, the adversary's intelligence service would have had the opportunity to intercept communications regarding an attack involving two Saudis and an Egyptian in specific locations and perhaps could have obtained the video bearing Owhali's image. These communications also created counterintelligence problems in the postattack environment. In the wake of the US embassy bombings, the United Kingdom's security service tracked the claim of credit to Fawwaz and sent him to a maximum-security prison for his aid to al Qa'ida.[279]

Before the US embassy and USS *Cole* attacks, Bin Laden issued an interview and a video, respectively, threatening an attack on US interests. In both media events, he included a "teasing" clue about the upcoming attacks—for the USS *Cole* attack video he wore a distinctive, curved Yemeni dagger in his belt.[280] Providing such a clue may have been a subtle way of making sure credit was given to al Qa'ida in the aftermath, but it also introduced some chance that the clue would be useful to those trying to prevent the attacks.

Al Qa'ida's publicity-campaign videos occasionally gave away sensitive information about the group. As Bin Laden became more popular in the Muslim world in the late 1990s, his "public" demanded more information about him. He obliged, and video interviews he granted to CNN, ABC, and al Jazeera gave away valuable information about his health and location.[281] Bin Laden claimed that he would regularly ride horseback for more than seventy kilometers—information that would be valuable for those assessing his health or those studying his modes of travel.

Al Qa'ida also subjected itself to potentially crippling counterintelligence weakness in its extensive travel. The four pilots for the 9/11 operation passed through US immigration and customs inspections seventeen times between 2000 and 2001. Ziad Jarrah alone entered the United States seven times.[282]

Al Qa'ida's reliance on personal connections for recruiting and advancement provided the group with counterintelligence advantages and disadvantages. On the one hand, personal connections provided al Qa'ida with a quick and low-cost vetting process. However, personal connections also muddied decision making about how to punish security violations. Bin Laden had a personal affiliation for 9/11 operative Khalid al-Mihdhar, and prevented KSM from excluding him from the 9/11 attacks after al-Mihdhar made an unauthorized departure from San Diego in 2000.[283] Shadi Abdalla, one of Bin Laden's bodyguards in

Afghanistan, enjoyed a special position of trust in al Qa'ida simply because Bin Laden's brother-in-law recruited him in Mecca and Ramzi Bin al Sheibh had good personal rapport with him.[284]

Personal connections may also create vulnerabilities if an intelligence service can link individuals through kinship ties. Nearly every "muscle" hijacker for the 9/11 operation could be linked to each other and other al Qa'ida members through kinship and friendship.[285]

Al Qa'ida's use of face-to-face communications also had its counterintelligence advantages and disadvantages. On the one hand, face-to-face meetings reduced al Qa'ida's communications profile, making the interception of those conversations nearly impossible. On the other hand, they take longer and require traveling, which allow intelligence services to monitor an operative's physical movements more easily. KSM reported that he would deliver oral updates to Bin Laden, which required him to travel for a day and a half in some instances.[286] This method of communication slowed the organization's response, in theory, to information that KSM was collecting in the field—information that could have related to counterintelligence problems that needed immediate fixing. Al Qa'ida's limited supply of trusted couriers probably also restricted its ability to move messages and funds quickly.[287] All of the 9/11 hijackers met occasionally in Las Vegas and Florida, traveling together to and from these locations,[288] which provided them with valuable face-to-face planning time but also could have implicated all of the hijackers if one of them had come under FBI scrutiny.

Al Qa'ida's strategy to provide its operational cells with a degree of autonomy generated several counterintelligence problems. First, operational planners did not always know whether their operatives were following security protocols. KSM reported that he instructed his hijackers not to talk to one another in the United States, but he had no way of checking up on them to make sure.[289] Second, planners could not easily discipline operatives when they violated protocol. KSM instructed al Qa'ida operative Zacarias Moussaoui not to mention airplanes in his communications with him or Bin al Sheibh, but Moussaoui nevertheless mentioned flight training in an email. The greatest punishment KSM could exact on Moussaoui was to cut him out of the operation and require other operatives to cut off communication with him.[290]

Operations that were even more autonomously designed had additional counterintelligence problems. Many al Qa'ida operations were partially or completely self-financed. Some of the self-financed operations relied on criminal activities to raise funds. Conducting criminal activities in some cases raised the operatives' profiles and exposed them to law enforcement.[291] Al Qa'ida operatives arrested while preparing for the millennium attack in Jordan had financed their operation with bank robberies, burglary, and forged checks. Even the 9/11 operation, which was fully funded, exposed itself to scrutiny when operatives remitted their "unspent funds" back to al Qa'ida before the attacks.[292]

Al Qa'ida also suffered from the theft of information by spies in this period. Following the group's move to Afghanistan in 1996, the husband of one of the Bin Laden's nieces surrendered himself to Saudi Arabian intelligence and divulged details of Bin Laden's funding network.[293] Member Jamal al-Fadl also gave himself to US authorities in 1996, providing the United States with a rare look at al Qa'ida's inner workings.[294]

Al Qa'ida's training in counterinterrogation, its dedication to compartmentation for big operations, and its careful handling of sensitive documents are all basic-denial techniques. The group showed some adaptive-denial aptitude when it negotiated the release of a captured operative for fear that he would divulge group secrets.

Summary. Al Qa'ida developed powerful adversaries in the Middle East and the West. Its structure in the 1996–2001 period remained relatively hierarchical, though the operatives deployed outside of Afghanistan retained some operational autonomy. Its access to financial resources, high-quality personnel, and controlled territories continued in this period. Its local popular support remained relatively low, but its international popularity increased substantially between 1996 and 2001. The increase was the result of a series of successful attacks and an increase in inflammatory public statements. Al Qa'ida's intelligence and counterintelligence capabilities were more sophisticated in this period.

Al Qa'ida enjoyed popular support in many locations and successfully co-opted locals into providing intelligence support. There is not much evidence that locals provided much counterintelligence support. However, the fact that al Qa'ida could work in a foreign theater without being "turned over" to local law enforcement gave the group a large counter-intelligence advantage. Its campaigns to generate popular support occasionally gave away sensitive information about its personnel and plans. In addition, al Qa'ida imperiled its relationship with the Taliban in its quest to generate widespread support, which could have caused it to lose its controlled territory—arguably one of its most precious counterintelligence resources. Al Qa'ida's contact with the media introduced counter-intelligence vulnerabilities as the group interacted with journalists by phone, by Internet, and in person.

AL QA'IDA GAINS NOTORIETY, FLEES AFGHANISTAN: 2001–2003

Key Factors

Organizational Structure. Al Qa'ida's structure in the 2001–2003 period became relatively loose because the core of the group in the Afghan–Pakistan border region was essentially cut off from its operatives deployed outside of Afghanistan. The al Qa'ida core in Afghan–Pakistan tribal areas continued to issue strategic and inspirational direction to some of its overseas operatives, although these individuals had greater operational and tactical autonomy.[295]

The organizational structure of al Qa'ida's core probably remained hierarchical. An internal al Qa'ida document dated March 20, 2002, laid out the requirements for joining the group: abiding by al Qa'ida rules, obeying leaders in charge without disobeying Islamic rules, and foregoing any connection between al Qa'ida membership and any other Islamic group.[296] Such requirements indicate that al Qa'ida retained a high degree of command over its local membership.

Al Qa'ida's international operatives appear to have enjoyed increased autonomy, though they continued to interact with the core. Abd al Rahim al Nashiri, the al Qa'ida operative responsible for the USS *Cole* attack, continued to plan terrorist operations in the Persian Gulf, including the attack against a French oil tanker in October 2002.[297] Nashiri formed the idea of the attack, picked the target and his operatives, and then asked for funds and the "green light" from the al Qa'ida military committee, which was headed by Sayf al-Adl.[298] The al Qa'ida core used videos released to the media to boost morale and provide strategic direction to operatives with whom it was able to maintain regular contact.[299]

Popular Support: Local. Local support for al Qa'ida increased dramatically following US Operation Enduring Freedom, the post-9/11 attack on Afghanistan. The group's exodus and relocation to the Afghan–Pakistan border region was facilitated by the Taliban in Afghanistan and by the Pashtun tribes of the Pakistan frontier area.

Al Qa'ida knew that fleeing its strongholds in Afghanistan was necessary when Operation Enduring Freedom began. It chose to retreat to Tora Bora, a mountainous fortress on the border of Pakistan. The tribal leaders in Tora Bora, the Eastern Shura, had the final word on what would happen to al Qa'ida in Tora Bora. The Eastern Shura had a favorable view of Bin Laden and his cohorts because they had brought commerce and employment opportunities to Afghanistan during their stay there.

To shore up al Qa'ida's popular base before moving to Tora Bora, Bin Laden held a *jirga* (tribal assembly) with regional Pashtun elders on November 10, 2001, where he announced that al Qa'ida intended on fighting the United States as the latter's forces advanced across Afghanistan. Bin Laden's close association with the Taliban, coupled with his mythical status as a hero of the anti-Soviet jihad, afforded him additional support from the tribal elders. The final pillar in al Qa'ida's escape strategy was to pay off regional tribal leaders in return for support against invading Western forces.[300]

As Bin Laden moved east from the Mileva Valley to Tora Bora, the "core of his close-quarters guards consisted of sixty men," according to villagers in the area. In addition to these bodyguards, a four-hundred-man force acted as lookouts on al Qa'ida's flanks. While the United States and its tribal allies fought up one side of the Tora Bora Valley, tribesman loyal to Bin Laden were helping to smuggle al Qa'ida members out of Tora Bora into Pakistan. The Eastern Shura also facilitated the delivery of food to al Qa'ida, even while the United States was bombing the area.[301]

Al Qa'ida continued to encourage Afghans to join the group during this time. Appeals for support were circulated by covert "night letters," *shabnama*. The distribution of "night letters" was a psychological warfare technique taught to the Afghans by the United States during the 1980s. The Taliban also put out night letters offering a bounty for specific special-forces personnel as well as for any foreigner.[302] Al Qa'ida provided clan leaders and local Pashtun village leaders with Pakistani rupees in return for support.[303]

Al Qa'ida did experience setbacks in popular support during its exodus, though. Member Fouad al Rabia recalls that group members could stay in a stranger's house for only a couple of days at a time because many villagers feared that renting a house to an Arab would result in their being shot or bombed.[304] This fear was reinforced when the US bombed the al Jazeera offices in Kabul. After the bombing, al Jazeera decided not to air any more al Qa'ida videotapes.[305]

Once al Qa'ida escaped to the Afghan–Pakistan border region, it received an additional measure of popular support. In both of the Pakistani provinces that border Afghanistan, Baluchistan and the Northwest Frontier Province, al Qa'ida-friendly Pashtun tribes were major players. These tribes subscribe to *pashtunwali*, a law of the Pashtuns that prizes providing hospitality and refuge to those in need. The border region stretches fifteen hundred miles—which Peter Bergen points out is approximately the distance from Washington, DC, to Denver—and is riddled with Pashtun tribes.[306]

Popular Support: International. Al Qa'ida international popular support continued to swell in the wake of the 9/11 attacks and Operation Enduring Freedom. Al Qa'ida restructured its public-media efforts in 2002, becoming even more prolific in its public outreach: it issued sixty public communications in 2002 and twenty-nine in 2003, in contrast to only four in 1999 and 2000.[307] Following the 9/11 attacks, Bin Laden and Zawahiri released an audio or video statement approximately once every six weeks.[308]

Al Qa'ida redoubled its public-relations offensive soon after the US invasion of Afghanistan. On the first day of the US bombing of Kabul, al Qa'ida released a videotape to al Jazeera in which Bin Laden and spokesperson Sulaiman Abu Ghaith called for a religious war to drive Americans out of the Muslim world.[309] Al Qa'ida had anticipated US airstrikes and had the professionally edited video ready to air as soon as the US campaign began.[310] Bin Laden gave his last television interview to al Jazeera in October 2001.[311] Atef telephoned *al Quds* editor Abdel Bari Atwan after the United States bombed Tora Bora to issue a communiqué to confirm that Bin Laden had lived through the assault.[312]

In part, the US invasion of Afghanistan was itself a source of increased support for al Qa'ida. The United States endeavored to minimize collateral damage, but the perception and reality of such damage were hard to eliminate. Media outlets reported large numbers of villagers killed and civilian homes destroyed,[313] which allowed al Qa'ida's to cast itself as the David to the US Goliath. Some of this support, however, was tempered by an idea circulating in the Islamic world that al Qa'ida had "lost" Afghanistan with its militant provocation.

Al Qa'ida used its Web site, www.alneda.com, to increase public support during this time as well. The Web site published a list of names of eighty-four al Qa'ida fighters captured in Pakistan following their exodus from Afghanistan, presumably to let their family members know they were still alive.[314] In February 2003, al Qa'ida released the fifth and sixth installment of Internet articles called "In the Shadow of Lances," where Sayf al-Adl provided advice on how to employ guerrilla tactics against US forces in their upcoming invasion of Iraq.[315] Al Qa'ida members probably also used chat rooms and online social-networking services to connect to and communicate with jihadist communities throughout the world.[316] Coupling dramatic video footage with digital photographs, stirring music, and audio clips most likely facilitated al Qa'ida's mission to create a community of sympathizers all over the world.[317] Despite obvious difficulties, al Qa'ida maintained contact with media personnel and organizations during this period. It sent an email to *al Quds* in October 2002 to claim credit for its attack on a French tanker in Yemen and again in November 2003 to claim credit for attacks in Istanbul, Turkey.[318]

Al Qa'ida's video production became more sophisticated during the 2001–2003 period. The group's video branch, the Sahab Institute for Media Production, was a professional video-production outfit. Sahab would produce multiple versions of videos with subtitles in various languages in order to increase its audience. It created the al Qa'ida video containing Bin Laden's address to Americans and Muslims in Iraq, released to al Jazeera on October 18, 2003.[319] And it probably helped Bin

Laden and Zawahiri make some of their twenty-six video statements between January 2002 and July 2005.[320]

For al Qa'ida, the downside of its video campaign was the pressure it put on the group to "deliver" on attacks. This dynamic produced tension between the operational elements of al Qa'ida, such as Abu Musab al Zarqawi's branch in Iraq, and the core leadership remaining in the Afghan–Pakistan border region.

Al Qa'ida was careful to shape its message in the 2001–2003 period in order to appeal to the largest possible audience. After the 9/11 attacks, al Qa'ida began to appeal directly to national groups subject to the greatest counterterrorism assault from the West, such as Pakistan, Saudi Arabia, Iraq, and the Palestinian territories. It continued to sell its mission as a religiously sanctioned defensive jihad—an act of self-defense of Muslim lands in response to Western aggression.[321]

At times, Bin Laden tried to portray himself as a statesman to make himself more palatable to Western audiences and moderate Muslims.[322] This approach appears to have paid off. In June 2003, the Pew Research Institute found that solid majorities in Indonesia, Jordan, Morocco, Pakistan, and the Palestinian territories believed that Bin Laden would do the right thing regarding world affairs.[323] Al Qa'ida was also sensitive to the collateral damage it created by its attacks on Western interests. The newsletter *al-Battar Military Camp* (*Mu'askar al-Battar*), published in Saudi Arabia, advised al Qa'ida members to know the nationalities of the likely victims of their attack because "nationalities determine the effect of the operation."[324]

Controlled Territory. Al Qa'ida suffered an initial shock when its controlled territory in Afghanistan was lost, but it then regained some controlled territory—albeit limited, most likely—along the Afghan–Pakistan border. This new controlled territory did not begin to match the controlled territory it had enjoyed in Afghanistan. In this particular period, controlled territory also created the disadvantage of subjecting the group to US military targeting. In some cases, al Qa'ida members were forced to evacuate their attacked facilities, carrying everything valuable they could find with them. Hamed Mir, a Pakistani journalist and Bin Laden's biographer, reported that every other al Qa'ida member fleeing camps in 2001 carried a laptop computer—and the adversary would know just where to look for those few laptops left behind.[325]

Other Important Factors

Resources: Local and International. Al Qa'ida's local and international resources remained relatively high in the 2001–2003 period. Its activity in this period included attacks on the French oil tanker *Limburg* on October 6, 2002; on an Israeli-owned hotel in Kenya on November 28, 2002; on the Cordoval Compound in Saudi Arabia on May 13, 2003; on the Spain House and Jewish cemetery in Morocco on May 16, 2003; on the Muhaya Housing Compound in Saudi Arabia on November 8, 2003; and on the HSBC Bank and British consulate in Turkey on November 20, 2003.[326]

Al Qa'ida continued to receive a great deal of financial support, though the United States moved to cut off its finances by freezing the assets of individuals and charities affiliated with al Qa'ida and the Taliban. Al Qa'ida's videos continued to inspire donors to contribute to the group's mission. Its finances also received a major boost after it was able to drop its exorbitant annual donation to the Taliban government.[327] It is unknown how much of these funds were redirected to tribal leaders in al Qa'ida's controlled territory in the Afghan–Pakistan border region, though.

Al Qa'ida's links and access to "international" fighters were also degraded by the US military action in Afghanistan. The US operation essentially eliminated al Qa'ida's training and logistical infrastructure in Afghanistan, which made it much harder to train, recruit, and plan on the same scale as the organization had done previously.[328]

Al Qa'ida members overseas tried to make up for this deficit by relying more heavily on indigenous resources in their areas of operation and on training available on the Internet. Saudi Arabia is one country that experienced marked growth in indigenous support for al Qa'ida. Operative Ahmed Omar Abu Ali offered his services to al Qa'ida operatives in Saudi Arabia in 2002. They provided Abu Ali with training in weapons and document forgery as well as with funds for a computer and a cell phone.[329] As noted, al Qa'ida also launched the newsletter *al-Battar Military Camp* in Saudi Arabia, targeted at Saudis interested in joining the jihad against the regime.[330] The al Qa'ida core's connections to the Saudi branch are demonstrated by the regular "column" the chief of al Qa'ida's military operations wrote for *al-Battar*.[331]

Al Qa'ida also made up for its controlled-territory deficit by creating a virtual quasi–safe haven on the Internet, where it could communicate with its followers and provide instruction on training, intelligence, and counterintelligence techniques. Before the 9/11 operation, al Qa'ida had known only one Web site, www.alneda.com, but that number grew to as many as fifty by 2006.[332] The *al-Battar* publication was available to jihadists online, and the first issue encouraged those who could not travel to training camps, saying: "In order to join the great training camps you don't have to travel to other lands. . . . [A]lone, in your home or with a group of brothers, you too can begin to execute the program."[333] Al Qa'ida operatives also used the Internet to communicate with one another. As late as September 16, 2002, al Qa'ida cells in Western countries reportedly used Internet-based phone services to communicate with operatives overseas.[334]

Adversary Counterterrorism Capability. After September 11, 2001, the United States dramatically increased resources devoted to locating and destroying al Qa'ida. It initiated Operation Enduring Freedom on October 7, 2001, in response to the al Qa'ida attacks in New York and Washington, DC. It assembled a coalition of twenty-four countries to accomplish this mission. The campaign began with a series of air strikes, and US intelligence personnel and special-operations forces worked with the Northern Alliance and with anti-Taliban Pashtun forces.[335] By November 12, coalition forces took the Afghan capital, Kabul, and by December 7 had taken key Taliban strongholds in Kunduz and Kandahar.

By March 2002, al Qa'ida had regrouped in the Shahi-Kot Valley and Arma Mountains southeast of Zormat. The US launched Operation Anaconda in order to slowly squeeze al Qa'ida forces in the region. US Predator drones circled overhead, while US and Afghan troops, along with soldiers from many other allied countries, patrolled the mountains.[336]

The United States also increased its efforts to find and disrupt al Qa'ida cells throughout the world. It began working more closely with liaison partners. Al Qa'ida's online presence increased in this time period as well, so the United Stats continued its efforts at shutting down Web sites and chat rooms where al Qa'ida was suspected of transmitting information or propaganda to its operatives.

Intelligence and Counterintelligence Outcomes

Intelligence: Local and International. There is a dearth of information about al Qa'ida's intelligence capabilities in the 2001–2003 period, though the group appears to have continued to conduct intelligence collection in support of its international operations.

Al Qa'ida's Internet-based intelligence training continued in this period. Sayf al-Adl wrote numerous articles that advised al Qa'ida operatives on how to conduct intelligence. The *al-Battar* publication featured al-Adl articles on the following topics: how to collect intelligence during conversations, how to set up a safe house, how to conduct an operational test for vetting weapons dealers, how to secure a location using remote surveillance, and how surveillance operations can differ based on the number of operatives involved.[337] Al Qa'ida also made an appeal in 2002 on one of its Web sites, www.alrakiza.com, for Muslims working at US airbases, naval bases, seaports, and airports in the Arabian Peninsula to provide intelligence to al Qa'ida. The Web site announcement asked "brothers" to post information, including the location of US naval vessel refueling stations and the type of fuel lines used at airbases, along with photographs and scanned commercial maps.[338]

Al Qa'ida probably continued to blend into local environments to conduct surveillance for its operations. Its attack in Kenya in November 2002 was preceded by months of surveillance by operatives posing as fishermen, according to a United Nations report.[339]

Espionage operations probably remained sporadic and opportunistic. Al Qa'ida may have made a series of penetrations of the Saudi government during this time. An al Qa'ida computer recovered after the fall of Kabul in 2001 contained some secret Saudi government documents, presumably passed to al Qa'ida by sympathetic Saudi bureaucrats.[340] The operatives involved in the attack in Saudi Arabia in 2003 were alleged to have had very detailed knowledge of the Vinnell Corporation's residential complex, a target of the attack, suggesting the group had recruited sources in the Saudi National Guard to provide information about the compound.[341]

It is likely that al Qa'ida members continued to use open sources to collect information on targets. In 2005, British al Qa'ida members were indicted on charges of carrying out reconnaissance of targets in New York, Newark, New Jersey, and Washington, DC. The men allegedly videotaped the targets and collected more than five hundred photographs of them, many of which they downloaded from the Internet.[342]

Local Counterintelligence: Basic Denial. Al Qa'ida's local counterintelligence procedures remained high and probably improved in the 2001–2003 period. It continued to demand that its recruits uphold an agreement to secrecy. An internal "contract" between al Qa'ida and its recruits, dated March 2002, stipulated that members would not talk about work assigned in al Qa'ida even with other al Qa'ida members except their "direct" commander. The same document outlines the responsibilities of al Qa'ida's security committee, which include providing necessary security for operations, promoting the feeling of security among personnel, and facilitating the administrative security procedures related to the host country.[343] The promotion of the "feeling of security" may relate to the cultivation of a counterintelligence awareness among its members to reduce espionage and information-leakage problems.

This same internal document also describes the duties of al Qa'ida's counterespionage section and its installations, personnel, and facilities security section. The counterespionage group, referred to as the Central Section, was responsible for uncovering espionage and penetration operations by the enemy, penetrating the enemy's defenses through agent recruitment, monitoring everything in the media related to al Qa'ida's work, and filing all gathered data either on paper or on computer.[344]

The facilities protection section, referred to as the Organizational Work Security Section, was responsible for al Qa'ida leaders' protective detail, guarding documents and facilities, conducting background checks on personnel handling sensitive documents, and selecting suitable locations for secure work facilities.[345] Interestingly, al Qa'ida's seem to have weighed the risk of keeping soft and hard copies of files and decided that it was better to keep them.

Al Qa'ida continued to use videos to promote its message despite the risks associated with producing and delivering such material to non–al Qa'ida personnel. One strategy it probably employed to reduce the information-leakage risk was to minimize the time between the delivery of a videotape and its airing. Videotape experts at the Virginia-based government contractor IntelCenter contend that typically videotapes were aired within two days of their being delivered to the media outlet.[346]

To keep core al Qa'ida operatives from exposing themselves to enemy law enforcement, lower-level members were used for logistical tasks, delivering messages by hand, and inputting Internet messages and communications at Internet cafes. Al Qa'ida operative Iyman Faris was reported to have helped al Qa'ida members arrange travel to Yemen by visiting a travel agency disguised as a member of an Islamic organization called "Tablighi Jamaat."[347]

Internet communications were also handled through lower-level members. Al Qa'ida leaders would record a communication on a disk and then send a low-level operative to upload the material on a computer at a cyber café. The al Qa'ida core group allegedly did not use the Internet directly for fear of being caught or tracked.[348]

Al Qa'ida's local security probably also received a boost as a result of having safe havens—or perhaps, more accurately, safe houses—in the Afghan–Pakistan border region. Not only is the region remote and free of Pakistani and Afghan government control, but nontribal entities in the region are easily identified by locals. Pakistan journalist Rahmullah Yusufzai reported that outsiders stick out immediately in the tribal region, so that nonlocals and even Arabs find it difficult to hide there.[349] Peter Bergen contends that even without the anti-US sentiment in the region, finding a few al Qa'ida members in this vast area is a daunting task. He describes how thousands of North Atlantic Treaty Organization soldiers spent more than a decade unsuccessfully hunting Bosnia–Serb war criminals in Bosnia, an area less rugged than and only two-thirds the size of Pakistan's Northwest Frontier Province.[350]

Al Qa'ida's connections to the Pashtun tribes in the region afforded its members even greater security as a result. The group's ties with the chiefs of southern Afghans heroin-trafficking networks may have allowed it to move fighters across the Afghanistan–Iran and Afghanistan–Pakistan borders.[351] It is telling that despite the $100 million reward offered by the United States for information leading to the capture of Bin Laden in the 2001–2003 period, not a single person stepped forward to offer such information.[352] Part of this reticence may have resulted from al Qa'ida's popularity and willingness to pay off locals. One tribal elder reported to a journalist: "Osama and his men are heroes for locals. . . . They are treated as honorable guests. They don't harm tribesmen, stay for a couple of nights, and pay [$175 to $300] before they leave."[353]

Despite its improving counterintelligence tradecraft, al Qa'ida faced a number of setbacks in the 2001–2003 period. First, the group continued to give away sensitive information about its personnel and locations in its videos. In one video, operatives are seen close-up in some rugged mountain setting with their faces and communications equipment in full view.[354] Although this video did not give away their exact location, intelligence services could have used the information to assess the group's general location, communication modus operandi, and overall physical and financial health. One tribal elder in Waziristan commented to a journalist: "The footage I saw on a local TV channel, looked to me like our area. . . . Osama was wearing a Waziristani woolen cap, shalwar kameez, and a scarf on his shoulder. The dress is of here and the terrain is familiar; I have walked these mountains all my life."[355]

In a video released on December 27, 2001, Bin Laden appeared gaunt and was not moving his left arm, probably as a result of injures from US strikes against al Qa'ida. The video, in theory, would allow al Qa'ida's adversaries to assess his health and perhaps speculate on the accuracy of intelligence they had received leading to the air strikes. Some videotapes of Bin Laden gave the impression that he was not living in a remote tribal region, but that he was in a secure, comfortable location where he was able to follow political developments with some ease.[356] This information was most likely valuable to intelligence services that were tracking Bin Laden's location based on such small clues.

Second, al Qa'ida risked exposure by trying to get its publicity products to media organizations. An October 2004 al Qa'ida video featured an interview in English with operative Azzam al-Amriki and was delivered to *ABC News* via a source known to have contacts with al Qa'ida in the tribal region of Pakistan.[357] As Peter Bergen notes, it is possible to exploit these contacts and sources by tracing the series of handoffs that must occur for the media product to reach the final source.[358] Several minor operatives were allegedly arrested after being spotted on closed-circuit television uploading al Qa'ida communications at Internet cafés.[359]

Al Qa'ida's basic-denial techniques included maintaining group documents that advised members about how to enhance their counterintelligence profiles, using low-level operatives who did not have access to sensitive information to perform tasks where the expected rate of capture was high, and relying on the hospitality and anonymity offered in Pakistan's tribal areas to hide from an adversary that would be unlikely to collect good intelligence in those areas.

International Counterintelligence: Basic Denial and Some Adaptive Denial. Al Qa'ida's international counterintelligence procedures probably remained high in the 2001–2003 period because the group seemed to capitalize on the counterintelligence advantages afforded by the Internet for communication and training.

Al Qa'ida continued to use code systems to communicate with its operatives. Operative Iyman Farris reported that he relayed information to his al Qa'ida managers by referring to gas cutters as "gas stations" and special operational equipment as "mechanics shops." For an additional measure of communications security, Farris's manager instructed him to access email only after opening other Internet sites first and never immediately after logging in.[360]

Al Qa'ida's loose organizational structure probably helped the group to evade some surveillance of its coded communications. According to Canadian al Qa'ida operative Muhammed Monsour Jabarah, captured in 2002 by Canadian authorities, code words were generally established by individual cells,[361] which would make it difficult for law enforcement to scan communications in general for a discrete number of "standard" code words.

Al Qa'ida members also employed some counterintelligence procedures when dealing with journalists. When al Jazeera journalist Yosri Fouda met with KSM and Bin al Sheibh in Pakistan in 2002, Fouda first had to meet an intermediary outside Karachi and was then blindfolded and driven to a safe house before meeting the al Qa'ida leaders.[362]

Al Qa'ida used the Internet to maintain the international reach of its media and operational campaigns while retaining a level of secrecy. During and immediately following Operation Enduring Freedom, al Qa'ida used the Web site www.alneda.com to boost morale among its operatives and to gain new support from sympathizers throughout the world. This Web site was irregularly operational through 2002, jumping from one Internet service provider to another as the US government tried to shut it down completely. In one eight-week period, it moved from a provider in Malaysia to one in Texas and finally to one in Michigan before being cut off.[363] In the cyber game of "cat and mouse," the difficulty of shutting down even a single Web site permanently is a testament to the current security advantage afforded to the "mouse." Perhaps the greatest natural advantage the Internet provides is its size. London-based Saudi dissident Muhammed al-Masri pointed out that "nine hundred million people use the Internet annually. . . . [I]t is impossible to keep it under random surveillance."[364]

Al Qa'ida may have adapted to some law enforcement techniques for tracing communications. *Al Quds* editor Atwan argues that some members may have used one-time email accounts or passed messages through a shared email account. These methods would thwart law enforcement efforts to monitor a suspect email account or intercept emails passed between accounts. Short-life Web sites, open for perhaps only a few hours, may also be used to pass information, thereby avoiding a direct email-to-email communication. Atwan argues that al Qa'ida members probably did not need to encrypt their Web site and chat-room communications, relying instead on the jihadi visitors' "sixth sense" of what was being communicated through the text and various signposts,[365] which would thwart law enforcement efforts to casually drop into a Web site forum and pick up hidden messages without a substantial background on the forum.

Sayf al-Adl wrote numerous articles that advised al Qa'ida operatives on counterintelligence practices. The *al-Battar* publication featured al-Adl articles on how to develop an effective cover, how to write and classify intelligence reports, how to physically secure sensitive information and documents, when to be particularly wary of monitoring by the adversary, and how to communicate with a limited number of coded references in order to avoid raising suspicion.[366]

Al Qa'ida suffered from a number of counterintelligence vulnerabilities in the 2001–2003 period. First, its increased media efforts required it to raise its operational profile on numerous occasions and to have regular access to video cameras, videotapes, production equipment, computers, editing equipment, and the Internet.[367] These efforts could potentially expose al Qa'ida members to law enforcement because the latter monitor the signatures and footprints left by the purchase and use of such material. Some of al Qa'ida videos display a distinctive mark, known as a "bug," to indicate which media shop produced the video. Its Sahab Institute for Media Production had a unique bug that indicated its handling and editing of a video.[368] Some al Qa'ida operatives also came out of hiding to give media interviews. Bin al Sheibh, for example, granted an interview to al Jazeera in 2002 while he was hiding in Karachi.[369]

During this period, al Qa'ida was also exposed to secondhand monitoring via its associations with non–al Qa'ida intermediaries and international media organizations, who were easier for governments to monitor. Increased monitoring occasionally deterred media organizations from dealing with al Qa'ida at all. An internal memo described the difficulty al Qa'ida was having finding volunteers to distribute its propaganda in the Persian Gulf due to security pressure from the governments in the region.[370]

Copies of al Qa'ida videos in the 2001–2003 period were occasionally held in clearinghouses, often based in London, from where they would be distributed internationally. Those managing these clearinghouses were easily monitored, and some may have been arrested and prosecuted.[371] When authorities could not track down al Qa'ida's intermediaries, they often tracked al Qa'ida's interactions with larger media organizations. British police raided the *al Quds* offices in London after the newspaper received an email from a suspected al Qa'ida operative in the wake of the Madrid bombings in 2004.[372]

Second, al Qa'ida's loss of controlled territory generated both counterintelligence advantages and vulnerabilities. Although the volunteers could no longer be traced to al Qa'ida through visits to training camps in Afghanistan, it is likely that the lack of formal training caused operatives' security tradecraft to suffer. In addition, al Qa'ida members who were known to have visited Afghanistan before Operation Enduring

Freedom were still hounded and sometimes arrested by intelligence services throughout the world.[373] The loss of a controlled territory may also adversely impact the fervor and dedication of the next generation of al Qa'ida recruits. Terrorism expert Brian Jenkins argues that "televised videotapes and virtual realms on the Internet may not suffice to maintain a high level of devotion."[374] A decrease in secrecy and security would likely accompany such a decline in devotion and commitment to the movement.

Third, al Qa'ida's increase in organizational looseness in 2001–2003 generated both counterintelligence advantages and vulnerabilities. Although operatives had fewer connections to al Qa'ida members known or monitored by law enforcement, their security tradecraft likely suffered as a result of increasingly self-managed training. In addition, al Qa'ida's core had to rely on less secure and more open channels for mass communicating with operatives whose access to secure Web sites and connections to other operatives were ambiguous.[375]

Al Qa'ida's relatively decentralized structure outside of Afghanistan and Pakistan militated against some basic-denial practices. Recruits and transnational operatives had to expose themselves in relatively overt channels in order to contact the group for guidance. The group successfully employed the use of coded language as a basic-denial technique. Al Qa'ida also showed some adaptive-denial proficiency by communicating through Web sites that were up for only a few hours, knowing that the adversary was monitoring Web sites more adeptly than before.

Summary. After September 11, 2001, the United States began to devote increasing amount of its resources to locating and destroying al Qa'ida. Al Qa'ida's structure in the 2001–2003 period became relatively loose because the group's core in the Afghan–Pakistan border region was essentially cut off from its operatives deployed outside of that region. Its local and international resources remained relatively high in this period, and its local popular support increased dramatically following the US Operation Enduring Freedom. The group's exodus and relocation to the Afghan–Pakistan border region was facilitated by local warlords in Afghanistan and by the Pashtun tribes of the Pakistan frontier area. Its international popular support also swelled in the wake of the 9/11 attacks and Operation Enduring Freedom. Al Qa'ida appears to have continued to conduct intelligence collection in support of its international operations. The group's local counterintelligence procedures remained high in the 2001–2003 period despite encountering new local security and counterintelligence challenges. Its international counterintelligence procedures probably remained high in this period as well.

Al Qa'ida enjoyed popular support in many locations and probably co-opted locals into providing intelligence support, especially in places such as Yemen, Saudi Arabia, and Indonesia. Its campaigns to generate popular support continued to offer its adversaries sensitive information about its personnel and plans. In addition, the group's contact with the media continued to introduce counterintelligence vulnerabilities. Its decentralization probably enhanced some aspects of its counterintelligence by diversifying the sources of its publicity campaign and the methods and codes of its international cells.

KEY FACTORS REVISITED

Organizational Structure. By maintaining a tight command-and-control structure, al Qa'ida was able to develop superior counterintelligence training and compartmentation. In Sudan and Afghanistan before October 2001, al Qa'ida trained its members in intelligence and counterintelligence techniques, and every member leaving a training camp was assured to have a basic competence in guerrilla fighting. When al Qa'ida had a surfeit of recruits in 1999, Bin Laden insisted that every recruit attend the training camps, regardless of overcrowding. Al Qa'ida's tight structure also allowed select members to train heavily in one intelligence or counterintelligence skill and serve as a specialist for the group. Jamal al-Fadl, for example, served as Bin Laden's chief of security. After October 2001, however, al Qa'ida had to rely more on Internet-based training guides and operational publications such as *al-Battar Military Camp* to provide worldwide operatives with a basic understanding of intelligence and counterintelligence procedures.

Al Qa'ida's tight command-and-control structure also made the group more vulnerable to its adversary's efforts to develop high-level penetrations and exploit the group's standardized counterintelligence procedures. When al Qa'ida had a looser structure, cells were responsible for devising a set of codes to communicate with cell members. With cell-based code selection, the discovery of one cell's codes would not necessarily compromise another cell's codes. Al Qa'ida's tight organization in its first period caused a major counterintelligence setback when turncoat Jamal al-Fadl was able to describe many details of the group's international organization to US authorities in 1996. Its international structure was generally looser than its local structure. In the second period, this loose international structure allowed cell members in Yemen to search for targets of opportunity in Aden Harbor rather than relying on top-down target selection. However, some constraints on innovation did exist, given that the Yemen cell had to report regularly to al Qa'ida leaders in Afghanistan.

Popular Support. Before al Qa'ida gained international notoriety, it sent a core-group member to do its intelligence collection for the US embassy attacks. After it gained popular support, it was able to exploit local networks to gather intelligence. The US seaman who provided details to al Qa'ida through a Web site was gathering intelligence on his US ship because he was an al Qa'ida sympathizer. There is some evidence that al Qa'ida continued to use its extensive Internet presence to solicit anonymous intelligence from sympathizers after 9/11. It presumably used the international recruits it trained in Afghanistan to conduct intelligence when they returned to their home countries. Although al Qa'ida did not enjoy local popular support in Sudan in the 1990s, the group was given access to the government's Delegation Office, which allowed it to collect valuable intelligence and counterintelligence data on the local population. There is some evidence that al Qa'ida used its international contacts to spot and vet new members, as it did in mosques in Saudi Arabia.

Al Qa'ida's campaign to win popular support appears to have caused some exploitable counterintelligence lapses. Bin Laden routinely leaked valuable information about his health, locations, and operational intentions in video interviews and tapes released to media organizations. Al Qa'ida leaders were in frequent contact with journalists, media organizations, and group members in the West networking regularly with the media. Zawahiri was on the telephone with a Pakistani journalist immediately before and after the US cruise-missile strikes in Afghanistan in 1998. From 1998 to 2000, al Qa'ida members made more than two hundred calls to Fawwaz to coordinate the group's media strategy. Any of these calls could have given away valuable information about the group's location and plans. In one case in order to arrange an immediate press release after an attack, al Qa'ida transmitted a message detailing the nationality and location of an operative before he performed his suicide mission. Terrorist planners might argue that this early notification is a risk worth taking because popular support is the most important component of waging a guerrilla war.

Controlled Territory. Al Qa'ida had superior communications security, physical security, and counterintelligence vetting inside its controlled territories. Within its territories, al Qa'ida leaders were trailed by an armed coterie, which would have made an assassination or seizure operation difficult. Bin Laden was able to change his residence every evening, lowering the chances he could be tracked by a single informant and targeted for a missile strike. Al Qa'ida members in the group's Afghanistan camps were well protected from exposure to outsiders. Even well-known journalists such as John Miller and Peter Bergen had to go through an extensive vetting procedure before getting access to the camps. In contrast, al Qa'ida members giving interviews and meeting with media organizations in Pakistan (such as KSM) and London (such as Fawwaz) did not have access to such controlled meeting and vetting procedures. Al Qa'ida's communications security was also better in its controlled territory. Members could meet face to face and did not have to rely on means of communications that could be intercepted.

The group's controlled territory also gave its adversaries a discrete geographical space on which to concentrate their military and intelligence resources. Al Qa'ida's large presence in Afghanistan may have allowed its adversaries to observe remotely the relative size and activity at its known training camps and bed-down locations. Individuals passing into and out of the training camps could also be subject to scrutiny simply based on the fact that they were traveling to certain locations in Afghanistan and Pakistan.

ADDITIONAL LESSONS FROM THE AL QA'IDA CASE

The al Qa'ida case study provides additional insights into terrorist counterintelligence. It highlights the natural tension between international and local counterintelligence. The most important tension arises as the group campaigns to increase its international popular support in ways that undermine its local support or local security. In addition, local security precautions can sometimes introduce international counterintelligence vulnerabilities. Al Qa'ida members were told to disperse from camps before major attacks, which could have compromised operational security for international cells had al Qa'ida camps been penetrated or monitored at the time.

A tight command structure introduces serious disadvantages for an organization conducting global terrorist operations. In most cases, it allows terrorist leaders to exercise more control over their organization by mandating counterintelligence training and basic communications-security procedures. However, ensuring secure communications among distant group members can become a fatal weakness of a tightly controlled global group. As a group spreads out across the globe, face-to-face communications become more difficult, and communications migrate to cell phones, email, the Internet, or courier. Using couriers becomes an impractically slow form of communication as distances grow, but it remains the most secure method when face-to-face meetings are not possible. Moreover, relying on couriers can become impractical if the group's supply of trusted couriers becomes limited. By covertly undermining a terrorist group's confidence in its couriers, counterterrorism practitioners almost certainly slow the transmission of messages, materials, and funds. Just as al Qa'ida did in the 1990s, terrorist groups that wish to retain control over their global operations will most likely opt for a "centralization of decision" and "decentralization of execution" model. In this model, communication with global cells occurs in infrequent, short bursts that minimize the chance of discovery.

State sponsorship provides many intelligence and counterintelligence benefits to a terrorist group but also introduces exploitable vulnerabilities. A key vulnerability may arise when a terrorist group shares information about its leaders, personnel, facilities, training and military

capabilities with its state sponsor. Thus, an adversary that cannot infiltrate the terrorist group may gain access to such information through
penetrations of the state sponsor's security and police service, whose
members may be more susceptible to standard human intelligence-re-
cruitment techniques.

5 / THE EGYPTIAN ISLAMIC GROUP

In the early 1990s, the Egyptian Islamic Group (IG, Gamaa al-Islami-yya), enjoyed widespread popular support in Egypt. IG's attacks on the tourism industry and Egyptian security forces left the Egyptian government struggling to fight back. By the end of the decade, IG lost most of its popular support, and many of its key leaders and operatives had been killed or imprisoned. Resigned to defeat, the group agreed to a cease-fire with the Egyptian government in 1998. After enjoying such great success in the early 1990s, why did IG collapse so quickly?

The case study shows that IG collapsed because the Egyptian government made dramatic improvements in its counterterrorism capabilities, whereas IG lost critical popular support as a result of audacious and unpopular attacks on civilians and the tourism industry. The case also highlights a number of interesting dynamics between counterintelligence, popular support, and an adversary's counterterrorism capabilities.

The IG case study is broken into two parts, as summarized in table 5.1. The first part depicts IG from 1989 to 1993, when the group faced a relatively weak Egyptian security force while enjoying widespread popular support, particularly among young men with a middle or lower middle class and rural or small-town background. The second part depicts IG from 1994 until its collapse in 1998, when the group faced a much stronger Egyptian government, and its popular support slipped away. Figure 5.1 shows the places where IG controlled territory from 1989 to 1998.

Table 5.1 Egyptian Islamic Group (IG) Case Study: Key Factors

IG	Organizational Structure	Popular Support	Controlled Territory	Resources	Adversary Counterterrorism Capability
1989–1993	Loose	High	Yes	High	Low
1994–1998	Loose	Low	Yes	High	High

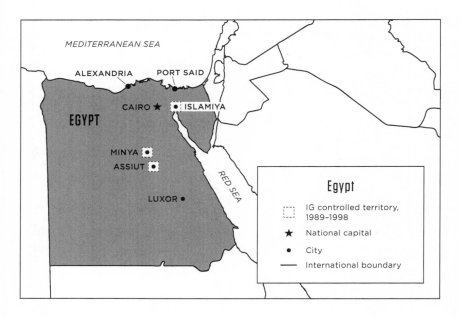

Figure 5.1 Egypt

OVERVIEW OF THE ISLAMIC GROUP

IG formed in the mid-1970s among young Islamic activists at universities across Egypt.[1] IG branches appeared first in the southern part of Egypt, known as Upper Egypt, and then in Cairo, but it played a role in spreading fundamentalist Islamic ideas in all of Egypt's universities.[2]

The group was at the helm of an Islamic resurgence, and within a few years many male students began growing their beards, and female students began wearing veils—practices that had not been witnessed for decades. IG's frustration with the Egyptian government's secular leanings slowly evolved into a more seditious mission. The group sought to overthrow the Egyptian regime and replace it with an Islamic government based on Islamic sharia law.[3]

IG did not have one supreme leader but rather organized itself in cells and followed the edicts of key Egyptian religious figures. Sheikh Omar Abdel Rahman, a professor of theology at Egypt's esteemed al Azhar University, was one such figure. To his many disciples, Rahman was known as the "Blind Sheikh"—he had been completely blind since childhood as a result of complications from diabetes. When Egyptian president Anwar al Sadat initiated efforts to dampen the influence of Islamists in Egypt in the 1970s, Rahman traveled to Saudi Arabia and other Arab countries to gather donations from patrons willing to support the Islamic resurgence.[4] Upon his return to Egypt, he was heralded as one of IG's primary leaders, and he issued a fatwa calling for Sadat's assassination. He was not convicted of conspiring to murder Sadat, however, and he eventually left Egypt to continue spreading IG's fundamentalist message.

As the years passed, IG attempted to leverage its popularity in Upper Egypt to inspire a mass movement. In 1989, the leaders of IG formed a military wing to spearhead the beginning of the group's violent rebellion in Egypt. IG's attacks against foreign tourists and Egyptian security personnel in the early 1990s caused widespread panic and resulted in a $1.5 billion loss in tourism income for the country. The government responded by capturing numerous IG members and sympathizers and passing aggressive antiterrorism legislation.[5] IG's violent turn ultimately did not inspire a popular movement but instead inflicted significant damage—IG killed more than five hundred civilians and security personnel between 1994 and 1998.[6]

IG's violence reached a tipping point in 1997, when it attacked a popular Egyptian tourist cite in Luxor that left sixty tourists dead. The Egyptian population was so repulsed by the attack and exasperated by the repeated shocks to their economically critical tourism industry that IG's demise was assured.[7] Weakened by a precipitous drop in popularity

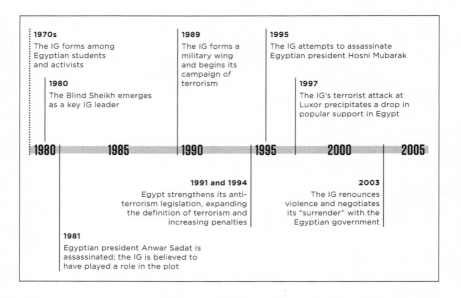

Figure 5.2 Abbreviated Timeline of Key Egyptian Islamic Group (IG) Activities and Events

and superlative Egyptian counterterrorism actions, IG renounced its violent rebellion in 2003. Figure 5.2 offers a summary of key events for the IG.

THE ISLAMIC GROUP EMERGES AND CHALLENGES THE EGYPTIAN GOVERNMENT: 1989–1993

Key Factors

Organizational Structure. IG's organizational structure in the 1989–1993 period was relatively loose and decentralized. IG's military branch was run collectively by a widely scattered network of leaders, some of whom were serving sentences in Egyptian prisons.[8] IG's cells were spread across Egypt and typically based out of local mosques. Mosques would provide a great cover for clandestine meetings or the passage of general directions from national leaders to local cells because government security forces would not be able to infiltrate every mosque in Cairo, nor could they arrest every charismatic sheikh and preacher without a major public backlash.

At the top of IG's organization was its spiritual leader or emir. Sheikh Omar Abdel Rahman, also known as "the Blind Sheikh," served as IG's spiritual and inspirational leader for a large part of its existence. He played mostly a symbolic or spiritual role rather than an organizational role in IG.[9]

Below Sheikh Rahman were the provincial emirs, who were also members of IG's consultative body, the Majlis al-Shura. Among other responsibilities, the Shura would elect IG's emir.[10] Falling under the command of each provincial emir was an emir designated for each town or village. Each of IG's small group cells within these towns and villages would also have an emir. The cell's emir would answer to a number of superiors, though command and control were poorly defined, and directions occasionally conflicted.[11] IG's large numbers of militants, preachers, and leaders created a sprawling organization,[12] which made it difficult for core IG's leaders to control group activity and decentralized decision making to the village and town level to a great extent. Members of a cell in one Upper Egypt village or Cairo slum would not know their colleagues in another village or slum.[13] IG's decentralized nature was occasionally evident in the aftermath of a terrorist attack, when some elements of IG claimed responsibility for the attack, but others denied having anything to do with it.[14]

Although IG cells had some freedom of action, they were not completely autonomous from one another. IG's top leaders issued general direction and religious rulings to its cells, which the cells obeyed for the most part because they were bound together by ideological kinship.[15] Very few IG leaders were universally known, however, probably because very few leaders had ultimate authority over the entire group or a full view of the network.[16]

Several important IG leaders operated under Sheikh Rahman.[17] Mustafa Hasan Hamza, thought to be the head military planner for IG, resided in Sudan and Afghanistan. Talaat Fouad Qassam, the spokesperson for IG, resided in Denmark. Rifai Ahmed Taha resided in Afghanistan and helped direct attacks inside Egypt. Sawfat Abdel-Ghani was convicted of ordering from his prison cell the 1992 assassination of human rights activist Farag Foda. Mohammed Abu Halima served as an assistant to Sheikh Rahman inside of Egypt. Ali Abdel Rahman Salama was head of the IG military wing in the Egyptian governates of Badari and

Assuit. Talaat Yassin Mohammed Hammam led IG members in Afghanistan and headed IG's security branch. Ahmed Salam was a senior operations officer for IG, and Ahmed Sayid was the IG leader in Upper Egypt.

IG's loose structure impacted the group both positively and negatively. On the one hand, its decentralized nature helped in recruiting members and cultivating new leaders. In addition, a decentralized
cell network would make far-reaching government infiltration of IG
extremely time consuming because most cells would need to be penetrated for the government to gain a full picture of the group's activities.
On the other hand, decentralization allowed for strong local leaders to
emerge and carry portions of the group in directions "unapproved" by
national and regional leaders,[18] which potentially would make it very
difficult for IG leaders to impose standardized, high-quality tradecraft
upon its many cells.

Popular Support. IG had high popular support in the 1989–1993 period. It dominated the Islamic activist scene on university campuses,
lead by its spiritual guide Sheikh Rahman. It had a solid following in the
towns of Upper and Middle Egypt, though it shared equal popularity
with another underground movement, Egyptian Islamic Jihad, in many
neighborhoods of Cairo, Alexandria, Islamiya, and Port Said. In contrast
to Egyptian Islamic Jihad, IG believed in displaying a public face, having a visible presence in the community, and taking responsibility for
its actions.[19] This approach undoubtedly gave IG an edge in the battle
for popular support. Its core sympathizers were young men—typically
younger than thirty—with a rural or small-town background, from the
middle or lower-middle class, and with some university education.[20] IG
also enjoyed widespread support among Egypt's rural populations and
among rural migrants in metropolitan locations.

Not surprisingly, IG flourished in areas where the Egyptian government failed to alleviate economic depression and high unemployment,
which accounted for a substantial portion of Upper Egypt.[21] IG enjoyed
a boost of support, particularly among Egyptian youth, when it initiated militant operations against the government.[22] The government's
widespread crackdown on the Islamic community in the wake of increased Islamic militancy in Egypt further strengthened IG's standing
in the community.[23] IG also mounted publicity campaigns that highlighted the government's use of corruption, lying, and torture to achieve

its goals.[24] It had some interaction with Western media organizations in Cairo, releasing statements to reporters following a militant attack or unpopular government action.[25]

Islamic groups in Egypt often responded to the community's needs more rapidly than the Egyptian government did. In the aftermath of an earthquake in 1992, such groups rushed in to provide relief, while the government moved much more slowly.[26] In the Cairo slum of Imbada, home to 1.2 million squatters without access to basic public services, IG opened mosques, schools, and medical clinics.[27] The IG leader in Imbada, Sheikh Gaber Mohamed Ali, was recognized in the community for ridding the slum of thieves and thugs. Worried that IG was beginning to gain control of Imbada, the Egyptian government conducted a week-long security sweep in which it arrested 650 suspected radicals.[28] The community of Imbada predictably became even more hostile to the government and more supportive of IG. Despite these gains, IG experienced occasional setbacks to its popularity in its slum territories. Girls and women were subject to harassment if they moved about without proper Islamic head coverings, and Christian residents were threatened and forced to pay taxes to IG.[29]

IG's popular support in the 1989–1993 period benefited the group immensely. Popular backing in the slums of Cairo provided it with small but critical pockets of controlled territory. IG took a "hands-on" approach to increasing its popularity, establishing mosques and provided public services. Its decision not to rely on media-based publicity campaigns provided it with some counterintelligence cover. Its simple message of Islamic values, coupled with the government's inept handling of Islamic resurgence in Egypt, allowed the group to maintain its popularity without exposing details of its leaders, organization, and plans.

Controlled Territory. Although the IG did not control large swathes of territory, it did control some areas and fielded a large number of militants and supporters. The government of Sudan, Egypt's southern neighbor, provided IG activists with housing, documentation, training, and safe haven.[30] This safe haven allowed IG to smuggle weapons into Egypt to supply its operatives. Sudan's intelligence service offered further support to IG operatives by providing them with information that enabled them to smuggle explosives along unguarded caravan trails across the Sudanese–Egyptian border.[31]

Other Important Factors

Resources. IG had significant resources at its disposal in this first period. These resources were reflected in its campaign to fight back against the Egyptian government. In addition to an antiforeigner and anti-Christian agenda, Egypt's tourism industry was one of the IG's most important targets. Tourism was the government's single-largest source of foreign currency—$3.3 billion annually—and IG believed it could turn the population against the government if Egypt's tourism industry were to falter.[32] Its attacks against foreign tourists and security personnel caused massive panic. Government income from tourism dropped to $1.5 billion by 1993. Attacks on policemen grew bolder across this time period, including daylight ambushes against senior police security officials and their bodyguards.[33]

IG's manpower also grew in this period. At its peak, IG's network of underground militants reached approximately 3,000 men, and its network of supporters and sympathizers was estimated to be between 10,000 and 100,000 people. By 1993, IG was thought to have a presence everywhere in Egypt, with a particularly strong presence in Cairo and the southern portion of the country.[34] Many of its members and sympathizers were poor, young, and unemployed, though not necessarily uneducated. Some of these individuals were recruited into the organization through a network of low-cost health clinics, inexpensive schools, and stores providing jobs.

Some of IG's operatives had valuable jihad experience in Afghanistan, which increased their skill in guerrilla conflict. When veterans from the Afghan jihad returned to continue their armed struggle in Egypt, the Egyptian government was taken offguard.[35]

IG's targets were diverse, ranging from Nobel Laureate Naguib Mahfouz to street police officers.[36] IG concentrated some of its attacks on areas where security forces had been rough with IG members. One of the group's most daring initial attacks was an attempted assassination of the interior minister Zaki Badr, who IG believed was responsible for the intensification of police attacks on the group's operatives.[37] Security-force fatalities increased dramatically in the early 1990s, from 14 in 1991 to 23 in 1992 to 120 in 1993.[38]

The group also aggressively targeted tourists and Westerners. Civilian fatalities also increased dramatically from 16 in 1991 to 39 in 1992 to 111 in 1993. Fatalities of IG members kept pace, with 4 in 1991, 32 in 1992, and 101 in 1993.[39]

IG probably subsisted on a modest financial income in addition to support provided by foreign state sponsors. It is alleged to have collected "Islamic" taxes in Coptic Christian neighborhoods, where inhabitants were encouraged to convert to Islam or continue paying rents.[40]

One of IG's most important resources in this period was its access to a large pool of recruits. The large number of recruits allowed IG to maintain a force of operatives that could overwhelm Egypt's security forces, numbering far beyond what the Egyptian government could monitor closely. The large number, however, made it difficult for IG to train and equip its operatives to the highest standards. The result was that the average IG member was more vulnerable to becoming a government informant—probably a price IG was willing to pay for the volume of operatives it could throw against the government. IG's decentralized structure also contributed to its large number of operatives, with local branches springing up more readily and taking on recruits without having to wait for "approval" from a central IG authority.

Adversary Counterterrorism Capability. The Egyptian government was the IG's chief adversary throughout the group's lifespan. It had battled numerous domestic opposition groups for decades, including the secretive and very capable Muslim Brotherhood.[41] Through hard-earned experience, it had developed expertise in how to address such threats. Despite this expertise, the government responded in a heavy-handed fashion to IG in the group's first period, perhaps overwhelmed by a sharp increase in violent opposition from multiple groups in the early 1990s. The IG was high on the government's list of targets because it was responsible for more than a thousand civilian and security personnel fatalities in the first half of the 1990s.[42]

The Egyptian government had very little intelligence on the group in this period because security forces most likely had not penetrated operationally active parts of the group with human assets. A great deal of the government's information came fortuitously during police investigations and from house-to-house searches and mass arrests. Frustrated by their overall lack of progress, "security forces resorted to collective punishment," which included demolishing homes, holding relatives of wanted terrorists in detention, imposing onerous curfews, and rounding up suspects en masse.[43] Some nighttime raids on suspected terrorist havens involved several hundred security-force personnel armed with heavy machine guns and rocket-propelled grenade launchers.[44] The security forces would then hold thousands of suspected militants in extended detention without charges or trial.[45]

In July 1991, Egypt passed antiterrorism legislation that mandated life imprisonment or death for those who committed terrorist offenses. Egypt would put to death ninety individuals in this period—the largest number of executions for political crimes in the country's history.[46] By mid-1993, thirty-one prisons in Egypt housed more than forty thousand convicts and political prisoners, including tens of thousands of Islamist activists with no connection to militant activities.[47] Judicial standards were "not very rigorous," so evidence against arrested individuals was frequently "thin."[48]

In March 1993, Egyptian security forces dramatically escalated their campaign against the Islamist militants. A massive wave of raids and arrests resulted in the deaths of forty-five people and the arrest of all bearded youths in numerous Islamist neighborhoods.[49] In one incident, security forces are said to have shot tear gas into a mosque in the southern Egyptian city of Aswan and then subsequently killed seven people and wounded fifteen others.[50]

Although the Egyptian government launched social welfare programs to combat its negative image, the Islamist welfare programs in Egypt were generally far superior in their quality.[51] IG welfare programs were also more strategically targeted than the government's programs, so the group did not need to compete with the government on all social programming. Thus, the government fought an uphill battle for hearts and minds.

The security forces' heavy-handed activities affected IG both positively and negatively. On the one hand, IG would benefit from an increase in popular support without having to campaign for it aggressively. The government's tactics alienated most of the Islamist population and some of the non-Islamist population as well. Thus, IG did not have to expose itself with complex media campaigns in order to cash in on increased support. On the other hand, the government's aggressive policing practices reduced the amount of territory and neighborhoods IG could control.

Intelligence and Counterintelligence Outcomes

Intelligence. The quality of IG's intelligence collection in this period is difficult to determine. By analyzing the quality of IG's attacks, it is possible to draw some limited conclusions about what intelligence would have been required to execute such operations.

IG had many successful and near-successful assassination attacks against "hard" targets, who took numerous security precautions. It killed Egypt's parliamentary speaker as well as numerous high-level security-force leaders—targets that would likely have had a cadre of well-trained security guards.[52] It also attempted but failed to assassinate several hard targets. The group made three attempts on an Egyptian minister of information, two attempts on ministers of the interior, one attempt on a minister of foreign affairs, and two attempts on President Hosni Mubarak.[53] Targets of this caliber would require a measure of relatively sophisticated surveillance methods. Each of these targets would have had armed escorts that would likely employ countersurveillance and counterattack procedures.

A few of IG's assassination targets held security positions that would have been unknown to the general public, which suggests that IG was penetrating security forces to identify these individuals. For example, on September 25, 1993, IG militants gunned down Abd al-Halim, a member of a secret task force monitoring Islamic militants, outside his house. A few days later IG assassinated a prison doctor they accused of facilitating torture inside one of the security forces' covert prisons.[54]

Counterintelligence: Basic Denial. IG's counterintelligence procedures in this period were relatively basic but sufficient to keep the group's key leaders and large operational plans secret. Its internal security group was one of its more counterintelligence-savvy branches. The security branch was led by Talaat Yassin Hammam, known as the "Ghost" to police forces due to the difficulty they had in locating and capturing him. Hammam's branch was responsible for special operations and counterespionage as well as for physical security for the group's public meetings, seminars, and demonstrations. Although Hammam's branch was mostly compartmented from IG's overt branches, his men would wear badges and provide crowd control at public meetings.[55] This practice was a significant counterintelligence oversight for Hammam because it probably afforded a watchful police service a chance to identify individuals with access to IG's most covert operatives simply by taking note of which IG members wore this special badge at public meetings.

Hammam exercised a great deal of personal security. He rarely met with anyone in IG, including his own security-branch personnel. He never appeared in public, unlike many other IG leaders. Many of his operatives maintained a high level of personal security as well. To avoid police scrutiny, they "held regular jobs, shaved their beards," and did not frequent IG mosques. The importance of maintaining a low profile was reinforced for IG operatives when the group's spokesperson was gunned down by undercover security forces in broad daylight on a Cairo street.[56]

Senior IG's operatives allegedly had instructions to commit suicide if they were caught and detained by security forces to ensure that no information would leak out during the brutal interrogation session. On one occasion, an IG operative fulfilled this command by jumping out the fifth-floor window of the police headquarters in Aswan during an interrogation.[57] Some of IG's operatives were not as well trained. After completing an attack against a German tour bus, one IG operative recruited in a hasty manner was quickly hunted down by local police forces.[58] And one of the men involved in the attack on Farag Foda was captured and gave police details about the operation.[59]

IG probably relied to some extent on tribal, kinship, and friendship ties to weed out informants and those at risk of becoming government agents.[60] When IG discovered a police informant in its ranks, the informant was killed.

IG also had a very public side to its activities, including its well-received social services. Compared to Ayman Zawahiri's clandestine Egyptian Islamic Jihad operatives, rank-and-file IG militants were probably easy for the Egyptian government to identify.[61] The sheer number of IG activists, however, made monitoring each militant impractical; in contrast, Egyptian Islamic Jihad members were probably hard to find but easy to monitor once found due to the group's relative small size.

IG's popular support helped it gain counterintelligence from the local population. Its political wing employed personnel that acted as community liaison officers. These IG members would work with the local population to facilitate communications, provide hospitality to couriers, and arrange hiding places for members on the run from the police.[62] IG political wing members would also select recruits from the local population, which almost certainly involved working with locals to weed out recruits regarding whom there might be potential counterintelligence concerns.

IG's communications with media organizations also exposed the group on a regular basis. It contacted numerous international media organizations in Cairo both by telephone and by fax to issue threats and to claim responsibility for attacks against tourists and security forces. In one instance, a key IG leader personally contacted foreign journalists to claim that his fighters had carried out a recent attack.[63] In another instance, IG operatives conducted an interview with a handful of Western and Egyptian journalists at an IG safe house used by clandestine operatives. They compounded their mistake by using their real names in the interview. Although these operatives were emboldened by the fact that they were inside their controlled territory in Imbada, this behavior reflects mediocre security tradecraft.

Overall, IG's relatively basic application of counterintelligence methods in this period reflected the fact that it was not able to impose a strict standard of counterintelligence awareness among its operatives. Although top-level operatives did employ strict security procedures, these habits did not filter down to lower levels. IG's large number of operatives, its quick recruiting cycle, and its relatively loose organizational structure provide some explanation for this deficit.

IG was able in part to compartment its public branches from its clandestine branches. Though there was some crossover between the two branches, the group seemed to keep these functions separate and therefore avoided getting large numbers of its covert militants arrested in this period. Interestingly, this strategy proved doubly effective because the government, in its frustration to locate true IG operatives among a mass of supporters and Islamic bystanders, resorted to mass arrests, which further drove the population into IG's arms.

IG successfully employed a number of basic-denial techniques, including the compartmentation of its clandestine armed wing from its political branch and the use of basic operational security procedures to keep its leaders safe. The group did not systematically employ adaptive-denial practices, although the decision that members should shave their beards and be discouraged from attending radical mosques indicates that it adapted to at least one profiling and intelligence-collection procedure used by the Egyptian government.

Summary. In the 1989–1993 period, IG had a loose organizational structure, a relatively incapable adversary, access to controlled territory, a relative abundance of popular support, and financial resources. Its pockets of controlled territory provided some guarantee that the Egyptian government would have difficulty gaining insight into its activities in these areas. Its public-support campaigns focused on social services, coupled with the Egyptian government's inept counterterrorism strategies, added an interesting wrinkle to the popular-support landscape: IG was able to gain support without having to expose itself to the general population too extensively in the media.

THE ISLAMIC GROUP LOSES ITS POPULAR-SUPPORT BASE AND COLLAPSES: 1994–1998

Key Factors

Organizational Structure. IG's organizational structure in the 1994–1998 period remained relatively decentralized. A collection of influential leaders continued roughly to direct the group's actions, though these leaders increasingly would do so from their prison cells or from overseas.

A number of crucial field commanders, both in Egypt and overseas, took these general directions from the most senior leaders and tailored their cells' operations to satisfy these strategic plans. An important overseas operative, Mustafa Hamza, trained and directed a cell of militants in Ethiopia to assassinate Egyptian president Hosni Mubarak.[64]

Hamza, along with Afghanistan-based IG leader Rifai Ahmed Taha, planned and directed a cell of militants to execute the Luxor Massacre in November 1997—a brutal attack that left more than sixty tourists dead and repulsed most Egyptians.[65] Talaat Hammam directed numerous cells in Egypt, and when security forces finally killed him, terrorist activities dropped sharply.[66]

The growing divisions in IG's leadership created a more decentralized overall organization. Ironically, the growing divisions may have also produced a collection of more centralized suborganizations. Divisions in the group developed between hardliners and moderates as well as between the internal Egyptian leaders and the external leaders. IG's many external leaders, known as the Diaspora Council, operated from Europe, Afghanistan, and North Africa and tended to support a hardline approach until they ratified the nonviolence initiative in March 1999. Key personalities on the council were Sheikh Rahman, Hamza, Mohammad Islambouli, Talaat Qassam, and Rafai Taha.[67] The divided leaders probably attempted to shape behavior more forcefully within their respective emerging divisions; whether they were successful in this endeavor is not evident from the available historical record, though.

While the hardliners continued to plan audacious attacks against Egyptian interests, the moderates realized that armed struggle would not achieve the group's goals. Sheikh Rahman—among the moderate members of the Diaspora Council—issued decrees and direction to IG members from a prison in the United States. Prominent moderate IG leader Khalid Ibrahim called for a general cease-fire in 1996, and many more IG leaders echoed the call in July 1997.[68] Many of these moderate leaders, who tended to be older than the hardliners, were languishing in Egyptian prisons when they called for the cease-fire.

The Luxor Massacre further shattered the group, driving moderates to bend even further to government demands. Rifai Taha, thought to have ordered the Luxor attack to scuttle the cease-fire movement, was forced to resign from the IG council.[69] Interestingly, when one IG source issued a claim of responsibility for the Luxor attack, it was quickly answered with a counterclaim from IG's "official" spokesperson that rogue IG members had perpetrated the attack.[70]

It is clear that the Egyptian government did not succeed in gaining a penetration of IG's leadership in Egypt or its Diaspora Council because the Luxor attack was a complete surprise to it. However, security forces were able to infiltrate a sufficient number of lower-level cells to disrupt many other plots and to capture many important leaders.

Popular Support. The precipitous decline in the Egyptian population's support for IG was perhaps the most dramatic change for the group in the 1994–1998 period. IG had calculated correctly that attacking the tourism industry would hobble the Egyptian government's economic base, but it had not accounted for the fact that doing so would also destroy the livelihoods of millions of regular Egyptians and turn them against the group. More than ten million Egyptians nationwide were directly or indirectly involved in the tourism trade and were thus negatively affected by the drop in tourism.[71] Moreover, the bulk of Egyptians did not support widespread violence against foreigners and venerated Egyptian intellectuals such as Naguib Mahfouz, so this targeting strategy almost certainly backfired on IG as well. Without the support of the population, IG had to retreat even farther into its inner strongholds in Upper Egypt. Its internal leaders, many of whom remained in prison, recognized that their defeat was inevitable and moved to endorse a cease-fire.

IG's strategic miscalculation highlighted an interesting dynamic between popular support and effective terrorist operations. IG had to find a plan of attack that struck at its enemy, the Egyptian government, without causing direct collateral damage to its base of support. The group's attacks on Egyptian security forces seemed to fulfill this objective: security forces overreacted and imposed unpopular collective punishments on the population, leaving IG only *indirectly* responsible for the collateral damage. IG's attacks on tourists led directly to the cancellation of tourists' trips to Egypt and thus to a loss of revenue. The lesson for terrorist groups is that populations will likely blame a group for causing direct collateral damage to the population but may be less likely to punish a group for indirectly inviting such collateral damage. The lesson for governments is that populations should always be reminded of the direct role the local terrorist group plays in bringing collateral damage upon that population.

Controlled Territory. The group's access to controlled territory continued in this period. IG would use Sudanese territory to train and operate unmolested by Egyptian security forces.[72] Sudanese support to IG may have been declining by 1996, but Sudan almost certainly remained a key safe haven in this period.[73] Although the Egyptian government began to push IG members from their traditional strongholds in Upper Egypt, the group would retain its core territories in Assiut and Minya.[74]

IG's support from foreign sponsors probably became increasingly important as the group was driven from its traditional strongholds within Egypt. This support also became one of IG's liabilities because its dependence on the foreign sponsors backfired once the Egyptian government began to track and eliminate those foreign connections.

Other Important Factors

Resources. IG maintained its access to resources in the 1994–1998 period. Its ability to carry out numerous terrorist operations was a testament to its access to recruits, money, and assistance from state sponsors. IG killed more than 550 civilians and security personnel between 1994 and 1998.[75] It also achieved its goal of destroying Egypt's tourism industry: five-star hotels were operating at only a 5 to 10 percent capacity; cancelled reservations totaled $1 billion; and tourism companies had to reduce employee salaries by 50 percent.[76]

IG would get some of its money from government-sponsored charities in Saudi Arabia and wealthy Saudi businessmen.[77] Other funds would come from membership dues, contributions from Egyptians living overseas, and donations from Islamic charities and foundations throughout the world.[78] According to various trial transcripts, IG was alleged to have received some of its money from Iran.[79] It would also receive logistical support from the Sudanese government. In one key instance, the Sudanese issued diplomatic passports to several IG cell members after they attempted to assassinate President Mubarak in Ethiopia.[80]

Many IG members remained well trained in this period, benefiting from years of guerrilla experience in the Afghan–Soviet War.[81] The group's access to recruits and fighters continued, even though the government had arrested and incarcerated an estimated twenty thousand militants by 1997.[82]

Adversary Counterterrorism Capability. The Egyptian government's counterterrorism capabilities increased dramatically in the 1994–1998 period. It improved its strategy in six key ways, according to terrorism expert Nachman Tal. First, the government succeeded in recruiting individuals to infiltrate IG as members and provide intelligence. Security forces began to recruit networks of informants and agents living among IG members in their communities.[83] These informants provided vital information to the security forces on many IG cells' local activities. In 1995, security forces were able to raid an IG cell safe house in Zawya al Hamra and kill seven militants as a result of an informant's tipoff.[84] Based on information received from terrorist-group penetrations, security forces were able to prevent planned terrorist operations in Cairo and the Nile Delta areas in 1995.[85] Information gleaned from interrogations of captured IG members also proved critical in the human intelligence effort.

Second, the government created a centralized database to track terrorist groups, their members, and their activities. This database contributed to the government's ability to track and kill terrorists—a total of 357 for 1994–1995 versus just 150 for 1992–1993.[86]

Third, security-force members received more extensive training, raising their level of professionalism. This better training led to more effective policing of borders, particularly along the border with Sudan, and ultimately to a reduction of weapons smuggled into Egypt.[87]

Fourth, the government targeted high-level IG members for assassination and capture and focused less attention on detaining and killing middle-level group members. Security forces were successful in this effort, killing more high-level commanders than they had in previous years.[88] The government was able to kill senior leader Talaat Yassin Hammam and his replacement, Ahmed Hassan Abdel Galil, in 1994.[89]

Fifth, the government began to study IG's international infrastructure and worked to exploit the vulnerabilities of its transnational support networks. IG's international infrastructure was not extensive, but it included cells of terrorist operatives in several European, Middle Eastern, and South Asian countries. In addition, some of its leaders and fund-raising elements were based outside of Egypt. Egypt's ability to work with foreign governments to facilitate the monitoring, arrest, and extradition of IG elements in those countries was an important component of this strategy.[90] The government worked more closely with Arab governments in the region and with Pakistan in particular to shut down IG training camps and track down IG members operating internationally.[91] Importantly, as the Egyptian government operated more effectively against IG within Egypt, IG members began to migrate increasingly to bases outside of Egypt, which rendered the government's ability to combat IG outside of Egypt progressively more important.

Sixth, the government passed emergency antiterrorism legislation that broadened the counterterrorism powers of the security forces under a more legitimate, publicly supported banner. The Egyptian Parliament ratified the three-year extension of the State of Emergency Act on April 11, 1994. In addition, the penalties for committing a terrorist act were made harsher, and the definition of terrorism was broadened to include "obstructing the work of the authorities."[92]

The Emergency Act had been effective since the assassination of President Anwar Sadat in 1981, but its extension and other antiterrorism legislation gave Egyptian security forces renewed cover for moving more aggressively against what it considered to be terrorist elements.[93] Police forces were given the authority to open fire and assassinate terrorist-group leaders in broad daylight if they felt it was warranted. Legislative changes were accompanied by government-sponsored media campaigns aimed at reducing IG's appeal by publicizing particularly shocking terrorist acts.[94]

By 1997, the Egyptian government had so battered IG that large elements of the group were ready to negotiate a cease-fire.[95] In July of that year, the Islamist lawyer Montassir al-Zayyat struck a deal between IG and the government known as the "nonviolence initiative."[96] In March 1999, IG's exiled leadership ratified the group's decision to cease IG operations.[97]

The Egyptian government made huge strides in its counterterrorism policy in this period, but it also continued many ineffective and counterproductive practices. Among these ineffective practices were the implementation of mass curfews, arrests, and searches; the mistreatment of civilians who came forward with information on terrorist activities; the consistent overcrowding of prisons; and the use of collective punishments for entire neighborhoods or families associated with militants.[98] Although the security crackdowns probably deterred some IG activities, brutal police tactics frequently backfired for the government.[99] Whether they provided a net loss or net gain for Egypt is difficult to judge.

Overall, however, the government's dramatic turnaround in counterterrorism tactics paid off remarkably well. The security forces' less-frequent use of collective punishments and a more legitimate legal platform almost certainly generated more public support for the government campaign. Even more important, the government's ability to penetrate IG cells would lead to a steady dismantling of the group. With greater and greater numbers of IG leaders dead or in prison, the group was forced to cave in to the government's demands.

Intelligence and Counterintelligence Outcomes

Intelligence. Determining IG's intelligence capabilities in this period is difficult, but it is possible to reach some conclusions about these capabilities by looking closely at the group's activities. IG monitored and assassinated several hard targets, which indicates that it had some advanced surveillance capabilities. For example, it assassinated the deputy chief of an elite police force, the Egyptian equivalent of the FBI. The murdered deputy had been using an unmarked car and had implemented counter-surveillance measures, so it is possible that IG's operations against this deputy and his three aides in previous incidents were aided by an IG penetration of the elite police force.[100] It is widely believed that the 1994 assassination of Major General Rauf Khayrat, a ranking veteran of the security services, required information accessible only to high-ranking security officers.[101] In either case, advanced surveillance and human penetrations suggest a fairly sophisticated intelligence-collection capability. IG also assassinated a number of police generals and high-ranking judges whom it blamed for the conviction of IG members.

Although IG ultimately failed to assassinate President Mubarak, it nearly succeeded during a presidential trip to Ethiopia. The assassination unit had trained for and rehearsed its attack in Khartoum, which demonstrates an additional layer of sophistication.[102] Many of these incidents suggest that IG at the very least had some insiders feeding them information about the locations of their targets. However, it is likely that most of these penetrations were somewhere fairly low in the security bureaucracy.

Counterintelligence: Limited Basic Denial. IG began to suffer from numerous counterintelligence lapses in this period, some of which stemmed from the government's increased capabilities and some of which stemmed from the group's hemorrhaging popular support. Prominent IG commander Talaat Hammam faced a number of counterintelligence failures just before he was captured by security forces. On February 16, 1994, Hammam's picture "ran on the front page of *al Akhbar* newspaper" with the offer of a reward.[103] Not only was the picture soon plastered on every coffee shop and public kiosk, but the fact that the security forces had acquired a picture of Hammam suggested a major security leak in IG. Hammam soon sent out a message over public radio canceling all IG meetings and movements for a week. The fact that he did not have any other way to transmit this message securely to the rest of his IG compatriots suggests that IG counterintelligence procedures were slipping as times became desperate.

With his group facing increasing pressure, Hammam was forced to meet "face to face with frontline operatives" rather than to send intermediaries. Police forces began to draw a progressively tighter circle around Hammam's activities until they finally cornered him in his apartment in the Cairo neighborhood of Hada'ak al Kubbah. One police official claimed that they found Hammam by monitoring militants overseas who they suspected would try to contact Hammam in Cairo. The government also alleged that they were led to Hammam by a penetration of this network.[104]

Seizing Hammam in his operations center and residence caused extensive damage to key IG networks. With documents recovered from Hammam's center, police were able to storm thirty-six other cells and arrest 120 of Hammam's confederates.[105] In addition, the police found numerous forged identification papers and passports, which probably allowed them to target for greater scrutiny those individuals with similar forged documents in circulation.

Examination of Hammam's operations center also revealed a number of the IG leader's personal counterintelligence strengths and vulnerabilities. First, Hammam lived with his wife and two children, which imposed additional counterintelligence weaknesses for him because his wife most likely was easier to track. Second, Hammam's center was located only a short distance from the headquarters of Egypt's elite police forces—an audacious move that could have gotten Hammam wrapped up even sooner. To Hammam's credit, he did not fit the profile of a typical slum-based IG member. Instead, he lived a bourgeois lifestyle and drove an expensive red Mitsubishi.[106]

Once captured, IG members most likely gave up information about the group to police interrogators. In the case of the attempted assassination of Mubarak, the terrorists arrested following the attacks identified the other militants involved.[107]

IG, however, also had several counterintelligence successes in this period. It partially stemmed the tide of police informants by monitoring and harassing suspected informants in their neighborhoods. In the Upper Egypt slum of Mallawi, it detained and killed more than forty informants in only four months in 1995.[108] Although the amount of information available to the adversary was reduced substantially by this action, the fact that IG had to fight a tide of informants may have been an indication that popular support was slipping. IG's international operations, including the assassination attempt on Mubarak, also indicated a level of sophistication. For the assassination attempt, IG established an operational infrastructure in Ethiopia that included safe houses, weapons, escape plans, communications, and forged documents.[109]

Despite the group's employment of these basic-denial techniques, declining popular support allowed police forces to develop a larger number of informants within and around the group in its areas of operations and controlled territories. IG's initiative to stage its leadership and some operations outside of Egypt is a testament to the fact that Egypt was becoming a hostile operating environment for the group. The government's augmented counterterrorism capabilities turned the conflict even more dramatically in the state's favor. Adept monitoring of militants overseas and exploitation of documents seized at crime scenes allowed the police to capitalize on IG's counterintelligence vulnerabilities.

Summary. In the 1994–1998 period, IG maintained a loose organizational structure and an abundance of resources and controlled territory. However, IG faced a much stronger adversary and a sharp reduction of popular support. Despite some continued success, IG made a critical strategic miscalculation in this period. It wagered that its attack on the tourism industry would harm the government but would not undercut its own popular appeal in Egypt. However, as the tourism industry faltered, occasionally on the heels of brutal civilian attacks, the public began to turn against IG. The goodwill that seemed to insulate IG from penetrations in the first period now faded away.

The government's dramatic increase in counterterrorism capabilities compounded IG's problems. The government was very successful at rounding up key IG leaders and operatives and keeping them in jail. As the number of key IG personnel in prison increased, the group slowly realized that it was on the brink of failure. It is difficult to judge whether the IG's counterintelligence challenges were a result of the fading popular support or the government's increased capabilities—most likely some combination of these two major changes.

KEY FACTORS REVISITED

Organizational Structure. By maintaining a loose command-and-control structure, IG had some difficulty developing superior counterintelligence training and compartmentation. IG's loose organizational structure in the 1989–1993 period prevented the group from imposing rigorous tradecraft upon its group members. The lack of counterintelligence standards occasionally backfired for IG because men who were captured by the police quickly gave up important operational details. IG became more fragmented in the 1994–1998 period, though each of the fragments may have become relatively tighter than the previous whole.

IG's loose structure also allowed for the emergence of strong local leaders, which militated against the creation of an IG-wide, standardized tradecraft and prevented the Egyptian government from exploiting groupwide plans and procedures. It meant that the government would have had to penetrate a large percentage of IG cells to understand and predict IG's behavior and upcoming plots.

Popular Support. There is evidence that the local population provided counterintelligence assistance to IG when the group enjoyed high levels of popular support. Support appears to have included identifying and vetting potential recruits, helping to secure courier-based communications, and providing hiding places for IG members on the run from the police. IG was very concerned about popular support, and, in contrast to groups such as Egyptian Islamic Jihad, it worked hard to cultivate a public-outreach program. It routinely reached out to local and international media outlets, telephoning and faxing media offices and granting interviews with journalists. All of this behavior risked exposing sensitive details about IG personnel and resources to the Egyptian government. In one instance, as noted, IG held an interview in an operational safe house—a dangerous move if undercover operatives ever wanted to use the safe house again. However, IG was able to gain popular support in ways that provided much less exposure to the media. First, it relied on providing social services through local mosques, health clinics, and schools, which directly increased popular support while giving up few important details about the group's membership and resources. Of course, the leadership of the mosques, health clinics, and schools would have had some connection to more central IG figures and thus would have been priority recruitment targets for the Egyptian government. IG also relied on the Egyptian government's heavy-handed missteps to gain additional support—a windfall the group forfeited when it began to attack civilians and the tourism industry more brutally.

Controlled Territory. IG's overall security clearly benefited from controlling territory. Egyptian security forces could not adequately police these areas and had to rely on mass sweeps and raids when venturing into them. Raids on this scale may have been easy to predict and may have given key leaders and operatives a chance to hide or escape police roundups.

IG's controlled territories, however, gave security forces an area to target, and mass arrests almost certainly netted some operatives and IG sympathizers. Egyptian forces would have captured militants who would give up some useful information in the course of an interrogation, but it is difficult to assess on balance whether such mass arrests served as a net gain or net loss for the Egyptian government.

ADDITIONAL LESSONS FROM THE ISLAMIC GROUP CASE

The IG case study provides additional insights into terrorist counterintelligence. It demonstrates the tension that arises between maintaining controlled territory and gaining popular support. In general, controlling territory leads to increased popular support when the group provides public goods to the population but demands relatively little in return. When the group can offer social services to the population while doing very little "social policing"—that is, punishing people for not adhering to the group's religious or social agenda—the population will most likely be supportive. This support can be further strengthened when frustrated government forces make heavy-handed incursions into controlled territory, further alienating the population to the government's cause. IG's ultimate failure to terrorize the Egyptian government without terrorizing its own population highlights the difficulty such groups face in pursuing a terrorist mission on home soil. Terrorist groups that conduct operations in territories that are separate from those they control and from which they derive popular support may avoid this predicament. Al Qa'ida, for example, largely avoided this problem in the 1990s by conducting terrorist operations in areas far removed from its core territories in Afghanistan. The trade-off, however, is that the terrorist group's adversary may be more willing to conduct military strikes against the group's controlled territory if it falls outside of the adversary's national jurisdiction.

The case highlights the challenges and trade-offs governments face when battling a group with controlled territory. On the one hand, government incursions into controlled territory have the potential to backfire dramatically if the government's counterterrorism nets snare numerous innocent bystanders—a likely outcome in territory with which security forces are unfamiliar. On the other hand, groups that control territory for long periods are likely to harbor numerous high-value terrorist targets and may have relaxed security practices because the territory is perceived as relatively impenetrable. Governments need to weigh these trade-offs carefully for each territory and its likely intelligence yield when planning mass arrests and raids.

The IG case highlights an interesting facet of the relationship between popular support and the adversary's counterterrorism capabilities. As the Egyptian government became more capable of protecting its forces against IG attacks, IG operatives were forced to attack less-protected and less-popular targets—civilians, Coptic Christians, and tourists. Thus, the government's success in hardening its security forces and installations became an indirect source of the IG's reduction in popular support.

Most terrorist groups do not last more than a few years.[1] Many collapse because of counterintelligence failures. This chapter chronicles the counterintelligence lapses of five groups that failed. The case studies illustrate the role of counterintelligence in dooming many embryonic terrorist groups. The Fort Dix Group, the Toledo Group, the Bronx Group, the Cambodian Freedom Fighters, and the Toronto 18 are considered homegrown terrorist groups because they had no connections to foreign terrorist organizations. Several of the groups were inspired by the post-9/11 jihadist movement to initiate terrorist operations, but each grew from likeminded, local contacts to form a new terrorist group.

The five groups are very different from the groups detailed in the earlier case studies, as noted in table 6.1: they were very small, lacked controlled territory, and at every stage were hounded by highly capable Western intelligence and law enforcement services.[2] Despite these differences, the five cases reinforce the key findings from the earlier case studies and in particular highlight how a terrorist group operating outside of controlled territory against a strong adversary faces uniquely challenging counterintelligence problems.

THE FORT DIX GROUP: 2005–2007

Sometime in 2005, six men in New Jersey formed a terrorist group with the objective of killing American soldiers stationed at military bases in the United States. The six foreign-born men—Mohammad Shnewer, Serdar Tatar, Dritan Duka, Eljvir Duka, Shain Duka, and Agron

Table 6.1 Embryonic Groups Case Studies: Key Factors

	Organizational Structure	Popular Support	Controlled Territory	Resources	Adversary Counterterrorism Capability
Fort Dix Group	Tight	Low/ None	No	Low	High
Toledo Group	Tight	Low/ None	No	Low	High
Bronx Group	Tight	Low/ None	No	Low	High
Cambodian Freedom Fighters (CFF)	Loose	Low	No	Medium	Medium
Toronto 18	Loose	Low/ None	No	Low	High

Abdullahu—were in their twenties and had spent their childhood years together in Cherry Hill, New Jersey. Shnewer, the leader, conducted surveillance of several US military installations in 2006 and picked Fort Dix, New Jersey, as the group's principle target. The group engaged in weapons and tactical terrorist training in New Jersey and Pennsylvania and aimed to kill at least a hundred American soldiers with light weapons and rocket-propelled grenades. By the time the group conducted its surveillance runs and training, however, it was already under close observation by the FBI, which had begun monitoring the group with human assets and technical devices after receiving a tipoff in January 2006 that the men were engaged in terrorist training. The tipoff came from a Circuit City store clerk in Mount Laurel, New Jersey, who called the police when he viewed a terrorist-training videotape that one of the

Fort Dix members had submitted to the store to be copied onto a DVD. The FBI arrested all six men in May 2007 before they committed any terrorist acts.

Key Factors

Mohammad Shnewer maintained a relatively tight command over the Fort Dix Group. This control was made easy by the fact that the group was small and met regularly to discuss training and proposed operations. Shnewer led group members in firearms training and surveillance exercises and encouraged group members to view and study terrorist-training videos. He directed group members to engage in a variety of operational activities, such as acquiring maps of targeted facilities, and was the most forward leaning with regard to committing a terrorist act.[3]

The Fort Dix Group did not try to establish any popular support but did show a desire to document its activities. Group members recorded themselves firing automatic weapons at a shooting range and ordered DVD copies of the video at the Circuit City store.[4] The group may have intended to use the video to attract recruits or foreign funding, but it is unknown if the group posted the video online or sent it to potential donors.

The group clearly did not control territory: it operated in territory highly controlled by US law enforcement and where the population was sensitized to possible terrorist attacks. The FBI quickly became aware of the Fort Dix Group's intentions when a local resident observed suspicious behavior and informed the police.

Following the tipoff, the FBI was easily able to swarm the group with human, technical, and investigative resources. The FBI showed a copy of the DVD to an individual familiar with the Muslim community in the New Jersey area, who helped identify several of the Fort Dix Group members. US Immigration and Customs Enforcement (ICE) checks showed that the brothers Dritan, Eljvir, and Shain Duka were illegally residing in the United States. In addition to providing the FBI and ICE with an arrestable offense, this illegal status prevented these group members from training at gun ranges or acquiring firearms legally,[5] which forced the group to increase its operational footprint to find illegal ways of acquiring weapons and weapons training.

Other Important Factors

The group's resources in term of recruits and weapons were minimal but sufficient to achieve its operational goals. The group amassed an arsenal of handguns, shotguns, and semiautomatic assault weapons, and in 2007 it ordered four AK-47 Kalashnikov fully automatic machine guns.[6] All group members had full-time jobs, allowing them to support themselves and contribute spare funds to group expenses.

The FBI's counterterrorism capabilities were extensive and impressive throughout the group's lifespan. The FBI conducted a fifteen-month investigation based heavily on human penetrations of the Fort Dix Group as well as on audio and video surveillance of the group's training, surveillance, and plotting.[7]

The FBI's key human penetration, Mahmoud Omar, was an Egyptian-born used-car salesman who had entered the US illegally in early 1990s. Omar came to the FBI's attention after he was arrested and faced deportation for bank fraud in 2004.[8] The FBI offered to help Omar on the condition that he assist the FBI in various investigations of radical Muslims in the United States. Omar took the offer and had helped in at least one investigation prior to the Fort Dix case. In 2006, the FBI recognized that Omar would make an ideal penetration of the Fort Dix Group after learning that he knew Mohammad Shnewer personally from visits to the Shnewer family's southern New Jersey grocery store. Omar had previously encountered Shnewer on several occasions and had heard him talk about how he hated Americans. With this prior contact, Omar's approach to Shnewer in March 2006 was normal enough not to set off any alarms and gave the FBI an enormous security advantage from the beginning of the case. Omar made himself more appealing to Shnewer by telling him that he had once served in the Egyptian military—a professional background Shnewer felt was missing from his small band of terrorists, which the FBI may have known and deftly exploited. By the end of the investigation, the FBI had recorded more than one hundred hours of Omar's conversations with the Fort Dix members.[9]

The FBI cultivated a second human penetration of the group, Besnik Bakalli, to gain access to the three Albanian members of the group—Dritan, Eljvir, and Shain Duka. The FBI instructed Bakalli, who was fluent in Albanian, to enter a coffee shop where the three Fort Dix members would meet after mosque and speak Albanian into his cell phone within earshot of them.[10] The men, eager to befriend an Albanian, invited Bakalli for coffee. The men took Bakalli fishing soon thereafter and trusted him enough to show him a jihadist video, which led to his recruitment into the terrorist group.

The FBI's control of the territory that the Fort Dix Group operated in allowed it to place their agents in contact with the group. Physical control also allowed the FBI to use technical surveillance to monitor the group and thus corroborate the information it was getting from Omar and Bakalli.[11] With this advantage, the FBI could test its human sources to verify their access to the group and the accuracy of their reporting or to challenge those sources if they attempted to report false information. The FBI was thus able to maintain a level of control over their human sources that would have been very difficult without multiple human and technical information-collection platforms.

Intelligence and Counterintelligence Outcomes

The Fort Dix group's intelligence-collection capabilities were very basic. The group conducted vehicular surveillance of the US Army bases at Fort Dix and Fort Manmouth in New Jersey; the US Air Force base in Dover, Delaware; and the US Coast Guard Building in Philadelphia. The surveillance provided the group with basic information about the facilities' perimeters and possible attack routes. Shnewer chose to attack Fort Dix because Serdar Tatar had entered the base on numerous occasions to deliver pizzas from his family's pizzeria and could acquire maps of the base. Tatar's knowledge of the base entry points and basic security procedures augmented the surveillance and may have offered the group a tactical advantage during an attack.[12]

The Fort Dix group's counterintelligence practices were unsophisticated and ad hoc and were limited to basic-denial tactics. The group's tight organizational structure allowed group leaders to provide some counterintelligence training to other members. On one occasion, Dritan Duka instructed another group member to used coded language when discussing the acquisition of AK-47s over the telephone.[13] Dritan also reminded group members that he believed US authorities were closely monitoring mosques, so group members needed to be careful about what they said.[14] Eljvir Duka and Mahmoud Omar discussed the need to use coded language when talking about weapons training in Pennsylvania.

Other group behaviors reflected its basic security training and counterintelligence awareness. Shnewer instructed members to avoid taking pictures during surveillance runs because he thought doing so would alert base security personnel. Dritan recognized the risk of revealing the members' identities and argued that they should not meet face to face with an unknown arms dealer. The group also considered the trustworthiness of Omar, the FBI penetration of their group, and at times sensed the risk that he posed. In November 2007, Tatar directly questioned Omar about whether he was an FBI agent. Tatar was only partially satisfied with Omar's response, and a few weeks later he cautioned Shnewer not to place too much trust in Omar. Shnewer, however, did not embrace Tatar's suspicion.[15]

The group unevenly applied its informal security practices and did not punish security violations. Shnewer committed an obvious violation of basic communications security when over the telephone he asked Omar to accompany him on a surveillance run at Dover Air Force Base.[16] It is also likely that the group did not conduct any counterinterrogation training. When Agron Abdullahu was arrested, he immediately waived his Miranda rights and agreed to be interviewed by FBI investigators.[17] Abdullahu eventually told FBI agents of the Fort Dix group's desire to attack US military targets. Had he known not to waive his Miranda rights, he may have been able to keep this crucial information from the FBI.

The group's poor vetting procedures and willingness to trust outsiders created additional vulnerabilities. Both FBI penetrations received minimal security vetting before they were brought into the group. Omar was trusted because Shnewer knew him as a friend from his family's grocery store and because Omar had related skills from his time in the Egyptian military.[18] Bakalli was trusted because he spoke Albanian and was apparently sympathetic to the jihadist message the three Albanians advocated in his company.[19] The group applied rudimentary vetting procedures to contacts outside the core group. Dritan queried Omar about whether Omar's arms dealer contact was trustworthy and religious and presumably was satisfied when Omar confirmed that the contact was Muslim.[20]

The Fort Dix Group would have been smart to vet its core members, such as Serdar Tatar, more carefully. Tatar appears to have developed second thoughts about his membership in the terrorist group after confronting Omar about working for the FBI. In November 2007, Tatar called a sergeant with the Philadelphia Police Department and reported that he had been approached by an individual who had pressured him to acquire maps of Fort Dix.[21] Several weeks later the FBI visited Tatar and asked him about his report. Tatar changed his story and denied having any connections to a plot targeting the base or knowing of any individuals who were engaged in plotting an attack.[22] The Fort Dix group's key security-vetting advantage—the fact that five of the group's core members had grown up together and three were brothers—ended up becoming a weakness because the group became dependent on outsiders for key skills and guidance.

The group's most devastating counterintelligence weakness was its lack of controlled territory. The FBI's extraordinary control of the environment allowed it to recruit sources that would be most appealing to the group and then to place these sources in front of the group in ways that would appear natural and unalerting. The FBI knew that the Albanian speaker, Bakalli, would get the attention of the three Albanian brothers and assessed correctly that they would initiate a relationship with him after overhearing him speak Albanian in a cell phone conversation. The FBI's access to ICE data allowed it to identify the three Albanian brothers as illegal residents and possible investigative leads. The FBI had such pervasive control of the territory that group members accidentally approached an undercover FBI agent while they were training at a shooting range in February 2007 to ask where they could purchase AK-47s and M-16s.[23] If the group had not already convinced the FBI of their commitment to a terrorist attack, their approach to the undercover officer provided ample evidence.

The group's small size offered the FBI an additional counterintelligence advantage. In relatively small groups, leaders can withhold only a few details of the timing and location of an attack from group members because almost all members will be required for critical tasks. Not surprisingly, both FBI penetrations in this case had access to vital details of the group's planning and weapons-acquisition strategies.

Interestingly, the Fort Dix Group seemed to be aware of its security weaknesses and yet continued on with its terror plot. When Dritan first attempted to acquire AK-47s for the group, he explained that he did not follow through with the transaction because he believed the FBI was setting him up. He later told group members: "I'm telling you, I almost bought a [sic] AK-47 from an agent." During a conversation with FBI informant Omar, Tatar commented: "I don't know you very much. . . . I don't know whether you're FBI. . . . Whether you are or [are] not [FBI] I'm gonna do it. It doesn't matter to me whether I get locked up, arrested, or get taken away, it doesn't matter. . . . I'm doing it in the name of Allah."[24] The group's continued plotting despite indications that the FBI had the group under surveillance suggests that the group members overestimated their planning capabilities or underestimated the FBI or both.

The group sporadically employed basic-denial techniques, such as the occasional use of coded language and vetting hurdles, but it showed little if any adaptive-denial techniques. The group knew very little about how the FBI was monitoring its members; as a result, it was unable to adapt to or counter FBI intelligence-collection methods, and it failed as a result.

THE TOLEDO GROUP: 2004–2006

In 2004, five men in Toledo, Ohio, formed a terrorist group with the objective of killing US soldiers overseas. The men—Mohammad Zaki Amawi, Marwan Othman El-Hindi, Wassim Mazloum, Zubair Ahmed, and Khaleel Ahmed—were similar to the Fort Dix Group insofar as they led apparently normal lives. Amawi was a dual US–Jordanian citizen and a travel agent; El-Hindi was a US citizen with several children; Mazloum was a legal permanent resident and operated a car dealership with his brother; and cousins Zubair and Khaleel Ahmed were US citizens from Chicago. Amawi, one of the leaders of the group, was born in Washington, DC, and became radicalized after an extended trip to

Jordan at age twenty-four. He told investigators later that he had attempted to enter Iraq from Jordan in 2004 to fight US soldiers before his family discouraged him from doing so.[25] When he returned to the United States at this time, he and his co-conspirators plotted to kill US forces in Iraq by first recruiting additional members and then conducting weapons, hand-to-hand combat, and explosives training in the United States before trying to enter Iraq.[26] The FBI, however, quickly had the group under close observation and by February 2006 had amassed enough evidence to convict each of the members on terrorism-related charges.

Key Factors

The Toledo Group was relatively tightly commanded, with Amawi and El-Hindi at its helm. El-Hindi sought to enhance the group's training by introducing group members to a former special-forces soldier who offered jihadist training.[27] He also organized training sessions for group members that he hoped would also increase their security and religious discipline. Amawi established a training regiment for group members and recruited Mazloum specifically to increase the size of their training sessions.[28]

The Toledo Group did not try to establish local or international popular support but sought to research and solicit funding sources for their training and operating costs.[29] Because the group was small and operating in the United States, it would have been impractical and highly counterproductive to initiate a campaign to generate local support. The group's efforts to gain private donations from sympathizers were likely unsuccessful.

No small jihadist group will be able to control territory in the United States. Like the Fort Dix group, the aspiring terrorists in Toledo operated in territory that was highly controlled by US law enforcement agencies, especially once the FBI had probable cause to monitor them. The FBI was aware of the group's activities and planning from inception largely because it was able to monitor the group extensively with technical information-collection devices and an informant. The group was mostly unable to detect these intelligence-collection platforms and was therefore highly vulnerable to penetration and manipulation. In November 2004, El-Hindi considered sending several members to the Middle East for terrorist training—he indicated that he was in contact with individuals there who were building a terrorist-training facility.[30] Had this training occurred, it would have been the group's only attempt to operate outside of territory that was controlled by a highly capable adversary.

Other Important Factors

The group's resources were extremely modest and may not have been adequate to achieve its operational goals of sending its members to Iraq to kill US soldiers. The group's members had regular jobs, which provided them with sufficient income to fund basic training and would have allowed for transportation to Iraq had the FBI not interrupted the group's plot.

The FBI's counterterrorism capabilities simply overwhelmed the amateur group. The FBI monitored the group with human penetrations and by technical means in an investigation that lasted approximately two years. The FBI's most important investigative asset was its human penetration of the group, Darren Griffin. Griffin was a former US special-forces soldier who was recruited by the FBI to pose as an extremist within the Muslim community in Toledo.[31] He had previously worked for the US Drug Enforcement Administration, spoke Farsi and rudimentary Arabic, and owned a private-security business called Direct Action Security.[32] After signing up with the FBI, he had spent months posing as an Islamic extremist and even convinced his family that he had become radicalized. He then joined a radical mosque, where he met El-Hindi and Amawi.[33] Griffin posed as a security specialist with an expertise in jihadist-style training, which the FBI knew would get the attention of radical Islamists looking to enhance their terrorist skills. In June 2004, El-Hindi introduced Griffin to Zubair and Khaleel and requested that Griffin provide them with training.[34] El-Hindi encouraged Griffin to share intelligence information that he had about US strategic plans in Iraq from his time in the US military.[35] The FBI's ability to place an extremist "dangle" inside a Muslim community harboring potential terrorists offered it a large advantage. Instead of waiting for terror groups to fully materialize, it could watch them mature and determine if they were going to be a threat. By gaining an early human penetration of a potential terror group, the FBI could more easily manipulate and direct the group down paths that made it easier both to monitor the group and to gather evidence against it.

Intelligence and Counterintelligence Outcomes

The Toledo Group's intelligence-collection mechanisms were very basic. It did not collect intelligence about specific targets, but it did collect information on the Internet about how to assemble and detonate improvised explosive devices and suicide vests. Its counterintelligence methods were similarly rudimentary. Despite the fact that the group was relatively tightly commanded, its members were unable to acquire sufficient security training because they did not have access to trainers or training materials. The group's leaders made an effort to acquire a trainer, from whom they requested counterintelligence and countersurveillance guidance, but the individual they selected was in fact an FBI recruit, Griffin, who was careful to provide only basic training.[36] They were forced to rely on Internet-based training to make up for this deficit, which came with a host of counterintelligence challenges. El-Hindi helped one group member register for access to a jihadist Web site on his computer, which included a training module on weapons and terrorist tactics. Although El-Hindi wisely cautioned that only a few group members should register at the site to reduce their operational footprint, the fact that they registered at all on such a Web site introduced security vulnerabilities. In fact, El-Hindi and Amawi in February 2005 discussed the US government's ability to monitor their Internet activity if they entered jihadist Web sites. Group leaders also were forced to coach members on operational security in the course of sensitive communications exchanges. In 2005, Amawi admonished a group contact for being too open during his communications while the two were trying to discuss the acquisition of chemical explosives.[37]

At times, the group successfully employed coded language to mask their plotting. Zubair and Khaleel Ahmed agreed to substitute *third* as a code word for "violent jihad," which they routinely used in their correspondence. Group members occasionally spoke in Arabic or Urdu in phone conversations to evade and complicate surveillance. Zubair discussed with another group member his concerns that the US government might be monitoring their phones and suggested using phones listed in other persons' names to counter potential surveillance.[38] Some group members talked about communicating by encrypted emails, but it is not clear if they acted on this plan.

The group's security-vetting procedures were limited and lacked sophistication. Although several of the group members had known each other for many years, others were mere acquaintances and were not well vetted. The vetting of group member Wassim Mazloum consisted only of his viewing videos of violent terrorist acts in Iraq and stating that he was committed to training and the employment of these tactics in Iraq. Mazloum then invited his younger brother, Bilal, to participate in at least one terrorist-training event even though he had doubts about Bilal's trustworthiness.[39]

Despite the group's lack of interest in any form of popular support, the group's leaders nonetheless endangered the group by trying to relate their personal stories and opinions to sympathetic audiences. El-Hindi posted numerous messages to a radical Islamic Web site known as "Ekhlass," where, in response to a video depicting an attack on US soldiers in Iraq, he stated his desire to kill Americans.[40] El-Hindi was a regular, registered user of the extremist Web site and was clearly undeterred by his belief that his postings could be monitored by US law enforcement agencies. In April 2005, Amawi discussed with Griffin the possibility of videotaping the group's outdoor training exercises, possibly to post the videos on the Internet or to gain foreign sympathizers.[41] The group did not in the end videotape themselves, but Amawi's impulse to do so shows the powerful pull many terrorist groups feel to document their stories for outsiders.

The group's greatest counterintelligence disadvantage was, again, the lack of controlled territory. From the group's inception, the FBI was closely observing its activities. The group could have leveraged the benefit of operating in uncontrolled territory by blending into Toledo's thriving Muslim community, but they lacked the training necessary to conduct their terrorist plotting and reached out through their Toledo mosque to find a trainer, who turned out to be an FBI informant. Once the FBI had the group on its radar screen, monitoring them with human assets and technical devices was not challenging. Griffin conducted audio surveillance of the men for about two years while they talked about training in explosives, guns, and sniper tactics in their homes and at a storefront mosque where they prayed together.[42] The group was forced to rely on practically unvetted contacts through Internet-based connections because they could not afford to travel out of the country to meet these contacts routinely, nor could their contacts easily travel to Ohio for meetings. Amawi developed an unvetted Syrian Internet contact with whom he discussed acquiring chemical explosives.[43] Operating in uncontrolled territory meant that the group's communications were highly vulnerable to monitoring and disruption and, furthermore, that the group would be unlikely to detect whether and how these communications were being tracked.

The group occasionally recognized the vulnerability of operating in uncontrolled territory and discussed using their businesses as cover for traveling in and out of Iraq and the Fourth of July holiday to mask their training on explosives.[44] Amawi told his boss at his travel agency that the US government was monitoring him and showed the boss a camera positioned on a utility pole outside of the store.[45] Like the Fort Dix Group, the Toledo Group leaders believed that they were being monitored, yet they nevertheless remained committed to their plotting. The Toledo Group occasionally employed basic-denial techniques but failed to develop adequate communications and operational security. It had very few opportunities to adapt to a far superior adversary with extensive control of the territory and a high-level penetration of the group, which gave that adversary nearly complete insight into the group leaders' plans and capabilities.

THE BRONX GROUP: 2008–2009

From June 2008 to May 2009, four men in New York conspired to use a surface-to-air guided-missile system to destroy military aircraft at an US Air National Guard base and improvised explosive devices to attack synagogues in the Bronx. The four men—James Cromitie, David Williams, Onta Williams, and Laguerre Payen—had extensive criminal records and had developed radical Islamic sympathies while serving time in prison together. Before the group began to work out the details of its terrorist plot, however, the FBI had penetrated it with an individual posing as an extremist financier. The informant allowed the FBI to eavesdrop on the group's discussions about the timing of its operation and its plans to acquire weapons. The informant helped the FBI to set up a complex sting operation, which began when the informant took the group to a storage facility in Newburgh, New York, to show them what they believed were several improvised explosive devices and a surface-to-air guided-missile system.[46] The FBI arrested the men in May 2009 as they prepared to detonate the mock improvised explosive devices in front of a synagogue in the Bronx.

Key Factors

The Bronx Group, led by Cromitie, was relatively tightly commanded. Cromitie did not lead the group in extensive training, but group members deferred to him for decision making about terrorist plotting. Because of the group's small size, it was probably relatively easy for Cromitie to maintain control over its weapons acquisition and attack plans. The Bronx Group, like other terrorist groups operating in the United States, did not try to establish any support within the regular population. It also did not videotape any aspects of its training or preparation for the attacks, nor did its members try to reach out to potential sympathizers on the Internet to tell their story. It did not control territory but rather operated in territory that was highly controlled by US law enforcement agencies. Between October 2008 and May 2009, the FBI and its Joint Terrorism Task Force, which consisted of agents from ICE and the Internal Revenue Service, US marshals, and New York City Police Department officers, monitored the group extensively through concealed audio and video devices.[47]

Other Important Factors

The Bronx Group's resources were very modest and likely would not have been sufficient to achieve its operational goals. Its financial resources were provided by the FBI through the informant. The infusion of cash allowed the group to purchase improvised explosive devices and a surface-to-air guided-missile system, all of which were nonfunctional as part of the FBI sting operation. Without this financial support, the group would not have progressed as far as it did, though it may have been successful with a less ambitious plan.

The FBI's counterterrorism capabilities were extensive throughout the group's lifespan, and its resources were bolstered by the multiagency Joint Terrorism Task Force. Its investigation was aided by multiple clandestine collection assets, the most important of which was a human penetration of the group. Its control of the local territory was enhanced by cooperation with the New York Police Department, which maintained a strong intelligence and counterterrorism capability of its own.

The informant, Shahed Hussein, had worked with the FBI for six years prior to the Bronx Group case, which allowed the FBI to vet Hussein comprehensively and to trust him to monitor the group reliably.[48] Hussein, a fifty-two-year-old Pakistani, came to the FBI's attention in 2002 when he pleaded guilty to taking part in a fraud scheme while working as a translator for the New York Department of Motor Vehicles and was sentenced to five years probation.[49] The FBI had used Hussein in 2004 to set up a sting operation against a Pakistani pizzeria owner and an Iraqi Kurd who offered to provide material support to a terrorist operation in the United States.[50] Hussein testified that the FBI sent him to Pakistan in 2008 to attend a terrorist-training camp, possibly to report on individuals attending the camp and to enhance his bona fides in jihadist circles.[51]

After returning to the United States, Hussein began targeting the Masjid al-Iklas, a mosque in Newburgh, New York, to ferret out extremists among the congregation. Although most mosque members avoided Hussein, Cromitie befriended him and over meals with him began to talk about his own jihadist aspirations.[52] Hussein's access to the group offered the FBI critical insights into the timing and methods of the group's planned terrorist attack. Before the sting operation, the FBI notified the targeted Bronx synagogue of the terrorist plot, which allowed the synagogue's leaders the opportunity to recommend that their congregation stay away from the synagogue the evening of the attack.[53] The FBI's extensive control of the territory allowed it to foil the terrorist plot and simultaneously reduce the likelihood that innocent bystanders would be injured in the operation. It engineered the sting to acquire the extensive evidence needed to convict the plotters on terrorism charges. As with other homegrown terrorist cases, it artfully balanced the need to prevent terrorist attacks with the need to collect enough information on the group to convict its members.

Intelligence and Counterintelligence Outcomes

The Bronx Group's intelligence-collection capabilities were very basic and unsophisticated. The group probably relied mostly on open-source information to select its targets and prepare for its operation. The group also conducted clandestine surveillance of synagogues and Jewish community centers in the Bronx.[54]

The Bronx Group's counterintelligence practices were severely lacking and provided the FBI with a significant intelligence-collection advantage. The group's vetting of operational contacts and the FBI informant was nearly nonexistent. Even during Cromitie's first meetings with Hussein, he expressed his interest in conducting jihad in the United States. Before long, Hussein was privy to the group's most closely held plans and was even brought along during a surveillance run of the Air National Guard base. The group also failed to vet the individuals from whom it was purchasing weapons. Williams arranged a weapons deal with an unknown and unvetted female gun supplier in Newburgh, New York, in April 2009. The group also trusted Hussein's "arms dealer" to obtain securely a surface-to-air guided-missile system—a transaction that could easily come to the attention of local law enforcement agencies.[55]

The Bronx Group occasionally employed basic communications security. Its members agreed to use code words when discussing various weapons and targets—for example, referring to synagogues as "joints" and airplanes as "spiral birds." The group also discussed the need to purchase new cell phones to communicate with one another during the operation, presumably to hedge against the possibility that their personal phones were already being monitored by law enforcement.[56]

The group also implemented several operational security measures before and during the terrorist operation. Cromitie stated that he would not wear traditional Muslim clothing during his surveillance of the synagogues in order to avoid raising suspicion among bystanders. During the group's drive to Connecticut to acquire its surface-to-air guided-missile system, one of its members noted that they were being followed by law enforcement, which prompted them to conduct a rudimentary surveillance-detection route around Newburgh, New York, to determine if the surveillance remained behind them.[57] During the terrorist operation, group members posted themselves around the vicinity of the synagogue to serve as lookouts for law enforcement.[58] Although this tactic may have offered the group an opportunity to terminate or modify the operation at the last minute, it would also have blown the operation if just one member had been subject to FBI monitoring.

The Bronx Group sporadically employed basic-denial techniques but mostly left its personnel and plans exposed. The group's lack of controlled territory played a large role in its inability to hide itself from the FBI and prevent a highly successful FBI sting operation.

THE CAMBODIAN FREEDOM FIGHTERS: 1998–2001

From 1998 to 2001, a group of several hundred men in Cambodia and California calling themselves the Cambodian Freedom Fighters (CFF) conspired to overthrow the Cambodian government. Like the Fort Dix, Toledo, and Bronx groups, the CFF had numerous counterintelligence problems, stemming in part from its inability to operate in territory it controlled. Unlike the other homegrown terrorist groups discussed in this chapter, the CFF's counterintelligence challenges were heightened by extensive and ill-advised media outreach. The CFF's leader and chief spokesman, Chhun Yasith, was based in California and commanded CFF soldiers living on the border of Cambodia and Thailand.[59] A naturalized US citizen who ran a successful accounting office in Long Beach, California, Yasith openly publicized the group's plans and took credit for its attacks in Cambodia. In February 1999, he ordered a grenade attack on a karaoke bar in Cambodia, which injured several bar patrons.[60] In June 2000, he ordered his fighters, most of whom were stationed near the Cambodian–Thai border, to initiate small attacks against bars, nightclubs, and other soft targets in the Cambodian capital of Phnom

Penh. In November 2000, when a group of seventy CFF fighters attacked government buildings in Phnom Penh with assault rifles, rocket-propelled grenades, and grenades, the Cambodian military quickly defeated the CFF forces, killing eight of them.[61] Yasith proudly recounted these attacks on the CFF Web site, where he also reported that the CFF was officially registered as a political organization by the State of California.[62] The Cambodian Criminal Court convicted Yasith in absentia, along with two co-conspirators, on terrorism charges in June 2001 and issued an Interpol warrant for his arrest. Yasith was arrested by US authorities in June 2005 and was found guilty of various terrorism-related charges in 2008.

Key Factors

The CFF was a relatively loosely commanded organization. The group's founding in 1998 included a verbal pact between Yasith and approximately sixty CFF commanders and rank-and-file members to overthrow the government of Samdech Hun Sen. Yasith was made president of the group and agreed to raise funds for the group while those remaining in Cambodia were tasked with acquiring weapons. Several months later Yasith recruited one of the group's key leaders, Richard Kiri Kim, when the two met in Oregon.[63] Yasith occasionally instructed the group to engage in various acts of violence, but he acted mostly as an inspirational leader and financier. After the failed coup attempt in November 2000, he boasted to a journalist that CFF would continue with additional plotting and would "attack the whole country" on the next attempt.[64] Yasith and Kim did not oversee or participate in routine training or security indoctrination of CFF members.

Yasith briefly tightened his command of the group prior to and during the November 2000 coup attempt. He traveled to the Cambodian–Thai border a month before the attack in order to rally CFF fighters staging near the border.[65] He initiated the coup on November 23, 2000, from his base on the Cambodian border by calling Kim, who was leading the terrorist attack in Phnom Penh.[66] Following the attack, Yasith devolved command to lower-ranking members. He told one journalist during an interview in Bangkok that he had to return to the United

States and his day job, saying, "[I]t's tax season . . . I have to prepare returns for almost 3,000 clients."[67]

The CFF did not establish popular support in the United States but hoped to achieve popularity in Cambodia. It believed that a base of likeminded Cambodians would welcome its attacks against the government. It prepared an official statement to be read on a local Cambodian television station following the coup.[68] Yasith boasted to journalists on numerous occasions and on the CFF Web site that his group was orchestrating additional attacks, possibly to enhance what he judged was growing popularity in Cambodia and to improve its relatively successful fund-raising efforts in the United States.

When the group staged its attacks in Phnom Penh, it did not control territory but rather operated in territory controlled by US authorities in California and by Cambodian authorities. Its best operating environment was the uncontrolled territory of the Cambodian–Thai border. The CFF made no attempt to hide its activities from US law enforcement. Yasith welcomed visits from the FBI and journalists writing exposés and maintained contact with US lawmakers. The group worked slightly harder to keep its activities in Cambodia hidden from Cambodian authorities. Yasith, Kim, and twenty other CFF fighters established a secret base on the Thailand side of the Cambodian–Thai border. From the secret base, Kim ordered CFF fighters to travel into Cambodia to contact active-duty Cambodian military personnel and offer them money and positions in a new government in exchange for their assistance and loyalty.[69]

Other Important Factors

The CFF had moderate resources in terms of recruits, money, and weapons. It had enough fighters to achieve some of its operational objectives, although they were not well trained and lacked sufficient strength to overthrow the Cambodian regime. One US official commented that some of the fighters were drug addicts and farmers and apparently were convinced to participate in the group's attack by the promise of financial compensation. One fighter testified in Cambodian court that he received $1,000 to $2,000 from Yasith at various times, which is a significant amount of money for the average Cambodian citizen.[70] The group had plenty of money to achieve its operational goals. Yasith held fund-raisers in Long Beach, California, and gathered as much as $300,000 from sympathizers. One of the fund-raisers, held on the *Queen Mary* cruise ship in Long Beach, attracted five hundred sympathizers, who pledged to help the CFF.[71]

The CFF's primary adversary was the Cambodian government. The Cambodian military and law enforcement's counterterrorism capabilities were modest but relatively effective. Following the coup attempt, the Cambodians detained approximately two hundred suspects within two weeks, including Richard Kiri Kim.[72] Only six months after the attacks and within a justice system aided by lenient detention rules and strict penalties for terrorism-related offenses, the Phnom Penh Supreme Court charged thirty-two suspects with terrorist crimes. The government offered immunity to some of the fighters in exchange for their testimony against key leaders and members.[73] The Cambodian authorities alleged that they had penetrations inside the group before the coup and had known of the timing and method of the attack.[74]

The Cambodians also petitioned the FBI for assistance in apprehending CFF fighters living in the United States. A Cambodian political officer at the country's embassy in Washington described the evidence his government had acquired against CFF and invoked 9/11 to add political pressure: "My government has asked the FBI to investigate. . . . We handed over weapons used by the CFF, documents found in Cambodia naming CFF members in the United States. How can America focus on terrorism and not care about these exile groups?"[75]

Intelligence and Counterintelligence Outcomes

The CFF's intelligence and counterintelligence capabilities were very basic. The group probably collected most of its information through open-source media, supplemented with information from CFF fighters on the ground in Cambodia. It made few attempts to mask its plans, personnel, and operational methods from US and Cambodian law enforcement. Yasith provided most of the group's sensitive details directly to journalists. After the failed coup attempt, he told a journalist: "We're definitely going to try again. There will be more operations. It won't be long."[76] He invited journalists to attend CFF operational planning meetings in California and to go to his secret hideout in Bangkok during the November coup attempt.[77]

On numerous occasions, Yasith provided journalists with details of the group's operations, which would have allowed any law enforcement agency to degrade and disrupt its activities. He invited a journalist to sit in during one operational planning session where he talked with CFF fighters preparing for attacks after the initial coup attempt. Among other security infractions, Yasith exposed the group's communication methods during an interview with a journalist. Picking through international calling cards in front of the journalist, he spoke with a militant commander in Cambodia who claimed that they had guns, weapons, and tanks and were ready to fight.[78] "When we came to Thailand," he told the journalist, "we didn't bring weapons or military supplies, we just gave them telephone cards to call us."[79] Yasith was also cavalier about his own personal security and listed his home address and telephone numbers on the CFF Web site. The group was careless about its security during its terrorist operations. The entire militant force, for example, wore matching CFF T-shirts during their attempted coup, which almost certainly helped government forces to determine who was CFF affiliated during and following the attack.[80]

The Cambodian authorities leveraged the CFF's poor operational security practices to collect intelligence about the group and arrest its remaining members in Cambodia. In the wake of the November 2000 coup attempt, Cambodian police quickly rounded up more than two hundred suspects.[81] After the Cambodian courts convicted numerous CFF ringleaders and low-level members on terrorism charges, the national head of the Cambodian police declared that the group had been largely dismantled.[82]

The CFF failed to implement even basic-denial techniques for much of its existence. Operational and communications security was not a priority, and the group struggled immensely to employ basic-denial techniques even when security protocols had been developed. Yasith told a journalist that each CFF member was assigned a code of letters and numbers for speaking to operatives in Cambodia, but he then admitted that the coding system was so complicated that he lost track of which code represented which agent.[83] The group's failure to employ rudimentary security measures and its appetite for publicity led to its swift and decisive demise.

THE TORONTO 18: 2005–2006

From March 2005 to June 2006, eighteen men in Toronto, Canada, conspired to commit acts of terrorism against the Government of Canada in retribution for the country's participation in military operations in Afghanistan. The group, led by Fahim Ahmad and Zakaria Amara, formulated plans to attack the Canadian Security Intelligence Service (CSIS) headquarters, the Toronto Stock Exchange, and the Canadian Parliament building.[84] CSIS investigators became aware of Ahmad and Amara's extremist views after noticing their communications with other extremists in Internet forums, such as ClearGuidance.com.[85] CSIS and the Royal Canadian Mounted Police (RCMP) conducted large-scale investigations of the group's training, personnel, and plans and began arresting group members on June 2, 2006, before they could attack any of their targets.

Key Factors

The Toronto 18 was relatively loosely commanded. Ahmad and Amara shared responsibility for leading the group until March 2006, when Amara decided to create his own faction. Even before the split, the Toronto 18 leaders only sporadically supplied the group with weapons and security training. Ahmad's only attempt to enlist a security expert failed when he recruited a CSIS informant posing as a security specialist.[86] The group appeared to be haphazardly compartmented. Whereas some group members had many details about the group's plans, others were unaware of their final target and knew only that the terrorist operation would take place in September 2006.[87]

The Toronto 18 did not try to establish popular support but, much like the CFF and the Toledo Group, attempted to tell its story to sympathetic audiences. It videotaped its terrorist-training exercises for the purpose of showing leaders in Afghanistan and select imams who the group's leaders believed would be sympathetic to their cause.[88] Amara commented that he wanted to use the video to impress jihadist leaders, but it is unclear whether he believed it would help the group recruit additional members or attract international funding or just show people that the group was serious about waging jihad.[89] The video was edited and mixed with jihadi music and sent overseas to a variety of sympathizers, including a notorious radical Islamic figure in Great Britain.[90] The group made only a minimal effort to mask the identities of its members in the video. Ahmad stated that "people were going to be shown the tape and that members of the group were going to be pioneers or leaders." One portion of the tape was choreographed to showcase Ahmad giving a rousing speech to group members sitting in a semicircle around him. In a separate video, Amara recorded himself triggering a remote-controlled detonator with his cell phone.[91] The group planned to engage more openly in a popular-support campaign following its first terrorist operation. Members discussed storming the Canadian Broadcasting Corporation building in downtown Toronto following their planned siege on the Canadian Parliament building in order to "take control of cameras to broadcast their message."[92]

The group did not control territory but rather operated in territory that was controlled by Canadian law enforcement agencies. From the group's inception, the CSIS and the RCMP were able to monitor it extensively. CSIS became interested in Ahmad and Amara when they first tried to establish extremist contacts in Internet chat rooms—a common practice and a persistent security vulnerability for groups operating in uncontrolled territory. Law enforcement entered Amara's and other group members' apartments and hotel rooms when they were absent or traveling. In several instances, the clandestine entries produced leads and evidence of terrorist plotting.[93]

The Toronto 18 almost certainly was aware that operating in uncontrolled territory introduced a host of security disadvantages. Ahmad clumsily removed a surveillance camera positioned near his apartment, believing that he was being monitored. Amara conducted his open-source intelligence collection at a public library with Internet searches on ammonium nitrate, turf fertilizer, and the al Qa'ida "tube bomb plot," probably to avoid having these searches traced back to his personal computer.[94] He chose to meet in public places with an individual (the CSIS informant) he believed could supply the group with explosives, probably to make their interactions look as normal as possible to anyone monitoring him.[95]

Other Important Factors

The group had relatively limited financial resources. It made up some of this deficit by stealing goods and equipment that it needed for training and operations. Several members who were asked to acquire items for a training camp shoplifted some of the requested items. Although the group had numerous recruits, it lacked critical security and explosives expertise. As a result, it was forced to rely on relatively unvetted individuals who possessed these skills.[96]

The Canadian police and intelligence service's counterterrorism capabilities were formidable throughout the group's lifespan. The two primary investigative agencies, CSIS and the RCMP, used hundreds of officers, penetrated the group with multiple informants, and captured more than eighty-two thousand phone calls in the course of their investigation.[97]

One of the Canadian's primary human penetrations, Mubinoddin Shaikh, was well known in Toronto's Muslim circles and worked as an official at the al-Noor Mosque and Islamic Center.[98] Shaikh's first encountered CSIS in 1997 when he notified the agency of inflammatory extremist material being passed out at a Toronto mosque. He contacted the agency years later to see about an intelligence job and was instead asked to participate as a source in the Muslim community.[99] After observing Ahmad and Amara's extremist proclivities on the Internet, CSIS identified Shaikh as an ideal penetration—he knew the concerns and vernacular of Toronto's Muslim community and had a strong urge to help law enforcement.[100] With the benefit of controlled territory, CSIS was able to engineer Shaikh's approach to the group to avoid an unnatural or alerting encounter. CSIS knew Ahmad and some of his group members would be at a particular banquet hall on November 27, 2005, and, after showing Shaikh fifteen photographs of the group, CSIS directed him to approach Ahmad to develop a friendship.[101] Shaikh's approach to Ahmad was successful and allowed him to spend the next seven months with the group reporting every important detail to Canadian authorities.

At the time of Shaikh's first meeting with the group, RCMP officers had already begun their own investigation. CSIS and the RCMP continued to run separate investigations but shared information and cooperated on the case—both had an incentive to cooperate because the only evidence admissible in court would be that collected by the RCMP.[102] As a result, CSIS transferred the responsibility of handling Shaikh to the RCMP in December 2006.[103] CSIS probably also coordinated some law enforcement activities with the Canadian border police. In August 2005, it likely alerted border officials to stop a car owned by Ahmad, and when the officials stopped the car, they found two group members with loaded weapons.[104] This discovery allowed them to take both individuals into custody and immediately reduce the number of personnel and weapons available to the Toronto 18.

The Canadians' second penetration of the group, Shaher Elsohemy, was recruited to help Canadian authorities when the Toronto 18 split into two factions in March 2006. Elsohemy was an old friend of Shareef Abdelhaleem, a group member close to Amara, who had contacted Elsohemy in February 2006 to say that he was contemplating terrorist acts and was looking for Elsohemy's advice. Elsohemy alerted CSIS and agreed to become a government informant.[105] CSIS encouraged Elsohemy to mention to Abdelhaleem that he was an agricultural engineer and that one of his relatives was in the chemical business. CSIS knew that this piece of information would be particularly enticing to the group because it was struggling to obtain explosive materials and expertise. Elsohemy met with Amara soon thereafter and arranged a fictitious purchase of three tons of ammonium nitrate fertilizer and other chemicals that were to be used to make truck bombs.[106] Elsohemy's information allowed Canadian authorities to set up a sting operation against the group and collect vital incriminating evidence for court proceedings.

Intelligence and Counterintelligence Outcomes

The Toronto 18's intelligence-collection capabilities were very basic. A large percentage of the group's intelligence likely came from open sources, such as newspapers and the Internet. In April 2006, a *Toronto Star* newspaper article about an FBI arrest of two Georgia men on terrorist charges induced some panic among the group's leaders because they were very close with one of the men arrested.[107] Amara conducted open-source research on a computer at a local public library to learn how to obtain and make explosives.[108] Group members also conducted basic, clandestine surveillance of their key targets, such as the Parliament building, and noted the times when politicians arrived and the types of weapons the building guards carried.[109]

The Toronto 18's counterintelligence practices were mostly unsophisticated and uneven, but the group employed some basic-denial techniques and exhibited an occasional burst of adaptation to Western counterterrorism intelligence-collection methods. The group's relatively loose organizational structure prevented most group members from knowing many details about the group's plots and targets. One group member commented later that he had known that the group was planning a terrorist operation but did not know the precise timing or intended target.[110] On several occasions, Ahmad reiterated to senior group members that personnel attending the training camps should not be told that the true purpose of the camps was to prepare for a terrorist operation in Canada.[111] Amara wrote down this reminder on a piece of paper, which law enforcement later discovered in his car: "Dealing with new recruits, do not tell them anything. Just give them jihad . . . give [a] false name, keep . . . on the down low."[112]

Despite the loose nature of the group's structure, Ahmad tried to regulate some group behavior. During one training camp, which took place in a secluded wooded area, Ahmad commanded the group members to refrain from talking about the camp with nongroup members. Ahmad developed a cover story about a religious retreat for group members to convey to family and friends if they were questioned about the weekend. However, security infractions persisted, and group leaders took few disciplinary measures against offending group members. Ahmad declared a "no cell phone" policy for the training camp, but many members violated this policy and were not punished. Some group members, described as "slackers" by CSIS informant Shaikh, arrived late to the training but were not disciplined for this infraction, possibly because they had critical computer skills that the group felt it needed.

One of the group members later admitted to Shaikh that he had been talking to people about the camps.[113]

In addition to these security weaknesses, the group employed unsophisticated vetting techniques. During Shaikh's first encounter with Ahmad in November 2005, Ahmad asked him more or less directly whether he was interested in participating in violent jihad. Ahmad was excited by the fact that Shaikh had a gun license and firearms training, and he believed Shaikh's cover story that he had been denied entry into Yemen and was subsequently grilled by CSIS about the matter.[114] Only two days after meeting Shaikh, Ahmad asked him if he would lead the group's sensitive, upcoming terrorist-training exercises, thus demonstrating his own immediate and mostly unfounded trust of the CSIS informant. Many of the group members knew each other from childhood, but several unvetted individuals in addition to Shaikh were accepted into the group. The second CSIS penetration, Shaher Elsohemy, was accepted into the group with little hesitation after he affected an outwardly fanatical approach to Islam. He, too, was soon provided with sensitive details about the group's terrorist plot.[115]

The Toronto 18's desire to recruit new members and tell its story to a potential international audience introduced additional counterintelligence vulnerabilities. Its decision to videotape itself in training exercises provided CSIS and the RCMP with valuable evidence against it: investigators used tapes seized in raids to convince arrested members to begin talking about the other members' role in the group.[116] Ahmad sent a copy of one of the training camp videos to unspecified contacts overseas without editing out group members' faces.[117] An intercepted transmission of the video over the Internet almost certainly would have implicated Ahmad and other members in terrorist plotting had Canadian authorities not already been monitoring the group extensively.

The group's limited resources also contributed to its security weaknesses. Due to their lack of funds, group members shoplifted items they needed for their training exercises, and on one occasion two members were arrested for this activity, which brought them unwanted scrutiny from law enforcement agents.[118] The group's need for capable recruits with useful expertise forced them to rely on less-vetted individuals and individuals who were already on Canadian law enforcement's radar. Shaikh's rapid acceptance into the group was aided by his coveted security and weapons expertise. If the group had been able to select from a large population of recruits with similar expertise, it could have raised its vetting threshold and reduced its exposure to hostile penetrations. Shaikh's background also resulted in his being consulted by group leaders on security and counterintelligence matters, which offered CSIS and the RCMP unprecedented insight into the group's plotting and vulnerabilities.

Like other homegrown terrorist groups' situation, the Toronto 18's lack of controlled territory produced large counterintelligence setbacks. In many instances, the group could not procure critical resources without engaging in alerting behavior. Its members welcomed Shaikh in November 2006 in part because he had a license to acquire firearms legally in Canada, which was something no other group member possessed.[119] The group's efforts to acquire weapons illegally in August 2005 had led to the arrest of two of its members. The group was also forced to reach out to likeminded extremists on the Internet rather than in person for advice and sympathy and could never be certain about how many of these communications were being monitored. Ahmad was a regular user of extremist chat forums on ClearGuidance.com and Islamic-Network.com and conversed with notorious extremists such as the UK-based Lashkar-e-Tayyiba facilitator Aabid Khan, who were likely being monitored by sister law enforcement services.[120]

The group's training camps suffered from security problems because they were not held in controlled territory. The group traveled ten hours north of Toronto to a remote wooded area for the training, and its outings to local stores and eateries drew unwanted attention. CSIS Shaikh testified: "One time we went to No Frills [grocery store] and people were literally jumping up from the aisles to get a better look at a bunch of brown guys in fatigues buying cans of tuna."[121] During their training, group members in fatigues made a daily visit to Tim Horton's eatery for food, drinks, and washroom breaks.[122]

By operating in territory that was controlled by its adversary, the group dramatically reduced its margin for error. Many of the group's security mistakes were exploited by law enforcement. One critical mistake was leaving sensitive group records unsecured in apartments and vehicles. The RCMP's covert entries in Amara's residence in April and May 2006 allowed it to recover incriminating evidence from Amara's computer.[123] Following the arrest of Toronto 18 members in June 2006, Canadian authorities seized many of their personal computers and found that most of these computers had extremist content and information on explosives.[124]

Some of the group's most sensitive discussions were monitored closely, often with the help of the government's informants. Nearly ten hours of discussion conducted on the way to a terrorist-training camp in February 2006 were recorded by a technical device implanted in the group's rental car. Technical monitoring provided CSIS and the RCMP with the added benefit of being able to verify the information they were getting from informants and occasionally to test the informants. In one instance, Shaikh lied to his law enforcement handler about the presence of a 9-mm handgun at the terrorist-training camp, but he later confessed; information from a variety of technical and surveillance platforms helped Shaikh's handler maintain control of the asset.[125]

Although the Toronto 18 made many counterintelligence blunders, it occasionally employed successful denial techniques. At times, it took care to hide its members' identities. Some of the members wore masks while they were videotaped at the terrorist-training camps.[126] The group discussed purchasing a safe house using an assumed non-Muslim-sounding name, knowing that a Muslim-sounding name would likely attract attention. Amara hoped to obtain fake identification and credit cards before renting the U-Haul vans he needed to conduct the terrorist attacks; although he did not expect to evade detection completely, he believed that if he could avoid being tracked down in the first twenty-four hours after an attack, then he would be able to escape to Pakistan.[127]

The group also took precautions to hide some of its members' operational activities. Amara provided the group members responsible for transporting and handling the raw explosive materials with shirts that read "Student Farmers" so that they might be able to justify their possession of ammonium nitrate if questioned.[128] This cover story was weak, but it might have been enough to alleviate the suspicion of curious bystanders. To evade law enforcement's technical surveillance platforms, Amara frequently met with the CSIS informant Elsohemy in public places to discuss the bombing plot.[129] Ahmad preferred to meet with CSIS informant Shaikh in Shaikh's car because he believed the mosque he attended was under technical surveillance.[130] Amara attempted to hide Internet research on explosives by using the public-library computer, which probably did not require that he submit any identifying information to perform the search.

Amara and several of the Toronto 18 group split from the main group in March 2006 in part because Amara felt Ahmad was insufficiently security conscious. Once Amara formed the subgroup, he implemented more sophisticated counterintelligence practices, including methods that approached adaptive denial. One of his first activities was to call Ahmad and send him emails that he believed would be monitored by CSIS to tell Ahmad that the group had "just quit everything" and that he wanted out of the plot.[131] Amara apparently hoped that CSIS would be listening and might be thrown off the scent of the terrorist plotting. What he did not realize, however, was that CSIS and the RCMP had multiple collection platforms observing the group's behavior, so feeding misinformation into only one collection channel was insufficient. Amara's action, therefore, can be considered only rudimentary adaptive denial because it was ineffective and undertaken without a clear picture of CSIS's intelligence-collection process. Nonetheless, Amara smartly recognized that contemporary counterterrorism efforts have benefitted from the interception of phone and email traffic. As a result, he instructed his subgroup to communicate through face-to-face meetings, memory sticks, and, on occasion, pagers and pay phones.[132]

A slightly more adaptive counterintelligence technique was inspired by Amara's analysis of the British discovery of an al Qai'da plot in February 2004. It was well publicized in Canada that British law enforcement covertly entered a storage facility where an al Qa'ida cell kept its explosives and replaced the explosives with an inert substance. Amara planned to avoid this type of covert tampering with his group's explosives by instructing members to place dots on their bags of explosives and candle wax along the base of the storage door to detect if bags had been replaced or the door had been open.[133]

Although the Toronto 18 understood its security weaknesses—in particular those resulting from operating in uncontrolled territory—it is intriguing that the group continued with its terrorist plotting. Amara and Ahmad received the first indication that they might be subject to

Canadian surveillance when CSIS officers visited Amara twice in 2005 to ask about his participation in extremist Internet chat rooms.[134] During both interviews, Amara admitted to CSIS officers that he visited extremist Web sites and posted radical messages. In January and February 2006, Amara told Ahmad over the phone that he thought he was under surveillance and that his phone was tapped.[135] A month before his arrest, Amara believed that his email was also being monitored and that CSIS had him and several group members under around-the-clock physical surveillance.[136] Despite these indicators, Toronto 18 members believed they could pull off a successful terrorist attack.

The Toronto 18 sporadically employed basic-denial techniques and on several occasions used rudimentary adaptive-denial methods. Its lack of insight into specific CSIS and RCMP intelligence-collection methods made the routine employment of adaptive-denial techniques nearly impossible. This disadvantage, coupled with the group's lack of control over group members and Canadian law enforcement's extensive control of its territory, left the Toronto 18 riddled with human and technical penetrations that gave CSIS and the RCMP an insurmountable intelligence advantage.

KEY FACTORS REVISITED

Organizational Structure. The Fort Dix, Toledo, and Bronx groups were relatively tightly commanded, which allowed them to engage in slightly more sophisticated and systematic security and weapons training than the CFF and the Toronto 18. The relatively small size of all of the groups facilitated a tighter command-and-control approach but also allowed their adversaries to penetrate the groups with high-level informants more easily. Both the CFF and the Toronto 18 were larger than the average group, which may have contributed to their command-and-control problems as well as to the increased challenge of penetrating them. Canadian authorities needed a second human penetration of the Toronto 18 as a result of the group's loose command structure and its fragmentation. Had the Toronto 18 been tightly commanded its entire existence, CSIS and RCMP likely would not have needed the second penetration.

The FBI recruited a second human penetration of the Fort Dix Group but probably did not need the second informant to uncover the group's core terrorist plot.

Popular Support. None of the groups established popular support, and only the CFF even attempted this feat. Nevertheless, all but one (the Bronx Group) of the organizations risked the exposure of sensitive details about their plans and personnel by making videos of their training, posting messages on chat forums, and trying to make contact with sympathizers overseas. The CFF went so far as to establish a group Web site that gave sensitive details about the group and to offer journalists access to operational methods and terrorist plots. Because none of the groups succeeded in gaining popular support, none of them benefitted from counterintelligence support from local populations.

Controlled Territory. None of the groups controlled territory. Instead, each of the groups operated in territory that was controlled by a very capable, hostile adversary. This factor was probably the single most challenging security problem for all of them. In each case, a capable adversary was able to monitor the group with human assets and technical intelligence-collection devices, allowing it to observe the group's terrorist plotting easily. Each group had severe problems in vetting new members and operational contacts because it could not easily check a contact's background. Meanwhile, its adversary could engineer operational contacts that looked authentic and fortuitous to the group and thereby lure the group into befriending the adversary's covert agents. The groups' security problems were similar to those faced by Fatah in the 1964–1967 period, when Israeli control of the West Bank left the Fatah riddled with informants and alienated from the local population. Importantly, operating in uncontrolled territory meant that these smaller groups were unlikely to learn much about their adversaries' intelligence-collection techniques, which prevented them from evolving in response to their adversaries' methods and employing adaptive-denial techniques.

All of the groups also enjoyed the brief benefit of anonymously operating in uncontrolled territory when their adversaries were unaware of their existence. However, as soon as the groups developed an operational footprint by contacting extremists on the Internet or by looking for like-minded terrorists in local venues, their adversaries were easily able to encircle them with human and technical surveillance assets.

ADDITIONAL LESSONS FROM TERRORIST GROUPS THAT FAILED

The experiences of the five terrorist groups discussed here offer some additional insights into terrorist counterintelligence. First, four of the five groups operating in uncontrolled territory judged that they were being monitored by hostile law enforcement agencies and yet still carried on with their terrorist plotting. Some of these groups may have believed that law enforcement intelligence collection was broad and diffused across many targets rather than specifically directed at them. One member of the Fort Dix Group commented to fellow militants that he had narrowly escaped an FBI attempt to ensnare him in an illegal weapons sale. This individual must have assumed that the FBI was fishing in general for criminals to entrap rather than targeting him specifically because he moved forward with other weapons-procurement plans unfazed. Another Fort Dix member confronted the FBI penetration in the group and told him that he did not care if the penetration was working for the FBI because the group was carrying out its religious duty. Leaders of the Toronto 18 believed they were under twenty-four-hour physical, phone, and email surveillance and still continued with their attack planning. This behavior suggests that the groups knew they were up against a formidable opponent but perhaps judged that greater forces were on their side. If this behavior is representative of an "overconfident" subset of the larger population of homegrown terrorist groups, it can present advantages and disadvantages for law enforcement agencies. A distinct disadvantage is that these types of groups are unlikely to be deterred from their terrorist missions even when provided with credible feedback that they are being monitored closely. One advantage, however, is that overconfident groups will likely invest less in security and may make more counterintelligence mistakes.

Second, of the five groups operating in uncontrolled territory, four were looking for someone with security expertise to improve their counterintelligence practices. Law enforcement and intelligence agencies exploited this objective in all four cases by cultivating informants who would offer security training to the group. This type of penetration was very productive for law enforcement and intelligence agencies because group leaders and members routinely consulted these "security experts" on operational planning and operational deficits. Apart from monitoring group behavior, law enforcement can use these penetrations to create paranoia within the group about untrustworthy members, draw the group's attention away from correcting real counterintelligence vulnerabilities, and distract the group with unimportant security problems.

Third, all of the groups demonstrated a desire to be part of a larger cause and often attempted to fulfill this ambition by telling their story to sympathetic audiences. The Fort Dix Group videotaped itself during its terrorist-training exercises and believed its members would become renowned as jihadist pioneers. On extremist Internet chat forums, the Toledo Group's leaders stated their desire to kill Americans. The leader of the Bronx Group was eager to meet people at his local mosque with whom he could discuss his jihadist aspirations. The CFF maintained a Web site and offered interviews to journalists where sensitive details about the group's leaders, plans, and personnel were routinely exposed. The Toronto 18 videotaped itself engaged in terrorist training and shared the video with numerous extremists to impress them and show them that the group was serious about conducting an attack. All of these activities helped the groups feel more connected to their international causes but simultaneously produced an operational footprint that was easy for law enforcement to identify and track. The need for connectedness may in fact become intensified in groups that operate in uncontrolled or hostile territory. Finding ways to exploit every homegrown group's desire to tell its story to a sympathetic audience will likely help to identify cells as well as to increase human penetrations and ease technical monitoring of such groups.

7 / TERRORISM AND COUNTERINTELLIGENCE

The practice of counterintelligence, whether for terrorist groups or for governments, is a discipline of calculated trade-offs. As in a game of chess, the majority of "moves" in the operational environment enhances some features of an organization's counterintelligence posture while weakening others: for example, advanced technologies offer counterintelligence benefits but usher in new technical counterintelligence vulnerabilities; an increased attack tempo wins more popular support for a terrorist group but also increases the group's operational profile; group record keeping enhances counterintelligence trend analysis but also leaves a paper trail of the organization's most sensitive personnel and activities. The case studies in this book underscore this fundamental dynamic by demonstrating that terrorist groups regularly grapple with the counterintelligence trade-offs posed by their organizational structure, popular support, and controlled territory. This final chapter compares insights from all the case studies and offers practical lessons for global counterterrorism efforts.

REVIEW OF THE KEY FINDINGS: ORGANIZATIONAL STRUCTURE

An organization's structure and its level of compartmentation deeply affect its counterintelligence fitness. Tightly structured organizations have the important advantage of being more capable of conducting superior training. The PIRA case provides the best support for this concept because the group's organizational structure rapidly tightened in the mid-1970s while all other factors stayed constant. As the PIRA tightened its structure, it was able to compartment its operations more effectively and train its members in counterinterrogation techniques. Both Fatah and BSO had tight structures and successfully trained their members in counterintelligence methods. From 1996 to 2001, al Qa'ida had a relatively tight command structure and was able to train its members in counterintelligence. When its structure began to loosen after 2001, its rank and file outside of Afghanistan had to rely on previous training or in some cases Internet-based training to develop and sharpen their counterintelligence practices, although, of course, some of the training deficits al Qa'ida experienced after 2001 resulted from its core group's being physically cut off from its overseas operatives rather than from its loosening organizational structure. The Egyptian IG had a loose structure its entire existence, which prevented it from imposing rigorous tradecraft on its members and led to a variety of basic counterintelligence vulnerabilities.

Although training can specifically augment counterintelligence procedures, it also can foster a general sense of discipline among group members. Before the PIRA began its standardized training, the British often referred to PIRA sloppiness as the "Paddy factor" due directly to the general lack of operational discipline. Tight organizations also enjoy superior strategic coordination, which is critical to systematic analysis and dissemination of lessons learned. In the late 1990s, al Qa'ida kept meticulous records of its members, which aided in identifying both ideal candidates for particular missions and internal counterintelligence threats. BSO was able to recover rapidly from an Israeli raid on its headquarters due to its tight organizational structure, quickly replacing agents, changing codes, and abandoning missions in the planning stages across the world.

The most important weakness of tightly structured organizations is their vulnerability to long-term penetrations. Like any tightly structured organization, the tightly structured terrorist group promotes low-level members to increasingly important positions over the course of their career. The teenage courier and low-level "lookout" eventually gets promoted to regional quartermaster and perhaps one day to senior adviser and then to the head of security for the entire organization. Recruiting the young, impressionable, and cash-strapped teenager and handling him until he becomes a senior commander may prove easier than recruiting the hardened senior leader. In addition, senior leaders in tight organizations are typically left in positions of influence until they retire. Therefore, once a senior leader is recruited, he is likely to maintain his access to sensitive information for many years. The British recruited the high-ranking PIRA counterespionage officer Freddie Scappaticci after the PIRA tightened its organizational structure in the mid-1970s, and he was an especially key informant because he had access to the PIRA's innermost secrets—upcoming missions, arms cache locations, travel and security details, bombing and assassination targets, and which PIRA volunteers were suspected of being informants. Scappaticci was able to protect himself from suspicion by rigging counterespionage investigations and framing PIRA members who were not British informants.[1] Loose organizations are better at avoiding this problem because group members are not necessarily promoted from local or regional cells to a centrally managed or administrated headquarters.

Standardization also has its benefits and drawbacks. It allows a group to establish uniform, high-quality training and operational procedures across the organization. The organization can then approach the operational environment with some assurance that each member is capable of performing certain activities, such as firing a weapon or resisting interrogation.

Standardization also makes an organization more predictable and therefore easier to monitor and manipulate, however. Fatah's use of standard codes allowed the Jordanian government to manipulate the organization by mimicking its communications. Standardization of special technology or training procedures also increases the risk that these special technologies will be exposed to the adversary. For example, one PIRA branch resisted sharing its radio-controlled bomb technology with the rest of the PIRA for fear of having it captured and studied by the British, which is exactly what happened when PIRA headquarters began to share the bomb technology with other PIRA units.[2] Standardization also risks leaving signatures, footprints, and patterns that the adversary can study and exploit over time. In the late 1990s, al Qa'ida established a formal system of using guesthouses and specific vetting procedures to screen recruits coming to its camps. Standardized vetting would allow a clever adversary to penetrate the camps by studying and testing the vulnerabilities in the group's vetting procedures. In addition, standardization allows spies and defectors to more easily identify key, uniform counterintelligence vulnerabilities, which may facilitate additional adversary recruitments. Al Qa'ida defector Jamal al-Fadl was able to describe many details of the group's international organization to US authorities through simple observation of the group's standard operating procedures.

Compartmentation has its benefits and drawbacks as well. it is designed to keep most of the members of one cell from knowing the members of another cell and dependent on top leadership for resources and direction. PIRA's compartmentation in the late 1970s made it difficult for a British interrogator to extract much information from any captured PIRA member.[3] Compartmentation also facilitates a group's counterintelligence investigations. Restricting the flow of information makes the list of suspects with access to the "compromised" information small, giving a potential mole far less room to maneuver. For the counterterrorism official, this point is critical. Understanding if and how a terrorist group is compartmented is an important step in managing penetrations of that group. For example, if a government acts on information provided by a terrorist-group member—about conducting a raid or bombing a specific location, for instance—it needs to be sure that several, if not many, individuals in the terrorist group had access to this information, or it will risk compromising its source. However, a government may have the opportunity to create paranoia in a terrorist group if the human source of actionable information is considered above reproach or believed not to have access to the compromised information. Thus, the government may act on this information for the purpose of causing the terrorist group to initiate an internal investigation that generates confusion and mistrust in their ranks.

However, compartmentation is an ideal that is probably seldom achieved. In organizations that recruit from particular families, ethnicities, or neighborhoods, many members will know other members even in distant, compartmented cells. For the PIRA, the British "supergrass" informants made this point painfully obvious when they gave evidence in court against former PIRA colleagues despite extensive formal compartmentation within the PIRA.[4] Too much compartmentation can also be harmful if leaders are killed or captured and remaining members are not fully briefed on the operational goals and plans. When a mixed Japanese–Palestinian BSO group attempted to hijack a Japanese airliner in July 1973, the mission planner was killed during the initial aircraft takeover. Because no other member of the hijacking team was fully briefed on the mission, the remaining terrorists had to abandon the operation.[5]

Compartmentation and secrecy more generally can also hinder the development of popular support. Organizational leaders and top commanders may opt for greater secrecy to avoid assassination, but this option will also conversely lower their public profile. Lowering their public profile can ultimately backfire if the popular-support base loses interest in an organization with no face or personality.

An additional insight provided by the cases is the fact that terrorist groups facing external threats appear to become increasingly centralized and tightly commanded over time. The PIRA leadership recognized explicitly in multiple internal documents that British counterterrorism capabilities had to be met with improved counterintelligence tradecraft. The PIRA deemed it essential to its survival to become more effective in developing counterinterrogation techniques, vetting new members, conducting investigations of suspected informants, and lowering members' operational profiles—all of which required tightening and compartmenting its structure. If the PIRA had not adapted so effectively, it probably would have been incapacitated, if not completely eliminated, by the end of the 1970s. Al Qa'ida maintained a tight organizational structure until it was unable to do so following the loss of its Afghanistan safe haven in 2001. Its near complete loss of its communications infrastructure in this period physically prevented the group's core from conveying commands to and receiving feedback from its international operatives in a manner reliable and timely enough to retain tight command over the organization.

Although terrorist groups seem to favor the tight command structure, that structure is not without its flaws, as described earlier. Interestingly, it may even facilitate catastrophic counterintelligence vulnerabilities, such as damaging, long-term penetrations by the group's adversary. However, because these catastrophic weaknesses are very difficult to detect and slow to develop, terrorist groups may be very far down the road to a tightened structure before they become aware of such vulnerabilities. Tightening command structure may also reflect the terrorist-group leader's preference to retain control over his organization, despite the attending counterintelligence disadvantages, real and perceived. Thus, tightening may not always be the most logical or efficient structure for the group, but rather one that favors the group leader's personal preferences. Furthermore, as a group becomes tighter organizationally, it will be increasingly easier for a powerful central leader to nurture this trend and defeat calls for decentralization.

Causal Mechanisms. The case studies suggest several driving forces behind these outcomes. First, loose organizations are less capable of monitoring and controlling and therefore training its members. With little oversight, members of loose organizations may be unwilling to implement good counterintelligence tradecraft. Good counterintelligence is often inconvenient and laborious. Members must refrain from many common conveniences and comforts to which they have grown accustomed, such as keeping in touch with family and friends. Members of loose organizations may also be incapable of implementing good counterintelligence tradecraft due to mentoring deficits or aggressive promotion of best practices. In addition, counterintelligence procedures are occasionally subtle or counterintuitive. Members will likely understand that they are forbidden from providing information directly to their adversary, but they may not be aware of the many indirect ways the adversary collects information on their organization, such as by means of subtle, peripheral "talent spotters"—sometimes called "access agents."

The inability to strictly control group members also impairs organizational compartmentation. A compartmented organization requires high levels of coordination between organizational units to prosecute its mission effectively—compartmentation without coordination and oversight results in organizational fragmentation and disintegration.

In the converse, because members of loose organizations are less controllable, they are also less predictable to the adversary. There are fewer "signature" styles of attacking, organizing covert cells, reaching out to the media, and communicating. In addition, loose organizations rarely assign individual members administrative responsibility for managing large portions of the organization, such as an accounting or security section. For the adversary facing a tightly commanded organization, these administrative sections are a prime target for high-level penetrations.

REVIEW OF THE KEY FINDINGS: POPULAR SUPPORT

Popular support and the processes required to gain and maintain popularity can both alleviate and create counterintelligence problems for a terrorist group. For most terrorist groups, gaining popular support is essential to survival, and the counterintelligence losses incurred in the process are necessary concessions. Fatah's leader Yasser Arafat embarked on a popular-support campaign in Jordan when he recognized that failure to gain popular support in the West Bank had been one of the group's early disadvantages.[6] Fatah soon began to fear, however, that Israeli assassination squads were exploiting its openness in order to track down its leaders.[7]

Popular support offers terrorist groups numerous, alluring benefits. It frequently results in increased recruitment. Osama Bin Laden's reputation was an important factor in drawing militants to Afghanistan. Journalist Peter Bergen argues that "something of a bin Laden cult was taking shape in [this] period," which "helped fuel an unprecedented volume of recruits to al Qa'ida's camps."[8] Support also ensures that local populations—and probably members of the terrorist group itself—are less likely to defect to and spy for the adversary.

The case studies indicate that a terrorist group with popular support, relative to one without popular support, will have greater counterintelligence support from the local population. The PIRA received crucial counterintelligence support from its Hen Patrols, members of the community who brashly alerted Republicans to incoming British patrols and raids. Fatah leaders could easily relocate from apartment to apartment in Beirut when the group was enjoying high popular support in the 1967–1984 period, but the group was constantly "ratted out" in the West Bank and Gaza in the low popular-support era from 1964 to 1967. Before al Qa'ida gained international notoriety, it sent core group members to do all of its intelligence collection for the US embassy attacks in East Africa. After it gained popular support, it was better able to exploit local networks to gather intelligence. For the IG, local support included the identification and vetting of potential recruits, aid in securing courier-based communications, and the provision of hiding places for IG members on the run from the police.

Al Qa'ida's shift to more Internet-based outreach and interaction may have provided some refuge from this popularity dynamic. Some of al Qa'ida's popularity is cultivated in chat rooms and on Web sites where many non–al Qa'ida members discuss the group's virtues; however, although this Internet exchange does not always expose details of the core group's personnel and plans, it does allow law enforcement to identify potential extremists and trends in al Qa'ida's local popularity, including what activities seem to generate the most and least interest.

Importantly, for clandestine organizations there is a natural tension between secrecy and popularity. Fatah encountered enormous popular-support difficulties when it prized secrecy over all other goals. One Fatah member described Fatah's obsessive secrecy in the 1964–1967 period: "We kept our secrets so close that the word Fatah would not be mentioned except to a member. Only Fatah members could see our two basic documents, the organizational structure and the political program."[9] After cultivating a far more public image in the late 1960s, Fatah leaders again tried to increase the group's secrecy in the early 1970s but found it difficult to go back "under ground" after exposing the group's leaders and organizational structure to the public.

The PIRA considered its compartmentation in the mid-1970s a net gain for counterintelligence, but it also felt the drain on its popular support. One PIRA member noted that increased secrecy drew PIRA volunteers away from daily interaction with the average citizen of Northern Ireland and that less contact with the population eventually resulted in less familiarity and trust between the PIRA and its base of popular support.[10]

The cases also show that a terrorist group with popular support will be more likely to expose sensitive information about itself in its efforts to gain and maintain its popularity. The PIRA routinely exposed its personnel and plans at PIRA marches, rallies, and pubs despite nonfraternization rules banning the mingling of known and unknown PIRA members. Al Qa'ida leaders were in frequent contact with journalists and media organizations, and group members in the West had regular liaison contact with the media. Bin Laden and other al Qa'ida leaders routinely revealed valuable information about their health, locations, and operational intentions in video interviews and tapes released to media organizations. The IG routinely reached out to local and international media outlets, telephoning and faxing media offices and granting interviews with journalists. All of this behavior risked exposing sensitive details about IG personnel and resources to the Egyptian government.

Causal Mechanisms. The case studies suggest several driving forces behind these outcomes. First, local populations that support a terrorist group will take a risk in providing material support to that group. As the risk of being detected by the adversary for providing support decreases and as the group's popularity increases, the instances and boldness of support will most likely increase. Decreasing popular counterintelligence support to terrorist groups must thus involve either increasing the risk of detection for providing support or decreasing the terrorist group's popularity.

Second, the process of winning popular support probably requires that a terrorist group divulge sensitive details about its plans, personnel, and organization to the public. People are often motivated by the human dimension of the terrorist group's cause—the personal struggle of the group's leader, the inspiring and daring plan to defeat the adversary, and the success and methods of recent attacks and victories. Terrorist-group leaders are occasionally seduced by their base of support as well and unknowingly end up offering valuable intelligence on the goals and health of the organization to their adoring populations and watchful adversaries alike. Terrorist groups sometimes earn popular support by default when a clumsy adversary alienates the population with heavy-handed tactics. This popular-support windfall comes with a price, however, because a heavy-handed adversary frequently will cause damage to both the offending terrorist group and the bystander population.

REVIEW OF THE KEY FINDINGS: CONTROLLED TERRITORY

A terrorist group's control of territory substantially impacts its counterintelligence strengths and vulnerabilities and almost certainly more so than any other factor. Control of territory affords members of a terrorist group the opportunity to live, communicate, and train together in the open. For example, PIRA-controlled territory in the countryside, such as South Armagh, allowed the PIRA to relax its counterintelligence profile and operate more openly.[11] This ability to operate more openly not only lifts the physical and financial counterintelligence burden of hiding personnel and property but also helps to alleviate the psychological counterintelligence burden that can wear heavily on members who would otherwise need to live a constant "cat and mouse" game with law enforcement.

The PIRA's controlled territories allowed the group to train its members more effectively and to coordinate its operations to mitigate its counterintelligence vulnerabilities. Al Qa'ida used its controlled territory to conduct secure training and enhanced vetting of its recruits. Before its recruits were granted access to the camp, they had to surrender all their personal belongings, thus enhancing al Qa'ida's counterintelligence control over trainees and training venues. In some cases, camp supervisors would personally assess a newcomer to determine if he were sincere in his commitment to al Qa'ida's goals.[12] When al Qa'ida controlled territory in Afghanistan, top leaders were able to change their location every evening, thus lowering the chances they could be tracked by a single informant and targeted for a cruise-missile strike. The group's communications security was also better in its controlled territory. Members could meet face to face and did not have to rely on means of communications that could be intercepted. For the IG, Egyptian security forces could not adequately police the group's controlled territories and had to rely on mass sweeps and raids when venturing into IG areas. Police raids on this scale were most likely easy to predict and probably gave key leaders and operatives a chance to hide or escape. But the controlled territories also gave security forces an area to target, and mass arrests almost certainly netted some IG operatives and sympathizers.

Fatah also enjoyed superior security in its controlled territories. Israel found it difficult to track and assassinate Fatah leaders in Lebanon because they were surrounded by bodyguards and were able to move between safe houses with ease. Operation Spring of Youth, in which Israeli special-forces units raided an apartment in Beirut and killed several high-ranking Fatah members, is an instance when Israel took the risk of attacking within Fatah's controlled territory. As noted in chapter 3, the half-hour-long operation cost Israel the lives of two of its soldiers

as well as hundreds of hours of surveillance of buildings and neighborhoods.[13] In contrast, Israel monitored and attacked BSO leaders in Europe
with relative ease once these individuals had been located there.

Controlled territory may have the disadvantage, however, of fostering a dangerously relaxed counterintelligence posture. For example, Bin
Laden's journey's within al Qa'ida's controlled territory of Afghanistan
sometimes followed a predictable path.[14] Operatives in noncontrolled
territory, living on the run, are almost certainly more likely to keep a
sharp counterintelligence mentality or will risk being detected and captured in short order.

Operating in noncontrolled territory can have additional counterintelligence advantages. Primary among these advantages is the relative
ease with which a terrorist in noncontrolled territory can remain anonymous and travel around undetected. For example, BSO members participating in the group's attack in Khartoum in the 1970s would have
been nearly impossible to detect because six of the operatives were flown
in on Jordanian passports and briefed on the operation only the day before the attack.[15] Operatives for BSO's operation in Munich were equally
well hidden. One Palestinian operative had lived in Germany for five
years, had attended the University of Berlin, and took a job as a civil
engineer in the Olympic Village to surveil BSO targets.[16] A second Palestinian had worked for a Munich oil company and took a job in the
Olympic Village as a cook to conduct surveillance.

Israel could relatively easily monitor the borders of Fatah's controlled
territories and thereby estimate its manpower and weapons supplies. In
contrast, the rank-and-file BSO members were more anonymous and
hidden among tens of thousands of noncombatants with similar biographical profiles. In many cases, BSO operatives were also legitimate
students and workers who, after participating in only one mission, would
leave very few operational footprints. Thus, the difficulty of locating
the group's operatives made estimation of its overall manpower, communications, and weapons supplies at any time very difficult. An important caveat to this hypothesis is that noncontrolled territory offers
the hypothesized benefits only if the territory is not under the control
of another hostile state or nonstate actor.

Operating in noncontrolled territory can also pose a serious counterintelligence risk if the territory is well policed by the adversary. For the

PIRA, concentrations of its members and supporters in noncontrolled urban areas lived under constant threat of British surveillance. One observer noted that the PIRA areas of the city resembled low-security prisons: "There were cameras and night sights, hidden spotters, bought informants, erratic patrols and undercover police, computer banks and those who kept track of milk delivered and clothes taken to the cleaners."[17]

The relationship between controlled territory, popular support, and the adversary's capabilities also offers insight into the counterintelligence benefits and drawbacks of controlled territory. On the one hand, controlled territory offers terrorist groups a chance to build an invaluable local support base within the territory by providing social services uninterrupted and unchallenged by their adversaries. In Fatah's controlled territory in Jordan, the group administered its own hospitals and provided service to widows, orphans, and the disabled.[18] Furthermore, an adversary's incursions into controlled territory have the potential to backfire dramatically if they snare numerous innocent bystanders—a likely outcome in territory with which security forces are not familiar—thus winning even more popular support for the territory's "freedom" fighters.

Adversary incursions into a terrorist group's controlled territory may conversely pay dividends to the adversary if the incursions net high-value terrorist targets. Further, they may alienate the population from the terrorist group as well as the adversary if the population views the terrorist group as the ultimate cause of the raids. A variation of this predicament beset al Qa'ida when it was driven from its safe haven in Afghanistan in 2001. Even as al Qa'ida portrayed itself as David to the US Goliath, the idea circulated in the Islamic world that al Qa'ida had sacrificed Afghanistan in its quest to attack the United States. The IG felt this trade-off even more sharply as it attacked the economic base of the Egyptian government and inadvertently undermined the economic livelihood of its local support base.

Causal Mechanisms. The case studies point to several factors driving these outcomes. First, controlled territory denies the adversary physical access to its most important targets. Although some intelligence and counterintelligence information can be acquired remotely, gaining physical proximity to terrorist-group personnel, meeting venues, and the popular-support base is almost certainly the most important intelligence objective for the adversary. An adversary that physically encounters terrorists can recruit terrorists to spy for it. An adversary that gains physical access to meeting venues can monitor those venues directly. An adversary that interacts directly with a terrorist group's base of support can psychologically influence that support base.

Second, controlled territory places a challenging but guaranteed high-value target directly in the adversary's sights. The adversary will have to devote much energy to penetrating the controlled territory with spies that blend in sufficiently, but once the territory has been penetrated with spies, the adversary may gain access to a large percentage of its highest-priority targets. In contrast, terrorist operatives scattered across noncontrolled territory will be less predictable but far more vulnerable to monitoring and attack once located.

Finally, when physically penetrating a controlled territory is impossible, governments may find that the high concentration of terrorist members in one area makes them more susceptible to remote monitoring. As terrorists congregate in small areas, governments may be able to use overhead imagery and technical measures to observe the group's size, key training facilities, and key meeting venues. Groups that are spread out over large urban areas will be far less susceptible to this type of monitoring.

REVIEWING OTHER IMPORTANT FACTORS

The Adversary's Counterterrorism Capabilities. The counterterrorism capabilities of a terrorist group's adversary affect that group's counterintelligence strengths and vulnerabilities. First, a strong adversary forces a terrorist group to adopt superior counterintelligence practices or face elimination. Some of al Qa'ida's counterintelligence awareness, for example, was a product of its members' guerrilla fighting and "underground" experience. Al Qa'ida leader Ayman al-Zawahiri led a clandestine underground organization in Egypt before he was sixteen and spent years evading the Egyptian security services.[19] Thus, somewhat paradoxically, strong adversaries play a critical role in many terrorist groups' counterintelligence evolution.

Terrorist-Group Resources. A terrorist group's resources can also dramatically affect its counterintelligence strengths and weakness. For the purposes of counterintelligence, having an abundance of resources almost certainly provides some advantage, whereas having too few resources can be a fatal deficit. Terrorist groups with meager finances may be particularly vulnerable. The PIRA suffered numerous counterintelligence problems when it could not pay its members. British forces were able to recruit many cash-deprived young Catholics during their interrogation by offering them a financial reward for spying on the PIRA.[20] Terrorist groups with a deficit of recruits also face challenges. For al Qa'ida, even before 2001, a limited supply of trusted couriers almost certainly restricted the group's ability to move messages and funds quickly.[21]

An abundance of resources can also present counterintelligence problems if those resources are not properly handled. Terrorist groups occasionally take on more recruits than they can train, which lowers the group's overall counterintelligence standards. Relying too heavily on a state sponsor for resources also ushers in counterintelligence problems. A key vulnerability in this situation is that terrorist groups sometimes share with their state sponsor information about their leaders, personnel, facilities, and training and military capabilities. Al Qa'ida's close relationship with the Sudanese and Taliban governments frequently exposed its most sensitive personnel and activities to many government officials who did not favor its cause. The US cruise-missile strikes in Afghanistan in 1998 taxed the patience of many Taliban officials.[22] Bin Laden further antagonized some Taliban officials by giving an inflammatory interview to al Jazeera's bureau chief in Pakistan in December 1998.[23] An adversary that cannot infiltrate the terrorist group may gain access to information about the group through penetrations of the state sponsor's security and police service, whose members may be more susceptible to standard recruitment techniques.

REVIEW OF THE KEY FINDINGS: BASIC DENIAL, ADAPTIVE DENIAL, AND COVERT MANIPULATION

The vast majority of counterintelligence strategies employed by the groups examined can be categorized as basic-denial techniques. In each of the cases, the terrorist group provided its members with aliases, discouraged contact with the adversary's security forces, and avoided communications that could be easily monitored. Importantly, a group's consistent application of basic-denial techniques may be sufficient for near-term survival and in some cases for longer-term survival.

Some of the groups employed more sophisticated adaptive-denial practices. The PIRA investigated members that had been captured or recruited by the British in order to adjust the group's counterintelligence and counterespionage procedures. Al Qa'ida recognized that its Web sites were being monitored by its adversaries and so began to communicate through sites that were active for only a few hours. In each case, the adaptive technique demonstrated a thoughtful effort to adjust to the group's unique counterintelligence vulnerability or to the adversary's unique intelligence-collection efforts.

Among the case studies, there are only a few examples of groups' employment of covert manipulation. As stated earlier, an overwhelming majority of terrorist groups will not engage in covert manipulation because of the complex coordination and sophisticated understanding of the adversary's methods that are required to execute such tasks. In a rare instance of systematic covert manipulation, the PIRA monitored the RUC's surveillance chatter and intentionally ran select PIRA members through the RUC surveillance operations to identify compromised members and safe houses.

The addition of adaptive-denial and covert-manipulation techniques to a terrorist group's repertoire may indicate that the group is devoting more resources to counterintelligence or that it has developed a more sophisticated analytic approach to counterintelligence. The emergence of these techniques may also indicate that the group's adversary is exposing its own intelligence tradecraft by increasing its operational tempo and footprint or is lowering its counterintelligence and security standards in order to make contact with its hardest targets. In either case, the emergence of adaptive denial and covert manipulation should be cause for concern and analytic investigation.

COUNTERINTELLIGENCE AND TERRORIST GROUPS: EXPLOITING THE VULNERABILITIES

Understanding the mechanics of terrorist-group counterintelligence allows for more efficient exploitation of terrorist counterintelligence vulnerabilities. Such exploitation can lead to improvements in intelligence collection on terrorist-group personnel, activities, and intentions, which will ultimately lead to improved counterterrorism operations. This section describes a number of ways counterintelligence vulnerabilities can be exploited to improve intelligence collection on and counterterrorism operations against terrorist groups.

Enhancing Paranoia and Mistrust

Secret organizations are by their nature prone to paranoia, mistrust, and suspicion. The common practice of compartmentation—the act of restricting information flow to prevent information leakage—testifies to the fact that the organization believes some percentage of its members cannot be trusted with sensitive information. Organizations often engage in "mirror imaging" their own conspiratorial strategies and plotting mindset onto their adversaries. As a secret organization faces existential crises and serious losses at the hand of its adversary, its tendency to mistrust members who may be trustworthy and to perceive conspiracies where there may be none will grow. The tendency toward paranoia and mistrust, particularly when a group's adversary enjoys a string of counterterrorism successes, offers fertile ground for governments to disrupt and manipulate terrorist-group behavior.

A group that is tightly commanded will tend to be more vulnerable to having its collective paranoia exploited if its leaders are already prone to paranoid views and conspiratorial theories that they transmit to the rest of the group. A tightly commanded group may also produce rank-and-file members that venerate or mythologize their leader, which makes the leader a good conduit for paranoia-inducing misinformation.

Sowing discord and mistrust in terrorist groups has yielded tremendous gains historically. The British frequently employed these techniques against the PIRA. For example, the British would announce that information from an informant inside the group had led to an arrest even when it had not or would announce an exaggeratedly high figure for the spoils of a PIRA bank robbery, which sometimes resulted in a spate of internal PIRA punishment shootings.[24] A PIRA spokesperson summed up the damage: "[The British] almost destroyed us. They created paranoia in the ranks and left us severely damaged."[25]

Increasing mistrust in terrorist groups can be achieved in numerous ways. First, every government should understand how its terrorist adversary conducts internal investigations: How do members come under suspicion of betrayal? What personal behavior or lifestyles are considered reasons for "alert"? What are the group's inaccurate assumptions about how its suspect spies collect intelligence and then pass this information to the adversary? Which members are already suspected of divided loyalty? What is the group's capacity for investigating suspected spies? How many and how thoroughly can the group investigate suspected spies concurrently? What assumptions does the group have about its own informant vulnerabilities? For example, if a group assumes that its foreign-born operatives are more susceptible to recruitment by the adversary, a government might plant in channels from which the terrorist group collects its information (e.g., a trusted newspaper or a double agent) the information that a record number of foreign-born operatives has been recruited this year or that a particular foreign-born operative provided sensitive details of the group's internal dynamics that led to a recent arrest. All of these paranoia-inducing untruths are more likely to work if they fit into the terrorist group's assumptions about its own vulnerabilities. Interestingly, a terrorist group's interrogation of a suspected spy—as with many mishandled and overly aggressive interrogation—may serve to draw out a false confession that simply feeds the group's sometimes inaccurate assumptions about its vulnerabilities. Engaging a terrorist group's propensity for paranoia, of course, needs to be carefully balanced with the government's need to protect its genuine spies within the group. The ideal strategy is one where the group's paranoia is directed—to the extent it can be controlled once unleashed—toward a valuable portion of the group that does not include government informants and that is otherwise unlikely to be penetrated.

The quasi-omniscient mystique that some government security agencies possess may offer another avenue for sowing discord and confusion within terrorist groups. Many terrorist groups assume that their state adversary occasionally lives up to the quasi-omniscient reputation that the popular media and culture tend to promote. Governments may benefit from augmenting this popular belief because terrorist groups will expend valuable resources to protect against illusory intelligence capabilities. Terrorist groups that assume their adversary has near-omniscience will be more likely to believe the adversary regularly compromises group members and critical internal communications pathways. Intelligence and security services can use agents within terrorist groups to spread rumors about "compromises" of sensitive information that *can only* have resulted from a novel government collection capability. Many groups will likely respond by scaling back a wide variety of operations and activities that might have been compromised by the novel but ultimately illusory capability. Groups that naturally assume their adversary is highly capable and cunning will more easily fall into this trap.

Intelligence and security services should ask the following questions: How does the terrorist group believe it is being monitored? What inaccurate assumptions has the group made about its adversary's technical and human collection capabilities? How can the group's paranoia about illusory technical threats be enhanced? For example, if a terrorist group erroneously thinks that its adversary is using a cutting-edge "chemical agent" to monitor where group members have been, it might be beneficial for the group's adversary to give it some credible feedback that this is precisely what is happening.[26] The more time the group spends worrying about and mitigating the risk of things such as "chemical agents," the less time it will spend thoughtfully addressing its true counterintelligence vulnerabilities and the more it will be potentially highlighting itself by trying to mitigate the illusory threat.

The key take-away is that to create paranoia in a terrorist group successfully, a government adversary must have an understanding of the group's counterespionage procedures, superstitions, and biases—including if and how its organizational structure, popular-support campaigns, and controlled territory impact these procedures. For terrorist groups whose leader acts as the final judge of counterespionage cases, knowing that leader's psychological biases, idiosyncratic paranoia, and past history with spy cases will also be critical.

Most, if not all, terrorist groups will be prone to paranoid thinking. Some counterterrorists, however, wait until their terrorist adversary shows signs of paranoia and mistrust before trying to exacerbate these tendencies opportunistically. Intelligence and security services should discard this opportunistic approach and instead routinely include among their counterterrorism weapons a plan to study and exploit the paranoid tendencies of every terrorist group they face.

Exploiting the Publicity Craving

If there is one affliction that all terrorist groups suffer from, it is the craving for publicity. The craving typically afflicts a group's leaders most severely and directly cuts against the group's need for secrecy and discretion.

Terrorist group leaders may come to believe their own rhetoric that they are the saviors of the populations whose grievances they promise to right. Leaders may also become fascinated with their newfound stardom. Regardless of cause, group leaders frequently are seduced by an adoring population's demands for information about their lives, activities, and the group's plans and personnel more generally. Bin Laden became close to Saudi Arabian journalist Jamal Khashoggi, for example, to whom he proudly recounted his exploits in Afghanistan.[27] Fatah leader Yasser Arafat was also easily seduced by his popular-support base and provided the local media with sensitive details, which in turn allowed the Israelis to track down Fatah leaders more easily. Individual group members can also fall victim to this seduction. Clandestine members of the PIRA marked a treaty negotiation victory by emerging in public to celebrate with their support base and known PIRA members, all in plain sight of the British.

A tightly commanded group will tend to be more vulnerable to having its publicity craving exploited. Groups with iconic leaders may already have a bias toward assuming their leaders are exceptional and deserving of popular praise. A group's iconic leader may also engender stiff competition among the group's second tier of leaders who may be vying for top leadership positions, which may inspire impulsive publicity maneuvers among that second tier.

Intelligence and security services might occasionally encourage this type of behavior by cultivating in terrorist-group leaders the conviction that their support base requires this type of close interaction. Group leaders should be encouraged to believe that their personal story is uniquely compelling and that they are uniquely capable of delivering the group's narrative to the media. Those leaders with a messianic self-image will almost certainly be more open to sharing details about themselves, the terrorist group, and its operational and strategic victories over the adversary. Cultivating the same sense of egotism in up-and-coming leaders may serve to increase damaging group publicity while simultaneously encouraging the formation of rifts among and challenges to top group leaders. Intelligence services may be able to use key penetrations of a terrorist group with access to senior group leaders to cultivate this sense of egotism. There may be a delicate balance to strike between encouraging leaders to share information about the group with the media for intelligence-collection purposes and preventing groups from gaining too much additional popularity as a result. This strategy is ideally implemented when it can be determined that the intelligence-collection benefit outweighs the cost of any increase in the group's popularity.

Intelligence and security services should ask the following questions: What is the terrorist group's plan for increasing popular support? What assumptions do the group and its leaders maintain about the need to tell their unique stories to their population? Which leaders are particularly susceptible to this egotistical thinking? Which up-and-coming leaders might have a similar egotism that may cause a rift in the group were they to believe their superiors are taking all the limelight? When (or where) does it make sense to allow a terrorist Web site or online magazine to remain operational rather than to take it down?

Exploiting Points of Exposure

A government may find that a terrorist group it is battling has very few counterintelligence weak points. Fortunately, terrorist groups frequently expose themselves to a variety of "liaison" partners, state sponsors, and other political entities whose counterintelligence postures may be far weaker than that of the terrorist group. For example, al Qa'ida provided its Sudanese liaison partners with volumes of sensitive data about its members and capabilities. Governments may gain access to a significant portion of these secrets by penetrating the weaker liaison partners rather than by trying to penetrate the terrorist group itself.

Terrorist groups occasionally create or at least consort with a political wing to carry the burden of generating popular support and negotiating with adversary politicians. These political wings are occasionally created to minimize the exposure of the clandestine wing's operatives and leaders. However, the political wing often has less sophisticated counterintelligence procedures and assumes some level of exposure to the adversary through regular negotiations and meetings. Because the group's clandestine wing almost certainly shares sensitive details about its personnel and plans with the political wing, the political wing presents a significant counterintelligence vulnerability to the group. Governments should focus on recruiting individuals within a terrorist group's political wing to gain intelligence on the group, including which members of the clandestine wing are most vulnerable to recruitment and manipulation.

Intelligence and security services should ask the following questions: With which state and nonstate actors does the group conduct formal and informal "liaison" exchange of information, weapons, or even personnel? Who among these other actors might be an easier target for penetration? What access would these alternative penetrations have to sensitive information about the terrorist group's personnel, plans, or capabilities? Which elements of the group, such as political or media-wing personnel who have access to sensitive information, might be an easier target for penetration than the group's security, military, or counterintelligence elements?

Exploiting the Bureaucratization of Counterintelligence

Terrorist groups often adopt counterintelligence procedures that are simple but effective. For example, a group may recruit only individuals from a particular clan or neighborhood, which can dramatically reduce the likelihood it will be infiltrated by its adversary.

Although bureaucratization and standardization of this practice often augments terrorist-group counterintelligence, any standardized practice can become a counterintelligence vulnerability if it is studied and covertly circumvented by the adversary. This can be particularly true for practices that are considered "simple and effective" because a terrorist group will be unlikely to suspect that these methods have been defeated. Al Qa'ida standardized the procedures by which a prospect recruit was vetted prior to gaining access to al Qa'ida training camps in Afghanistan, and its adversaries could have methodically studied these procedures and over time gained a penetration of the camps by some trial and error.[28]

The tendency toward bureaucratization will most likely be exacerbated by a tight organizational structure and controlled territory, or, put another way, tightly commanded organizations will be more likely to create and impose standardized, bureaucratic procedures. Controlled territory will likely provide the group with the sense of safety that will stimulate bureaucratic practices, reliance on counterintelligence and security facilities, and long-term stable communications procedures.

A government should look for opportunities to turn a terrorist group's standardized and trusted counterintelligence procedures against it. A group's methods for identifying and vetting new members, investigating and interrogating suspected informants, and recruiting its own penetrations of its adversary can be mapped out and defeated over time. A government should also seek a deeper understanding of the bureaucracy of the terrorist group's counterintelligence and counterespionage units. For example, many terrorist counterintelligence units will perform auxiliary tasks that distract them from spy hunting—such as providing physical security to group leaders on the move or chasing down counterintelligence leads supplied by the local population. Just as Cold War adversaries occasionally attempted to overwhelm and degrade each other's counterintelligence systems by sending fake "walk-in" informants to each other's embassies—which would tie up resources because the walk-ins were handled as if they were genuine—intelligence services should look for opportunities to overwhelm terrorist-group counterintelligence procedures. If all counterespionage personnel work in the same safe house or facility with static filing and computer systems, a government security service should make the surveillance or destruction of that facility a priority; if counterintelligence personnel investigate most leads provided to them by the local population, the security service should find ways to feed false leads to the group through the population; not only will such leads tie up precious resources, but they may also undermine the group's confidence in a sometimes reliable source of counterintelligence leads. The more time these individuals spend on worthless or administrative tasks, the less time they will be spending looking for true spies.

Questions that probe all these exploitable vulnerabilities should be incorporated into a terrorist-group counterintelligence checklist that every intelligence and security service trying to monitor, penetrate, or disrupt a terrorist group might find useful. Table 7.1 is a sample checklist of intelligence requirements beyond the obvious questions about basic counterintelligence practices. Although some of the intelligence requirements on the checklist will be difficult to collect, many of them will be relatively easy to estimate and should provide an immediate boost to counterintelligence analysis.

APPLYING THE FINDINGS TO CONTEMPORARY TERRORIST GROUPS

The findings can be applied to a variety of contemporary terrorist groups. Contemporary groups can be compared to the case-study groups by organizing the groups into "types" according to the key factors (see table 7.2 for an overview of this "terrorist-group typology"). A Type I group is one that has controlled territory, high popular support, and a tight organizational structure. The PIRA from 1976 to 1994 and Fatah from 1967 to 1982 are Type I groups. Based on these cases, it is clear that a tightly commanded group operating in controlled territory has the potential to develop sophisticated counterintelligence procedures. In both cases, the groups maintained security and counterintelligence branches with dedicated facilities. They leveraged local support to vet their recruits and to assist in intelligence and counterintelligence collection, but they also exposed sensitive details about themselves in the local and international media.

Table 7.1 Terrorist Counterintelligence: Questions and Requirements

Organizational Structure

1. Does the group have a tight or loose command-and-control structure?

2. Does the group have a single branch or set of individuals responsible for groupwide counterintelligence, counterespionage, or security? Can any of these individuals be targeted for recruitment to spy against the group?

3. How often does the group rotate its security and counterintelligence personnel to other units or tasks? How well and how often does it investigate these individuals? How does the group select members to serve in its security or counterintelligence branch?

4. Does the group mandate or offer counterintelligence training to members or appear to have uniform counterintelligence, counterinterrogation, or operational security practices? How might the uniformity of these practices be exploited?

Popular Support

1. Does the group have popular support in its areas of operation?

2. Does the group have an active publicity or media outreach campaign?

3. What assumptions does the group maintain about the need to tell its unique stories to its popular base? Which leaders are particularly susceptible to being drawn into the media limelight? How can these leaders be manipulated into giving up even more information to their popular base?

Controlled Territory

1. Does the group control territory?

2. Does the group have a fixed headquarters or other facilities? Where does it keep its sensitive files and personnel information? How does it secure sensitive hard-copy and electronic information?

3. Is the group a "guest" within a state or nonstate actor's controlled territory? If so, what security vulnerabilities does this produce?

Paranoia and Mistrust Vulnerabilities

1. How does the group believe it is being monitored and penetrated by spies?

2. What inaccurate assumptions has it made about its adversary's technical and human collection capabilities? How can a security service take advantage of or aggravate these assumptions?

3. How do members come under suspicion of spying? What personal behavior or lifestyles alert the group as signs of spying?

4. What is the group's capacity for investigating suspected spies?

Points of Exposure

1. With which state and nonstate actors does the group conduct formal and informal liaison exchange of information, weapons, or personnel?

2. Who among these other actors might be the easiest target for penetration?

3. What access would these alternative penetrations have to sensitive information about the terrorist group's personnel, plans, or capabilities?

4. Which elements of the group, such as political or media-wing personnel who have access to sensitive information, might be an easier target for penetration than the group's security, military, or counterintelligence elements?

Bureaucratization Vulnerabilities

1. Does the group have standardized vetting procedures? What are they?

2. Does the group have standardized communications protocols or codes?

3. Does the group have standardized investigatory procedures? Is there a general profile for group members who have been accused of spying?

4. Are there commonalities among members who have been accused of spying and then exonerated? What personal or situational factors insulate a member from being accused of spying or, if accused, being expelled from the group?

5. How does the group deal with members who have been detained by the adversary and released? What does it take for the group to accept them back as trusted insiders? Can the vulnerabilities of this reintegration process be exploited to recruit detained individuals as spies?

6. How do the group's cultural, tribal, or religious beliefs shape its security, vetting, investigation, and counterespionage procedures? How might these beliefs be leveraged to enhance intelligence operations against the group?

Table 7.2 Terrorist-Group Typology

Type	Organizational Structure	Popular Support	Controlled Territory	Case-Study Examples	Contemporary Examples
Type I	Tightly commanded	High support	Yes	PIRA (1976–1994); Fatah (1967–1982)	Hamas; Hizballah; Lashkar-e-Tayyiba; Kongra-Gel
Type II	Loosely commanded	High support	Yes	PIRA (1969–1972, 1972–1976); al Qa'ida (2001–2003); IG (1989–1993)	al Qa'ida; al-Shabaab
Type III	Tightly or loosely commanded	Low support	Yes	al Qa'ida (1988–1996, 1996–2001); IG (1994–1998)	Abu Sayyaf Group; Shining Path
Type IV	Tightly or loosely commanded	High or low support	No	Fatah (1964–1967); BSO (1971–1978); Toronto 18; Fort Dix Group; Toledo Group; Bronx Group; CFF	Aum Shinrikyo; November 17; Libyan Islamic Fighting Group; Tamil Tigers; and various "home-grown" groups in the United States, Canada, and Europe

Both PIRA and Fatah faced very capable adversaries that moderated counterterrorism actions to win public sympathies while focusing on recruiting penetrations, interrogating detainees, and seizing troves of sensitive documents during raids. Both groups also suffered from high-level penetrations recruited by their adversaries. Contemporary groups that fit this profile are Hamas (Gaza Strip), Hizballah (Lebanon), Lashkar-e-Tayyiba (South Asia), and Kongra-Gel (Kurdish Iraq and Turkey).

A Type II group is one that has controlled territory, high popular support, and a loose organizational structure. The PIRA from 1969 to 1972 and 1972 to 1976, al Qa'ida from 2001 to 2003, and the IG from 1989 to 1993 are Type II groups. These cases show that controlled territory offers a powerful counterintelligence advantage, but that a loose organization structure is a formidable barrier to developing standardized, high-quality counterintelligence procedures or cultivating counterintelligence professionals. Each group used popular support in its controlled territory to thwart its adversaries' intelligence-collection efforts. These groups struggled, however, with the combination of a loose organizational structure and aggressive media strategies. In every case, the loose organizational struggle promoted uncoordinated media outreach that was occasionally detrimental to the group's counterintelligence fitness.

These groups faced a mix of highly capable and less capable adversaries. The highly capable adversaries leveraged harsh but popularly supported counterterrorism legislation to combat the groups, and less capable adversaries relied more on massive raids and detentions, which frequently alienated local populations. None of these Type II terrorist groups maintained security branches, and as a result their adversaries were unable to recruit counterintelligence penetrations that offered insight into group-wide security procedures and investigations. Contemporary groups that fit this profile are al Qa'ida (as a conglomeration of regional affiliates) and the Somalia-based al-Shabaab.

A Type III group is one that has controlled territory but limited popular support and may have either a tight or a loose command structure. The IG from 1994 to 1998 and al Qa'ida from 1988 to 1996 and 1996 to 2001 are Type III groups. The IG was forced to harass and intimidate the local population in order to maintain its controlled territory and prevent informants from spying for the Egyptian government. It could not sustain this practice, and its lack of popular support was a leading factor in its demise.

Al Qa'ida, in each of its periods, relied on a state sponsor to provide a safe haven within which the group controlled territory. It benefitted from two layers of security with a state sponsor because its adversaries would have to evade both its and its state sponsor's security and counterintelligence forces to penetrate the group's controlled territory. In each period, however, al Qa'ida's counterintelligence fitness was reduced as a result of its dependence on its government sponsor, particularly so during its stay in Sudan.

In all of these cases, the groups were likely aware of their vulnerability to intelligence collection performed by local informants or their state sponsor. The IG's "informant" killing spree in the Egyptian slum of Mallawi in 1995 was almost certainly a paranoid overreaction to the fear of Egyptian government penetrations. Such an overreaction most likely further reduced the group's popularity and made it even more reliant on counterproductive intimidation techniques. Groups that lack popular support in their controlled territory are probably generally aware of the vulnerable position they are in vis-à-vis the local population or a state sponsor. This awareness makes them vulnerable to paranoia about the size of their adversaries' informant network or about their own state sponsors' intentions. Contemporary groups that fit this profile are the Philippines-based Abu Sayyaf Group and the Peru-based Shining Path.

A Type IV group is one that does not have controlled territory. Fatah from 1964 to 1967, BSO from 1971 to 1978, the Toronto 18, the Bronx Group, the Toledo Group, and the Fort Dix Group are Type IV groups. These cases show the core benefits and drawbacks of operating without controlled territory. All groups had some success in hiding from their adversaries among the general population as long as group members did not leave a significant operational footprint. In each case, however, the group members were vulnerable to their adversaries' tracking and locating capabilities once they were discovered among the general population. Without the benefit of the counterintelligence and countersurveillance resources afforded by a sympathetic population, state sponsor, or a group security branch, group members could never be certain who was monitoring them.

In each case, the counterintelligence deficits incurred by operating on uncontrolled or hostile territory outweighed the benefits gained by having a tight organizational structure or high popular support. Groups in this position may be particularly prone to manipulation, paranoia, and second-guessing of their plans and leadership. US Central Intelligence Agency director Michael Hayden commented on this principle when he spoke about al Qa'ida's dwindling controlled territory in Afghanistan in November 2008: "By making a safe haven feel less secure, we keep al-Qaeda guessing. We make them doubt their allies; question their methods, their plans, even their priorities."[29]

In the cases listed here as Type IV groups, the groups' adversaries smartly focused on methodically hunting down group members one by one, intercepting group communications, and recruiting informants to break up individual cells in multiple countries. Contemporary groups that fit this profile are Aum Shinrikyo in Japan, the November 17 group in Greece, the Tamil Tigers in Sri Lanka (following their defeat in 2009), and the Libyan Islamic Fighting Group.

APPLYING COUNTERINTELLIGENCE LESSONS TO OTHER VIOLENT NONSTATE ACTORS

The mechanics of terrorist-group counterintelligence may offer lessons for exploiting the counterintelligence vulnerabilities of other violent, clandestine organizations that resemble terrorist groups, including some organized criminal groups, drug-trafficking organizations, and large, transnational street gangs.

Organized criminal groups, drug-trafficking organizations, and large street gangs are obviously different than the terrorist groups investigated in this book and perhaps in ways that affect whether and how the group's counterintelligence fitness varies based on the key factors. A rigorous examination of each of these armed group types is required before firm conclusions can be drawn, but a preliminary assessment suggests some important similarities. Beyond the obvious similarity that all of them are relatively small nonstate organizations, each type maintains among its primary objectives the goal of remaining clandestine while performing "operations"—whether such operations involve moving or selling drugs, assassinating rival group members, recruiting informants, or covertly attacking government installations—and evading a possibly large number of adversaries, all of which may be trying to target the group for penetration or attack.

On its face, there is no reason to think that a tightly commanded criminal group would be any different than a tightly commanded terrorist group in its capacity to train its members in counterintelligence techniques or in its vulnerability to high-level law enforcement penetrations. In other words, a criminal group's operations—buying, moving, and selling illegal goods—does not necessarily have a significant impact on how its organizational structure, controlled territory, and popular support affect its counterintelligence fitness.

Less-sophisticated street gangs may be less likely to take advantage of the counterintelligence strengths that come with a tightly commanded structure or controlled territory and more likely to suffer from counterintelligence vulnerabilities that accrue in these conditions, depending on the sophistication of their law enforcement adversary. However, the basic relationships between the gang's counterintelligence fitness and the key factors are likely to be observable and exploitable.

If a law enforcement or intelligence service entity is trying to collect information on a street gang, and it is known that the gang is tightly commanded, the entity might plan its operations in a way that assumes the group will more efficiently disseminate counterintelligence "lessons learned" to other parts of the group over time. The tightly commanded street gang might also have a single person or subgroup responsible for security, which would make a good target for a confidential informant; a loosely commanded group would be less likely to establish such a position. If a large gang controls territory and believes that it can operate securely within this space, it may be more likely to have a rudimentary headquarters where it keeps records and holds important meetings—which perhaps would be a good target for a technical intelligence-collection operation. If a gang has popular support, this support may allow the group to create an informal intelligence-collection network among the local population, which may alter the way law enforcement entities police or even enter the group's territory. If the group does not have popular support, it may expose valuable information about its personnel, operations, and plans in an effort to gain popularity. A law enforcement entity may be able to subtly alter the gang's perception of its popular support in order to induce gang behavior that leads to the exposure of this type of information.

Organized criminal groups, drug-trafficking organizations, and street gangs—much like terrorist groups—are probably vulnerable to mistrust and paranoia as a result of their being clandestine or quasi-clandestine organizations under constant threat of penetration and elimination. Aggravating the paranoid tendencies of clandestine organizations by playing on their assumptions about their own counterintelligence vulnerabilities is likely to disrupt a wide variety of their operations and may hasten their demise.

Most important, no clandestine organization can maintain perfect secrecy; nearly every counterintelligence innovation introduces new vulnerabilities. This is as true for terrorist organizations as it is for nation-state intelligence services, making counterterrorist and counterintelligence analysts natural companions. Hard-earned insights gained from the practice and study of counterterrorism have much to offer to the field of counterintelligence and vice versa. One key to success in both endeavors is the recognition that almost every operational act has its counterintelligence advantages and disadvantages. Incorporating these insights into our counterterrorism efforts will likely inspire inventive methods for monitoring and disrupting terrorist groups.

1. INTRODUCTION

1. See the discussion in Bruce Hoffman, "The Modern Terrorist Mindset," in *Terrorism and Counterterrorism: Understanding the New Security Environment*, ed. R. D. Howard and R. L. Sawyer, 229–256 (Guilford, CT: McGraw Hill, 2002).

2. Audrey Kurth Cronin, "How al-Qaida Ends: The Decline and Demise of Terrorist Groups," *International Security* (Summer 2006): 7–48.

3. Brendan O'Brien, *The Long War: The IRA and Sinn Fein 1985 to Today* (Dublin: O'Brien Press, 1993), 161.

4. Bruce Hoffman, *Inside Terrorism* (London: Victor Gollancz, 1998), 43.

5. Daniel Byman, *Deadly Connections: States That Sponsor Terrorism* (Cambridge, UK: Cambridge University Press, 2005), 8.

6. Seth G. Jones and Martin C. Libicki, *How Terrorist Groups End: Lessons for Countering al Qa'ida* (Santa Monica, CA: RAND Corporation, 2008), 12.

7. Walter Laqueur, *Guerrilla: A Historical and Critical Study* (Boulder, CO: Westview Press, 1984), xi.

8. Large street gangs may not have national political agendas, but many have local political agendas that they attempt to achieve with violence and intimidation of local populations.

9. Double-agent and "dangle" operations—where "feed" material is passed to the adversary to convince the adversary of the double's bona fides and willingness to spy—are considered covert manipulation if the overarching purpose of the operation is to provide disinformation to the adversary. The operations are considered adaptive denial if the purpose is to learn about the adversary's intelligence requirements—the secrets the adversary is asking the double agent to steal from the group—and about the adversary's spy-recruiting and handling methods.

10. Brian Jackson, "Groups, Networks, or Movements: A Command and Control Driven Approach to Classifying Terrorist Organizations and Its Applications to al Qa'ida," *Studies in Conflict and Terrorism* 29 (2006), 243.

11. Donald James Goodspeed, *The Conspirators: A Study of Coup d'État* (New York: Viking Press, 1961), 222; Edward Luttwak, *Coup d'État: A Practical Handbook* (London: Wildwood House, 1979), 102–103; James T. Quinlivan, "Coup-Proofing: Its Practice and Consequences in the Middle East," *International Security* 24, no. 2 (Autumn 1999), 151; Charles W. Thayer, *Guerrilla* (London: Michael Joseph, 1963), 87–88.

12. Mark Irving Lichbach, *The Rebel's Dilemma* (Ann Arbor: University of Michigan Press, 1995), 201.

13. Wayne E. Baker and Robert R. Faulkner, "The Social Organization of Conspiracy: Illegal Networks in the Heavy Electrical Equipment Industry," *American Sociological Review* 58, no. 6 (December 1993), 848; Gordon H. McCormick and Guillermo Owen, "Security and Coordination in a Clandestine Organization," *Mathematical and Computer Modelling* 31 (2000), 176.

14. Robert Meade Jr., *Red Brigades: The Story of Italian Terrorism* (London: MacMillan, 1990), 51, 95.

15. Mark Bowden, "Jihadists in Paradise," *Atlantic Monthly* (March 2007), available at http://www.theatlantic.com/magazine/archive/2007/03/jihadists-in-paradise/5613/, accessed September 15, 2011.

16. Nathan Leites and Charles Wolf Jr., *Rebellion and Authority: An Analytical Essay on Insurgent Conflicts* (Chicago: Markham, 1970), 10.

17. Geographical space is defined, at a minimum, as a large neighborhood or collection of neighborhoods. Controlled geographical space may also span hundreds of square miles.

18. Larry Margasak, "Philippines Reports Show Terrorists' Careful Plans," Associated Press, April 7, 2003.

19. Hoffman, *Inside Terrorism*, 250.

20. Byman, *Deadly Connections*, 36–50.

21. Walter Laqueur argues that rural guerrilla groups tend to be large organizations, whereas urban-based terrorist groups tend to be much smaller (see Laqueur, *Guerrilla*, 147). Even if this distinction were generally true, it does not negate the impact of the key factors but suggests that certain terrorist-group types vary systematically along the factors that would be impacted by group size—for example, insurgent-type groups may tend to be larger and therefore may also tend to need and acquire more controlled territory.

2. THE PROVISIONAL IRISH REPUBLICAN ARMY

1. Peter Taylor, *Provos: The IRA and Sinn Fein* (London: Bloomsbury, 1997), 60. Republicans and Loyalists are typically considered extreme versions of Nationalists and Unionists, respectively.

2. Tim Pat Coogan, *The IRA: A History* (Niwot, CO: Roberts Rinehart, 1993), 251.

3. J. Bowyer Bell, *The IRA, 1968–2000: Analysis of a Secret Army* (London: Frank Cass, 2000), 175.

4. Ibid., 267.

5. Brian A. Jackson, John C. Baker, Kim Cragin, John Parachini, Horacio R. Trujillo, and Peter Chalk, *Aptitude for Destruction, Volume Two: Case Studies of Organizational Learning in Five Terrorist Groups* (Santa Monica, CA: RAND Corporation, 2005), 96.

6. Ed Moloney, *A Secret History of the IRA* (New York: W. W. Norton, 2002), 87.

7. Bell, *The IRA*, 226.

8. Brendan O'Brien, *The Long War: The IRA and Sinn Fein 1985 to Today* (Dublin: O'Brien Press, 1993), 39.

9. Bell, *The IRA*, 162.

10. Moloney, *A Secret History of the IRA*, 107.

11. Ibid., 88.

12. Patrick Bishop and Eamonn Mallie, *The Provisional IRA* (London: Heinemann, 1987), 136.

13. Ibid., 141.

14. Ibid., 137.

15. M. L. R. Smith, *Fighting for Ireland? The Military Strategy of the Irish Republican Movement* (London: Routledge, 1995), 119.

16. Bell, *The IRA*, 142.

17. Raymond Gilmour, *Dead Ground: Infiltrating the IRA* (London: Little Brown, 1998), 21.

18. Smith, *Fighting for Ireland?* 93.

19. Quoted in Taylor, *Provos*, 83.

20. Bishop and Mallie, *The Provisional IRA*, 127.

21. Tony Geraghty, *The Irish War* (London: HarperCollins, 1998), 52.

22. Moloney, *A Secret History of the IRA*, 117.

23. Taylor, *Provos*, 87.

24. Ibid., 88.

25. Bishop and Mallie, *The Provisional IRA*, 152.

26. Jackson et al., *Aptitude for Destruction*, 104.

27. O'Brien, *The Long War*, 51.

28. J. Bowyer Bell, *The Secret Army: The IRA* (New Brunswick, NJ: Transaction, 1997), 382.

29. Moloney, *A Secret History of the IRA*, 87; Jackson et al., *Aptitude for Destruction*, 98.

30. Bishop and Mallie, *The Provisional IRA*, 108.

31. Coogan, *The IRA*, 128.

32. Ibid., 113; Moloney, *A Secret History of the IRA*, 103.

33. Moloney, *A Secret History of the IRA*, 107; Jackson et al., *Aptitude for Destruction*, 98; Taylor, *Provos*, 108.

34. Bell, *The IRA*, 81, 225.

35. Moloney, *A Secret History of the IRA*, 112.

36. Peter Taylor, *Beating the Terrorists? Interrogation at Omagh, Gough, and Castlereagh* (Middlesex, UK: Penguin Books, 1980), 20.

37. Nicholas Davis, *Ten Thirty Three: The Inside Story of Britain's Secret Killing Machine in Northern Ireland* (Edinburgh: Mainstream, 1999), 32.

38. Ibid.

39. Taylor, *Beating the Terrorists?* 19.

40. Davis, *Ten Thirty Three*, 33.

41. Ibid.

42. Colonel Michael Dewar, *The British Army in Northern Ireland* (London: Arms and Armour Press, 1996), 49.

43. Ibid., 64

44. Tim Pat Coogan, *The Troubles: Ireland's Ordeal 1966–1996 and the Search for Peace* (Lanham, MD: Roberts Rinehart, 1996), 112.

45. Taylor, *Provos*, 92.

46. Ibid., 93.

47. Bell, *The Secret Army*, 381.

48. Coogan, *The IRA*, 127.

49. Bishop and Mallie, *The Provisional IRA*, 172.

50. Bell, *The IRA*, 241.

51. Bishop and Mallie, *The Provisional IRA*, 127.

52. Bell, *The IRA*, 276.

53. Quoted in Bishop and Mallie, *The Provisional IRA*, 149.

54. Quoted in Taylor, *Provos*, 109.

55. Ibid.

56. Bishop and Mallie, *The Provisional IRA*, 159.

57. Geraghty, *The Irish War*, 55.

58. Ciaran de Baroid, *Ballymurphy and the Irish War* (London: Pluto Press, 2000), 78; Gilmour, *Dead Ground*, 21.

59. Bishop and Mallie, *The Provisional IRA*, 117.

60. Dewar, *The British Army in Northern Ireland*, 71.

61. Brendan Anderson, *Joe Cahill: A Life in the IRA* (Dublin: O'Brien Press, 2002), 223.

62. Taylor, *Provos*, 92.

63. Bell, *The IRA*, 244.

64. Peter Taylor, *Brits: The War Against the IRA* (London: Bloomsbury, 2001), 133.

65. Sean O'Callaghan, *The Informer* (London: Bantam Press, 1998), 27.

66. Bell, *The IRA*, 226.

67. Geraghty, *The Irish War*, 48.

68. Bishop and Mallie, *The Provisional IRA*, 145.

69. Taylor, *Beating the Terrorists?* 19.

70. Geraghty, *The Irish War*, 63.

71. Bishop and Mallie, *The Provisional IRA*, 159.

72. Moloney, *A Secret History of the IRA*, 104.

73. Bishop and Mallie, *The Provisional IRA*, 133.

74. Ibid., 138.

75. Ibid., 157.

76. Gilmour, *Dead Ground*, 25.

77. Moloney, *A Secret History of the IRA*, 113.

78. Bell, *The Secret Army*, 399, 405.

79. Bell, *The IRA*, 233; Bishop and Mallie, *The Provisional IRA*, 246.

80. Moloney, *A Secret History of the IRA*, 160.

81. Quoted in ibid.

82. Bishop and Mallie, *The Provisional IRA*, 202.

83. Bell, *The Secret Army*, 406.

84. Ibid.

85. Bishop and Mallie, *The Provisional IRA*, 254.

86. Ibid., 232.

87. O'Callaghan, *The Informer*, 85.

88. Bell, *The IRA*, 233.

89. O'Callaghan, *The Informer*, 30.

90. Bishop and Mallie, *The Provisional IRA*, 228.

91. Ibid.

92. Taylor, *Brits*, 158.

93. Ibid.

94. Bishop and Mallie, *The Provisional IRA*, 228.

95. Gilmour, *Dead Ground*, 40.

96. Ibid.

97. Bishop and Mallie, *The Provisional IRA*, 173.

98. Bell, *The IRA*, 226.

99. Bell, *The Secret Army*, 393.

100. Moloney, *A Secret History of the IRA*, 117, 233.

101. Ibid., 233, 128, 133.

102. Bell, *The IRA*, 227.

103. Ibid.

104. Allen Feldman, *Formations of Violence: The Narrative of the Body and Political Terror in Northern Ireland* (Chicago: University of Chicago Press, 1991), 88.

105. Ibid.

106. Taylor, *Provos*, 174.

107. Quoted in Coogan, *The IRA*, 345.

108. Moloney, *A Secret History of the IRA*, 125.

109. Davis, *Ten Thirty Three*, 34.

110. Bell, *The Secret Army*, 400.

111. Geraghty, *The Irish War*, 137.

112. Moloney, *A Secret History of the IRA*, 134, 141.

113. Taylor, *Brits*, 149.

114. Taylor, *Beating the Terrorists?* 145, 146.

115. Moloney, *A Secret History of the IRA*, 156.

116. Bishop and Mallie, *The Provisional IRA*, 187.

117. Quoted in Coogan, *The IRA*, 267.

118. Taylor, *Provos*, 162.

119. Bell, *The Secret Army*, 404, 411, 424; Coogan, *The IRA*, 190.

120. Taylor, *Provos*, 173.

121. Taylor, *Brits*, 158.

122. Bishop and Mallie, *The Provisional IRA*, 200; Coogan, *The IRA*, 293; Taylor, *Provos*, 155.

123. Moloney, *A Secret History of the IRA*, 149.

124. Ibid.

125. Ibid., 125.

126. Bell, *The Secret Army*, 405.

127. Taylor, *Provos*, 155.

128. Bishop and Mallie, *The Provisional IRA*, 228.

129. Ibid., 230.

130. Quoted in ibid.

131. Ibid., 201.

132. Taylor, *Brits*, 149.

133. Moloney, *A Secret History of the IRA*, 134.

134. Coogan, *The Troubles*, 266, 267.

135. Moloney, *A Secret History of the IRA*, 138.

136. Taylor, *Provos*, 162.

137. Taylor, *Brits*, 135.

138. Moloney, *A Secret History of the IRA*, 120.

139. Ibid.

140. Bishop and Mallie, *The Provisional IRA*, 254.

141. Moloney, *A Secret History of the IRA*, 123.

142. Bell, *The Secret Army*, 406.

143. Coogan, *The IRA*, 353.

144. Quoted in Moloney, *A Secret History of the IRA*, 155.

145. Taylor, *Provos*, 152–158; Coogan, *The Troubles*, 159–160.

146. Taylor, *Provos*, 156, 197.

147. Coogan, *The Troubles*, 345.

148. Ibid., 205.

149. Ibid., 345–347, appendix A.

150. In spite of the push to reorganize the entire PIRA, the restructuring process was not uniform across the organization. Units in rural areas fought harder to retain their old structures and operational habits.

151. Mark Urban, *Big Boys' Rules: The SAS and the Secret Struggle Against the IRA* (London: Faber and Faber, 1992), 31.

152. Taylor, *Provos*, 211.

153. Ibid., 213.

154. Bell, *The IRA*, 227.

155. Moloney, *A Secret History of the IRA*, 158.

156. Ibid., 317.

157. Ibid., 148.

158. Bell, *The IRA*, 136; Kevin J. Kelley, *The Longest War: Northern Ireland and the IRA* (Westport, CT: Lawrence Hill, 1988), 285.

159. Taylor, *Provos*, 257.

160. Smith, *Fighting for Ireland?* 189.

161. Ibid., 263.

162. Matthew Teague, "Double Blind: The Untold Story of How British Intelligence Infiltrated and Undermined the IRA," *Atlantic Monthly* (April 2006), available at http://www.theatlantic.com/magazine/archive/2006/04/double-blind/4710/, accessed September 15, 2011.

163. Jackson et al., *Aptitude for Destruction*, 129.

164. De Baroid, *Ballymurphy and the Irish War*, 205.

165. Moloney, *A Secret History of the IRA*, 160.

166. Ibid.

167. Ibid.

168. Jackson et al., *Aptitude for Destruction*, 125.

169. Bell, *The Secret Army*, 592–593.

170. Quoted in Moloney, *A Secret History of the IRA*, 171.

171. Bell, *The IRA*, 212.

172. Ibid., 235.

173. Bishop and Mallie, *The Provisional IRA*, 250; Moloney, *A Secret History of the IRA*, 317.

174. Bell, *The Secret Army*, 440.

175. Irish Republican Army, General Headquarters, *A Handbook for Volunteers of the Irish Republican Army* (n.p.: n.p., 1956), 7 .

176. Dewar, *The British Army in Northern Ireland*, 117.

177. Smith, *Fighting for Ireland?* 145; O'Brien, *The Long War*, 161.

178. O'Brien, *The Long War*, 161.

179. Ibid., 206.

180. Quoted in Coogan, *The Troubles*, 214.

181. Bell, *The Secret Army*, 470.

182. Bell, *The IRA*, 138.

183. Dewar, *The British Army in Northern Ireland*, 161.

184. O'Brien, *The Long War*, 161.

185. Gilmour, *Dead Ground*, 178, 229.

186. Moloney, *A Secret History of the IRA*, 292; Taylor, *Provos*, 277; O'Brien, *The Long War*, 129.

187. Bell, *The Secret Army*, 438.

188. Ibid., 566.

189. O'Brien, *The Long War*, 206.

190. Geraghty, *The Irish War*, 206.

191. O'Brien, *The Long War*, 280.

192. Taylor, *Provos*, 202.

193. Ibid., 256.

194. O'Brien, *The Long War*, 162; Geraghty, *The Irish War*, 131.

195. Coogan, *The Troubles*, 210.

196. Coogan, *The IRA*, 245.

197. Taylor, *Provos*, 268.

198. Ibid.

199. Taylor, *Beating the Terrorists?* 193.

200. Geraghty, *The Irish War*, 157.

201. Coogan, *The Troubles*, 195.

202. Davis, *Ten Thirty Three*, 36.

203. Ibid., 111.

204. Taylor, *Beating the Terrorists?* 61.

205. Taylor, *Provos*, 276.

206. Geraghty, *The Irish War*, 131.

207. Bell, *The IRA*, 206.

208. Bell, *The Secret Army*, 615.

209. Ibid., 470.

210. Ibid., 597.

211. Bell, *The IRA*, 227.

212. Ibid., 228.

213. O'Brien, *The Long War*, 163.

214. Bell, *The IRA*, 229.

215. Ibid., 247; Taylor, *Beating the Terrorists?* 269–271.

216. Geraghty, *The Irish War*, 114.

217. Coogan, *The Troubles*, 194–196; Taylor, *Beating the Terrorists?* 158; Bell, *The Secret Army*, 443.

218. Taylor, *Provos*, 258.

219. Taylor, *Beating the Terrorists?* 157.

220. Bell, *The IRA*, 229.

221. Bell, *The Secret Army*, 451.

222. The PIRA's telephone taps in the British Telecom Network included the private line on the Dunmurry residence of the army general commanding the army garrison. See Bell, *The IRA*, 246; Bell, *The Secret Army*, 474.

223. Bell, *The IRA*, 246.

224. Bell, *The Secret Army*, 474.

225. Bell, *The IRA*, 246.

226. Bishop and Mallie, *The Provisional IRA*, 323.

227. Bell, *The IRA*, 247.

228. Gilmour, *Dead Ground*, 177.

229. Jackson et al., *Aptitude for Destruction*, 126.

230. Ibid., 125; Bishop and Mallie, *The Provisional IRA*, 320.

231. Taylor, *Beating the Terrorists?* 97.

232. Ibid., 275.

233. Gilmour, *Dead Ground*, 40.

234. Liam Clarke, *Broadening the Battlefield: The H-Blocks and the Rise of Sinn Fein* (Dublin: Gill and Macmillan, 1987), 67.

235. Quoted in Bishop and Mallie, *The Provisional IRA*, 273.

236. Ibid., 320.

237. Gilmour, *Dead Ground*, 223.

238. Bishop and Mallie, *The Provisional IRA*, 322.

239. Bell, *The Secret Army*, 631.

240. O'Brien, *The Long War*, 203.

241. Moloney, *A Secret History of the IRA*, 157.

242. Jackson et al., *Aptitude for Destruction*, 123–125.

243. Smith, *Fighting for Ireland?* 145.

244. Taylor, *Provos*, 257; Coogan, *The Troubles*, 345–347.

245. Moloney, *A Secret History of the IRA*, 154; Gilmour, *Dead Ground*, 96.

246. Bishop and Mallie, *The Provisional IRA*, 320, 321, 322.

247. Gilmour, *Dead Ground*, 279.

248. Bishop and Mallie, *The Provisional IRA*, 256.

249. Gilmour, *Dead Ground*, 105.

250. Bishop and Mallie, *The Provisional IRA*, 256, 288.

251. Ibid., 206; Urban, *Big Boys' Rules*, 120.

252. Irish Republic Army, *A Handbook for Volunteers of the Irish Republican Army*.

253. Gilmour, *Dead Ground*, 99, 100.

254. Taylor, *Beating the Terrorists?* 155, 223; Geraghty, *The Irish War*, 83.

255. Montgomery Cybele Carlough, "Pax Brittanica: British Counterinsurgency in Northern Ireland, 1969–1982," PhD diss., Yale University, 1994, 252.

256. Feldman, *Formations of Violence*, 44.

257. Bishop and Mallie, *The Provisional IRA*, 323.

258. O'Brien, *The Long War*, 214, 277.

259. Irish Republican Army, *A Handbook for Volunteers of the Irish Republican Army*, 1.

260. Geraghty, *The Irish War*, 83, 84–87, 90.

261. O'Brien, *The Long War*, 155.

262. Jackson et al., *Aptitude for Destruction*, 133.

263. Taylor, *Provos*, 268.

264. Gilmour, *Dead Ground*, 105.

265. O'Brien, *The Long War*, 207.

266. Ibid., 263.

267. Gilmour, *Dead Ground*, 230.

268. Dewar, *The British Army in Northern Ireland*, 127.

269. Bell, *The IRA*, 250.

270. Moloney, *A Secret History of the IRA*, 155.

271. Coogan, *The IRA*, 265.

272. O'Callaghan, *The Informer*, 200.

273. Moloney, *A Secret History of the IRA*, 316.

274. Coogan, *The Troubles*, 277.

275. Gilmour, *Dead Ground*, 322.

276. Bell, *The IRA*, 246.

277. Taylor, *Provos*, 295.

278. Gilmour, *Dead Ground*, 216.

279. Ibid.

280. Clarke, *Broadening the Battlefield*, 80.

281. Richard English, *Armed Struggle: The History of the IRA* (New York: Oxford University Press, 2003), 230.

282. Taylor, *Provos*, 211.

283. Ibid., 257.

284. Moloney, *A Secret History of the IRA*, 335, 155.

285. Smith, *Fighting for Ireland?* 188.

286. Moloney, *A Secret History of the IRA*, 160.

287. O'Brien, *The Long War*, 143.

3. FATAH AND BLACK SEPTEMBER

1. Edgar O'Ballance, *Arab Guerilla Power: 1967–1972* (London: Archon Books, 1973), 26.

2. Said K. Aburish, *Arafat: From Defender to Dictator* (New York: Bloomsbury, 1998), 41.

3. O'Ballance, *Arab Guerilla Power*, 28.

4. Aburish, *Arafat*, 74.

5. Michael Bar-Zohar and Eitan Haber, *The Quest for the Red Prince* (New York: Morrow, 1983), 103.

6. Simon Reeve, *One Day in September* (New York: Arcade, 2000), 176.

7. Bruce Hoffman, "All You Need Is Love: How the Terrorists Stopped Terrorism," *Atlantic Monthly* (December 2001), available at http://www.theatlantic.com/past/docs/issues/2001/12/hoffman.htm, accessed September 15, 2011.

8. Ehud Yaari, *Strike Terror: The Story of Fatah* (New York: Sabra Books, 1970), 77, 107.

9. Ibid., 128; Anat N. Kurz, *Fatah and the Politics of Violence: The Institutionalization of a Popular Struggle* (Brighton, UK: Sussex Academic Press, 2005), 48.

10. Yaari, *Strike Terror*, 128.

11. Ibid,. 131.

12. Riad El-Rayyes and Dunia Nahas, *Guerrillas for Palestine* (London: Portico, 1976), 8.

13. Yaari, *Strike Terror*, 130.

14. Zeev Schiff and Raphael Rothstein, *Fedayeen: Guerrillas Against Israel* (New York: David McKay, 1972), 86.

15. John K. Cooley, *Green March, Black September* (London: Frank Cass, 1973), 109.

16. Ibid.; John Laffin, *Fedayeen: The Arab–Israeli Dilemma* (London: Cassell, 1973), 95.

17. Yaari, *Strike Terror*, 111.

18. Ibid., 74.

19. O'Ballance, *Arab Guerilla Power*, 40.

20. Schiff and Rothstein, *Fedayeen*, 203.

21. Barry Rubin and Judith Colp Rubin, *Yasir Arafat: A Political Biography* (Oxford: Oxford University Press, 2003), 39.

22. Ibid., 203.

23. Aburish, *Arafat*, 60.

24. Schiff and Rothstein, *Fedayeen*, 86.

25. Ibid., 62.

26. Aburish, *Arafat*, 60.

27. Rubin and Rubin, *Yasir Arafat*, 39.

28. Tony Walker and Andrew Gowers, *Arafat: The Biography* (London: Virgin Books, 2003), 37.

29. Rubin and Rubin, *Yasir Arafat*, 58.

30. Yaari, *Strike Terror*, 22.

31. Aburish, *Arafat*, 74.

32. Ibid.; Yaari, *Strike Terror*, 141.

33. Schiff and Rothstein, *Fedayeen*, 77.

34. Aburish, *Arafat*, 74.

35. O'Ballance, *Arab Guerilla Power*, 40.

36. Cooley, *Green March, Black September*, 98.

37. O'Ballance, *Arab Guerilla Power*, 40.

38. Schiff and Rothstein, *Fedayeen*, 85.

39. Yaari, *Strike Terror*, 109.

40. Ibid., 43, 66, 69, 78.

41. Carlos Marighella, *The Minimanual of the Urban Terrorist*, available at http://www.marxists.org/archive/marighella-carlos/1969/06/minimanual-urban -guerrilla, accessed August 22, 2006.

42. O'Ballance, *Arab Guerilla Power*, 39.

43. Yaari, *Strike Terror*, 111.

44. Ibid., 10; Aburish, *Arafat*, 47.

45. O'Ballance, *Arab Guerilla Power*, 26.

46. Yaari, *Strike Terror*, 127.

47. O'Ballance, *Arab Guerilla Power*, 28.

48. Cooley, *Green March, Black September*, 95.

49. Ibid., 97.

50. O'Ballance, *Arab Guerilla Power*, 29.

51. Quoted in Walker and Gowers, *Arafat*, 24.

52. Yaari, *Strike Terror*, 88.

53. Ibid, 107.

54. Schiff and Rothstein, *Fedayeen*, 86.

55. Yaari, *Strike Terror*, 128.

56. Ibid.; Rubin and Rubin, *Yasir Arafat*, 39.

57. O'Ballance, *Arab Guerilla Power*, 60.

58. Ibid., 39.

59. Cooley, *Green March, Black September*, 98.

60. O'Ballance, *Arab Guerilla Power*, 39.

61. Yaari, *Strike Terror*, 143, 145.

62. Christopher Dobson, *Black September: Its Short Violent History* (New York: Macmillan, 1974), 26.

63. Bar-Zohar and Haber, *The Quest for the Red Prince*, 100.

64. Ibid.

65. Aburish, *Arafat*, 74.

66. Cooley, *Green March, Black September*, 98.

67. Ibid., 69.

68. Reeve, *One Day in September*, 30.

69. O'Ballance, *Arab Guerilla Power*, 31.

70. Rubin and Rubin, *Yasir Arafat*, 46, 47.

71. Kurz, *Fatah and the Politics of Violence*, 52.

72. Rubin and Rubin, *Yasir Arafat*, 46.

73. Walker and Gowers, *Arafat*, 52, 53.

74. Ibid., 59.

75. Yaari, *Strike Terror*, 245.

76. O'Ballance, *Arab Guerilla Power*, 87.

77. Helena Lindholm Schulz, with Juliane Hammer, *The Palestinian Diaspora: Formation of Identities and Politics of Homeland* (London: Routledge and the Taylor and Francis Group, 2003), 121; O'Ballance, *Arab Guerilla Power*, 91.

78. Jullian Becker, *The PLO: The Rise and Fall of the Palestine Liberation Organization* (New York: St. Martin's Press, 1984), 150.

79. The PLO was created in 1964 to represent Palestinian people throughout the world. The PLO also became an umbrella organization for numerous terrorist groups, including Fatah. Fatah was its largest and most politically influential component. As head of Fatah, Yasser Arafat also became the head of the PLO in 1969.

80. Becker, *The PLO*, 188.

81. Yaari, *Strike Terror*, 245.

82. Schulz, *The Palestinian Diaspora*, 46.

83. O'Ballance, *Arab Guerilla Power*, 60.

84. Bar-Zohar and Haber, *The Quest for the Red Prince*, 105.

85. O'Ballance, *Arab Guerilla Power*, 57.

86. Reeve, *One Day in September*, 29.

87. Kurz, *Fatah and the Politics of Violence*, 55.

88. Schiff and Rothstein, *Fedayeen*, 86.

89. Kurz, *Fatah and the Politics of Violence*, 52.

90. O'Ballance, *Arab Guerilla Power*, 64, 122, 170.

91. Reeve, *One Day in September*, 33.

92. El-Rayyes and Nahas, *Guerrillas for Palestine*, 22.

93. Becker, *The PLO*, 95.

2

94. O'Ballance, *Arab Guerilla Power*, 122.

95. El-Rayyes and Nahas, *Guerrillas for Palestine*, 31.

96. Schulz, *The Palestinian Diaspora*, 55.

97. Schiff and Rothstein, *Fedayeen*, 218; Richard A. Gabriel, *Operation Peace for Galilee: The Israeli–PLO War in Lebanon* (New York: Hill and Wang, 1984), 42.

98. O'Ballance, *Arab Guerilla Power*, 210, 231.

99. Dan Bavly and Eliahu Salpeter, *Fire in Beirut: Israel's War in Lebanon with the PLO* (New York: Stein and Day, 1984), 38.

100. Cooley, *Green March, Black September*, 131.

101. Kurz, *Fatah and the Politics of Violence*, 102.

102. Bavly and Salpeter, *Fire in Beirut*, 178.

103. Ibid., 79.

104. O'Ballance, *Arab Guerilla Power*, 38.

105. Aburish, *Arafat*, 79.

106. Schiff and Rothstein, *Fedayeen*, 74.

107. Aburish, *Arafat*, 79.

108. Steve Posner, *Israel Undercover: Secret Warfare and Hidden Diplomacy in the Middle East* (Syracuse, NY: Syracuse University Press, 1987), 72.

109. Becker, *The PLO*, 148.

110. Ibid., 188.

111. Walker and Gowers, *Arafat*, 139.

112. Becker, *The PLO*, 93.

113. Rubin and Rubin, *Yasir Arafat*, 80, 41.

114. Reeve, *One Day in September*, 28.

115. O'Ballance, *Arab Guerilla Power*, 57.

116. Ibid., 47.

117. Walker and Gowers, *Arafat*, 66, 67.

118. Ibid., 51, 80, 6.

119. Bar-Zohar and Haber, *The Quest for the Red Prince*, 108.

120. El-Rayyes and Nahas, *Guerrillas for Palestine*, 22; O'Ballance, *Arab Guerilla Power*, 182.

121. Schiff and Rothstein, *Fedayeen*, 237.

122. Ibid., 218; Gabriel, *Operation Peace for Galilee*, 42.

123. Becker, *The PLO*, 100.

124. Posner, *Israel Undercover*, 47.

125. George Jonas, *Vengeance: The True Story of an Israeli Counter-Terrorism Team* (New York: Simon and Schuster, 2005), 185.

126. Aburish, *Arafat*, 151.

127. Ibid., 171.

128. Ibid., 137, 140.

129. Marighella, *The Minimanual of the Urban Terrorist*.

130. Walker and Gowers, *Arafat*, 66.

131. Becker, *The PLO*, 101.

132. Ibid., 146.

133. Dobson, *Black September*, 124.

134. O'Ballance, *Arab Guerilla Power*, 51.

135. Schiff and Rothstein, *Fedayeen*, 78.

136. Yaari, *Strike Terror*, 11, 267.

137. Ibid., 357–359.

138. Becker, *The PLO*, 96, 99.

139. Cooley, *Green March, Black September*, 114.

140. Yaari, *Strike Terror*, 356.

141. Bar-Zohar and Haber, *The Quest for the Red Prince*, 118; Yaari, *Strike Terror*, 197.

142. Yaari, *Strike Terror*, 375, 378.

143. O'Ballance, *Arab Guerilla Power*, 168.

144. Yaari, *Strike Terror*, 187.

145. Aburish, *Arafat*, 151.

146. Bar-Zohar and Haber, *The Quest for the Red Prince*, 160, 213.

147. El-Rayyes and Nahas, *Guerrillas for Palestine*, 106.

148. Bavly and Salpeter, *Fire in Beirut*, 178.

149. "Information Bank Abstracts," *New York Times*, March 16, 1969.

150. Cooley, *Green March, Black September*, 129.

151. Gabriel, *Operation Peace for Galilee*, 62.

152. Ibid., 107.

153. Posner, *Israel Undercover*, 47.

154. Dobson, *Black September*, 124.

155. Gabriel, *Operation Peace for Galilee*, 114.

156. Posner, *Israel Undercover*, 10.

157. Ibid., 62.

158. Daniel Byman, *Deadly Connections: States That Sponsor Terrorism* (Cambridge, UK: Cambridge University Press, 2005), 127.

159. James Dorsey, "Syria Tries to Discredit PLO: A Tale of Intrigue and Murder," *Christian Science Monitor*, August 5, 1981.

160. Byman, *Deadly Connections*, 128.

161. Ibid., 127.

162. Marighella, *The Minimanual of the Urban Terrorist*.

163. Becker, *The PLO*, 147.

164. Marighella, *The Minimanual of the Urban Terrorist*.

165. Yaari, *Strike Terror*, 282.

166. Dobson, *Black September*, 124, 129.

167. Posner, *Israel Undercover*, 76.

168. Aburish, *Arafat*, 174.

169. Bar-Zohar and Haber, *The Quest for the Red Prince*, 103.

170. El-Rayyes and Nahas, *Guerrillas for Palestine*, 24.

171. Reeve, *One Day in September*, 34.

172. Aburish, *Arafat*, 124.

173. Bar-Zohar and Haber, *The Quest for the Red Prince*, 97, 111.

174. Aaron J. Klein, *Striking Back: The 1972 Munich Olympics Massacre and Israel's Deadly Response* (New York: Random House, 2005), 33.

175. Bar-Zohar and Haber, *The Quest for the Red Prince*, 119.

176. Cooley, *Green March, Black September*, 123.

177. Klein, *Striking Back*, 33.

178. Jonas, *Vengeance*, 144.

179. Dobson, *Black September*, 47.

180. "Information Bank Abstracts," *New York Times*, March 8, 1973.

181. "Information Bank Abstracts," *New York Times*, March 5, 1973.

182. Bar-Zohar and Haber, *The Quest for the Red Prince*, 165; "A Blacker September," *Time Magazine*, March 19, 1973.

183. Cooley, *Green March, Black September*, 90.

184. Klein, *Striking Back*, 143.

185. Reeve, *One Day in September*, 228.

186. O'Ballance, *Arab Guerilla Power*, 216; Reeve, *One Day in September*, 169.

187. Cooley, *Green March, Black September*, 90; Yaari, *Strike Terror*, 40.

188. Aburish, *Arafat*, 56.

189. Schiff and Rothstein, *Fedayeen*, 76.

190. Yaari, *Strike Terror*, 39.

191. Bar-Zohar and Haber, *The Quest for the Red Prince*, 146; Dobson, *Black September*, 136.

192. "Rome Guerrilla Base," *Sydney Morning Herald*, December 20, 1973.

193. Bar-Zohar and Haber, *The Quest for the Red Prince*, 151.

194. Dobson, *Black September*, 137, 138.

195. Ibid., 135.

196. Ibid., 143.

197. John Kifner, "West Beirut Bids Farewell to the PLO," *New York Times*, August 23, 1982.

198. Dobson, *Black September*, 45.

199. Reeve, *One Day in September*, 35.

200. Ibid.

201. Bar-Zohar and Haber, *The Quest for the Red Prince*, 103, 104, 119.

202. "Information Bank Abstracts," *New York Times*, March 8, 1973.

203. Christopher M. Andrew and Vasili Mitrokhin, *The World Was Going Our Way: The KGB and the Battle for the Third World* (New York: Basic Books, 2005), 257.

204. Klein, *Striking Back*, 138.

205. Reeve, *One Day in September*, 211.

206. Bar-Zohar and Haber, *The Quest for the Red Prince*, 114.

207. Reeve, *One Day in September*, 161.

208. Ibid., 161, 162.

209. Ibid., 164, 167, 169, 38.

210. Ibid., 176, 184.

211. Walker and Gowers, *Arafat*, 92.

212. Bar-Zohar and Haber, *The Quest for the Red Prince*, 161.

213. Reeve, *One Day in September*, 205.

214. Hoffman, "All You Need Is Love."

215. Dobson, *Black September*, 65; Cooley, *Green March, Black September*, 124.

216. Dobson, *Black September*, 47.

217. Cooley, *Green March, Black September*, 124.

218. Bar-Zohar and Haber, *The Quest for the Red Prince*, 118.

219. O'Ballance, *Arab Guerilla Power*, 216.

220. Reeve, *One Day in September*, 200, 2, 3.

221. Ibid., 169.

222. Bar-Zohar and Haber, *The Quest for the Red Prince*, 135.

223. Reeve, *One Day in September*, 173.

224. Dobson, *Black September*, 39.

225. Aburish, *Arafat*, 35.

226. Klein, *Striking Back*, 32.

227. O'Ballance, *Arab Guerilla Power*, 215.

228. Dobson, *Black September*, 43.

229. O'Ballance, *Arab Guerilla Power*, 216.

230. Dobson, *Black September*, 118.

231. Reeve, *One Day in September*, 43, 44, 46.

232. Cooley, *Green March, Black September*, 124.

233. Bar-Zohar and Haber, *The Quest for the Red Prince*, 110.

234. Cooley, *Green March, Black September*, 124.

235. Bar-Zohar and Haber, *The Quest for the Red Prince*, 118, 135.

236. Ibid., 160.

237. Dobson, *Black September*, 43.

238. Klein, *Striking Back*, 212.

239. Ibid., 231.

240. Dobson, *Black September*, 131.

241. Reeve, *One Day in September*, 1.

242. Ibid., 36.

243. Ibid., 185.

244. Bar-Zohar and Haber, *The Quest for the Red Prince*, 160.

245. Ibid., 157.

246. Klein, *Striking Back*, 231.

247. Dobson, *Black September*, 131.

248. Reeve, *One Day in September*, 190.

249. Bar-Zohar and Haber, *The Quest for the Red Prince*, 164.

250. Reeve, *One Day in September*, 201.

251. Dobson, *Black September*, 47.

252. Reeve, *One Day in September*, 172.

253. Becker, *The PLO*, 108.

254. Dobson, *Black September*, 131.

255. Reeve, *One Day in September*, 184.

256. Bar-Zohar and Haber, *The Quest for the Red Prince*, 151.

257. Ibid., 155.

258. Reeve, *One Day in September*, 173, 174.

259. Klein, *Striking Back*, 160, 168.

4. AL QAʾIDA

1. It is important to note that the evidence offers examples of potentially exploitable vulnerabilities as opposed to vulnerabilities that were necessarily exploited by al Qaʾida's adversaries. Al Qaʾida's potential vulnerabilities are a purer measure of its counterintelligence deficits because the vulnerabilities that are actually exploited represent the nexus of the adversaries' capabilities and the group's vulnerabilities.

2. Lawrence Wright, *The Looming Tower: Al-Qaʾida and the Road to 9/11* (New York: Knopf, 2006), 133–141; Thomas H. Kean, Chair, *The 9/11 Commission Report: Final Report of the National Commission on Terrorist Attacks Upon the United States* (New York: W. W. Norton, 2004), 55–56.

3. Quoted in Wright, *The Looming Tower*, 141.

4. Ibid.

5. Kean, *The 9/11 Commission Report*, 57.

6. Ibid., 59.

7. Steve Coll, *Ghost Wars: The Secret History of the CIA, Afghanistan, and Bin Laden from the Soviet Invasion to September 10, 2001* (New York: Penguin, 2004), 324.

8. Kean, *The 9/11 Commission Report*, 63–65.

9. Jason Burke, *Casting a Shadow of Terror* (London: I. B. Taurus, 2003), 5; Wright, *The Looming Tower*, 302.

10. Kean, *The 9/11 Commission Report*, 149.

11. IntelCenter, *Al-Qaʾida Operational Tempo—Madrid Follow-on Attack Assessment—V.1.0* (Alexandria, VA: IntelCenter/Tempest, March 14, 2004).

12. Kean, *The 9/11 Commission Report*, 56.

13. Joseph Felter, Jeff Bramlett, Bill Perkins, Jarrett Brachman, Brian Fishman, James Forest, Lianne Kennedy, Jacob N. Shapiro, and Tom Stocking, *Harmony and Disharmony: Exploiting al-Qa'ida's Organizational Vulnerabilities*, Combating Terrorism Center, United States Military Academy, February 14, 2006, available at http://www.ctc.usma.edu/posts/harmony-and-disharmony-exploiting-al-qaidas -organizational-vulnerabilities, accessed September 15, 2011, from US Military Academy Document Archive, Document No. AFGP-2002-000080, in an appendix to this work that includes documents recovered from various war zones.

14. Ibid., 32.

15. Peter Bergen, *The Osama Bin Laden I Know: An Oral History of the al Qa'ida Leader* (New York: Free Press, 2006), 55.

16. Coll, *Ghost Wars*, 269.

17. Rohan Gunaratna, *Inside al Qa'ida: Global Network of Terror* (New York: Columbia University Press, 2002), 35.

18. Bergen, *The Osama Bin Laden I Know*, 155.

19. Coll, *Ghost Wars*, 324.

20. Felter et al., *Harmony and Disharmony*, from Document No. AFGP-2002-000080.

21. Bergen, *The Osama Bin Laden I Know*, 32, 74, 83.

22. Burke, *Casting a Shadow of Terror*, 75.

23. Wright, *The Looming Tower*, 199.

24. Bergen, *The Osama Bin Laden I Know*, 87; Burke, *Casting a Shadow of Terror*, 158.

25. Abdel Bari Atwan, *The Secret History of al Qaida* (London: Saqi Books, 2006), 15; Jane Corbin, *Al-Qa'ida: In Search of the Terror Network That Threatens the World* (New York: Thunder's Mouth Press, 2003), 57.

26. Christopher M. Blanchard, *Al Qa'ida: Statements and Evolving Ideology*, Order Code RS21973 (Washington, DC: Congressional Research Service, November 16, 2004), 2.

27. Bergen, *The Osama Bin Laden I Know*, 150.

28. Ibid., 134.

29. Coll, *Ghost Wars*, 267.

30. Wright, *The Looming Tower*, 164.

31. Burke, *Casting a Shadow of Terror*, 130.

32. Bergen, *The Osama Bin Laden I Know*, 121; Peter Bergen, *Holy War, Inc.: Inside the Secret World of Osama Bin Laden* (New York: Simon and Schuster, 2001), 82.

33. Corbin, *Al-Qa'ida*, 55.

34. Wright, *The Looming Tower*, 187.

35. Coll, *Ghost Wars*, 268.

36. *United States v. Usama Bin Ladin et al.*, US District Court, Southern District of New York, S(7) 98 Cr. 1023 (March 2001), 2.

37. Ibid.

38. Burke, *Casting a Shadow of Terror*, 142.

39. Wright, *The Looming Tower*, 128, 133.

40. Bergen, *The Osama Bin Laden I Know*, 79.

41. Wright, *The Looming Tower*, 141, 142.

42. Burke, *Casting a Shadow of Terror*, 9.

43. Ibid.

44. Kean, *The 9/11 Commission Report*, 55.

45. National Commission on Terrorist Attacks Upon the United States, *Monograph on Terrorist Financing*, staff report, 20, available at http://govinfo.library.unt
.edu/911/staff_statements/index.htm, accessed September 15, 2011.

46. Bergen, *The Osama Bin Laden I Know*, 107.

47. Marc Sageman, *Understanding Terror Networks* (Philadelphia: University of Pennsylvania Press, 2004), 44.

48. Wright, *The Looming Tower*, 205.

49. Burke, *Casting a Shadow of Terror*, 9.

50. Gunaratna, *Inside al Qa'ida*, 159.

51. Kean, *The 9/11 Commission Report*, 62, 109.

52. Brian Michael Jenkins, *Countering al Qa'ida* (Santa Monica, CA: RAND Corporation, 2002), 6.

53. *United States v. Usama Bin Ladin et al.*, 4.

54. Burke, *Casting a Shadow of Terror*, 95.

55. Bergen, *The Osama Bin Laden I Know*, 118.

56. Wright, *The Looming Tower*, 181.

57. Bergen, *Holy War, Inc.*, 85.

58. Ibid., 198.

59. Montasser al-Zayyat, *The Road to al-Qa'ida: The Story of Bin Laden's Right Hand Man* (London: Pluto Press, 2004), 18.

60. Wright, *The Looming Tower*, 127, 128.

61. Corbin, *Al-Qa'ida*, 40.

62. Ibid.

63. *United States v. Usama Bin Ladin et al.*, Day 2; Gunaratna, *Inside al Qa'ida*, 32.

64. Bergen, *The Osama Bin Laden I Know*, 133; *United States v. Usama Bin Ladin et al.*, Day 7.

65. Gunaratna, *Inside al Qa'ida*, 33.

66. *United States v. Usama Bin Ladin et al.*, Day 2.

67. Ibid., Day 7.

68. Wright, *The Looming Tower*, 192.

69. Bergen, *The Osama Bin Laden I Know*, 81.

70. Ibid., 84.

71. Wright, *The Looming Tower*, 197.

72. *United States v. Usama Bin Ladin et al.*, Day 2.

73. Peter Bergen, "The Long Hunt for Osama," *Atlantic Monthly* (October 2004), available at http://www.theatlantic.com/magazine/archive/2004/10/the-long-hunt-for-osama/3508/, accessed September 15, 2011.

74. Wright, *The Looming Tower*, 193.

75. Bergen, *The Osama Bin Laden I Know*, 136–143.

76. Wright, *The Looming Tower*, 165.

77. Kean, *The 9/11 Commission Report*, 62.

78. Corbin, *Al-Qa'ida*, 62.

79. Kean, *The 9/11 Commission Report*, 3.

80. National Commission on Terrorist Attacks Upon the United States, *Monograph on Terrorist Financing*, 1–9.

81. Bergen, *The Osama Bin Laden I Know*, 78.

82. Wright, *The Looming Tower*, 179.

83. *United States v. Usama Bin Ladin et al.*, Day 2.

84. Ibid., Day 4.

85. Kean, *The 9/11 Commission Report*, 67.

86. Corbin, *Al-Qa'ida*, 79.

87. Wright, *The Looming Tower*, 318.

88. Burke, *Casting a Shadow of Terror*, 209.

89. Kean, *The 9/11 Commission Report*, 145, 149, 150.

90. *United States v. Zacarias Mousaoui*, Criminal Case no. 01-455-A (July 2002), Defendant's Exhibit 941, Interrogation of Khaled Sheikh Mohammed, 3, 31.

91. Kean, *The 9/11 Commission Report*, 152.

92. Ibid., 152, 153.

93. *United States v. Usama Bin Ladin et al.*, Day 20.

94. Corbin, *Al-Qa'ida*, 180.

95. Burke, *Casting a Shadow of Terror*, 150.

96. Jarret M. Brachman and William F. McCants, *Stealing al-Qa'ida's Playbook* (New York: Combating Terrorism Center at West Point, February 2006), 5.

97. Bergen, *The Osama Bin Laden I Know*, 159; Coll, *Ghost Wars*, 327.

98. Ibid., 328; Daniel Byman, *Deadly Connections: States That Sponsor Terrorism* (Cambridge, UK: Cambridge University Press, 2005), 199.

99. Burke, *Casting a Shadow of Terror*, 164.

100. Kean, *The 9/11 Commission Report*, 171.

101. Bergen, *The Osama Bin Laden I Know*, 161.

102. Gunaratna, *Inside al Qa'ida*, 40.

103. Coll, *Ghost Wars*, 285.

104. Bergen, *The Osama Bin Laden I Know*, 160.

105. Byman, *Deadly Connections*, 194.

106. Wright, *The Looming Tower*, 262.

107. Bergen, *The Osama Bin Laden I Know*, 219.

108. Burke, *Casting a Shadow of Terror*, 164.

109. Bergen, *The Osama Bin Laden I Know*, 241.

110. Quoted in Alan Cullison, "Inside al-Qa'ida's Hard Drive," *Atlantic Monthly* (September 2004), available at http://www.theatlantic.com/magazine /archive/2004/09/inside-al-qaeda-rsquo-s-hard-drive/3428, accessed September 15, 2011.

111. Daniel Benjamin and Steven Simon, *The Age of Sacred Terror* (New York: Random House, 2002), 155.

112. Burke, *Casting a Shadow of Terror*, 168.

113. Ibid., 158.

114. Gunaratna, *Inside al Qa'ida*, 41.

115. Bergen, *The Osama Bin Laden I Know*, 258.

116. IntelCenter, *Al-Qa'ida Attack/Messaging Statistics V.1.0* (Alexandria, VA: IntelCenter/Tempest, August 22, 2003), 10.

117. Coll, *Ghost Wars*, 341.

118. Bergen, *The Osama Bin Laden I Know*, 426.

119. Kean, *The 9/11 Commission Report*, 54.

120. Blanchard, *Al Qa'ida*, 2, 3.

121. Bergen, *The Osama Bin Laden I Know*, 161.

122. Atwan, *The Secret History of al Qaida*, 16.

123. Bergen, *The Osama Bin Laden I Know*, 202.

124. *United States v. Usama Bin Ladin et al.*, Day 20.

125. Kean, *The 9/11 Commission Report*, 69.

126. Burke, *Casting a Shadow of Terror*, 158, 159.

127. Kean, *The 9/11 Commission Report*, 69, 70.

128. Yossef Bodansky, *Bin Laden: The Man Who Declared War on America* (Roseville, CA: Prima, 2001), 289, 293.

129. Bergen, *The Osama Bin Laden I Know*, 170.

130. Blanchard, *Al Qa'ida*, 1.

131. Felter et al., *Harmony and Disharmony*, from Document No. AFGP-2002-600321.

132. *United States v. Zacarias Mousaoui*, Interrogation of Khaled Sheikh Mohammed, 2; Kean, *The 9/11 Commission Report*, 150.

133. Corbin, *Al-Qa'ida*, 66.

134. Bergen, *The Osama Bin Laden I Know*, 258.

135. Kean, *The 9/11 Commission Report*, 191.

136. Corbin, *Al-Qa'ida*, 81.

137. Burke, *Casting a Shadow of Terror*, 163.

138. Cited in Bodansky, *Bin Laden*, 295.

139. Burke, *Casting a Shadow of Terror*, 163.

140. Kean, *The 9/11 Commission Report*, 233.

141. Gunaratna, *Inside al Qa'ida*, 48.

142. Quoted in Burke, *Casting a Shadow of Terror*, 150.

143. Wright, *The Looming Tower*, 247.

144. Kean, *The 9/11 Commission Report*, 59, 248.

145. Burke, *Casting a Shadow of Terror*, 151.

146. Kean, *The 9/11 Commission Report*, 157.

147. Burke, *Casting a Shadow of Terror*, 156, 157.

148. *United States v. Zacarias Mousaoui*, Defendant's Exhibit 767, Mohammad Rashed Daoud al-Owhali Interrogation, 5.

149. Wright, *The Looming Tower*, 303, 302.

150. Bergen, *The Osama Bin Laden I Know*, 245.

151. Burke, *Casting a Shadow of Terror*, 13.

152. Sageman, *Understanding Terror Networks*, 48.

153. Burke, *Casting a Shadow of Terror*, 5; Wright, *The Looming Tower*, 302.

154. Bergen, *The Osama Bin Laden I Know*, 258.

155. Burke, *Casting a Shadow of Terror*, 152.

156. Atwan, *The Secret History of al Qaida*, 53.

157. Kean, *The 9/11 Commission Report*, 55; Gunaratna, *Inside al Qa'ida*, 62.

158. Kean, *The 9/11 Commission Report*, 170.

159. National Commission on Terrorist Attacks Upon the United States, *Monograph on Terrorist Financing*, 26, 28.

160. Ibid., 25.

161. Lorenzo Vidino, *Al Qa'ida in Europe: The New Battleground of International Jihad* (New York: Prometheus Books, 2006), 81.

162. Corbin, *Al-Qa'ida*, 150.

163. Gunaratna, *Inside al Qa'ida*, 140.

164. Burke, *Casting a Shadow of Terror*, 189.

165. Wright, *The Looming Tower*, 297.

166. Felter et al., *Harmony and Disharmony*, from Document No. AFGP-2002-000080.

167. Kean, *The 9/11 Commission Report*, 112, 114–115.

168. Ibid., 116, 117.

169. Ibid., 131.

170. Ibid., 142.

171. Bergen, *The Osama Bin Laden I Know*, 308.

172. Felter et al., *Harmony and Disharmony*, from Document No. AFGP-2002-000080.

173. Kean, *The 9/11 Commission Report*, 149.

174. Felter et al., *Harmony and Disharmony*, from Document No. AFGP-2002-000080.

175. *United States v. Iyman Faris*, US District Court for the District of Eastern Virginia, Criminal Case No. 03-4865 (June 2006), Statement of Facts.

176. Atwan, *The Secret History of al Qaida*, 34.

177. Haroun Fazul letter in Nairobi, acquired by PBS *Frontline*, available at http://www.pbs.org/wgbh/pages/frontline/shows/binladen/upclose/computer.html, accessed September 15, 2011.

178. *United States v. Zacarias Mousaoui*, al-Owhali Interrogation, 5.

179. *United States v. Usama Bin Ladin et al.*, Day 11, Day 12.

180. Bergen, *The Osama Bin Laden I Know*, 427.

181. *United States v. Jamal Ahmed Mohammed Ali al-Badawi, et al.*, S(12) 98 Cr. 1023 (KTD) (May 2003), Southern District Court of New York.

182. Kean, *The 9/11 Commission Report*, 158–159.

183. Sharad S. Chauhan, *The al Qa'ida Threat* (New Delhi: APH, 2003), 103.

184. Bruce Hoffman, *The Use of the Internet by Islamic Extremists*, testimony before the Permanent Select Committee on Intelligence, US House of Representatives, 109th Cong., 2d sess., May 4, 2006, 11.

185. Chauhan, *The al Qa'ida Threat*, 14.

186. Burke, *Casting a Shadow of Terror*, 144.

187. *United States v. Usama Bin Ladin et al.*, Day 12.

188. *United States v. Babar Ahmed and Azzam Publications*, District of Connecticut, Criminal Complaint, Docket Number 3:04M240 (WIG) (2004).

189. Coll, *Ghost Wars*, 471.

190. Kean, *The 9/11 Commission Report*, 65.

191. *United States v. Zacarias Mousaoui*, al-Owhali Interrogation, 3.

192. Bergen, *The Osama Bin Laden I Know*, 263.

193. *United States v. Iyman Faris*, Statement of Facts.

194. Bergen, *The Osama Bin Laden I Know*, 406.

195. Wright, *The Looming Tower*, 264.

196. Bergen, *The Osama Bin Laden I Know*, 180.

197. Bergen, "The Long Hunt for Osama."

198. Bergen, *The Osama Bin Laden I Know*, 181.

199. Bergen, "The Long Hunt for Osama."

200. Atwan, *The Secret History of al Qaida*, 23, 33.

201. Bergen, *The Osama Bin Laden I Know*, 241.

202. Daniel Byman, "Strategic Surprise and the September 11 Attacks," *Annual Review of Political Science* 8 (2005), 165; Gunaratna, *Inside al Qa'ida*, 42.

203. Bergen, *The Osama Bin Laden I Know*, 263, 261.

204. Simon Reeve, *The New Jackals: Ramzi Yousef, Osama Bin Laden, and the Future of Terrorism* (Boston: Northeastern University Press, 1999), 193.

205. Bergen, *The Osama Bin Laden I Know*, 265.

206. Coll, *Ghost Wars*, 500.

207. Kean, *The 9/11 Commission Report*, 112.

208. Ibid., 69, 250.

209. Wright, *The Looming Tower*, 331, 356.

210. Felter et al., *Harmony and Disharmony*, from Document No. AFGP-2002-000078.

211. Ibid., Document no. AFGP-2002-000112.

212. *United States v. Zacarias Mousaoui*, al-Owhali Interrogation, 4.

213. Bergen, *The Osama Bin Laden I Know*, 264.

214. Cullison, "Inside al-Qa'ida's Hard Drive."

215. Reeve, *The New Jackals*, 206.

216. Cullison, "Inside al-Qa'ida's Hard Drive."

217. Kean, *The 9/11 Commission Report*, 127.

218. Felter et al., *Harmony and Disharmony*, from Document No. AFGP-2002-000112.

219. Cullison, "Inside al-Qa'ida's Hard Drive."

220. Atwan, *The Secret History of al Qaida*, 55.

221. Wright, *The Looming Tower*, 283.

222. Ibid., 264.

223. *United States v. Zacarias Mousaoui*, Interrogation of Khaled Sheikh Mohammed, 31.

224. Wright, *The Looming Tower*, 247.

225. Quoted in Bergen, *The Osama Bin Laden I Know*, 250.

226. Corbin, *Al-Qa'ida*, 79.

227. Cullison, "Inside al-Qa'ida's Hard Drive."

228. Atwan, *The Secret History of al Qaida*, 62.

229. Benjamin and Simon, *The Age of Sacred Terror*, 153.

230. Kean, *The 9/11 Commission Report*, 67.

231. John Miller and Michael Stone, with Chris Mitchell, *The Cell: Inside the 9/11 Plot and Why the FBI and CIA Failed to Stop It* (New York: Hyperion, 2003), 260.

232. Bergen, *The Osama Bin Laden I Know*, 403.

233. Bodansky, *Bin Laden*, 289.

234. Chauhan, *The al Qa'ida Threat*, 46.

235. *United States v. Ahmed Omar Abu Ali*, Criminal Case No. 1:05CR53 (February 2005).

236. Kean, *The 9/11 Commission Report*, 167.

237. Chauhan, *The al Qa'ida Threat*, 83, 163, 164, 168.

238. *United States v. Zacarias Mousaoui*, Interrogation of Khaled Sheikh Mohammed, 21, 24.

239. Ibid., 25.

240. Ibid., 26.

241. Phil Hirschkorn, "Trial Spotlights America's Top Terrorist Threat," *Journal of Counterterrorism & Security International* 7, no. 4 (Summer 2001), available at http://www.lexisnexis.com/hottopics/lnacademic/?verb=sr&csi=244681, accessed September 15, 2011.

242. *United States v. Usama Bin Ladin et al.*, Day 20.

243. Burke, *Casting a Shadow of Terror*, 188.

244. Kean, *The 9/11 Commission Report*, 158.

245. Burke, *Casting a Shadow of Terror*, 222.

246. Kean, *The 9/11 Commission Report*, 167.

247. *United States v. Zacarias Mousaoui*, al-Owhali Interrogation, 2.

248. Burke, *Casting a Shadow of Terror*, 193.

249. Vidino, *Al Qa'ida in Europe*, 34.

250. Kean, *The 9/11 Commission Report*, 69.

251. Haroun Fazul letter, written in Nairobi, acquired by PBS *Frontline*.

252. Reeve, *The New Jackals*, 192.

253. *United States v. Usama Bin Ladin et al.*, Day 12.

254. Kean, *The 9/11 Commission Report*, 245.

255. *United States v. Zacarias Mousaoui*, Interrogation of Khaled Sheikh Mohammed, 30.

256. Corbin, *Al-Qa'ida*, 217.

257. National Commission on Terrorist Attacks Upon the United States, *Monograph on Terrorist Financing*, 26.

258. Cullison, "Inside al-Qa'ida's Hard Drive."

259. *United States v. Usama Bin Ladin et al.*, Day 12.

260. *United States v. Zacarias Mousaoui*, al-Owhali Interrogation, 14.

261. *United States v. Zacarias Mousaoui*, Interrogation of Khaled Sheikh Mohammed, 10.

262. Chauhan, *The al Qa'ida Threat*, 51.

263. Vidino, *Al Qa'ida in Europe*, 81.

264. Kean, *The 9/11 Commission Report*, 169.

265. *United States v. Ahmed Omar Abu Ali*.

266. National Commission on Terrorist Attacks Upon the United States, *9/11 and Terrorist Travel*, staff report, n.d., 56, available at http://govinfo.library.unt.edu/911/staff_statements/index.htm, accessed September 15, 2011.

267. Sageman, *Understanding Terror Networks*, 111, 121, 159.

268. Chauhan, *The al Qa'ida Threat*, 60.

269. Ibid., 92.

270. Kean, *The 9/11 Commission Report*, 156.

271. *United States v. Zacarias Mousaoui*, Interrogation of Khaled Sheikh Mohammed, 41.

272. Tight command-and-control structures may produce disadvantages for a global terrorist group if the increased need for transnational communication results in communications that are easier to monitor based on their elongated signal path.

273. Stephen Ulph, "Intelligence War Breaks Out on the Jihadi Forums," *Terrorism Monitor* 3, no. 14 (April 11, 2006), available at http://www.jamestown.org/programs/gta/single/?tx_ttnews[tt_news]=732&tx_ttnews[backPid]=239&no_cache=1, accessed September 15, 2011.

274. *United States v. Usama Bin Ladin et al.*, Day 20.

275. Burke, *Casting a Shadow of Terror*, 193.

276. *United States v. Zacarias Mousaoui*, al-Owhali Interrogation, 6.

277. Gunaratna, *Inside al Qa'ida*, 161.

278. Burke, *Casting a Shadow of Terror*, 160.

279. Corbin, *Al-Qa'ida*, 89.

280. Wright, *The Looming Tower*, 331; Bin Laden's "teasing clue" in his June 1998 interview with *ABC News* was his statement that he predicted a black day for Americans when they would bring their civilians and soldiers home in coffins—two months later al Qa'ida attacked the US embassies in Kenya and Tanzania.

281. Corbin, *Al-Qa'ida*, 91.

282. National Commission on Terrorist Attacks Upon the United States, *9/11 and Terrorist Travel*, 7.

283. *United States v. Zacarias Mousaoui*, Interrogation of Khaled Sheikh Mohammed, 21.

284. Bergen, *The Osama Bin Laden I Know*, 262.

285. Sageman, *Understanding Terror Networks*, 50.

286. *United States v. Zacarias Mousaoui*, Interrogation of Khaled Sheikh Mohammed, 55.

287. National Commission on Terrorist Attacks Upon the United States, *Monograph on Terrorist Financing*, 26.

288. Sageman, *Understanding Terror Networks*, 167.

289. *United States v. Zacarias Mousaoui*, Interrogation of Khaled Sheikh Mohammed, 36.

290. Ibid., 49.

291. Javier Jordan and Robert Wesley, "The Madrid Attacks: Results of Investigations Two Years Later," *Terrorism Monitor* 4, no. 5 (March 9, 2006), available at http://www.jamestown.org/programs/gta/single/?tx_ttnews[tt_news]=696&tx_ttnews[backPid]=181&no_cache=1, accessed September 15, 2011.

292. Gunaratna, *Inside al Qa'ida*, 116.

293. Atwan, *The Secret History of al Qaida*, 53.

294. Bergen, *The Osama Bin Laden I Know*, 155.

295. For the purposes of this case study, al Qa'ida operatives in the 2001–2003 period are considered to be those who had some direct logistical, financial, or communications connection to the al Qa'ida core in the Afghan–Pakistan region. Individuals who were inspired by al Qa'ida and adopted its mission but did not have any logistical or material connection to the al Qa'ida core are not considered a part of al Qa'ida.

296. Felter et al., *Harmony and Disharmony*, from Document No. AFGP-2002-600045.

297. Bergen, *The Osama Bin Laden I Know*, 253; Kean, *The 9/11 Commission Report*, 153.

298. Bergen, *The Osama Bin Laden I Know*, 253.

299. Ben Venzke, *Evolution of Jihadi Video V1.0* (Alexandria, VA: IntelCenter, May 11, 2005), 9.

300. Philip Smucker, *Al Qa'ida's Great Escape: The Military and the Media on Terror's Trail* (Washington, DC: Brassey's, 2004), 57, 45, 46.

301. Ibid., 51, 52, 50.

302. Ibid., 72, 80.

303. Corbin, *Al-Qa'ida*, 265–269.

304. Bergen, *The Osama Bin Laden I Know*, 328.

305. Corbin, *Al-Qa'ida*, 261.

306. Bergen, "The Long Hunt for Osama."

307. IntelCenter, *Al-Qa'ida Attack/Messaging Statistics V.1.0*, 10.

308. Bergen, *The Osama Bin Laden I Know*, 377.

309. Felter et al., *Harmony and Disharmony*, from Document No. 2RAD-2004-600457; Corbin, *Al-Qa'ida*, 260.

310. Hoffman, *The Use of the Internet by Islamic Extremists*.

311. Bergen, *The Osama Bin Laden I Know*, 321.

312. Atwan, *The Secret History of al Qaida*, 25.

313. Bodansky, *Bin Laden*, 283.

314. Timothy Thomas, "Al Qa'ida and the Internet: The Danger of 'Cyberplanning,'" *Parameters* (Spring 2003), 117.

315. Bruce Hoffman, *Combating al Qa'ida and the Militant Islamic Threat*, testimony before the Armed Services Committee, Subcommittee on Terrorism, Unconventional Threats, and Capabilities, US House of Representatives, 109th Cong., 2d sess., February 16, 2006.

316. Steve R. Corman and Jill S. Schiefelbein, *Communication and Media Strategy in the Jihadi War of Ideas*, Report No. 0601 (Phoenix: Consortium for Strategic Communication, Arizona State University, April 20, 2006), 17.

317. Hoffman, *The Use of the Internet by Islamic Extremists*.

318. Atwan, *The Secret History of al Qaida*, 120–121.

319. Ben Venzke, *Jihadi Master Video Guide V1.1* (Alexandria, VA: IntelCenter, May 18, 2006), 5–33.

320. IntelCenter, *Al Qa'ida Warning Cycle Completion for CONUS, V1.1* (Alexandria, VA: IntelCenter/Tempest, December 9, 2005), 32.

321. Blanchard, *Al Qa'ida*, 5, 6.

322. Ibid., 5.

323. Steven Simon and Jeff Martini, "Terrorism: Denying al Qa'ida Its Popular Support," *Washington Quarterly* (Winter 2004–2005), 136.

324. *Al-Battar Military Camp* (*Mu'askar al-Battar*) (newsletter), no. 10, May 23, 2004.

325. Cited in Atwan, *The Secret History of al Qaida*, 122.

326. IntelCenter, *Al-Qa'ida Operational Tempo—Madrid Follow-on Attack Assessment—V.1.0*.

327. Byman, *Deadly Connections*, 217.

328. Ibid.; Burke, *Casting a Shadow of Terror*, 232.

329. *United States v. Ahmed Omar Abu Ali*.

330. Bergen, *The Osama Bin Laden I Know*, 376.

331. Ibid.

332. Hoffman, *The Use of the Internet by Islamic Extremists*.

333. Quoted in ibid.

334. Thomas, "Al Qa'ida and the Internet," 112.

335. Byman, *Deadly Connections*, 216.

336. Wright, *The Looming Tower*, 372.

337. *Al-Battar Military Camp*, nos. 6, 9, 14, and 16 (January–November 2004).

338. This request was posted to http://www.alrakiza.com and accessed on November 19, 2002.

339. Marc Lacey, "Terrorists in Kenya Killings Posed as Fishermen," *New York Times*, November 6, 2003.

340. *Imperial Hubris: Why the West Is Losing the War on Terror* (Washington, DC: Brassey's, 2004), 72.

341. "US Intelligence: Al Qa'ida Infiltrated Saudi Arabia's Elite National Guard," *al Bawaba*, May 19, 2003.

342. Hoffman, *The Use of the Internet by Islamic Extremists*.

343. Felter et al., *Harmony and Disharmony*, from Document No. AFGP-2002-600045.

344. Ibid.

345. Ibid.

346. Ibid.

347. *United States v. Iyman Faris*, Statement of Facts.

348. Atwan, *The Secret History of al Qaida*, 130.

349. Bergen, "The Long Hunt for Osama."

350. Bergen, *The Osama Bin Laden I Know*, 395.

351. *Imperial Hubris*, 64.

352. Ibid., 51.

353. Quoted in Owais Tohid, "Tribesmen Take Cash, Count Blessings from al Qa'ida," *Christian Science Monitor*, October 29, 2003.

354. Venzke, *Jihadi Master Video Guide V1.1*.

355. Quoted in Tohid, "Tribesmen Take Cash, Count Blessings from al Qa'ida."

356. Atwan, *The Secret History of al Qaida*, 229.

357. IntelCenter, *Al Qa'ida Warning Cycle Completion for CONUS*, 27.

358. Bergen, "The Long Hunt for Osama."

359. Atwan, *The Secret History of al Qaida*, 130.

360. *United States v. Iyman Faris*, Statement of Facts.

361. Bergen, *The Osama Bin Laden I Know*, 274.

362. Ibid., 302.

363. Hoffman, *The Use of the Internet by Islamic Extremists*.

364. Quoted in Atwan, *The Secret History of al Qaida*, 130.

365. Ibid., 133, 135.

366. *Al-Battar Military Camp*, nos. 3, 10, 16, and 22 (January–November 2004).

367. Hoffman, *The Use of the Internet by Islamic Extremists*.

368. Venzke, *Jihadi Master Video Guide v1.1.*, 12.

369. Burke, *Casting a Shadow of Terror*, 223.

370. Felter et al., *Harmony and Disharmony*, from Document No. AFGP-2002-003251.

371. Evan F. Kohlmann, "The Real Online Terrorist Threat," *Foreign Affairs* 85, no. 5 (September–October 2006), 115.

372. Atwan, *The Secret History of al Qaida*, 121.

373. Felter et al., , *Harmony and Disharmony*, 21.

374. Jenkins, *Countering al Qa'ida*, 10.

375. Felter et al., *Harmony and Disharmony*, 33.

5. THE EGYPTIAN ISLAMIC GROUP

1. "Islamic Gema'at" is a more or less generic name for Islamic student groups that have existed in Egypt since the 1960s, but they are not organizationally connected to the IG that emerged in the 1970s.

2. Lawrence Wright, *The Looming Tower: Al-Qa'ida and the Road to 9/11* (New York: Knopf, 2006), 41.

3. Nachman Tal, *Islamic Fundamentalism: The Case of Egypt and Jordan* (Tel Aviv: University of Tel Aviv, 1999), 45.

4. Ibid., 56–57.

5. Caryle Murphy, *Passion for Islam, Shaping the Modern Middle East: The Egyptian Experience* (New York: Scribner, 2002), 85.

6. Tal, *Islamic Fundamentalism*, 154.

7. Wright, *The Looming Tower*, 257.

8. Murphy, *Passion for Islam*, 77.

9. Abdulrahman al-Hadlag, "Repression and Peoples' Political Violence in Egypt: The Case of al-Jama'a al-Islamiyya," PhD diss., University of Idaho, 1994, 100.

10. Michael Collins Dunn, "Fundamentalism in Egypt," *Middle East Policy* 2, no. 3 (1993), 75.

11. Murphy, *Passion for Islam*, 65.

12. Montasser al-Zayyat, *The Road to al-Qa'ida: The Story of Bin Laden's Right Hand Man* (London: Pluto Press, 2004), 71.

13. G. G. LaBelle, "Abdel-Rahman's Following in Egypt," Associated Press, July 18, 1993.

14. Murphy, *Passion for Islam*, 88.

15. LaBelle, "Abdel-Rahman's Following in Egypt."

16. Mary Anne Weaver, *A Portrait of Egypt: A Journey Through the World of Militant Islam* (New York: Farrar, Straus and Giroux, 1999), 112.

17. Charles Davidson, "Political Violence in Egypt: A Case Study of the Islamic Insurgency 1992–1997," PhD diss., Turfs University, 2005, 288.

18. Stanley Reed, "The Battle for Egypt," *Foreign Affairs* (September–October 1993), available at http://www.foreignaffairs.com/articles/49197/stanley-reed/the -battle-for-egypt, accessed September 15, 2011.

19. Weaver, *A Portrait of Egypt*, 29, 88, 68.

20. Gilles Kepel, *Jihad: The Trail of Political Islam* (New York: I. B. Tauris, 2006), 285; Davidson, "Political Violence in Egypt," 277.

21. Kepel, *Jihad*, 28.

22. Al-Zayyat, *The Road to al-Qa'ida*, 71.

23. Weaver, *A Portrait of Egypt*, 147.

24. Murphy, *Passion for Islam*, 85.

25. Murphy, *Passion for Islam*, 83.

26. Weaver, *A Portrait of Egypt*, 249.

27. Khaled Dawoud, "The Battle for the Mosque: Government vs. Extremists," Associated Press, December 24, 1993.

28. Dalia Baligh, "Crackdown on Extremists Winds Down in Cairo Neighborhood," Associated Press, December 15, 1992.

29. Weaver, *A Portrait of Egypt*, 147.

30. Ibid., 29.

31. Wright, *The Looming Tower*, 185.

32. Ibid., 184; Murphy, *Passion for Islam*, 81.

33. Murphy, *Passion for Islam*, 82.

34. Ibid., 82, 65.

35. Murphy, *Passion for Islam*, 85; Tal, *Islamic Fundamentalism*, 28.

36. Wright, *The Looming Tower*, 184.

37. Murphy, *Passion for Islam*, 77, 78.

38. Tal, *Islamic Fundamentalism*, 154.

39. Ibid.

40. Ibid., 114.

41. Although the Muslim Brotherhood fluctuated between violent and non-violent resistance strategies, the group ultimately settled on an essentially nonviolent strategy due in part to the efforts of its very capable state adversary.

42. Jason Burke, *Casting a Shadow of Terror* (London: I. B. Taurus, 2003), 139.

43. Murphy, *Passion for Islam*, 113, 115.

44. Chris Hedges, "Egypt's War with Militants: Both Sides Harden Positions," *New York Times*, April 3, 1993.

45. Al-Zayyat, *The Road to al-Qa'ida*, 95; Murphy, *Passion for Islam*, 76.

46. Murphy, *Passion for Islam*, 7.

47. Tal, *Islamic Fundamentalism*, 116; Burke, *Casting a Shadow of Terror*, 139.

48. Wright, *The Looming Tower*, 185.

49. Weaver, *A Portrait of Egypt*, 115.

50. Reed, "The Battle for Egypt."

51. Weaver, *A Portrait of Egypt*, 147.

52. Tal, *Islamic Fundamentalism*, 95; Murphy, *Passion for Islam*, 82.

53. Murphy, *Passion for Islam*, 82.

54. "Jemmah Islamiya Reported to Have Killed Policeman in Asyut," Agence France Presse, September 25, 1993.

55. Murphy, *Passion for Islam*, 77, 74.

56. Ibid., 74, 77, 79.

57. "Egypt's New Security Strategy: No Dialogue, No Retreat in All-Out War," *Mideast Mirror*, April 22, 1993.

58. Murphy, *Passion for Islam*, 81.

59. Tal, *Islamic Fundamentalism*, 97.

60. Marc Sageman, *Understanding Terror Networks* (Philadelphia: University of Pennsylvania Press, 2004), 147.

61. Weaver, *A Portrait of Egypt*, 88.

62. Tammy Arbuckle, "Egypt's Catch-22," *Jane's International Defense Review* 26, no. 12 (December 1, 1993), available at http://articles.janes.com/articles

/International-Defence-Review-93/EGYPT-S-CATCH-22.html, accessed September 15, 2011.

63. Tal, *Islamic Fundamentalism*, 95.

64. Tal, *Islamic Fundamentalism*, 110.

65. Wright, *The Looming Tower*, 257.

66. Murphy, *Passion for Islam*, 96.

67. Tal, *Islamic Fundamentalism*, 29.

68. Al-Zayyat, *The Road to al-Qa'ida*, 70.

69. Ibid., 30.

70. "Most Jamaa Leaders Favor End to All Attacks," Agence France Presse, December 11, 1997.

71. Weaver, *A Portrait of Egypt*, 267.

72. LaBelle, "Abdel-Rahman's Following in Egypt."

73. James Adams, "Americans Move to Destabilise Sudanese Regime," *Sunday London Times*, November 17, 1996.

74. Hassan Mekki, "Security Forces Kill Top Militant in New Blow to Fundamentalists," Agence France Presse, November 17, 1994.

75. Tal, *Islamic Fundamentalism*, 154.

76. Weaver, *A Portrait of Egypt*, 267; Tal, *Islamic Fundamentalism*, 99.

77. Robert Fisk, "Might of the Sword Menaces Christians," *The Independent*, February 9, 1995.

78. Murphy, *Passion for Islam*, 87.

79. Tal, *Islamic Fundamentalism*, 88.

80. Sageman, *Understanding Terror Networks*, 42.

81. Murphy, *Passion for Islam*, 92.

82. Mark Huband, "Luxor Masterminds in Afghanistan Exile," *London Financial Times*, November 20, 1997.

83. Tal, *Islamic Fundamentalism*, 119; Youssef M. Ibrahim, "Egyptian Police, Sweep, Seize Suspects in Killing of Greeks," *New York Times*, April 20, 1996.

84. Murphy, *Passion for Islam*, 92.

85. Tal, *Islamic Fundamentalism*, 124; Mekki, "Security Forces Kill Top Militant."

86. Tal, *Islamic Fundamentalism*, 124, 154.

87. Ibid., 149.

88. Ibid.

89. Ibid., 121; Murphy, *Passion for Islam*, 93.

90. Tal, *Islamic Fundamentalism*, 119, 120.

91. Ibid., 149; Murphy, *Passion for Islam*, 86.

92. Murphy, *Passion for Islam*, 85.

93. Wright, *The Looming Tower*, 215.

94. Tal, *Islamic Fundamentalism*, 133.

95. Although the Egyptian government had co-opted the Muslim Brotherhood to a limited extent, it is unclear what insight the government gained into IG activities by way of potential "liaison" contact with Muslim Brotherhood elements.

96. Wright, *The Looming Tower*, 40.

97. "Cairo Frees 1,200 Gama'a Members Following Cessation of Violence," *Mideast Mirror* 13, no. 79 (April 27, 1999): page numbers unavailable.

98. Tal, *Islamic Fundamentalism*, 150.

99. Sarah Gauch, "Egypt Uses Fear to Fight Islamic Extremists," *Christian Science Monitor*, April 3, 1995.

100. Murphy, *Passion for Islam*, 91.

101. Joseph Kechichian and Jeanne Nazimek, "Challenges to the Military in Egypt," *Middle East Policy* 5, no. 3 (September 1997), available at http://www.mepc.org/journal/middle-east-policy-archives/challenges-military-egypt, accessed September 15, 2011.

102. Tal, *Islamic Fundamentalism*, 110.

103. Murphy, *Passion for Islam*, 90.

104. Ibid., 93, 95.

105. Ibid., 94.

106. Ibid., 95.

107. Tal, *Islamic Fundamentalism*, 110.

108. Robert Fisk, "Terror Stalks Egypt's Forgotten Towns," *The Independent*, February 8, 1995.

109. Tal, *Islamic Fundamentalism*, 110.

6. FAILURE IN EMBRYONIC TERRORIST GROUPS

1. See the discussion in Bruce Hoffman, "The Modern Terrorist Mindset," in *Terrorism and Counterterrorism: Understanding the New Security Environment*, ed. R. D. Howard and R. L. Sawyer, 229–256 (Guilford, CT: McGraw Hill, 2002).

2. It is likely that many terrorist groups that fail to survive more than a few years have a similar profile: they tend not to have widespread popularity (because they are not around long enough to earn it); they tend to have relatively strong adversaries (because this factor contributed to their early demise); and they tend to be small and lacking controlled territory (possibly as a result of being relatively unpopular and hounded by strong adversaries).

3. *United States of America v. Mohamad Ibrahim Shnewer et al.*, Criminal Complaint, US District Court of New Jersey, Case 1:07-cr-00459-RBK, filed January 15, 2008.

4. Geoff Mulvihill, "Fort Dix Plot Tipster: 'I Don't Feel Like a Hero,'" Associated Press, May 29, 2007.

5. *United States v. Mohamad Ibrahim Shnewer et al.*, Criminal Complaint.

6. Ibid.

7. Ibid.

8. George Anastasia, "From Star FBI Witness to Ostracism, Loss," *Philadelphia Inquirer*, June 27, 2010.

9. Amanda Ripley, "The Fort Dix Conspiracy," *Time Magazine*, December 6, 2007.

10. "Informants Key at Suspects' Trial in Fort Dix Case," Associated Press, December 19, 2008.

11. *United States v. Mohamad Ibrahim Shnewer et al.*, Criminal Complaint.

12. Ibid.

13. Ibid.

14. Kevin Coyne, "Informer Appears at Trial, but His Recordings Talk," *New York Times*, November 2, 2008.

15. *United States v. Mohamad Ibrahim Shnewer et al.*, Criminal Complaint.

16. Ibid.

17. *United States of America v. Agron Abdullahu*, US District Court of New Jersey, Mag. No. 07-2050 (JS), filed May 16, 2007, Memorandum of Law of the United States in Opposition to Defendant Agron Abdullahu's Motion for Bail.

18. John Martin, "Prosecutors' Star Witness Testifies in Fort Dix Terror Case," *New Jersey Star-Ledger*, October 28, 2008.

19. "Informants Key at Suspects' Trial in Fort Dix Case."

20. *United States v. Mohamad Ibrahim Shnewer et al.*, Criminal Complaint.

21. Ripley, "The Fort Dix Conspiracy."

22. *United States v. Mohamad Ibrahim Shnewer et al.*, Criminal Complaint.

23. Ibid.

24. Ibid.

25. *United States of America v. Mohammad Zaki Amawi, Marwan Othman El-Hindi, and Wassim I. Mazloum*, US District Court for the Northern District of Ohio, Western Division, Case No. 3:06CR719, filed October 5, 2009, Government's Sentencing Memorandum.

26. Ibid., Indictment.

27. *United States of America v. Zubair Ahmed and Khaleel Ahmed*, US District Court for the Northern District of Ohio, Western Division, Case No. 1:07CR647, filed July 1, 2010, Government's Sentencing Memorandum.

28. *United States of America v. Mohammad Zaki Amawi, Marwan Othman El-Hindi, and Wassim I. Mazloum*, Indictment and Government's Sentencing Memorandum.

29. Ibid., Indictment.

30. Ibid.

31. Michael Isikoff, "The Secret Agent," *Newsweek*, July 3, 2008.

32. Christopher Evans, Mark Rollenhagen, and Mike Tobin, "Terror Case Informant Has Had Money Woes: Toledoan Declared Bankruptcy in 1999," *Cleveland Plain Dealer*, April 28, 2006.

33. "Toledo Terror Trial," Associated Press, June 14, 2006.

34. Isikoff, "The Secret Agent."

35. *United States v. Mohammad Zaki Amawi, Marwan Othman El-Hindi, and Wassim I. Mazloum*, Government's Sentencing Memorandum.

36. *United States v. Zubair Ahmed and Khaleel Ahmed*, Indictment.

37. *United States v. Mohammad Zaki Amawi, Marwan Othman El-Hindi, and Wassim I. Mazloum*, Indictment.

38. *United States v. Zubair Ahmed and Khaleel Ahmed*, Government's Sentencing Memorandum and Indictment.

39. *United States v. Mohammad Zaki Amawi, Marwan Othman El-Hindi, and Wassim I. Mazloum*, Government's Sentencing Memorandum.

40. Ibid.

41. Ibid., Indictment.

42. "Toledo Terror Trial."

43. *United States v. Mohammad Zaki Amawi, Marwan Othman El-Hindi, and Wassim I. Mazloum*, Government's Sentencing Memorandum.

44. Ibid., Indictment.

45. Evans, Rollenhagen, and Tobin, "Terror Case Informant Has Had Money Woes."

46. *United States of America v. James Cromitie, David Williams, Onta Williams, and Laguerre Payen*, Southern District Court of New York, 09 Mag 1237, May 19, 2009, Sealed Complaint.

47. Ibid.

48. Ibid.

49. Javier C. Hernandez and Sewell Chan, "N.Y. Bomb Plot Suspects Acted Alone, Police Say," *New York Times*, May 22, 2009.

50. Michael Wilson, "Jury Convicts Two Albany Men in Missile Sting," *New York Times*, October 11, 2006.

51. Chris Dolmetsch, "Bomb-Plot Informant Testifies FBI Sent Him to Terrorist Camp in Pakistan," *Bloomberg*, September 16, 2010.

52. Hernandez and Chan, "N.Y. Bomb Plot Suspects Acted Alone, Police Say."

53. Al Baker and Javier C. Hernandez, "Four Accused of Bombing Plot at Bronx Synagogues," *New York Times*, May 21, 2009.

54. *United States v. James Cromitie et al.*, Sealed Complaint.

55. Ibid.

56. Ibid.

57. Ibid.

58. Ibid., Indictment.

59. David Kihara, "The Cambodian Freedom Fighters, One Year After the Attack," *Cambodia Daily*, September 15, 2001.

60. Josh Gerstein, "California Man Arrested for Plot Against Cambodia," *New York Sun*, June 2, 2005.

61. Sebastian Strangio, "Geopolitics Behind a Cambodian Conviction," *Asia Times*, July 7, 2010.

62. Daljit Singh and Anthony L. Smith, eds., *Southeast Asian Affairs 2002* (Singapore: Institute of Southeast Asian Studies, 2002).

63. Kihara, "The Cambodian Freedom Fighters."

64. Strangio, "Geopolitics Behind a Cambodian Conviction."

65. Kay Johnson, "By Night, a Fierce Rebel," *Time Magazine*, January 8, 2001.

66. Joshua Kurlantzick, "The Strip-Mall Revolutionaries," *New York Times*, March 21, 2004.

67. Quoted in Johnson, "By Night, a Fierce Rebel."

68. Verghese Mathews, "Cambodia's Bizarre Freedom Fighters," *On Line Opinion*, July 6, 2005, available at http://www.onlineopinion.com.au/view.asp?article=3626, accessed September 15, 2011.

69. Kurlantzick, "The Strip-Mall Revolutionaries."

70. Kihara, "The Cambodian Freedom Fighters."

71. Kurlantzick, "The Strip-Mall Revolutionaries."

72. Strangio, "Geopolitics Behind a Cambodian Conviction."

73. Kihara, "The Cambodian Freedom Fighters"; Human Rights Watch, *World Report 2003* (New York: Human Rights Watch, 2003).

74. "Cambo Execs Say They Knew of the Raid in Advance," *Philippine Daily Inquirer*, November 26, 2000.

75. Quoted in Joshua Kurlantzick, "Guerillas in Our Midst: Is the United States Harboring Terrorists?" *The American Prospect*, June 2, 2002.

76. Quoted in John Marston, "Cambodia: Transnational Pressures and Local Agendas," in Singh and Smith, eds., *Southeast Asian Affairs 2002*, 101.

77. Kurlantzick, "The Strip-Mall Revolutionaries."

78. Ibid.

79. Quoted in Eric Pape, "The Plotting Fields," *LA Weekly*, January 19, 2001.

80. Johnson, "By Night, a Fierce Rebel."

81. Strangio, "Geopolitics Behind a Cambodian Conviction."

82. Marston, "Cambodia," 102.

83. Kurlantzick, "The Strip-Mall Revolutionaries."

84. Ontario Superior Court of Justice, Court File No. YC-07-1587, CanLII 51935 (September 25, 2008).

85. Isabel Teotonio, "The Toronto 18," *The Star*, n.d., available at http://www3.thestar.com/static/toronto18/, accessed September 15, 2011.

86. Ontario Superior Court of Justice, Court File No. YC-07-1587 (September 25, 2008).

87. Ontario Superior Court of Justice, Court File No. DR(F)2541/08, CanLII 24539 (May 20, 2008).

88. Ibid.

89. Teotonio, "The Toronto 18."

90. Ontario Superior Court of Justice, Court File No. CRIMJ(F)2025/07, CanLII 84786 (December 22, 2009).

91. Ontario Superior Court of Justice, Court File No. YC-07-1587.

92. Jackie Bennion, "The Group Next Door: The Radical Informant," *PBS Frontline/World*, January 30, 2007, available at http://www.pbs.org/frontlineworld /stories/canada602/shaikh.html, accessed September 15, 2011.

93. Teotonio, "The Toronto 18"; Government of Canada, *R. v. Saad Khalid*, Court File No. CRIMJ(F)2025/07 (May 20, 2008), Statement of Uncontested Facts, available at http://beta.images.theglobeandmail.com/archive/00208/Terror _case__Uncont_208021a.pdf, accessed September 15, 2011.

94. Ontario Superior Court of Justice, Court File No. YC-07-1587.

95. Government of Canada, *R. v. Saad Khalid*, Statement of Uncontested Facts.

96. Ontario Superior Court of Justice, Court File No. YC-07-1587.

97. Teotonio, "The Toronto 18."

98. Bennion, "The Group Next Door."

99. Teotonio, "The Toronto 18."

100. Bennion, "The Group Next Door."

101. Ontario Superior Court of Justice, Court File No. YC-07-1587.

102. Teotonio, "The Toronto 18."

103. Ontario Superior Court of Justice, Court File No. YC-07-1587.

104. Teotonio, "The Toronto 18."

105. Ibid.

106. Ontario Superior Court of Justice, Court File No. CRIMJ(F)2025/07.

107. Ontario Superior Court of Justice, Court File No. YC-07-1587.

108. Ontario Superior Court of Justice, Court File No. DR(F)2541/08.

109. Ontario Superior Court of Justice, Court File No. YC-07-1587.

110. Ontario Superior Court of Justice, Court File No. DR(F)2541/08.

111. Ontario Superior Court of Justice, Court File No. YC-07-1587.

112. Ontario Superior Court of Justice, Court File No. DR(F)2541/08.

113. Ontario Superior Court of Justice, Court File No. YC-07-1587.

114. Teotonio, "The Toronto 18."

115. Colin Freeze, "How a Police Agent Cracked a Terror Group," *Globe and Mail*, September 2, 2009.

116. Ontario Superior Court of Justice, Court File No. YC-07-1587.

117. Teotonio, "The Toronto 18."

118. Ontario Superior Court of Justice, Court File No. YC-07-1587.

119. Ibid.

120. Teotonio, "The Toronto 18."

121. Ibid.

122. Ontario Superior Court of Justice, Court File No. YC-07-1587.

123. Ibid.

124. Government of Canada, *R. v. Saad Khalid*, Statement of Uncontested Facts.

125. Teotonio, "The Toronto 18."

126. Ontario Superior Court of Justice, Court File No. YC-07-1587.

127. Government of Canada, *R. v. Saad Khalid*, Statement of Uncontested Facts.

128. Ontario Superior Court of Justice, Court File No. DR(F)2541/08.

129. Government of Canada, *R. v. Saad Khalid*, Statement of Uncontested Facts.

130. Ontario Superior Court of Justice, Court File No. YC-07-1587.

131. Ibid.

132. Government of Canada, *R. v. Saad Khalid*, Statement of Uncontested Facts.

133. Teotonio, "The Toronto 18."

134. Ibid.

135. Ontario Superior Court of Justice, Court File No. YC-07-1587.

136. Teotonio, "The Toronto 18."

7. TERRORISM AND COUNTERINTELLIGENCE

1. Matthew Teague, "Double Blind: The Untold Story of How British Intelligence Infiltrated and Undermined the IRA," *Atlantic Monthly* (April 2006), available at http://www.theatlantic.com/magazine/archive/2006/04/double-blind /4710/, accessed September 15, 2011.

2. Ed Moloney, *A Secret History of the IRA* (New York: W. W. Norton, 2002), 160.

3. Peter Taylor, *Provos: The IRA and Sinn Fein* (London: Bloomsbury, 1997), 211.

4. Ibid.

5. Christopher Dobson, *Black September: Its Short Violent History* (New York: Macmillan, 1974), 47.

6. Ehud Yaari, *Strike Terror: The Story of Fatah* (New York: Sabra Books, 1970), 245.

7. Edgar O'Ballance, *Arab Guerilla Power: 1967–1972* (London: Archon Books, 1973), 87.

8. Peter Bergen, *The Osama Bin Laden I Know: An Oral History of the al Qa'ida Leader* (New York: Free Press, 2006), 258.

9. Quoted in Walker and Gowers, *Arafat*, 24.

10. Brendan O'Brien, *The Long War: The IRA and Sinn Fein 1985 to Today* (Dublin: O'Brien Press, 1993), 161.

11. Patrick Bishop and Eamonn Mallie, *The Provisional IRA* (London: Heinemann, 1987), 159.

12. Bergen, *The Osama Bin Laden I Know*, 264.

13. Aaron J. Klein, *Striking Back: The 1972 Munich Olympics Massacre and Israel's Deadly Response* (New York: Random House, 2005), 160.

14. Steve Coll, *Ghost Wars: The Secret History of the CIA, Afghanistan, and Bin Laden from the Soviet Invasion to September 10, 2001* (New York: Penguin, 2004), 500.

15. Michael Bar-Zohar and Eitan Haber, *The Quest for the Red Prince* (New York: Morrow, 1983), 165; "A Blacker September," *Time Magazine*, March 19, 1973.

16. Simon Reeve, *One Day in September* (New York: Arcade, 2000), 2.

17. Quoted in J. Bowyer Bell, *The Secret Army: The IRA* (New Brunswick, NJ: Transaction, 1997), 470.

18. O'Ballance, *Arab Guerilla Power*, 122.

19. Montasser al-Zayyat, *The Road to al-Qa'ida: The Story of Bin Laden's Right Hand Man* (London: Pluto Press, 2004), 18.

20. Nicholas Davis, *Ten Thirty Three: The Inside Story of Britain's Secret Killing Machine in Northern Ireland* (Edinburgh: Mainstream, 1999), 34.

21. National Commission on Terrorist Attacks Upon the United States, *Monograph on Terrorist Financing*, staff report, 26, available at http://govinfo.library.unt.edu/911/staff_statements/index.htm, accessed September 15, 2011.

22. Jason Burke, *Casting a Shadow of Terror* (London: I. B. Taurus, 2003), 164.

23. Bergen, *The Osama Bin Laden I Know*, 241.

24. Bishop and Mallie, *The Provisional IRA*, 187.

25. Quoted in Tim Pat Coogan, *The IRA: A History* (Niwot, CO: Roberts Rinehart, 1993), 267.

26. Such a "chemical agent" might be reminiscent of the infamous "spy dust" employed by the KGB.

27. Lawrence Wright, *The Looming Tower: Al-Qa'ida and the Road to 9/11* (New York: Knopf, 2006), 199.

28. Thomas H. Kean, Chair, *The 9/11 Commission Report, Final Report of the National Commission on Terrorist Attacks Upon the United States* (New York: W. W. Norton, 2004), 67.

29. Michael Hayden, "State of al-Qaeda Today," presentation to the Atlantic Council, November 13, 2008, Washington, DC, available at http://www.acus.org/http:/%252Fwww.acus.org/event_blog/cia-director-event-transcript, accessed April 7, 2011.

Aburish, Said K. *Arafat: From Defender to Dictator*. New York: Bloomsbury, 1998.

Adams, James. "Americans Move to Destabilise Sudanese Regime." *Sunday London Times*, November 17, 1996.

Alexander, Yonah. *Counterterrorism Strategies: Successes and Failures of Six Nations*. Washington, DC: Potomac Books, 2006.

Anastasia, George. "From Star FBI Witness to Ostracism, Loss." *Philadelphia Inquirer*, June 27, 2010.

Anderson, Brendan. *Joe Cahill: A Life in the IRA*. Dublin: O'Brien Press, 2002.

Andrew, Christopher M. and Vasili Mitrokhin. *The World Was Going Our Way: The KGB and the Battle for the Third World*. New York: Basic Books, 2005.

Arbuckle, Tammy. "Egypt's Catch-22." *Jane's International Defense Review* 26, no. 12 (December 1, 1993). Available at http://articles.janes.com/articles /International-Defence-Review-93/EGYPT-S-CATCH-22.html. Accessed September 15, 2011.

Atwan, Abdel Bari. *The Secret History of al Qaida*. London: Saqi Books, 2006.

Al-Awadi, Hesham. *In Pursuit of Legitimacy: The Muslim Brothers and Mubarak, 1982–2000*. London: I. B. Tauris, 2005.

Baker, Al and Javier C. Hernandez. "Four Accused of Bombing Plot at Bronx Synagogues." *New York Times*, May 21, 2009.

Baker, Wayne E. and Robert R. Faulkner. "The Social Organization of Conspiracy: Illegal Networks in the Heavy Electrical Equipment Industry." *American Sociological Review* 58, no. 6 (December 1993): 837–860.

Bakier, Abdul Hameed. "The Evolution of Jihadi Electronic Counter-Measures." *Terrorism Monitor* 4, no. 17 (September 8, 2006). Available at http://www.james town.org/programs/gta/single/?tx_ttnews[tt_news]=894&tx_ttnews[backPid] =181&no_cache=1. Accessed September 15, 2011.

Baligh, Dalia. "Crackdown on Extremists Winds Down in Cairo Neighborhood." Associated Press, December 15, 1992.

Bar-Zohar, Michael and Eitan Haber. *The Quest for the Red Prince*. New York: Morrow, 1983.

Al-Battar Training Camp (Mu'askar al-Battar) (newsletter). Issues 3, 6, 9, 10, 16, 17, 22 (January–November 2004). Provided by SITE, RAND Voices of Jihad Database. Available at http://homelandsecurityus.com/archives/3294. Accessed September 15, 2011.

Bavly, Dan and Eliahu Salpeter. *Fire in Beirut: Israel's War in Lebanon with the PLO*. New York: Stein and Day, 1984.

Becker, Jullian. *The PLO: The Rise and Fall of the Palestine Liberation Organization*. New York: St. Martin's Press, 1984.

Bell, J. Bowyer. *The IRA, 1968–2000: Analysis of a Secret Army*. London: Frank Cass, 2000.

——. *The Secret Army: The IRA*. New Brunswick, NJ: Transaction, 1997.

Benjamin, Daniel and Steven Simon. *The Age of Sacred Terror*. New York: Random House, 2002.

Bennion, Jackie. "The Group Next Door: The Radical Informant." *PBS Frontline/World*, January 30, 2007. Available at http://www.pbs.org/frontlineworld/stories/canada602/shaikh.html. Accessed September 15, 2011.

Bergen, Peter. *Holy War, Inc.: Inside the Secret World of Osama Bin Laden*. New York: Simon and Schuster, 2001.

——. "The Long Hunt for Osama." *Atlantic Monthly* (October 2004). Available at http://www.theatlantic.com/magazine/archive/2004/10/the-long-hunt-for-osama/3508/. Accessed September 15, 2011.

——. *The Osama Bin Laden I Know: An Oral History of the al Qa'ida Leader*. New York: Free Press, 2006.

Bishop, Patrick and Eamonn Mallie. *The Provisional IRA*. London: Heinemann, 1987.

"A Blacker September." *Time Magazine*, March 19, 1973.

Blanchard, Christopher M. *Al Qa'ida: Statements and Evolving Ideology*. Order Code RS21973. Washington, DC: Congressional Research Service, November 16, 2004.

Bloom, Mia M. "Palestinian Suicide Bombing: Public Support, Market Share, and Outbidding." *Political Science Quarterly* 119, no. 1 (Spring 2004): 61–88.

Bobbitt, Randolph H., Jr., and Orlando Behling. "Organizational Behavior: A Review of the Literature." *Journal of Higher Education* 52, no. 1 (January–February 1981): 29–44.

Bodansky, Yossef. *Bin Laden: The Man Who Declared War on America*. Roseville, CA: Prima, 2001.

Bowden, Mark. "Jihadists in Paradise." *Atlantic Monthly* (March 2007). Available at http://www.theatlantic.com/magazine/archive/2007/03/jihadists-in-paradise/5613/. Accessed September 15, 2011.

Brachman, Jarret M. "High-Tech Terror: Al-Qa'ida's Use of New Technology." *Fletcher Forum of World Affairs* 30, no. 2 (Summer 2006): 149–164.

Brachman, Jarret M. and William F. McCants. *Stealing al-Qa'ida's Playbook*. New York: Combating Terrorism Center at West Point, February 2006.

Brass, Daniel J., Kenneth D. Butterfield, and Bruce C. Skaggs. "Relationships and Unethical Behavior: A Social Network Perspective." *Academy of Management Review* 23, no. 1 (January 1998): 14–31.

Bromley, David G. "Linking Social Structure and the Exit Process in Religious Organizations: Defectors, Whistle-Blowers, and Apostates." *Journal for the Scientific Study of Religion* 37, no. 1 (March 1998): 145–160.

Burke, Jason. *Casting a Shadow of Terror*. London: I. B. Taurus, 2003.

Byman, Daniel. *Deadly Connections: States That Sponsor Terrorism*. Cambridge, UK: Cambridge University Press, 2005.

——. "Strategic Surprise and the September 11 Attacks." *Annual Review of Political Science* 8 (2005): 145–170.

"Cairo Frees 1,200 Gama'a Members Following Cessation of Violence." *Mideast Mirror* 13, no. 79 (April 27, 1999): page numbers not available.

"Cambo Execs Say They Knew of the Raid in Advance." *Philippine Daily Inquirer*, November 26, 2000.

Canadian Security Intelligence Service. "Irish Nationalist Terrorism Outside Ireland: Out-of-Theatre Operations 1972–1993." *Commentary*, no. 40 (February 1994). Available at http://www.csis-scrs.gc.ca/pblctns/cmmntr/cm40-eng.asp. Accessed September 15, 2011.

Carlough, Montgomery Cybele. "Pax Britannica: British Counterinsurgency in Northern Ireland, 1969–1982." PhD diss., Yale University, 1994.

Chattopadhyay, Prithviraj, William H. Glick, and George P. Huber. "Organizational Actions in Response to Threats and Opportunities." *Academy of Management Journal* 44, no. 5 (October 2001): 937–955.

Chauhan, Sharad S. *The al Qa'ida Threat*. New Delhi: APH, 2003.

Clapman, Christopher, ed. *African Guerillas*. Oxford, UK: James Currey, 1998.

Clark, Robert. *The Basque Insurgents: ETA 1952–1980*. Madison: University of Wisconsin Press, 1984.

Clarke, Liam. *Broadening the Battlefield: The H-Blocks and the Rise of Sinn Fein*. Dublin: Gill and Macmillan, 1987.

Coll, Steve. *Ghost Wars: The Secret History of the CIA, Afghanistan, and Bin Laden from the Soviet Invasion to September 10, 2001*. New York: Penguin, 2004.

Coogan, Tim Pat. *The IRA: A History*. Niwot, CO: Roberts Rinehart, 1993.

——. *The Troubles: Ireland's Ordeal 1966–1996 and the Search for Peace*. Lanham, MD: Roberts Rinehart, 1996.

Cooley, John K. *Green March, Black September*. London: Frank Cass, 1973.

Corbin, Jane. *Al-Qa'ida: In Search of the Terror Network That Threatens the World*. New York: Thunder's Mouth Press, 2003.

Corman, Steve R. and Jill S. Schiefelbein. *Communication and Media Strategy in the Jihadi War of Ideas*. Report No. 0601. Phoenix: Consortium for Strategic Communication, Arizona State University, April 20, 2006.

Coyne, Kevin. "Informer Appears at Trial, but His Recordings Talk." *New York Times*, November 2, 2008.

Cronin, Audrey Kurth. "How al-Qaida Ends: The Decline and Demise of Terrorist Groups." *International Security* (Summer 2006): 7–48.

Cullison, Alan. "Inside al-Qa'ida's Hard Drive." *Atlantic Monthly* (September 2004). Available at http://www.theatlantic.com/magazine/archive/2004/09/inside-al-qaeda-rsquo-s-hard-drive/3428. Accessed September 15, 2011.

Davidson, Charles. "Political Violence in Egypt: A Case Study of the Islamic Insurgency 1992–1997." PhD diss., Turfs University, 2005.

Davis, Nicholas. *Ten Thirty Three: The Inside Story of Britain's Secret Killing Machine in Northern Ireland*. Edinburgh: Mainstream, 1999.

Dawoud, Khaled. "The Battle for the Mosque: Government vs. Extremists." Associated Press, December 24, 1993.

De Baroid, Ciaran. *Ballymurphy and the Irish War*. London: Pluto Press, 2000.

Dewar, Colonel Michael. *The British Army in Northern Ireland*. London: Arms and Armour Press, 1996.

Dobson, Christopher. *Black September: Its Short Violent History*. New York: Macmillan, 1974.

Dolmetsch, Chris. "Bomb-Plot Informant Testifies FBI Sent Him to Terrorist Camp in Pakistan." *Bloomberg*, September 16, 2010.

Dorsey, James. "Syria Tries to Discredit PLO: A Tale of Intrigue and Murder." *Christian Science Monitor*, August 5, 1981.

Dunn, Michael Collins. "Fundamentalism in Egypt." *Middle East Policy* 2, no. 3 (1993): 68–78.

"Egypt's New Security Strategy: No Dialogue, No Retreat in All-Out War." *Mideast Mirror*, April 22, 1993.

El-Rayyes, Riad and Dunia Nahas. *Guerrillas for Palestine*. London: Portico, 1976.

English, Richard. *Armed Struggle: The History of the IRA*. New York: Oxford University Press, 2003.

Erickson, Bonnie H. "Secret Societies and Social Structure." *Social Forces* 60, no. 1 (September 1981): 188–210.

Evans, Christopher, Mark Rollenhagen, and Mike Tobin. "Terror Case Informant Has Had Money Woes: Toledoan Declared Bankruptcy in 1999." *Cleveland Plain Dealer*, April 28, 2006.

Feldman, Allen. *Formations of Violence: The Narrative of the Body and Political Terror in Northern Ireland*. Chicago: University of Chicago Press, 1991.

Felter, Joseph, Jeff Bramlett, Bill Perkins, Jarrett Brachman, Brian Fishman, James Forest, Lianne Kennedy, Jacob N. Shapiro, and Tom Stocking. *Harmony and Disharmony: Exploiting al-Qa'ida's Organizational Vulnerabilities*. Combating Terrorism Center, United States Military Academy, February 14, 2006. Available at http://www.ctc.usma.edu/posts/harmony-and-disharmony-exploiting-al-qaidas-organizational-vulnerabilities. Accessed September 15, 2011.

Fisk, Robert. "Might of the Sword Menaces Christians." *The Independent*, February 9, 1995.

——. "Terror Stalks Egypt's Forgotten Towns." *The Independent*, February 8, 1995.

Freeze, Colin. "How a Police Agent Cracked a Terror Group." *Globe and Mail*, September 2, 2009.

Gabriel, Richard A. *Operation Peace for Galilee: The Israeli–PLO War in Lebanon*. New York: Hill and Wang, 1984.

Gates, Scott. "Recruitment and Allegiance: The Microfoundations of Rebellion." *Journal of Conflict Resolution* 46, no. 1 (February 2002): 111–130.

Gauch, Sarah. "Egypt Uses Fear to Fight Islamic Extremists." *Christian Science Monitor*, April 3, 1995.

Geraghty, Tony. *The Irish War*. London: HarperCollins, 1998.

Gerstein, John. "California Man Arrested for Plot Against Cambodia." *New York Sun*, June 2, 2005.

Gilmour, Raymond. *Dead Ground: Infiltrating the IRA*. London: Little Brown, 1998.

Gladstein, Deborah L. and Nora P. Reilly. "Group Decision Making Under Threat: The Tycoon Game." *Academy of Management Journal* 28, no. 3 (September 1985): 613–627.

Goodspeed, Donald James. *The Conspirators: A Study of Coup d'État*. New York: Viking Press, 1961.

Greer, Steven. "Towards a Sociological Model of the Police Informant." *British Journal of Sociology* 46, no. 3 (September 1995): 509–527.

Gunaratna, Rohan. *Inside al Qa'ida: Global Network of Terror*. New York: Columbia University Press, 2002.

Al-Hadlag, Abdulrahman. "Repression and Peoples' Political Violence in Egypt: The Case of al-Jama'a al-Islamiyya." PhD diss., University of Idaho, 1994.

Hansen, Wendy L., Neil J. Mitchell, and Jeffrey M. Drope. "The Logic of Private and Collective Action." *American Journal of Political Science* 49, no. 1 (January 2005): 150–167.

Hawthorn, H. B. "A Test of Simmel on the Secret Society: The Doukhobors of British Columbia." *American Journal of Sociology* 62, no. 1 (July 1956): 1–7.

Hayden, Michael. "State of al-Qaeda Today." Presentation to the Atlantic Council, November 13, 2008, Washington, DC. Available at http://www.acus.org

/http:/%252Fwww.acus.org/event_blog/cia-director-event-transcript. Accessed April 7, 2011.

Hazelrigg, Lawrence E. "A Reexamination of Simmel's 'The Secret and the Secret Society': Nine Propositions." *Social Forces* 47, no. 3 (March 1969): 323–330.

Hedges, Chris. "Egypt's War with Militants: Both Sides Harden Positions." *New York Times*, April 3, 1993.

Herbst, Jeffrey. "African Militaries and Rebellion: The Political Economy of Threat and Combat Effectiveness." *Journal of Peace Research* 41, no. 3 (May 2004): 357–369.

Hernandez, Javier C. and Sewell Chan. "N.Y. Bomb Plot Suspects Acted Alone, Police Say." *New York Times*, May 22, 2009.

Hirschkorn, Phil. "Trial Spotlights America's Top Terrorist Threat." *Journal of Counterterrorism & Security International* 7, no. 4 (Summer 2001). Available at http://www.lexisnexis.com/hottopics/lnacademic/?verb=sr&csi=244681. Accessed September 15, 2011.

Hoffman, Bruce. "All You Need Is Love: How the Terrorists Stopped Terrorism." *Atlantic Monthly* (December 2001). Available at http://www.theatlantic.com /past/docs/issues/2001/12/hoffman.htm. Accessed September 15, 2011.

——. *Combating al Qa'ida and the Militant Islamic Threat.* Testimony before the Armed Services Committee, Subcommittee on Terrorism, Unconventional Threats, and Capabilities, US House of Representatives, 109th Cong., 2d sess., February 16, 2006.

——. *Inside Terrorism.* London: Victor Gollancz, 1998.

——. "The Modern Terrorist Mindset." In *Terrorism and Counterterrorism: Understanding the New Security Environment*, ed. R. D. Howard and R. L. Sawyer, 229–256. Guilford, CT: McGraw Hill, 2002.

——. *The Use of the Internet by Islamic Extremists.* Testimony before the Permanent Select Committee on Intelligence, US House of Representatives, 109th Cong., 2d sess., May 4, 2006.

Horowitz, Ruth. "Community Tolerance of Gang Violence." *Social Problems* 34, no. 5 (December 1987): 437–450.

Huband, Mark. "Luxor Masterminds in Afghanistan Exile." *London Financial Times*, November 20, 1997.

Human Rights Watch. *World Report 2003.* New York: Human Rights Watch, 2003.

Ibrahim, Youssef M. "Egyptian Police, Sweep, Seize Suspects in Killing of Greeks." *New York Times*, April 20, 1996.

Imperial Hubris: Why the West Is Losing the War on Terror. Washington, DC: Brassey's, 2004.

"Informants Key at Suspects' Trial in Fort Dix Case." Associated Press, December 19, 2008.

"Information Bank Abstracts." *New York Times*, March 16, 1969; March 5, 1973; March 8, 1973.

IntelCenter. *Al-Qa'ida Attack/Messaging Statistics V.1.0.* Alexandria, VA: IntelCenter/Tempest, August 22, 2003.

——. *Al Qa'ida Messaging/Attacks Timeline V5.0.* Public-release version. Alexandria, VA: IntelCenter/Tempest, September 29, 2006.

——. *Al-Qa'ida Operational Tempo—Madrid Follow-on Attack Assessment, V.1.0.* Alexandria, VA: IntelCenter/Tempest, March 14, 2004.

——. *Al Qa'ida Warning Cycle Completion for CONUS, v1.1.* Alexandria, VA: IntelCenter/Tempest, December 9, 2005.

Irish Republican Army, General Headquarters. *A Handbook for Volunteers of the Irish Republican Army.* N.p.: n.p., 1956.

Isikoff, Michael. "The Secret Agent." *Newsweek*, July 3, 2008.

Jackson, Brian. "Groups, Networks, or Movements: A Command and Control Driven Approach to Classifying Terrorist Organizations and Its Applications to al Qa'ida." *Studies in Conflict and Terrorism* 29 (2006): 241–262.

Jackson, Brian A., John C. Baker, Kim Cragin, John Parachini, Horacio R. Trujillo, and Peter Chalk. *Aptitude for Destruction, Volume Two: Case Studies of Organizational Learning in Five Terrorist Groups.* Santa Monica, CA: RAND Corporation, 2005.

"Jemmah Islamiya Reported to Have Killed Policeman in Asyut." Agence France Presse, September 25, 1993.

Jenkins, Brian Michael. *Countering al Qa'ida.* Santa Monica, CA: RAND Corporation, 2002.

Johnson, Kay. "By Night, a Fierce Rebel." *Time Magazine*, January 8, 2001.

Johnson, Norman J., Richard H. Hall, and J. Eugene Haas. "Organizational Size, Complexity, and Formalization." *American Sociological Review* 32, no. 6 (December 1967): 903–912.

Jonas, George. *Vengeance: The True Story of an Israeli Counter-Terrorism Team.* New York: Simon and Schuster, 2005.

Jones, Seth G. and Martin C. Libicki. *How Terrorist Groups End: Lessons for Countering al Qa'ida.* Santa Monica, CA: RAND Corporation, 2008.

Jordan, Javier and Robert Wesley. "The Madrid Attacks: Results of Investigations Two Years Later." *Terrorism Monitor* 4, no. 5 (March 9, 2006). Available at http://www.jamestown.org/programs/gta/single/?tx_ttnews[tt_news]=696&tx_ttnews[backPid]=181&no_cache=1. Accessed September 15, 2011.

Kassimeris, George. *Europe's Last Red Terrorists: The Revolutionary Organization 17 November.* London: Hurst, 2001.

Kauffman, S. A. *The Origins of Order.* New York: Oxford University Press, 1993.

Kean, Thomas H., Chair. *The 9/11 Commission Report, Final Report of the National Commission on Terrorist Attacks Upon the United States.* New York: W. W. Norton, 2004.

Kechichian, Joseph and Jeanne Nazimek. "Challenges to the Military in Egypt." *Middle East Policy* 5, no. 3 (September 1997). Available at http://www.mepc.org/journal/middle-east-policy-archives/challenges-military-egypt. Accessed September 15, 2011.

Kelley, Kevin J. *The Longest War: Northern Ireland and the IRA.* Westport, CT: Lawrence Hill, 1988.

Kent, Robert B. "Geographical Dimensions of the Shining Path Insurgency in Peru." *Geographical Review* 83, no. 4 (October 1993): 441–454.

Kepel, Gilles. *Jihad: The Trail of Political Islam.* New York: I. B. Tauris, 2006.

——. *The Roots of Radical Islam.* London: Saqi Books, 2005.

Kienle, Eberhard. *Grand Delusion: Democracy and Economic Reform in Egypt.* London: I. B. Tauris, 2000.

Kihara, David. "The Cambodian Freedom Fighters, One Year After the Attack." *Cambodia Daily*, September 15, 2001.

Kifner, John. "West Beirut Bids Farewell to the PLO." *New York Times*, August 23, 1982.

Klein, Aaron J. *Striking Back: The 1972 Munich Olympics Massacre and Israel's Deadly Response.* New York: Random House, 2005.

Kohlmann, Evan F. "The Real Online Terrorist Threat." *Foreign Affairs* 85, no. 5 (September–October 2006): 115–124.

Kurlantzick, Joshua. "Guerillas in Our Midst: Is the United States Harboring Terrorists?" *The American Prospect*, June 2, 2002.

——. "The Strip-Mall Revolutionaries." *New York Times*, March 21, 2004.

Kurz, Anat N. *Fatah and the Politics of Violence: The Institutionalization of a Popular Struggle.* Brighton, UK: Sussex Academic Press, 2005.

LaBelle, G. G. "Abdel-Rahman's Following in Egypt." Associated Press, July 18, 1993.

——. "Charges of Terrorism, Claims of Democracy Mix Blur of Sudan." Associated Press, March 28, 1996.

Lacey, Marc. "Terrorists in Kenya Killings Posed as Fishermen." *New York Times*, November 6, 2003.

Laffin, John. *Fedayeen: The Arab–Israeli Dilemma.* London: Cassell, 1973.

Laqueur, Walter. *Guerrilla: A Historical and Critical Study.* Boulder, CO: Westview Press, 1984.

Leites, Nathan and Charles Wolf Jr. *Rebellion and Authority: An Analytical Essay on Insurgent Conflicts.* Chicago: Markham, 1970.

Lichbach, Mark Irving. *The Rebel's Dilemma.* Ann Arbor: University of Michigan Press, 1995.

Lowry, Ritchie P. "Toward a Sociology of Secrecy and Security Systems." *Social Problems* 19, no. 4 (Spring 1972): 437–450.

Luttwak, Edward. *Coup d'État: A Practical Handbook*. London: Wildwood House, 1979.

Manheim, Jarol B. and Robert B. Albritton. "Insurgent Violence Versus Image Management: The Struggle for National Images in Southern Africa." *British Journal of Political Science* 17, no. 2 (April 1987): 201–218.

Margasak, Larry. "Philippines Reports Show Terrorists' Careful Plans." Associated Press, April 7, 2003.

Marighella, Carlos. *The Minimanual of the Urban Terrorist*. Available at http://www .marxists.org/archive/marighella-carlos/1969/06/minimanual-urban -guerrilla/. Accessed September 15, 2011.

Marion, Russ and Mary Uhl-Bien. "Complexity Theory and al Qa'ida: Examining Complex Leadership." Paper presented at the conference "Managing the Complex IV: A Conference on Complex Systems and the Management of Organizations," Fort Meyers, FL, December 2002.

Marston, John. "Cambodia: Transnational Pressures and Local Agendas." In Daljit Singh and Anthony L. Smith, eds., *Southeast Asian Affairs 2002*, 95–108. Singapore: Institute of Southeast Asian Studies, 2002.

Martin, John. "Prosecutors' Star Witness Testifies in Fort Dix Terror Case." *New Jersey Star-Ledger*, October 28, 2008.

Marx, Gary T. "Thoughts on a Neglected Category of Social Movement Participant: The Agent Provocateur and the Informant." *American Journal of Sociology* 80, no. 2 (September 1974): 402–442.

Mathews, Verghese. "Cambodia's Bizarre Freedom Fighters." *On Line Opinion*, July 6, 2005. Available at http://www.onlineopinion.com.au/view.asp?article=3626. Accessed September 15, 2011.

McCormick, Gordon H. and Guillermo Owen. "Security and Coordination in a Clandestine Organization." *Mathematical and Computer Modeling* 31 (2000): 175–192.

Meade, Robert, Jr. *Red Brigades: The Story of Italian Terrorism*. London: MacMillan, 1990.

Mekki, Hassan. "Security Forces Kill Top Militant in New Blow to Fundamentalists." Agence France Presse, November 17, 1994.

Mileti, Dennis S., Doug A. Timmer, and David F. Gillespie. "Intra and Interorganizational Determinants of Decentralization." *Pacific Sociological Review* 25, no. 2 (April 1982): 163–183.

Miller, John and Michael Stone, with Chris Mitchell. *The Cell: Inside the 9/11 Plot and Why the FBI and CIA Failed to Stop It*. New York: Hyperion, 2003.

Moloney, Ed. *A Secret History of the IRA*. New York: W. W. Norton, 2002.

Moore, Joan, Diego Vigil, and Robert Garcia. "Residence and Territoriality in Chicano Gangs." *Social Problems* 31, no. 2 (December 1983): 182–194.

Moore, Robin. *The Hunt for Bin Laden: Task Force Dagger.* New York: Random House, 2003.

Moore, Will H. "Rational Rebels: Overcoming the Free-Rider Problem." *Political Research Quarterly* 48, no. 2 (June 1995): 417–454.

"Most Jamaa Leaders Favor End to All Attacks." Agence France Presse, December 11, 1997.

Mulvihill, Geoff. "Fort Dix Plot Tipster: 'I Don't Feel Like a Hero.'" Associated Press, May 29, 2007.

Murphy, Caryle. *Passion for Islam, Shaping the Modern Middle East: The Egyptian Experience.* New York: Scribner, 2002.

National Commission on Terrorist Attacks Upon the United States. *9/11 and Terrorist Travel.* Staff report, n.d. Available at http://govinfo.library.unt.edu/911/staff_statements/index.htm. Accessed September 15, 2011.

——. *Monograph on Terrorist Financing.* Staff report, n.d. Available at http://govinfo.library.unt.edu/911/staff_statements/index.htm. Accessed September 15, 2011.

Nojumi, Neamatollah. *The Rise of the Taliban in Afghanistan.* New York: Palgrave, 2002.

O'Ballance, Edgar. *Arab Guerilla Power: 1967–1972.* London: Archon Books, 1973.

Oberschall, Anthony. "Explaining Terrorism: The Contribution of Collective Action Theory." In "Theories of Terrorism: A Symposium," special issue of *Sociological Theory* 22, no. 1 (March 2004): 26–37.

O'Brien, Brendan. *The Long War: The IRA and Sinn Fein 1985 to Today.* Dublin: O'Brien Press, 1993.

O'Callaghan, Sean. *The Informer.* London: Bantam Press, 1998.

O'Neill, Bard, William Heaton, and Donald Alberts, eds. *Insurgency in the Modern World.* Boulder, CO: Westview Press, 1980.

Pape, Eric. "The Plotting Fields." *LA Weekly,* January 19, 2001.

Pedahzur, Ami and Arie Perliger. "The Changing Nature of Suicide Attacks: A Social Network Perspective." *Social Forces* 84, no. 4 (June 2006): 1987–2008.

Pershing, Jana L. "To Snitch or Not to Snitch? Applying the Concept of Neutralization Techniques to the Enforcement of Occupational Misconduct." *Sociological Perspectives* 46, no. 2 (Summer 2003): 149–178.

Posner, Steve. *Israel Undercover: Secret Warfare and Hidden Diplomacy in the Middle East.* Syracuse, NY: Syracuse University Press, 1987.

Quinlivan, James T. "Coup-Proofing: Its Practice and Consequences in the Middle East," *International Security* 24, no. 2 (Autumn 1999): 131–165.

Reed, Stanley. "The Battle for Egypt." *Foreign Affairs* (September–October 1993). Available at http://www.foreignaffairs.com/articles/49197/stanley-reed/the-battle-for-egypt. Accessed September 15, 2011.

Reeve, Simon. *The New Jackals: Ramzi Yousef, Osama Bin Laden, and the Future of Terrorism*. Boston: Northeastern University Press, 1999.

——. *One Day in September*. New York: Arcade, 2000.

Regan, Patrick M. and Daniel Norton. "Greed, Grievance, and Mobilization in Civil Wars." *Journal of Conflict Resolution* 49, no. 3 (June 2005): 319–336.

Reichman, Nancy. "Breaking Confidences: Organizational Influences on Insider Trading." *Sociological Quarterly* 30, no. 2 (Summer 1989): 185–204.

Ripley, Amanda. "The Fort Dix Conspiracy." *Time Magazine*, December 6, 2007.

"Rome Guerrilla Base." *Sydney Morning Herald*, December 20, 1973.

Ronfeldt, David and John Arquilla. *Networks and Netwars: The Future of Terror, Crime, and Militancy*. Santa Monica, CA: RAND Corporation, 2001.

Roucek, Joseph S. "Sociology of Secret Societies." *American Journal of Economics and Sociology* 19, no. 2 (January 1960): 161–168.

Rubin, Barry. *Islamic Fundamentalism in Egyptian Politics*. New York: St. Martin's Press, 1990.

Rubin, Barry and Judith Colp Rubin. *Yasir Arafat: A Political Biography*. Oxford: Oxford University Press, 2003.

Sageman, Marc. *Understanding Terror Networks*. Philadelphia: University of Pennsylvania Press, 2004.

Schanzer, Jonathan. *Al Qa'ida's Armies: Middle East Affiliate Groups and the Next Generation of Terror*. Washington, DC: Specialist Press International, 2005.

Scheuer, Michael. "The New York Plot: The Impact of Bin Laden's Campaign to Inspire Jihad." *Terrorism Focus* 3, no. 28 (July 18, 2006). Available at http://www.jamestown.org/programs/gta/single/?tx_ttnews[tt_news]=846&tx_ttnews[backPid]=239&no_cache=1. Accessed September 15, 2011.

——. *Through Our Enemies' Eyes: Osama Bin Laden, Radical Islam, and the Future of America*. Washington, DC: Potomac Books, 2006.

Schiff, Zeev and Raphael Rothstein. *Fedayeen: Guerrillas Against Israel*. New York: David McKay, 1972.

Schulz, Helena Lindholm, with Juliane Hammer. *The Palestinian Diaspora: Formation of Identities and Politics of Homeland*. London: Routledge and the Taylor and Francis Group, 2003.

Seale, Patrick. *Abu Nidal: A Gun for Hire*. New York: Random House, 1992.

Shultz, Richard. "Breaking the Will of the Enemy During the Vietnam War: The Operationalization of the Cost–Benefit Model of Counterinsurgency Warfare." *Journal of Peace Research* 15, no. 2 (1978): 109–129.

Simon, Steven and Jeff Martini. "Terrorism: Denying al Qa'ida Its Popular Support." *Washington Quarterly* (Winter 2004–2005): 131–145.

Sims, Jennifer. "Understanding Friends and Enemies: The Context for American Intelligence Reform." In *Transforming U.S. Intelligence*, ed. Jennifer Sims and Burton Gerber, 14–31. Washington, DC: Georgetown University Press, 2005.

Singh, Daljit and Anthony L. Smith, eds. *Southeast Asian Affairs 2002.* Singapore: Institute of Southeast Asian Studies, 2002.

Smith, M. L. R. *Fighting for Ireland? The Military Strategy of the Irish Republican Movement.* London: Routledge, 1995.

Smucker, Philip. *Al Qa'ida's Great Escape: The Military and the Media on Terror's Trail.* Washington, DC: Brassey's, 2004.

Staw, Barry M. and Eugene Szwajkowski. "The Scarcity–Munificence Component of Organizational Environments and the Commission of Illegal Acts." *Administrative Science Quarterly* 20, no. 3 (September 1975): 345–354.

Strangio, Sebastian. "Geopolitics Behind a Cambodian Conviction." *Asia Times*, July 7, 2010.

Sullivan, Denis J. and Sana Abed-Kotob. *Islam in Contemporary Egypt: Civil Society vs. the State.* London: Lynn Rienner, 1999.

Tal, Nachman. *Islamic Fundamentalism: The Case of Egypt and Jordan.* Tel Aviv: University of Tel Aviv, 1999.

——. *Radical Islam in Egypt and Jordan.* Brighton, UK: Sussex Academic Press, 2005.

Tarazona-Sevillano, Gabriela. *Sendero Luminoso and the Threat of Narcoterrorism.* Center for Strategic and International Studies Washington Papers. New York: Praeger, 1990.

Taylor, Peter. *Beating the Terrorists? Interrogation at Omagh, Gough, and Castlereagh.* Middlesex, UK: Penguin Books, 1980.

——. *Brits: The War Against the IRA.* London: Bloomsbury, 2001.

——. *Provos: The IRA and Sinn Fein.* London: Bloomsbury, 1997.

Teague, Matthew. "Double Blind: The Untold Story of How British Intelligence Infiltrated and Undermined the IRA." *Atlantic Monthly* (April 2006). Available at http://www.theatlantic.com/magazine/archive/2006/04/double-blind /4710/. Accessed September 15, 2011.

Teotonio, Isabel. "The Toronto 18." *The Star*, n.d. Available at http://www3.thestar .com/static/toronto18/. Accessed September 15, 2011.

Thayer, Charles W. *Guerrilla.* London: Michael Joseph, 1963.

Thomas, Timothy. "Al Qa'ida and the Internet: The Danger of 'Cyberplanning.'" *Parameters* (Spring 2003): 112–123.

Tohid, Owais. "Tribesmen Take Cash, Count Blessings from al Qa'ida." *Christian Science Monitor*, October 29, 2003.

"Toledo Terror Trial." Associated Press, June 14, 2006.

Ulin, Robert C. "Peasant Politics and Secret Societies: The Discourse of Secrecy." *Anthropological Quarterly* 59, no. 1 (January 1986): 28–39.

Ulph, Stephen. "Intelligence War Breaks Out on the Jihadi Forums." *Terrorism Monitor* 3, no. 14 (April 11, 2006). Available at http://www.jamestown.org

/programs/gta/single/?tx_ttnews[tt_news]=732&tx_ttnews[backPid]=239&no
_cache=1. Accessed September 15, 2011.

Urban, Mark. *Big Boys' Rules: The SAS and the Secret Struggle Against the IRA*. London: Faber and Faber, 1992.

"US Intelligence: Al Qa'ida Infiltrated Saudi Arabia's Elite National Guard." *Al Bawaba*, May 19, 2003.

Vaughan, Diane. "The Dark Side of Organizations: Mistake, Misconduct, and Disaster." *Annual Review of Sociology* 25 (1999): 271–305.

——. "Transaction Systems and Unlawful Organizational Behavior." *Social Problems* 29, no. 4 (April 1982): 373–379.

Venzke, Ben. *Evolution of Jihadi Video. V1.0*. Alexandria, VA: IntelCenter, May 11, 2005.

——. *Jihadi Master Video Guide. V1.1*. Alexandria, VA: IntelCenter, May 18, 2006.

Vidino, Lorenzo. *Al Qa'ida in Europe: The New Battleground of International Jihad*. New York: Prometheus Books, 2006.

Vinci, Anthony. "The Problems of Mobilization in the Analysis of Armed Groups." *Parameters* (Spring 2006): 49–62.

Walker, Tony and Andrew Gowers. *Arafat: The Biography*. London: Virgin Books, 2003.

Weaver, Mary Anne. *A Portrait of Egypt: A Journey Through the World of Militant Islam*. New York: Farrar, Straus and Giroux, 1999.

Wilson, Michael. "Jury Convicts Two Albany Men in Missile Sting." *New York Times*, October 11, 2006.

Woodworth, Paddy. *Dirty War, Clean Hands: ETA, the GAL, and Spanish Democracy*. Cork, Ireland: Cork University Press, 2001.

Wright, Lawrence. *The Looming Tower: Al-Qa'ida and the Road to 9/11*. New York: Knopf, 2006.

Yaari, Ehud. *Strike Terror: The Story of Fatah*. New York: Sabra Books, 1970.

Al-Zayyat, Montasser. *The Road to al-Qa'ida: The Story of Bin Laden's Right Hand Man*. London: Pluto Press, 2004.

INDEX

Note: page numbers followed by *f* and *t* refer to figures and tables, respectively. Those followed by n refer to notes, with note number.

al Qa'ida, U.S. attacks against: in
Afghanistan, 121, 124, 137, 166,
242; and al Qa'ida popular
support, 125, 163
al Qa'ida adversaries,
counterterrorism capability of,
104t, 112–13, 129–30, 155–56;
captured records and, 117; limited
early response to al Qa'ida,
112–13. *See also* United States
counterterrorism measures
al Qa'ida controlled territory, 104t,
118, 148, 166; advantages and
disadvantages of, 15, 139, 166,
238; in Afghanistan, 105f, 106,
107f, 120, 126; in Afghan-Pakistan
border region, 153–54, 158–59;
and counterintelligence, 133,
158–59, 162–63, 166, 167, 257;
Internet as substitute for, 155, 163;
in Sudan, 105, 106, 107f, 108, 110
al Qa'ida counterintelligence, 118,
148–49; aliases and disguises, 117,
134, 142; awareness of
vulnerabilities, 116; captured
records and, 117; controlled
territory and, 133, 158–59, 166, 167;
counterterrorism capabilities of
adversary and, 241; defectors, 1,
115, 165; document and records
security, 138–39, 142, 148, 153–54,
157; false documents and identities,
143–44; internationally, 116–17,
139–49, 160–63, 164; local and
international forms, tension
between, 167; locally, 114–16,
133–39, 157–60, 164; media
campaign and, 137–38, 158,
159–60, 162, 164, 165–66, 167,
287n280; members' experience
with, 114; misinformation, 144;

operational security, 140–42;
organizational structure and, 163,
164–65; personal connections and,
146–47; and popular support,
efforts to gain, 103; standardization
of, 231–32, 250; vulnerabilities in,
115–16, 137–39, 145–48, 162–63
al Qa'ida intelligence gathering, 118,
164; internationally, 113–14,
131–33, 156–57; locally, 113, 131,
156–57; local support networks
and, 133, 235; open sources and,
131, 132, 157
al Qa'ida media campaign, 103, 106,
109, 150; after U.S. invasion,
151–53, 161; Bin Laden on
importance of, 122–23; as
counterintelligence vulnerability,
5, 126, 137–38, 145–46, 158,
159–60, 162, 164, 165–66, 167,
236–37, 287n280; government
efforts to suppress, 162; internal
debate on, 121; Internet and, 161,
165; and popular support, 122–25;
and pressure to perform, 153;
security procedures for, 134–35;
sophistication of, 152–53; Taliban
concerns about, 121, 126, 138, 242
al Qa'ida organizational structure,
104t, 107, 118–20, 148, 149–50, 163,
164–65; Advice and Reformation
Committee, 109; Advisory Council
of, 105, 107; Central Section, 157;
command structure, 4; and
counterintelligence, 163, 164–65,
230; decentralized "venture
capital" model for, 118–20, 141,
167; information committee of,
136; loss of territory and, 233;
Organizational Work Security
Section, 157

Aum Shinrikyo, 254*t*, 257
Azzam, Abdullah, 104, 108
Azzam, Jihad al, 138

Badr, Zaki, 176
Bahaji, Said, 142
Bahri, Nasser al- (Abu Jandal), 139
Bakalli, Besnik, 199, 200–201
Bana, Sabi Khalila (Abu Nidal), 85
Bashir, Omar al, 106, 108
basic denial: by al Qa'ida, 114–16,
    116–17, 139, 148, 157–60; basic
    strategies of, 8–9; by BSO, 93–98;
    as commonly-used strategy, 10,
    242–43; definition of, 8, 11*f*; by
    Egyptian Islamic Group, 182,
    189–90; by Fatah, 71–74, 82–85;
    by Fort Dix Group, 199–202; in
    PIRA, 21*t*, 31–33, 35, 40–43,
    53–59; popular support and, 13;
    by Toledo Group, 207; by Toronto
    18, 220, 225
Basque Homeland and Freedom. *See*
    Euskadi Ta Askatasuna (ETA)
Battle of Karameh, Fatah public
    relations victory in, 75
behavior of members, monitoring of,
    as basic denial strategy, 9
Belfast Agreement (1998), 23*f*, 24
Belfast Brigade, 24
Bell, Ivor, 42
Bell, J. Bowyer, 24, 25, 34, 47, 50
Bergen, Peter, 128, 134, 151, 160, 166,
    235
Bin al Sheibh, Ramzi, 134, 140, 141,
    147, 160, 162
Bin Attash, Khallad, 132, 142, 144–45
Bin Laden, Osama: al Qa'ida
    anticipation of retaliatory strikes
    and, 136; and al Qa'ida
    counterintelligence, 138; and al

Qa'ida media campaign, 5, 121,
    122–24, 126, 134–35, 138, 146,
    151–52, 159, 165–66, 236–37, 242,
    247, 287n280; and al Qa'ida
    training, 164; attack planning by,
    106, 113, 119, 141; Bureau of
    Services and, 108–9, 111; and
    communications security, 136;
    confidants of, 1; data archive of,
    131; early U.S. response to, 112;
    expulsion from Sudan, 106, 109;
    family of, as security vulnerability,
    116; flight from Saudi Arabia, 105,
    110; and founding of al Qa'ida,
    104–5, 107, 107*f*; image
    management by, 109, 124, 153;
    marriage to fifth wife, 126; media
    experience of, 108–9; membership
    database of, 114; Mullah Omar
    and, 121–22, 122–23; personal
    fortune of, 111, 127, 128; personal
    security measures, 114, 115–16,
    135, 166, 239; recruitment
    expertise, 111; reputation, and al
    Qa'ida recruiting, 128, 235;
    reputation as soldier, 108, 150;
    retreat to Afghan-Pakistan border
    region, 150–51; role in al Qa'ida,
    107, 119; Saudi assassination
    attempt against, 135; in Sudan,
    105, 108, 110; and test runs of
    operations, 132; U.S. attempts to
    strike, 129–30; U.S. reward for
    capture of, 159; on U.S. terrorist
    watch list, 112; and vetting of al
    Qa'ida recruits, 116
Black September Organization. *See*
    BSO
Boudia, Mohammed, 89, 92, 96
Brigade 055 guerrilla unit (al Qa'ida),
    120

British counterterrorism capabilities, 21*t*, 28–29; counterintelligence, lack of, 29; improvements after 1972, 34, 36–39; improvements after 1976, 48; technological sophistication of, 49

British counterterrorism measures: adaptation of PIRA to, 20, 23, 42, 43–46, 51, 53–59, 243; "confidential phone" operation, 40; detentions, 37–38; heavy-handedness of, and loss of support, 25–26, 27, 29, 33, 35, 46; heavy-handedness of, and loss of territory, 26–27, 29; increase over time, 20, 21*t*; Operation Demetrius, 23*t*, 27, 29, 31, 32; Operation Hawk, 51, 59; Operation Motorman, 23, 23*f*, 37; popular support of PIRA and, 35–36; sowing of paranoia and mistrust, 38–39, 49, 244–45. *See also* prisoner interrogations, by British; spies and informants, British, in PIRA

British intelligence gathering: early lack of, 28; improvements in, 37–38; surveillance, thoroughness of, 47, 60, 240; technical surveillance, 38, 48; terrorist database, 49

British Internal Security Service (MI5), anti-PIRA measures, 28, 38, 48

British Special Air Service, 48, 56

British Special Intelligence Service (MI6), anti-PIRA measures, 28

Bronx Group, 207–11; classification by group type, 254*t*, 256; controlled territory, lack of, 208; counterintelligence failures,

210–11; FBI surveillance of, 208–9; goals of, 207; history of, 207–8; intelligence gathering, 210; organizational structure, 208, 225; resources, 208–9

BSO (Black September Organization): assassinations by, 92, 93, 98; classification by group type, 254*t*, 256; disconnection from Fatah, 66, 87, 94; end of, 92; establishment of, 63, 66, 67*f*, 87; Israeli tracking and killing of, 66–67; Khartoum hostage raid, 88, 239; leadership of, 87; mission of, 66, 87; Munich Olympics attacks, 66, 67*f*, 80, 91, 93, 94, 95–96, 239; recruiting, 87, 96; retreat from Europe, after Israeli counterterrorism efforts, 92; state sponsorship of, 90

BSO controlled territory, 6, 89–90, 98, 100, 239

BSO counterintelligence, 87–88, 93–98; counterproductive aspects of, 97, 232–33; damage control strategies, 96, 97; disinformation campaigns, 95, 96, 97–98; false documents and disguises, 96; Israel capture of files and, 97, 99; leaders' counterintelligence experience, 94; in Lebanon, 95; shunning of publicity, 94–95, 98, 99; state sponsorship and, 101–2; success of, 101

BSO intelligence gathering, 92–93

BSO organizational structure, 4, 87–88, 97, 98, 99, 230

BSO popular support, 88–89, 98, 99; Fatah resources and, 88–89, 98; and intelligence gathering, 93; shunning of publicity and, 94–95

organizational structure and, 163, 164–65; personal connections and, 146–47; and popular support, efforts to gain, 103; standardization of, 231–32, 250; vulnerabilities in, 115–16, 137–39, 145–48, 162–63

counterintelligence by Bronx Group, 210–11

counterintelligence by BSO, 87–88, 93–98; counterproductive aspects of, 97, 232–33; damage control strategies, 96, 97; disinformation campaigns, 95, 96, 97–98; false documents and disguises, 96; Israel capture of files and, 97, 99; leaders' counterintelligence experience, 94; in Lebanon, 95; shunning of publicity, 94–95, 98, 99; state sponsorship and, 101–2; success of, 101

counterintelligence by Cambodian Freedom Fighters, 211, 213, 213–14

counterintelligence by Egyptian Islamic Group, 179–82, 189–90; controlled territory and, 192; mosques as cover, 172; popular support and, 192; public relations campaign and, 192

counterintelligence by Fatah, 63–65, 65t, 71–74, 82–86; BSO creation as response to lapses in, 87; controlled territory, impact of, 83–85; impact on recruitment, 83; Israel capture of files and, 70, 72, 73, 84, 101; Jihaz al Razd counterespionage unit, 73, 85–86, 87; *Minimanual of the Urban Terrorist* and, 85; misinformation campaigns, 86; and popular support, 68, 75, 82, 99;

standardization in, 231; state sponsorship and, 101–2

counterintelligence by Fort Dix Group, 196, 197–98, 199–202, 226

counterintelligence by PIRA, 21t, 31–33, 40–43; amnesty programs for British informants, 40; counterforensics operations, 55–56, 59; improvements after 1976, 53–59; intelligence capability and, 61; misinformation campaigns, 56–57; PIRA prison inmates' contributions to, 40, 41; popular support and, 40, 44, 56, 58, 59, 235; recruiting of bureaucrats as spies, 3, 35; standardization and, 231; stifling effect of, 58. *See also* spies and informants, British, in PIRA

counterintelligence by Toledo Group, 205

counterintelligence by Toronto 18, 217–18, 220–25, 226

counterterrorism activities, effective: applying to criminal groups, 257–59; components of, 16; exploiting craving for publicity, 13, 247–48; exploiting of exposure points, 248, 253t; and forcing terrorists to target less-popular targets, 193–94; knowledge of groups' organizational structure and, 232; sowing of paranoia and mistrust, 232, 244–47, 253t; standardized counterintelligence procedures, exploitation of, 249–51, 253t; strategies for, 244–51, 252t–253t; terrorist counterintelligence capacity, overwhelming of with false alerts, 250–51; undermining faith in

206, 226; by Toronto 18, 216–17, 221, 226, 228

Doherty, Anthony, 42

Doyle, William, 50

Duka, Dritan, 195, 197, 199, 200, 201, 202

Duka, Eljvir, 195, 197, 199, 200

Duka, Shain, 195, 197, 199

Eastern Shura, 150

East Germany, support of BSO, 90–91

Echo 4 Alpha surveillance unit, 48

Egypt: expulsion of Fatah, 69–70; popular anger with, as source of IG popularity, 174–75; pressure on Sudan to expel al Qa'ida, 108, 112; support of BSO, 90; support of Fatah, 78, 86

Egyptian counterterrorism capability, 170*t*, 177–79, 183–84, 186–88

Egyptian counterterrorism measures: antiterrorism legislation, passage of, 171, 172*f*, 178, 187; assassination of IG members, 186; counterproductive actions, persistence in, 187–88; database of terrorists, 186; and diffuseness of Egyptian Islamic Group, 172, 177, 180–81; heavy-handedness of, and IG popular support, 174–75, 177–79, 181–82, 192; improvements in, 186–88, 190, 191; mass arrests, 171, 175, 178, 186, 192, 238; media campaign, 187. *See also* spies and informants, within Egyptian Islamic Group

Egyptian Islamic Group (IG; Gamaa al-Islamiyya): ceasefire agreement, 169, 172, 172*f*, 183, 184, 187; classification by group type, 254*t*, 255–56; formation of, 170, 172*f*;

goals of, 171, 176; history of, 170–72, 172*f*; internal conflict in, 183, 191; leadership of, 171, 172–73, 172*f*, 182–83; military wing, establishment of, 171, 172*f*; recruiting by, 176, 181; size of, 176; strategy of, as mistake, 184; Sudan's support for, 175, 184–85

Egyptian Islamic Group controlled territory, 170*f*, 170*t*, 175, 182, 184–85, 191, 192, 238

Egyptian Islamic Group counterintelligence, 179–82, 189–90; controlled territory and, 192; mosques as cover, 172; popular support and, 192; public relations campaign and, 192

Egyptian Islamic Group intelligence gathering, 179, 188–89

Egyptian Islamic Group members: demographic profile of, 174, 176; large number of, 176, 177, 180–81; training of, 177, 180, 181, 186, 190, 191

Egyptian Islamic Group organizational structure, 170*t*, 171, 172–74, 182, 182–84, 191; and counterintelligence capability, 181, 230; Diaspora Council, 183; Egyptian exploitation of, 186–87; internal security group, 179–80; Majlis al-Shura consultative body, 173

Egyptian Islamic Group popular support, 169, 170*t*, 174–75, 182, 192; collapse of, 169, 171–72, 172*f*, 184, 191, 240, 255–56; and counterintelligence, 181, 235, 237; as product of Egyptian government ineptness, 174–75, 177–79, 181–82, 192

Sahab Institute for Media Production, 152, 162

Salam, Ahmed, 174

Salama, Ali Abdel Rahman, 173–74

Salameh, Ali Hassan: and BSO, 87, 90, 95, 97; death of, 92; early duties in Fatah, 73; Israeli efforts to find, 95, 101; personal security measures, 83, 95, 96

Saudi Arabia: al Qa'ida in, 153, 154–55, 156–57; assassination attempt against Bin Laden, 135; Bin Laden's flight from, 105; embassies, BSO attacks on, 88, 96, 239; pressure on Sudan to expel al Qa'ida, 108; U.S. troops in, as cause of al Qa'ida anger, 105–6, 109

Sayid, Ahmed, 174

Scappaticci, Freddie, 45, 231

September 11th terrorist attacks: al Qa'ida anticipation of retaliatory strike, 136; communication security in, 3; counterintelligence vulnerabilities, 148; planning of, 106, 119, 141, 142, 144; and U.S. invasion of Afghanistan, 106, 107f

Shaikh, Mubinoddin, 218–19, 220–22, 223–24

Sharif, Sayyid Imam al (Dr. Fadl), 111

Shehhi, Marwan al, 141

Shining Path, 254t, 256

Shnewer, Mohammad, 195, 196, 199, 200

Sinn Fein: British spies and, 40; negotiations by, 23–24; and public support, 33

Six Day War (1967), 70, 78–79

Somalia, al Qa'ida attack planning in, 113

Soviet Union: support of BSO, 90; support of Fatah, 78

spies and informants, British, in PIRA, 3, 4, 37–38, 40, 42, 45, 231; amnesty and relocation programs for, 49; PIRA amnesty for, 40, 57; PIRA execution of, 23f, 33, 53, 56; PIRA torture of, 56; popular support in identification of, 56; recruiting of, 37, 242

spies and informants, double agents: in adaptive denial, 9, 261n9; BSO use of, 95, 98; in covert manipulation, 10, 11f, 261n9

spies and informants, Israeli, in BSO: BSO measures against, 93, 97–98; double agents, 95

spies and informants, Israeli, in Fatah, 70, 80, 84–85; Fatah measures against, 72, 73, 85

spies and informants, of adversary: assessment of damage done by, as adaptive denial strategy, 9–10; interrogation of, as adaptive denial strategy, 9; popular support as deterrent of, 5, 235; as threat, 11; verifying information from technical surveillance, 199, 223; vulnerability to, structural organization and, 4, 230–31

spies and informants, of al Qa'ida, 133, 156, 165–66

spies and informants, of CSIS, in Toronto 18, 218–19, 220–22, 223, 225

spies and informants, of Egyptian Islamic Group, 179, 188, 189

spies and informants, of Fatah, in Jordanian army, 81

spies and informants, of FBI: in Bronx Group, 208, 209; in Fort Dix Group, 198–99, 200–201, 202, 226; in Toledo Group, 204–5 spies and informants, of PIRA, 3, 35, 52

spies and informants, of terrorist group: as adaptive denial strategy, 9–10; in covert manipulation, 10

spies and informants, within al Qa'ida, 139, 148

spies and informants, within Cambodian Freedom Fighters, 213

spies and informants, within Egyptian Islamic Group, 184, 186; killing of, 180, 190, 256

Staff Report (PIRA), 43

standardization of counterintelligence procedures, as vulnerability, 231–32, 249–51, 253t

State of Emergency Act (Egypt), 187

state sponsored groups: advantages and disadvantages of sponsorship, 6, 17, 167–68, 242; exploitation of exposure points of, 249; imperfect control of territory and, 14; and resource availability, 16–17. See also Afghanistan, al Qa'ida in; Jordan, Fatah in; Lebanon, Fatah in; Sudan, al Qa'ida in; Syria, support of Fatah

Staunton, William, 50–51

strategies for counterintelligence, wide variation in, 3

Sudan: al Qa'ida counterintelligence support for, 114; al Qa'ida in, 105, 107f, 110; al Qa'ida popular support in, 107–8; as counterintelligence vulnerability for al Qa'ida, 116; expulsion of al Qa'ida, 106, 108, 109, 112–13; support for al Qa'ida, 110, 114, 242; support of Egyptian Islamic Group, 175, 184–85; as terrorist

haven, 110; U.S. attacks on al Qa'ida in, 107f

"supergrass" informants, 49, 58

Suri, Abu Mousab al, 127

Syria: arrest of Arafat, 85; Fatah flight to, 77, 79; invasion of Lebanon, 78, 85; Israel attacks on Fatah in, 77; measures against Fatah, 78, 85, 102; pressure on Sudan to expel al Qa'ida, 112; support of Fatah, 70–71, 77, 78, 85, 86

Taha, Rifai Ahmed, 173, 183

Tal, Nachman, 186

Tal, Wasfi, 92

talent spotters, 234

Taliban: and al Qa'ida, relationship with, 7–8, 106, 120–22, 127, 133, 138, 149, 150, 242; concerns about attention generated by al Qa'ida, 121, 126, 138, 242

Tamil Tigers, 254t, 257

Tatar, Serdar, 195, 199, 200, 201, 202

technical surveillance: by British, 38, 47, 48, 60, 240; by Canadian authorities, 218, 223; by FBI, 203, 208; and informants, management of, 199, 223; by Israel, 72, 84, 97

territory, control of. See controlled territory

terrorism, scholarship on, 2

terrorist groups: challenges faced by, 1; classification of by type, 251–57, 254t; definition of, 7, 18; rural vs. urban, size of, 262n21; types of, and characteristic counterintelligence profiles, 18; vast range of, 18; vs. insurgent groups or criminal groups, 7–8, 257–58. See also failed terrorist groups

United States counterterrorism measures (*continued*) 242; Bin Laden, attempts to capture, 129–30, 159; increase in after 9/11 attacks, 155–56, 163; limited early response to al Qa'ida, 112–13; Operation Anaconda, 155; pressure on Sudan to expel al Qa'ida, 108, 112. *See also* al Qa'ida adversaries, counterterrorism capability of; United States invasion of Afghanistan

United States embassy in Nairobi and Mombasa, al Qa'ida bombing of, 106, 107*t*, 121; al Qa'ida anticipation of retaliatory strike, 136; attack planning and implementation, 112, 113–14, 125, 129, 141; communications security and, 145, 146; trial of perpetrators, 115; U.S. strikes in response to, 121, 124, 130, 242

United States intelligence gathering, limited information on al Qa'ida, 130

United States invasion of Afghanistan, 106, 107*f*, 155; al Qa'ida media campaign following, 151–53, 161; and al Qa'ida popular support, 152, 163; and al Qa'ida retreat to Afghan-Pakistan border region, 150–51, 155, 163; and al Qa'ida training camps, elimination of, 154, 162; civilian deaths and damage, 152

Urduni, Abu Turub al-, 141

USS *Cole*, al Qa'ida attack on, 106; and adaptive denial, 144–45; al Qa'ida anticipation of retaliatory strike, 136; planning and implementation of, 132, 142, 143,

145; and popular support for al Qa'ida, 125

Valente, Peter, 52, 53

Wazir, Khalil Ibrahim al- (Abu Jihad), 94

weapons: PIRA acquisition of, 27, 47–48; PIRA protection of, through compartmentation, 54. *See also* resources

Williams, David, 207–8

Williams, Onta, 207–8

witnesses and incidental informants, as threat, 11

World Islamic Front, 123

World Trade Center, 1993 al Qa'ida attack on, 112

Wright, Seamus, 41

Yasith, Chhun, 211–13, 214–16

Yassin, Fawaz, 88

Yemen, al Qa'ida ties to, 126

Yusuf, Abdullah (Paulo Jose de Almeida Santos), 113

Yusufzai, Rahmullah, 124, 125, 158

Zawahiri, Ayman al-: on al Qa'ida advisory council, 105; al Qa'ida anticipation of retaliatory strikes and, 136; as al Qa'ida leader, 113; and al Qa'ida media campaign, 124, 138, 151, 153, 165–66; captured computer of, 137; disguises and aliases, 117; experience with counterintelligence, 114, 180, 241; recruiting by, 110–11

Zayyat, Montassir al-, 187

Zwaiter, Wael, 91, 97